AF288066

I SAY THANK YOU FROM MY HEART

To all the wonderful women and men who supported me in the creation of this book. To those who felt called by my request and regularly attended the group evenings. I thank you for the laughter, the amazement, and the valuable exchange. My thanks go to all who exposed their innermost selves and courageously shared their stories publicly. I know all too well how much courage it takes to see one's own process published in a book. A very special thanks goes to the mothers, because it is truly not easy to face the truths of one's own children. I also thank all the seekers, researchers, helpers, and healers who accompany other people daily and have the courage to repeatedly look deep into their own biography and the abysses of their selves. These abilities and gifts are rare, yet I am convinced that they will form the foundation for personal and collective growth of humanity in the future.

About me

Natalie Christine Walther, born in 1970 in Traunstein, Germany, with roots from Greece and Croatia, holding a degree in Business Administration and residing near Munich. My two children were the catalyst for my own deep self-development 23 years ago. After further education in Identity-oriented Psychotrauma Theory with and according to Prof. Dr. Franz Ruppert (IoPT) and Dreamwork with and according to Ortrud Grön (TAOG), I am now able to reveal the deepest causes and buried truths from every aspect of life, spanning across generations. May we no longer live in lies and denial, but in love for our inherent truth, love, authenticity, and joy of life.

**»The Little Prince«**
by Antoine de Saint-Exupéry
(1900 – 1944)


»Grown-ups never understand anything by themselves,
and it is tiresome for children
to be always and forever
explaining things to them.«

Natalie Christine Walther

# LISTEN TO US AT LAST!

## CHILDREN BETWEEN PAIN AND LOVE

A wake-up call to all adults

2025

This publication contains links to third-party websites. We assume no liability for their contents, as we do not adopt them as our own, but merely refer to their status at the time of initial publication.

Bibliographical information of the German National Library: The German National Library lists this publication in the German National Bibliography; detailed bibliographical data is available on the Internet at http://dnb.dnb.de.

ISBN: 978-3-7693-2633-8

© January 2025, Natalie Christine Walther

Original in German: »Hört uns endlichzu!«, published 2024

Titel picture: Canva

Cover design & translation: Natalie Christine Walther

Publisher: BoD · Books on Demand GmbH, In de Tarpen 42, 22848 Norderstedt, bod@bod.de

Print: Libri Plureos GmbH, Friedensallee 273, 22763 Hamburg

Printed in Germany

❀ Website: www.dreamsandsoul.com

❀ YouTube Kanal: @dreamsandsoul

❀ Also available as e-book.

**»ON CHILDREN«**

**by Khalil Gibran (1883 – 1931)**

**from the book »The Prophet«**


»Your children are not your children.
They are the sons and daughters
of Life's longing for itself.
They come through you but not from you,
and though they are with you yet they belong not to you.


You may give them your love
but not your thoughts,
for they have their own thoughts.
You may house their bodies
but not their souls,
for their souls dwell in the house of tomorrow,
which you cannot visit,
not even in your dreams.


You may strive to be like them,
but seek not to make them like you.
For life goes not backward
nor tarries with yesterday.


You are the bows from which your children
as living arrows are sent forth.
The archer sees the mark upon the path of the infinite,
and He bends you with His might that
His arrows may go swift and far.
Let your bending in the archer's hand
be for gladness;
for even as He loves the arrow that flies,
so He loves also the bow that is stable.«

# CONTENT

# 1. INTRODUCTION

## 1.1 PREFACE

We don't know each other and that's why I want to warn you in advance: This book is not intended for the inexperienced or for people who are easily triggered. It is also not meant for people who are not interested in causes or think that children today are too spoiled, teenagers too lethargic, parents should toughen up their children, or that medication can solve many problems. If you find yourself getting annoyed maybe already with the first chapter that you bought this book, then pause. Take a deep breath and ask yourself: Why did I buy this book? Does the topic maybe relate to my own biography? How did I actually feel as a child at the age of two or five? Can I even remember my childhood?

I am a mother of two children, but even before their birth, it was clear to me: Every child is right, every child is wonderful. Every child is full of love, joy, equipped with an incredible potential for capacity to love, curiosity, and a sense of adventure. Today, I know: Every child is a miracle; from the very beginning. It is primarily the parents' responsibility to protect, love, and provide a safe haven for this miracle. For me, there is no greater task on this planet than being a mother and loving and supporting my two children.

From the moment they were born, I asked myself: The minor and major illnesses and emotions? What am I not seeing? Where am I heading in the wrong direction? What do I need to change about myself? And so began my journey to the center of my self, a journey of deep self-development. A journey that increasingly merged from a pure internal view with the world around me. Even though I have integrated many aspects of my inner child and continue to work on them, it was only through my book that I began to delve deeper into the question of what children truly reflect back to us.

The idea for this book has many roots, but everything started in 2020, four years ago. A time when many fears were activated by the Corona pandemic, leading to significant changes that also had a massive impact on my fledgling self-employment. Feeling lost, I asked for

11

help from an energy healer for the first time in my life. During the reading, she drew the card of children three times. She told me that it would be part of my life's work to help children, teach them, and guide them. Me? The one who took two decades to even begin to unravel all the entanglements and deepest wounds of my childhood? The one who had to sift through family stories from three countries – Greece, Croatia, and Germany? Me, who tries to be truly a mother to my own children, but is plagued time and again by feelings of guilt and inadequacy? She said that childhood traumas are often not talked about, that it is a taboo subject, and that people are therefore very closed off. It is a nagging problem, but it frightens people. Because trauma, family burdens, and karma converge and weigh heavily on the children.

Almost at the same time, I began working as a family coordinator and school assistant. I was with families seeking help from the youth welfare office and thus gained insight into massive marital problems, saw the effects of divorce, the helplessness of the children, the overwhelming nature of the parents, and a school onto which so many unresolved conflicts were projected. I had many challenging conversations with mothers and fathers, experts, and institutions. I also tried to explain the extent of the suffering, to show the catastrophic effects of the lockdowns on children and teenagers in my circle of acquaintances and friends. Now, I was an experienced conversationalist, but time and again I encountered a wall of lack of empathy, disbelief, or avoidance. Even though I had delved deep into my own psyche, had countless experiences in groups both nationally and globally, and therefore always spoke from practical knowledge and experience, pointing to causes and reasons – the ears and hearts of most people remained closed. I simply could not articulate my experiences in a way that could be received without fear or resentment. The people around me preferred to look away, point fingers at me, or immerse themselves in proxy issues and conflicts. How often had I been angry and hurt because of this. I was also angry because I had to realize how little courage and how much more stupidity existed around me. I was also angry at the parents who did not want to take responsibility and unconsciously – and alarmingly often consciously – projected and transferred their issues onto the children. Corona literally put the icing on the cake.

12

All this frustration within me was the spark that ignited this book. Without thinking twice, it was clear to me that I would turn it into a research project. A project in which I wanted to involve the entire German- and English-speaking IoPT[1] community. It was important to me to really illuminate all the thematic blocks – from conception, pregnancy, birth, the first three years of life, until reaching adulthood at 18 years old. So, I announced my plan and offered open evenings. About twice a month for 1 ½ years, we met online in small groups. Eventually, nearly 40 themes and 400 pages of notes came together.

And that's how this book came to be. An unusual book. A book that gives you the opportunity to look directly into the souls of children. It is a book that will take you on a journey through the earliest origins of human development. It is a book that will even take you further into the past, on a journey through generations of family secrets. It questions the origins of institutions and technological inventions. Above all, it has become a book that candidly speaks the truth, making the deepest wounds and pains visible. And at the same time, it shows what a miracle life is, what wisdom and intelligence children bring from conception, and how a different future could look.

I know that all of this sounds very strange. Don't you need a machine for time travel? How can events from the distant past be stored or retrieved when they are long lost and forgotten? Oh no. That is not correct. Time travel is actually possible and it does not require machines, technology, science, or technical expertise. For this journey, all you need is yourself. You are the miracle that makes all of this possible. The only things you need are perseverance, a spirit of inquiry, a lot of courage, and love for yourself and for children. I am speaking from my own experience. If I hadn't experienced all of this myself, I wouldn't be able to believe some of the statements and conversations. Indeed, I would even consider them impossible. But as is the case in life: When one experiences it firsthand, everything changes.

Never would I have thought or dreamt of what would be revealed in these works. It's not that I don't know how it feels to not be wanted, not loved, not seen, to have no voice, and have to fight too often for

---

[1] I trained in the Identity-oriented Psychotrauma Theory (IoPT) according and with Professor Dr. Franz Ruppert and have been familiar with his methods and theories for over 20 years.

13

one's own life. I am all too familiar with the burden passed down through generations onto a child. However, all my personal and practical experiences could only prepare me for what I saw, heard, felt, and learned during my book project. The sheer magnitude of how little we actually know about children, childhood, and being human. In my naivety and idealism – yes, I still dream of unicorns on rainbows... really! – I actually thought the works would bring some additional aspects to light, but overall round up or summarize my previous experiences. Instead, what was revealed was an unforeseen extent of relational disconnect, attachment and loss trauma, lack of contact, familial and institutionalized violence that not only continues to affect countless lives to this day, but is also very much present and active, influencing our future.

So, this book has become what it likely aims to be: a book that reveals the needs, emotions, wounds, and traumas of our children and adolescents with depth and clarity, not holding back. It has become a book that raises many questions and provides answers at the same time. It has become a book that not only points out the wound but also offers healing. Disillusionment and possibility, chaos and new creation, trauma and self-awareness – to finally uncover ancient patterns so they can be healed. Because only truth heals.

I am aware that by writing this book (and the others that will follow on this topic), I am making myself vulnerable to public criticism. Especially because I also publish my own works. »Who does she think she is? What does she know or understand? This is not a scientific method or therapeutic approach! It's different for us; our children don't have these problems. It's good that they are in therapy and taking medication.« But I will not stop the process that began within me some years ago. Even though I am often unsure and constantly question myself. The time has come for us to decide and take responsibility. For our inner child (and trust me, there are many inner child parts that want to find a home within us!), for the next generations (related to the topic of a healthy generational contract), for a partnership on equal footing and in appreciation, and for coexisting on this wonderful earth. I didn't bring my children into this world to be sacrificed in the next war.

14

I hope that with my book I can contribute to a life-affirming, peaceful coexistence. The key to this is self-awareness, authenticity, and love. Only when each individual confronts their own issues with dignity and respect, courage and willingness, women and men, mothers and fathers, alone and together – and if we manage to finally speak openly about it, something new can emerge. First within us, then in families, in groups, and hopefully in the entire human family (one is still allowed to dream big).

I cordially invite you to join me on this journey into the innermost depths of children's souls. I promise you that none of the topics in this book will leave you untouched. And perhaps, just perhaps, you will see your children or the children around you in a slightly different light. Maybe you will even have the courage to lighten their load a bit. Whether you are a mother or father, sister or brother, aunt, uncle, grandmother, or grandfather. Open your hearts. The children will thank you.

Natalie Christine Walther

Fürstenfeldbruck, October 2024

## 1.2 METHODS AND PROCEDURES

*»If you want to find the secrets of the universe,*
*think in terms of energy, frequency and vibration.«*
*Nikola Tesla (1856 – 1943)*
*Electrical engineer and visionary inventor*

My research for this book was based on the Identity-oriented Psychotrauma Theory (IoPT) according to Professor Dr. Franz Ruppert from Munich, Germany. For those who want to learn more, I refer them to his numerous books. The method for processing deep-seated traumas is called the »Intention Method« by him . It served as a model for all group work.

### Decades of practical experience

I myself have decades of personal experience with the method and approach, and since my formation, I also have experience in the theory. I would like to say in advance that I did not strictly adhere to the methodology of Professor Dr. Franz Ruppert. On the one hand, I am my own person, and on the other hand, I followed my intuition during each work. Some might therefore consider it unorthodox or creative, but it was and is important to me to remain authentic, to follow my gut feeling, and not to impose any limitations on myself and my work. Furthermore, it was important to me during the general-encounters to dive into the deeper layers of inner and collective truths in order to be able to show as many different perspectives as possible in a single work. And since the general-encounters – unlike the self-encounters – are still a young field, there is still much to discover and explore.

### Self-Encounter and Generic-Encounter

Self-encounter refers to one's own personal work. This term is part of the IoPT vocabulary and, in my opinion, expresses the essence and goal very well. Even though in »classical self-encounter« the focus is on trauma, at least for me, the work has actually evolved more into a »self-encounter«. It is an encounter with oneself and one's own parts. Each person who wants to have a self-encounter chooses their intention and also selects the participants who resonate with every single word of the intention. This means there is no intervention.

Every single piece of information is stored in the cells of our body. We vibrate at a certain frequency and, like a radio, can tune into or resonate with the frequencies of other people. This allows us to access all experiences, wounds, and traumas that lie behind a word or intention. An incredible experience for anyone who has practically gone through it. It is eye-opening, painful, surprising, and in all the truth of brutal honesty and beauty.

However, if one were to consider a general topic from a neutral perspective, that is, not from a personal one, then I have simply called the work »general-encounter«. The wonder within us not only allows us to resonate with ourselves or for others but also with any given topic. Whether it's an idea, an institution, a technology, and much more.

I would like to tell you about a beautiful image experienced during a session in which she wanted to connect with her inner child aspects. The image that emerged was that of a tree. Although this session was not part of this research project, its content speaks of timeless truth and beauty, so I would like to dedicate a special place to it in my book:

»I am the tree. Like a May-tree, I was sawn off, painted and set up.[2] Literally and metaphorically. Because that's what happens when we are deeply hurt as children.

Though a part of us still remains in life, symbolized by the trunk, the vibrancy of the original tree - as one envisions when nesting in the mother's womb - is no longer there. All the other parts (severed and fallen leaves) lie scattered on the ground; sometimes closer, sometimes further away, and they are now just a shadow of the original. These are the countless child parts at various stages of age. Each with

---

[2] The erection of a tree trunk, painted and decorated, is a tradition here in Bavaria (and also in other parts of Germany and Europe). On May 1st, a national holiday, it is erected (in some cities it is also standing all year round). In many villages, people celebrate and dance with exuberance.

its own unique emotions, desires, and needs. But is there still hope for me? Yes. Every inner change, every realization, every desire to retrieve, every inner welcome, every honest feeling for oneself and these inner child parts make me alive again. There are countless scattered child parts like the leaves of a tree in autumn.«

**Intention Method**

The goal or also the intention is the prerequisite for every self-encounter or general-encounter. The more concrete the intention, the more concrete the answers as well. The longer and more mixed the intention is, and the less heart or interest in the work there is, the more confused the result will be.

There are many ways to formulate one's intention: It can be a sentence, a question or, for example, a dream. In brevity, there really is power. Practice has shown that the number 3 is a good fit. This means choosing a maximum of three words for an intention.

In general encounters, I was more flexible regarding the number of words. The intention depended on the number of participants; it was important to me that each participant should have the opportunity to resonate. I usually chose the intention. It was important to me to sometimes (but not always) include technical terms of a diagnosis or illness in the purpose. For example, ADHD or depression. Because in every symptomatology, illness, or diagnosis, a multitude of important information is already contained, which I wanted to make visible. And I wanted to give not only the children but also these words a space.

**Group Participants**

The groups started in late 2022 and took place online via Zoom, first in English and from the end of November 2023 also in German. The groups consisted of a maximum of six participants, with women in the majority.

**Profile of the Participants**
o Age: between 30 years and the end of 60
o Gender: female and male

18

- More than 10 countries of origin: Germany, Austria, Great Britain, Isle of Man, Ireland, Poland, Croatia, Romania, Bulgaria, the Netherlands, Greece, Iran, Brazil and China.
- Some have their roots in these countries, but were born elsewhere because their parents had emigrated. Some were still very young when their parents left with them their home country. Some had two or three different cultural backgrounds.
- All participants came from the narrow or wider field of the IoPT community and were therefore familiar with the method through their own work.
- With a few exceptions, no participant knew the previous history of the intention holder during the self-encounters. There was no information or very little information shared in advance.

All sessions were recorded and transcribed by me. I have made very few changes, shortened, or summarized in order not to disrupt the flow. As a result, the written text may seem a bit clunky at times. However, it is more important to me to preserve the original essence of the work. This also applies to the translation from English to German or German to English. Because this book will be published in both languages.

**Topics**

Before starting the group work, I made a list of topics and divided them into five categories.
- Conception,
- pregnancy,
- birth,
- the first 3 years,
- from 4 to 18 years of age.

In doing so, I wanted to achieve a balance of themes across all five categories. Over time, some topics have changed or new ones were added.

**Results**

I would like to emphasize that a single work can never fully depict the complete picture of a topic, but only ever a fragment, an approximation of a topic. There is no singular, universally valid truth. There is also no right or wrong. Like a puzzle with billions of pieces, each work reveals further aspects and clarifies perspectives.

Moreover, every resonance is dependent on the personality, biography, and inner development of both the presenter of the intention and the recipient of the resonance. Therefore, the results provide a good overview but can never be taken as a blueprint for another person or topic. Nevertheless, it is always astonishing to see how much truth each work holds and how the »right« individuals come together for a given topic.

# 1.3 HOW CHILDHOOD INFLUENCES OUR ENTIRE LIFE

Relationship patterns, behaviors, beliefs, fears, blockages and much more – the time of childhood influences our lives from the beginning to our end.

For example, very few people think about how they were conceived. Yet, even here, there is a wealth of themes and clues. With these few questions, I want to show how much one must already absorb and process in the first nine to ten months. How much joy and love, but also suffering, violence, and traumas a person can experience early on.

o Was it a planned pregnancy?
o What was the connection between mother and father and their own parents?
o Was the conception under the influence of violence, alcohol or drugs?
o Was there incest and rape?
o Were there any previous miscarriages or deceased children?

- How long did the parents know each other? Were they married?
- Did they love each other or was the connection more rational, politically motivated or socially opportune?
- How old were the parents? What was the age difference?
- Did any of the parents have a family and children before?
- Was the conception in a country other than the birth?
- Did the parents come from different countries? From a particular population group?
- What was the financial situation? The religious views?
- Do egg and sperm cells come from mother and father or from artificial insemination or surrogate mother or sperm donor?
- And how safe was the environment, the place, the land?

During the nine months of pregnancy, further questions are asked:

- How did the mother feel with the life she was carrying?
- How was the contact with the biological father?
- Did the parents argue a lot?
- Was the mother under stress, for example because a house was built, the financial resources were scarce, she had no support before her or the family of the man?
- Did she have to work physically hard, as is often the case in agriculture?
- Was she satisfied that her body became more and more round and soft?
- What pregnancy tests were there?
- Were there any problems such as diabetes, thrombosis or even a fallopian tube pregnancy?
- Did one have to take medication?
- Did the cervix open before birth?

And then the birth itself:

- What was the birth of one's own parents like?
- How did the mother prepare for childbirth?
- Was there an interaction between mother and child?
- How was the father doing?
- Were fears rising, feelings of loneliness, abandonment?

o Where was birth taking place? In a loving or rather sterile environment? Secretly on a toilet or even on the run?
o Were there any complications?
o What was the reaction of the doctors and midwife?
o Was it a natural birth or was untied by caesarean section or suction cup?
o Was one disappointed that it became »only a girl« or »only a boy«?

The research of the last 100 years – especially in the prenatal and perinatal areas – has brought to light countless new knowledge and many connections. In recent decades, the link between trauma and psychological and physical symptoms has increasingly come into focus. In this chapter, I would like to highlight certain stages of life and quote individuals who have made outstanding contributions in their respective fields. I am aware that my selection reflects only a tiny fraction of the findings, but I hope it can help you better contextualize the main part of this book.

**The Beginning**

In a well-read article by Dr. Jürgen Wettig, Senior Hospital Physician for Neurology, Psychiatry and Psychotherapy, published in 2006 in the German Medical Journal, is right at the beginning:[3]

»The well-known psychologist Paul Watzlawick once expressed: "One cannot be careful enough in the choice of one's parents." This statement describes the enormous formative responsibility of the closest caregivers in early childhood. Even the moment of conception is subject to vastly different circumstances. Is it a planned child, a "surprise", or even the result of sexual violence? On the other hand, pregnancy is sometimes used as a last resort to salvage fragile relationships. Thus, "meaning of life children, marriage glue children, or

---

[3] German Medical Journal, »Eltern-Kind-Bindung: Kindheit bestimmt das Leben.« [Parent-child bond: childhood determines life ], Dtsch Arztebl 2006; 103(36): A-2298 / B-1992 / C-1922 https://www.aerzteblatt.de/archiv/52567/Eltern-Kind-Bindung-Kindheit-bestimmt-das-Leben

gender role defining children" serve as commodities, where nothing is left to chance in their production.

The demographic crisis portrays children as a humane resource and contributors to social systems. In contrast, newborns found in dumpsters, the establishment of baby hatches in charitable institutions, or signs of physical abuse indicate childhood disasters that occur before childhood has truly begun. (...)

Is the father strict and pedantic, physically ill, addicted to alcohol or violent? Is the mother depressed, religious, ambitious or chronically overwhelmed? Does the parents' divorce create a sharp divide in a conflict-ridden family environment, demanding unreasonable partiality from the child? Is sibling rivalry fueled carelessly through unequal attention until it leads to destructive hatred? In the family, is there shared conversation, meals, arguments, play, and laughter, or does a spirit of strict rituals, cold distance, and aseptic cleanliness prevail, devoid of spontaneity?

The unequal and random rules of childhood can be endless. Nowadays, children are often faced with urbanization and traffic. Play spaces and open areas are becoming increasingly scarce. This results in a retreat to indoor spaces and media worlds, leading to delayed motor skills and obesity.

From birth, humans have a biological need for bonding. Attachment means a long-lasting emotional bond with very specific individuals who are not arbitrarily interchangeable.«

A study from Harvard, published in July 2010, shows that serious effects on the body, health and brain structure begin much earlier:

»Health in the earliest years – actually beginning with the future mother's health before she becomes pregnant – lays the groundwork for a lifetime of well-being. (…)

That is to say, developmental and biological disruptions during the prenatal period and earliest years of life may result in weakened physiological responses (e.g., in the immune system), vulnerabilities to later impairments in health (e.g., elevated blood pressure), and altered brain architecture (e.g., impaired neural circuits).«

**Center on the Developing Child at Harvard University (USA)**
»The Foundations of Lifelong Health Are Built in Early Childhood.«
https://developingchild.harvard.edu/resources/the-foundations-of-lifelong-health-are-built-in-early-childhood/

## Conception and Pregnancy

Our life does not begin only at birth. A fact that is still vehemently denied. I am sure that many of you will also be surprised when you read this. Those who research or deeply engage with themselves know that an embryo is a feeling, breathing, living, and knowing being. Some of you may have accessed fragments of such memories through a dream, meditation, physical treatment, regression, or self-encounter. It is astonishing how many unconscious memories we store in our bodies and can retrieve at any time.

For those who have the courage to embark on a journey through cause and effect, I can only recommend this. And to those who believe that we do not know enough, need to explore more, require further studies, well, I can say: No. It is not a question of knowledge, but of practical implementation.

»That we are usually already nine months old when we "come into the world" is something we know. That our psychological life also begins before birth is not yet common knowledge. Otherwise, we would behave differently towards unborn life – in our partnerships, within our families, in prenatal care, obstetrics, or even in so-called assisted reproduction.«

**Franz Ruppert (Deutschland)**
Professor for Psychology and Clinical Psychotherapist
Book »Frühes Trauma – Schwangerschaft, Geburt und erste Lebensjahre«, p. 11
[Early Trauma – Pregnancy, Birth and First Years of Life]

24

»There are various stressors that can significantly influence the prenatal bond between expectant parents and the baby. These stressors include psychosocial factors such as poverty and job loss; traumatic childhood experiences related to deprivation, violence, and separation; difficulties with conception; and mental health issues in the mother like substance abuse and depression. A particular psychological stress for many women today arises from prenatal diagnosis, which has become a routine examination in prenatal care. (...)

Importantly, the transfer of stress hormones through the placenta, especially in cases of significant traumatic experiences for the mother, is crucial. This adaptive mechanism ensures that a child born into an insecure environment develops stronger survival mechanisms compared to a child whose mother had a calm and relaxed pregnancy. Postnatally, trauma-related consequences could include symptoms of ADHD, role reversals with mentally ill parents, or depressive withdrawal—these represent adaptive survival patterns, albeit with stress.«

**Karl Heinz Brisch (Deutschland)**
Specialist in child and youth psychiatry, psychiatry and
psychosomatic medicine and psychotherapy as well as neurology
Book »Bindung und psychische Störungen –
Ursachen, Behandlung und Prävention«, p. 23
[Attachment and mental disorders – Causes, treatment and prevention]

I would like to quote Franz Ruppert once again. He wrote a groundbreaking book that demonstrates the developmental risks of early trauma through a variety of examples. Together with colleagues, he presented backgrounds and examples from conception to unfulfilled desire for children, violence, and adoption in 16 detailed individual contributions. I would like to highlight just one example here regarding the topic of **premature birth:** a young woman who became pregnant at 16 and then again at 17. The second child, Son Peter, was born in the 35th week of pregnancy:

25

»The life history of premature babies often shows disturbances or even ruptures in the relationship with their parents even before birth. Significant events in the mother's life and experience have consequences for the child. In the case of Dagmar and her son Peter, there were situations before birth that were unbearable for Dagmar and so burdensome for Peter that he just wanted to "get out and away", even from this life. In the meantime, Dagmar had written contact with her son and confirmed to me in another conversation that her son still thinks today: Others should take care of my well-being.«

**Franz Ruppert (Deutschland)**

Professor of Psychology and Clinical Psychotherapist

Book »Frühes Trauma – Schwangerschaft, Geburt und erste Lebensjahre«,

p. 172

[Early trauma - pregnancy, birth and first years of life]

What about a child who has an **abortion**? If the abortion fails and the child survives? One point that is completely lost in the discussion about women's rights: how does a child feel who has to be aborted? How do twins feel when one has been aborted and the other survives? How are children who survive multiple abortion attempts? Or how do children whose mothers want to kill themselves? Professor Dr. Franz Ruppert wrote on the subject of abortion attempts and suicide attempts of the mother in the above-mentioned book from page 118 onwards:

»The ideal of pregnancy as a time of carefree development and joyful anticipation, or of being warmly welcomed, can no longer be spoken of after an abortion attempt. The profoundly significant experience of being wanted, of being allowed to exist in safety, and of lovingly responding to its needs is missing for the child from the very beginning after existential prenatal threat. Even mothers who considered taking their own lives during pregnancy led the child in their womb into a traumatizing near-death experience and the associated consequences. It is now undisputed that traumatic experiences during the prenatal period leave lasting marks (Alberti 2012, Bauer 2002, Birnbaumer 1996, Deneke 1999, Huber 2013, Hochauf 2007, Hüther and Krenz

2013, Janov 2011, Janus 2013, Krüll 1997, Noble 1996, Singer 2002, Sonne 1997). The child feels fundamentally betrayed from the start with effects particularly on its "flourishing", its future need for security, its capacity for love/relationships, and its self-respect. The life stories of most of the children who have bravely defied attacks on their lives remain unknown to the public. (...) This can be so deeply internalized that these individuals find it difficult to find a secure place in life or to feel permanently connected; they may subject themselves, often repeatedly, to environments where they experience painful bullying, or they may, in a way, repeatedly push themselves away by (unconsciously) creating situations where their own – often steep – careers suddenly halt or looming successes are suddenly prevented or destroyed.«

**Birth**

Let's move on to the subject of birth. I am dismayed at how much the **caesarean section** rate has increased in Germany in recent years. And I am appalled at how midwives are being pushed further and further out and how childbirth has become a male-dominated process. According to the Federal Statistical Office in Germany, we now have a caesarean section rate of almost 31% (in some cases even 35!). »The statisticians also pointed out that fewer and fewer hospitals in Germany are offering obstetrics at all.«[4]

It is interesting that the older age of women giving birth is often mentioned as an argument, although women today are often physically fitter and healthier than they were 40 years ago.

If you delve deeper into the history of the caesarean section, you will find some remarkable information. Dr. Gerd Reuther's book on the 2500-year history of European medicine, which is well worth reading, contains the following:

---

[4] German Medical Journey, »Krankenkasse: Kaiserschnittrate steigt auf fast 35 Prozent«, [Health insurance: Caesarean section rate rises to almost 35 percent] from May 6, 2024, https://www.aerzteblatt.de/nachrichten/151183/Krankenkasse-Kaiserschnittrate-steigt-auf-fast-35-Prozent

27

»Until the 16th century, men had no direct influence on gynecology, and even access to pregnant women and births was denied to clergy. As a result, the church imposed restrictive oversight over the midwifery profession. All practices had to be combined with prayers instead of pre-Christian customs. (...)

Under pressure from the church, midwives also performed cesarean sections – not to save the lives of the mother and child, but solely to baptize the child (known as emergency baptism). Documents reveal that the cesarean section almost always meant a death sentence for the mother. According to church guidelines, the emergency baptism of a non-viable fetus took precedence over the mother's life. Cesarean sections that were survived by birthing individuals were not documented in Germany until 1264 and in England until 1790.«

**Gerd Reuther**

Specialist doctor with teaching authorization for radiology

Book »Heilung Nebensache – Eine kritische Geschichte der europäischen Medizin von Hippokrates bis Corona«, p. 314

[Healing as a minor matter – A critical history of European medicine from Hippocrates to Corona]

Since the birth of my children, I have also been wondering why the birthing process is not mainly supported and carried out by experienced mothers? And why do we not tap into ancient knowledge and healing practices? Lately, I have been contemplating whether the place where we give birth or are born also has an impact on our biography. I found an interesting article from Australia that refers to scientific studies involving Aborigines.

»In the first of nine papers, Wiradjuri and Ngemba Wayilwan author, Fleur Magick Dennis and her midwife share four compelling pregnancy and birthing journeys that give a unique insight into the cultural richness and healing that Birthing on Country can bring. These stories illustrate how important the transition during pregnancy and birth is for the "health" of the baby, mother, father, family and community.

The author also provides a rare insight into the vital role of Aboriginal fathers in the cultural and spiritual process of birth. It is a deeply personal journey. Critically, the stories highlight the importance of understanding and respecting the cultural choices for birthing that women make. (…)

Women, supported by midwives, Aboriginal health workers, Aboriginal Community Controlled Health Organisations and researchers are clearly 'reclaiming' rich ancestral wisdom and bringing culture and spirituality back into birth to enrich our contemporary health care systems to foster a nurturing birth environment to support parents through this important transitional life event.«

**Australian College of Midwives (ACM)**

»Women and Birth Journal«, Volume 32, Issue 5 (9 papers)

Article: https://www.ckn.org.au/content/reclaiming-ancestral-wisdom-through-birth-ing-country-australia-special-edition-women-and

Elsevier: https://www.clinicalkey.com.au/nursing/#!/browse/toc/1-s2.0-S1871519219X00050/null/journalIssue

## Dreams

Dr. Ludwig Janus is a luminary in prenatal and perinatal psychology and medicine. He was President of the International Society for Prenatal and Perinatal Psychology and Medicine from 1995 to 2005 and has written 26 books on this topic. [5] Dreams were an integral part of his work:

»Another example is the report by Klaus Bieback, a German primary therapist, about a twenty-two-year-old woman whose coming-of-age is hindered by archaic fears:

„The fact of the matter in this woman's life story is that her mother almost lost her child when she was on vacation with her in the third month of pregnancy – bleeding had started. The cervix had opened 25 millimeters, and the doctors at the hospital initially thought it was an artificially induced abortion, but this was not the case. The mother had

---

[5] Wikipedia, »Ludwig Janus«, https://de.wikipedia.org/wiki/Ludwig_Janus

to lie totally still for five days and was not allowed to move. The doctors said she had a five percent chance of making it. She was given Valium and all her vital movements became very, very slow. The bleeding stopped. The child was then born healthy after another six months of normal pregnancy.

In the following dream report of the young woman there is a bizarre translation of fear from archaic times:

"(…) At the top of the platform is our car. (...) Dad is steering and his sister is next to him. Mother and I are outside. I now have to direct father how to drive, once forwards, once backwards. It's a matter of millimeters; I can't even look at it. It's a matter of life and death, and I have full responsibility and didn't want to and couldn't actually do it. (...) Everything very, very slowly. You can't actually do it. You could crash. (...)"

I would like to give the dream a title like the one I gave the young woman. It read: "Life has the right of way before the crash – very, very slowly." (...) This report makes it clear how symbolic descendants of prenatal trauma can become present in dreams and in the communication of the therapeutic situation, the revival of which is necessary in order to gain independence in adult life through subsequent processing.«

**Ludwig Janus**
Psychotherapist and Psychoanalyst
Book »Wie die Seele entsteht.« p. 84
[How the soul is created]

### Attachment and Education

Bonding between the parents and the unborn child, but above all between mother and child, is vital. Dr. Karl Heinz Brisch writes in his book »Bindung und psychische Störungen« [Attachment and mental disorders]:

»Gerhard Roth, one of the most important neurobiologists in our country, pointed out several years ago on the basis of empirical findings that the main causes of mental disorders are the traumatization of the mother before and during pregnancy as well as the child's experience of trauma in the first 2-3 years of life. Genetic-epigenetic aspects only explain a variance of 10-20% on (Roth & Strüber 2014).«

**Karl Heinz Brisch**

Univ.-Prof., Dr. Med. habil

Specialist in child and adolescent psychiatry, psychiatry,

psychosomatic medicine and psychotherapy as well as neurology,

psychoanalyst

Book »Bindung und psychische Störungen –

Ursachen, Behandlung und Prävention«, p. 28

[Attachment and mental disorders – Causes, treatment and prevention]

In 2006, an article by Dr. Jürgen Wettig, doctor of neurology, psychiatry and psychotherapy and now head of the department of the ZSP Rheinblick (Centre for Social Psychiatry). He wrote:[6]

»Early childhood experiences, on the other hand, before the age of three, are stored in implicit (unconscious) memory. Freud coined the term "infantile amnesia" for this. From a neuroscientific perspective, there is no doubt today that early childhood experiences are significantly involved in the construction of the neuron network in the brain and thus shape future personality. For example, if a two-year-old child is frequently yelled at by their caregiver, the brain processes this stimulus directly in the cerebral cortex. The unconscious perception of the loud rejection becomes indelibly inscribed in implicit memory (priming, "scar") and may potentially cause an anxiety disorder or insecure social skills in adulthood, without the individual being consciously aware of the actual cause.«

---

[6] German Medical Journey »Eltern-Kind-Bindung: Kindheit bestimmt das Leben«, [Parent-child bond: childhood determines life] 2006; 103(36): A 2298-2301, https://www.aerzteblatt.de/archiv/52567/Eltern-Kind-Bindung-Kindheit-bestimmt-das-Leben

**Jürgen Wettig**

Doctor of Neurology, Psychiatry and Psychotherapy

Senior physician at the Forensic Clinic Vitos in the Rheingau, Germany

»Education should start with the parents' education from the birth of the child. The most powerful means of education is love, provided that it is shared equally among all children and not given in excess. One of the worst common parenting mistakes is to spoil children because it takes their courage and self-confidence, but it is also dangerous to use severe punishments. The child's self-confidence, his personal courage is his greatest happiness. «

**Adolf Adler (1870 – 1937)**

Doctor and psychotherapist

Founder of individual psychology [7]

## Education System

Gerhard Hüther and Uli Hauser start their book »Jedes Kind ist hoch begabt« [Every child is gifted] with a quote from John Lennon:

»When I was 5 years old, my mother always told me that happiness was the key to life. When I went to school, they asked me what I wanted to be when I grew up. I wrote down "happy". They told me I didn't understand the assignment, and I told them they didn't understand life.«

»Children can do more than squinting at school reports, we humiliate them by reducing their performance to the grades they have earned in

---

[7] Alfred Adler Institut Mainz, Individualpsychologie Alfred Adlers (Eine Einführung), [Individual Psychology Alfred Adlers (An introduction),] of Dr. H. Khoshrouy-Sefat, Frankfurt
https://www.google.com/url?sa=t&rct=j&q=&esrc=s&source=web&cd=&ved=2ahU
KEwiO2JGojbmDAxU3S_EDHcV5CZ84ChAWegQI-
AxAB&url=https%3A%2F%2Fwww.adler-institut-
mainz.de%2Fuploads%2Fmedia%2FIndividualpsychologie.pdf&usg=AOv-
Vaw1HVXlkYurT_Yfor4NkimSp&opi=89978449

school. More and more parents see themselves as managers or trainers of their children. This idea is based on the attitude that children are basically defective, because they lack something, the parents have to intervene. But the children are tired of being constantly corrected and criticized, they don't deserve it either. They are competent and want to take responsibility, for themselves and in the best case also for others. They are, from a young age, their own personalities with their own needs. You have gained your own memories and experiences, acquired your own skills and abilities. They belong to no one but themselves. They are eagles, not soup chickens.«

**Gerald Hüther**
Former professor of neurobiology at the
Psychiatric Clinic at the University of Göttingen, Germany
Book »Jedes Kind ist hoch begabt«, p. 31
[Every child is gifted]

In his world-famous 2006 speech at the TED conference (short for »Technology, Education, Design«), Ken Robinson, who has dedicated his entire life to the subject of education, said:

»If you think of it, the whole system of public education around the world is a protracted process of university entrance. And the consequence is that many highly talented, brilliant, creative people think they're not, because the thing they were good at school wasn't valued, or was actually stigmatized. And I think we can't afford to go on that way.

In the next 30 years, according to UNESCO, more people worldwide will be graduating through education than since the beginning of history. More people, and it's the combination of all the things we've talked about -- technology and its transformation effect on work, and demography and the huge explosion in population. Suddenly, degrees aren't worth anything. Isn't that true? When I was a student, if you had a degree, you had a job. If you didn't have a job it's because you didn't want one. And I didn't want one, frankly. But now kids with degrees are often heading home to carry on playing video games, because you need an MA where the previous job required a BA, and now you need a PhD[8] for the other. It's a process of academic inflation. And it indicates the whole structure of education is shifting beneath our feet. We need to radically rethink our view of intelligence.«

**Sir Ken Robinson, UK**
Professor and Head of the National Commission on Creativity,
Education and the Economy for the UK Government
TED-Talk »Do schools kill creativity?«
https://www.youtube.com/watch?v=iG9CE55wbtY

### Elites – Do they have it easier?

For those who believe that antiquated or brutal child-rearing is a thing of the past, I would like to draw your attention to the parenting style of long-established, wealthy families – the so-called elites. To this day, early separation of mother and child is promoted as ideal.

While the woman may bear offspring (preferably a son), child rearing itself is not her responsibility. Isn't it better to keep the child away from an excessive motherly care? Emotions and attachment are generally seen as disruptive. They spoil character and hinder one's upward climb on the career ladder. Therefore, changing nannies, housekeepers, and private tutors take over the upbringing. Even access to nature is systematically restricted or serves a specific purpose only, such as horseback riding, rowing, or fishing. In this way, outsiders gain access and control over the minds and bodies of the little ones right from birth.

Once these children outgrow their childhood, the process continues without a break. They are sent away from home to boarding schools where privacy is a foreign concept and often strictly segregated by genders. Suddenly, boys are faced with immense pressure to conform, strict rules, opaque hierarchies, and sometimes brutal punishment methods and initiation rites. An environment that is a torture especially for sensitive children.

---

[8] Master of Arts (MA), Bachelor of Arts (BA), Doctor of Philosophy (Ph.D.; scientific doctoral degree)

If they survive this time, some of them are then sent to military academies for toughening up, discipline, patriotism, and preparation for future wars. Their fathers only pay attention to them when they perform. Few of them know the warmth, affectionate physical contact with their mother and father.

In an article published in 2015 by the British newspaper »The Guardian«, author Alex Renton describes the experience at elite English boarding schools – which are still considered the gold standard worldwide – as follows:[9]

»I once knew an American psychoanalyst who worked in a Bangkok practice, specialising in expats. (…) "Middle-aged, middle-class Brits who went to your crazy private schools may just about be the most damaged social sub-group I've ever come across." (…) In the 20th century a clutch of authors, from George Orwell to Roald Dahl, wrote in their different ways about the systemic cruelty, psychological and physical, and of its wider effects. One of those was the establishment of the principle, among the elite and the ordinary, that to have been brutalized at a boarding school was key to becoming the right sort of Briton – one that might run an empire or a corporation, or a cricket team. Naturally, as the proven best way to educate a ruling caste, the system spread across the English-speaking world. Psychology seems to have taken a long time to catch up with the issue, perhaps because Freud famously dismissed most of his child patients' allegations of abuse by adults as fantasy. (…)

Joy Schaverien coined the term "boarding school syndrome" only a decade ago, though she follows in the footsteps of Nick Duffell, a psychotherapist who started work in the field in 1990 and wrote a passionate and influential book about the wounds boarding can inflict, *The Making of Them.* (…)

The many hundreds of emails I've received make it pretty clear that the schools of the elite suffered the same cover-ups and the same astonishing failings in regulation and in policing as did the hospitals,

---

[9] Alex Renton, »Boarding School Syndrome review – education and the pain of separation« from June 08, 2015, The Guardian, https://www.theguardian.com/books/2015/jun/08/boarding-school-syndrome-joy-schaverien-review

35

care homes and young offenders' prisons. The difference? (…) "Boarders cannot console themselves with the thought that their parents did not want them to go," Professor Schaverien states. Their parents chose to send them from home into hell or prison – words her patients frequently use – and so to break the bond with their child.«

John Bowlby, also from the UK and founder of attachment theory, grew up in a well-off family himself. His father was a respected surgeon and he is said to have only seen his mother for about an hour a day.

»However, Bowlby's own nanny took on a caring role for him, but left the family when he was three years old. At the age of eight he was sent to boarding school and after the First World War he entered the Royal Naval College in Dartmouth. At the age of seventeen, he decided to study medicine and psychology at Trinity College, Cambridge. In 1951, John Bowlby's study on the relationship between maternal care and mental health, commissioned by the WHO, was published. It was a contribution to the UN's program for the welfare of homeless children.«[10]

Throughout his life, John Bowlby was preoccupied with attachment, which he missed so sorely. In his 1988 book »A Secure Base« he wrote at the very beginning:[11]

»To be a successful parent means a lot of very hard work. Looking after a baby or toddler is twenty-four hour-a-day job seven days a week, and often a very worrying one at that. And even if the load lightens a little as children get older, if they are to flourish they still

---

[10] Wikipedia, »John Bowlby«, https://de.wikipedia.org/wiki/John_Bowlby

[11] John Bowlby, »A SECURE BASE, Parent-Child Attachment and Healthy Human Development.« Lecture 1, page 8 and following, https://www.google.com/url?sa=t&source=web&rct=j&opi=89978449&url=https://www.increaseproject.eu/images/DOWNLOADS/IO2/HU/CURR_M4-A13_Bowlby_(EN-only)_20170920_HU_final.pdf&ved=2ahUKEwjtrb7y7puFAx-UzXfEDHW5JCtEQFnoECBMQAQ&usg=AOvVaw1TfQSELD-DxfSZEZ25WM2y

36

require a lot of time and attention. For many people today, these are unpalatable truths. Giving time and attention to children means sacrificing other interests and other activities. (...) Study after study (...) attest that healthy, happy, and self-reliant adolescents and young adults are the products of stable homes in which both parents give a great deal of time and attention to the children. (...) Paradoxically it has taken the world's richest societies to ignore these facts. Man and woman power devoted to the production of material goods counts a plus in all our economic indices. Man and woman power devoted to the production of happy, healthy, self-reliant children in their own homes does not count at all. We have created a topsy-turvy-world. (...) It is evident, however, that attachment behavior is in no way confined to children. Although usually less readily aroused, we see it also in adolescents and adults of both sexes whenever they are anxious or under stress. No one should be surprised therefore when a woman expecting a baby or a mother caring for young children has a strong desire to be cared for and supported herself.«

**John Bowlby (1907 – 1990), UK**
Pediatrician, child psychiatrist and psychoanalyst
Founder of the attachment theory

It is interesting that as soon as people climb the career ladder or come into money, they emulate the pattern of the so-called elites without hesitation. Throughout their lives, their entire aspiration is geared towards career and the accumulation of money. Without hesitation, they make the same mistakes with their children and deny them what they themselves craved most: Love, time, attention, relationship and recognition. But the goal of getting to the top is probably more desirable than secure, stable, family ties.

In order to avoid having to feel their own pain, the pain is passed on from one generation to the next. Even more devastating: these traumatized elites determine the social interaction and lives of millions of people. As a result, they multiply their personal suffering and pain in institutions, foundations, companies and politics, the film and entertainment industry, as well as research and development. Their negative self-image and bleak visions of the future lead them to invent one survival strategy and destructive technology after another to involve us all in their perpetual internal and external wars.

**Rape, Institutionalized Violence and Wars**

For centuries and millennia, the history of mankind has been marked by violence, wars, assaults and torture. Of incest, abuse and abortions, of envy, resentment, rivalry, greed and avarice. The burden weighs on generations of families. Buildings, areas, regions and even nations are marked by it. These experiences, stored in every cell of our body and in the soil of Mother Earth, are passed on to our children and grandchildren from generation to generation. Often unconsciously, but sometimes very consciously.

At the University Hospital in Ulm, Germany, a team of experts for the first time over a period of four years (2013 to 2017) » accompanied the influence of positive and negative maternal childhood experiences on the relationship with one's child and its development. (…) In the study »Meine Kindheit – Deine Kindheit«[12],[13] [»My childhood – Your childhood«] risk and protective factors should be revealed that contribute to whether and how abuse, mistreatment and neglect experiences are passed on to the next generation. The study was divided into five substudies and started shortly after the birth of the child and lasted until the age of seven, that is to say school start. Physicians, biologists and psychologists accompanied about 158 families. It has been shown that

---

[12] University Clinic Ulm, Germany »My childhood – Your childhood«, Study on the Influence of Mothers' Childhood Experiences on their Children from Birth to School Age, (Study period from 2013 to 2017), https://www.uniklinik-ulm.de/kinder-und-jugendpsychiatriepsychotherapie/sektionen-und-arbeitsgruppen/sektion-paedagogik-jugendhilfe-bindungsforschung-und-entwicklungspsychopathologie/meine-kindheit-deine-kindheit/trans-gen.html

[13] Ulm News, Weblog »Meine Kindheit, Deine Kindheit: Studie untersucht Einfluss von Kindheitserfahrungen auf Mütter und deren Kinder« [My childhood, Your childhood: Study examines the influence of childhood experiences on mothers and their children] from April 27, 2021, https://www.ulm-news.de/weblog/ulm-news/view/dt/3/article/80625/Meine_Kindheit_Deine_Kindheit%3A_Studie_untersucht_Einfluss_von_Kindheitserfahrungen_auf_M-uumltter_und_deren_Kinder.html

mental stress had a negative effect on the body and lead to chronic and inflammatory diseases.[14]

The study has now been running for eight years; also during the time of the corona pandemic. In an article in FOCUS, Claudia Buß, professor at the Institute for Medical Psychology at the Charité in Berlin, said:

»Not only beatings are violence – psychological violence in the form of humiliation, threats or silence can also harm children. (...).

Approximately every third child is a victim of abuse and/or neglect. It is not only those affected who often carry these experiences with them for the rest of their lives. They apparently also pass on the risks. Researchers looked at the health of the subsequent generation and found connections with maternal abuse experiences. A team led by Buß reported on this in the specialist journal "The Lancet – Public Health". They analyzed data from over 4300 mother-child pairs.

According to the study, the offspring of women who had been abused and/or neglected as children had a higher risk of various illnesses: Precursors of depression and anxiety disorders, attention deficit disorder ADHD, autism and asthma. The daughters of these mothers were also more likely to be overweight than their sons. (...)

"The question of mental stress should be more closely integrated into general medical care, for example in gynaecology and pediatric medicine."«[15]

Institutionalized violence runs like a red line through history. What is frightening to me is seeing how doctors and psychologists willingly become accomplices. Especially the medical profession, which has sworn the Hippocratic Oath and is dedicated to healing people,

---

[14] Regio TV, »Ulmer Forscher können Kindheitstraumata im Blut nachweisen« [Ulm researchers can detect childhood trauma in the blood] from April 18, 2018, https://www.regio-tv.de/cmms-embed/amp/15007
[15] FOCUS online, »Wenn du jetzt nicht schläfst, dann knallt es! – Emotionale Misshandlungen von Kindern können gesundheitliche Folgen haben« [»If you don't sleep now, it's going to blow-up! – Emotional abuse of children can have health consequences«] from May 07, 2023, https://www.focus.de/familie/mm_id_192876075.html

repeatedly finds itself entangled with politics, churches, lobbyists, and powerful financiers. The massive perpetration of crimes against children often takes one's breath away:

»The use of medicines in children's homes was already discussed in the final report of the "Roundtable on Children's Home Care" published as early as 2010. Those affected reported the administration of medications without medical justification. (...)

Medical violence was facilitated by a perception of mental illnesses as primarily biological and therefore hereditary. Previous experiences of violence, such as abuse within the family, and resulting mental health issues or developmental delays were rarely taken into account during diagnosis. Consequently, the decision to admit individuals to an institution or clinic for the mentally ill or disabled was seldom questioned, and any failure of therapies was attributed to the young patients themselves, with their constitution being seen as the cause of their suffering.«

**Nora Wohlfarth**

State Archives of Baden-Württemberg

»Medizinische Gewalt«

[Medical Violence]

https://www.leo-bw.de/themenmodul/heimkindheiten/alltag/gewalt-einfuhrung/medizinische-gewalt

Krieg öffnet Tür und Tor für das Dunkelste und Schrecklichste. Ein Beispiel aus der NS-Zeit ist das Projekt »Lebensborn«[16], das 1935 begann:

»Approximately 700,000 abortions performed annually negatively affected the desired high birth rate. Unmarried women at the time opted for abortion to avoid defamation and social exclusion. Concerned that

---

[16] Wer mehr zu diesem Thema wissen möchte, ich kann die Bücher von Gisela Heidenreich empfehlen (nur auf Deutsch erhältlich).

40

these children would not be "lost" to the German Reich, Heinrich Himmler came up with the idea of creating opportunities for discreet childbirth. He believed this would eliminate the need for abortions. This was the birth of the "Lebensborn e.V." The organization was founded on December 6, 1935, and was administratively linked to the SS. In the German Reich (including Austria), it operated nine obstetric and two children's homes. To bring the illegitimate children of German occupying troops under German influence during the war, it established a total of 13 obstetric and children's homes in Belgium, France, Luxembourg, and Norway, with ten of them solely in Norway. Between 1936 and 1945, 8,000 to 9,000 children were born in its German homes, almost half of whom were born out of wedlock. Additionally, a total of 9,000 children, mostly illegitimate, were born in Norway. (...)

From 1942, the "Lebensborn" organization participated in the Germanization of several hundred children and adolescents aged from a few months to 17 years old. These individuals had been abducted to Germany against the will or without the knowledge of their parents or legal guardians from the former Yugoslavia, Norway, Poland, or the former Czechoslovakia. The "Lebensborn" gave them German names, educated them in its homes in what was deemed the German way of life, or placed them in German foster families for future adoption purposes. Simultaneously, new birth certificates were issued to them with German nationality.

According to the racial ideologies of the "Lebensborn" officials, the selection of expectant mothers aimed to prevent the birth of "inferior" offspring. Nevertheless, children with severe disabilities were born in the "Lebensborn" homes. They were immediately transferred to so-called children's specialist departments, where they were murdered as part of the "child euthanasia" program. Up to now, 17 killed "Lebensborn" children are known.

**Lebendiges Museum Online**

»The "Lebensborn e.V." of the SS«

https://www.dhm.de/lemo/kapitel/ns-regime/innenpolitik/
der-lebensborn-ev-der-ss.html

Child Uthanasie? Gerhard Schmidt wrote in his book »Selektion in der Heilanstalt 1939 – 1945«[17] [Selection in the Sanatorium 1939 - 1945] on pages 37 and 38:

»Eugenic-scientific slogans

That the purification of species was the goal of exterminating those under care, is evident not least from publications by race eugenicists. In 1940, a Nazi hereditary biologist felt compelled to shake up his colleagues with a conceptual design. One side of this Janus-faced "renewal program" was the control and promotion of reproduction among the healthy.

„For the actual breeding selection problem – these researchers have hardly shown any interest so far... For those who consider themselves engaged in the biological selection of their people..., the question is not whether they should produce offspring or not, but only with whom. We are looking for demonstrably healthy clans... Ruthlessly and with a clear marching order... If it was supposed to be the fundamental idea of the SS units from the very beginning, to be a biological selection... That alone has always been the purpose of marriage permission, and from this alone arose the call to the soldiers..., to overcome inevitable death through new life in various ways. A similar thought underlies the unique institution of the "Lebensborn" (Fountain of Life)... (...) Here lies... the secular task and significance of the Western biological sciences of our time... (»Der Biologe«, 1940). [»The Biologist«, 1940]"

(...)

In addition to this, a Munich racial biologist applauded in an open letter dated November 5, 1940, entrusted to the NS lecturer association and the NS lecturer union, and exaggerated in reference to

---

[17] The book is a documentation of what he found when he was appointed in June 1945 as »acting director of the health and nursing institution Eglfing/Haar near Munich, and analyzes what happened at this state institution, which was transformed from its then head into an NS-model-institution had been expanded, from 1939 to 1945.«

unspecified but assumed as known "government measures" into a hymn to the "New German Psychiatry":

"(…) The most recent events of government order, which need not be further elaborated here, have brought to the awareness of each of our professional colleagues, right into the deepest corner of psychiatric-medical life and psychiatric research, that, to what extent and in which direction this unique transformation in the history of psychiatry, involving a reevaluation of all values, is taking place. Here, just as in the past, a revolutionary change of all concepts and medical practices is being completed to an extent that has hardly been seen in any other field of science, and which can be directly linked to the influence of National Socialist ideology on a German field of science... Looking back and looking forward lead to the following new basic attitude: Away from lives deemed unworthy to be lived – towards treatable and curable fellow countrymen. Away from biologically inferior – towards biological excellence..."«

Even after the war, the children's suffering did not stop. Under the guise of health or relief for parents, incredible suffering was inflicted on the so-called »children of the deportation«:

»The transfers took place from the post-war period until the 1990s for two to six weeks in children's homes and – healing centers. Infants were sent together or alone, including children from the age of two (...)

In many deportation homes, there was a long-term strict treatment of children, some of which were still influenced by the Nazi ideology. It was propagated by Johanna Haarer in her book Die deutsche Mutter und ihr erstes Kind [The German mother and her first child] (sold 1934 to 1987). These included beatings of obedience, strict cleanliness requirements, physical coercion and the diktat of the clock. Suffered also mental and physical violence.«[18]

---

[18] Wikipedia, »Verschickungskinder«, [children of the deportation ]https://de.wikipedia.org/wiki/Verschickungskinder

43

In an article that appeared in 2024 in the BRIGITTE magazine, it was reported about » forced feeding, visitation bans, toilet bans, beatings, speech bans, mail censorship, terrible homesickness, fear of death«. Memories slowly came back to the now adult woman. At that time, she couldn't speak to her parents. »I was too young to find words for it; it remains only to suppress it.«

That's the detour. However, anyone who believes that such things no longer exist or can exist in the modern world, in the 21st century, is gravely mistaken. The self-encounters and general-encounters in this book bear witness to that.

# 2. PREGNANCY AND BIRTH

## 2.1 DESIRE TO HAVE CHILDREN

*General-Encounter (3 words)*
*German: Frau – Mann – Kinderwunsch*
*English: Woman – Man – Desire to have children (abbreviation "Desire")*

From what point in time should we talk about the desire to have children? Who wants the child? And what prerequisites are needed to make it work? A wonderful encounter in which there was much laughter. Well, it could all be so easy.

**Woman**
»I am totally fixated on the man. I think he's great, I think he's really awesome, and I'm trying to flirt. I would like to do something alone with him. He's my man, my partner. I would love to cuddle with him right now. All this endless chatter is distracting me. I have the impression that it's my turn as a woman now. There needs to be a right order: I'm with the man first, then us, then something develops, and then the desire for children comes. We need to get closer first.

I wish there was more intimacy. We don't have time to talk. I like it a little more romantic. Then we talk and then of course we do l'amour [love]. But I have to talk to him. You can't do both. And it takes a little bit of time. And I want it to be romantic and beautiful. Without me the "Desire" does not come forward.«

**Man**
»I am now looking at the "Desire" and honestly, I don't know what to do with you. But I find you super interesting! Why do you have to wait? One thing leads to another. Why do we need to discuss this for a long time? Without sex, there's no point in discussing the desire for children.«

**Desire**

»Someone made the wish, otherwise I wouldn't be here; I feel like a genie out of a bottle, the genie. As in the book of Michael Ende, the wunschalkoholischen Wunschpunsch[19] [wish-alcoholic wish-punch]. And now I sit here and have to wait until you're done flirting. I'm a little offended and thinking the whole time: "Do you want a child now or not? What do you wish for?" I'm not allowed to be a child yet. I'm just the wish-punch.«

o **Desire:** But someone called me!
o **Man:** That was me. I just noticed, when there are some little kids running around, I would love to have them and also some children. Kind of little terrorists.
o **Woman:** Right now, I find it exciting that the "Man" says he has the wish.
o **Man:** Such little kids, of whom you know, they are half of me and the other half of the "Woman" I love very much! That's cool!
o **Woman:** You have it clear for yourself. I think that's great. We already agree on that, but you speak differently than me.
o **Man:** Love, romance, desire for children, sex are all four things that belong together but they are all separate issues. Sometimes I'm romantic, sometimes not. The "Desire" is independent of that. And I find the "Desire" cool. "Desire", do you hear me?
o **Desire** Yes, unfortunately. It's really embarrassing! I have to listen to all the chatter. I feel like a teenager who sees the parents by accident!
o **Man:** How old are you, by the way?
o **Desire:** Well, I am only a wish and I'm already embarrassed by what I have to hear. And I don't even want to know what it's like when you stop talking and then do something.
o **Man:** For your 18th birthday, I will do a slide show and say: »In the tent, you were created!«

---

[19] The title of Michael Ende's book is actually »Der satanarchäolügenialkohöllische Wunschpunsch« [Trying to translate it into English, the book is called something like »The satanic archeological lies alcoholic hellish desire Punch«. The original was published in 1989. More on Michael Ende's website:
https://michaelende.de/buch/der-satanarchaeoluegenialkohoellische-wunschpunsch

o **Desire:** Nooo! I think I have to vomit! I don't want to know how I was made!
o **Man:** "Desire" is right. It's a bit confusing. We both don't say it from the heart, from the feeling »Yes, we want children. Now, we do one.« How doesn't matter. We're both not saying that. We're both letting it happen.
o **Woman:** You are talking about me right now, "Man". But I clearly stated earlier: It's all moving too fast for me. I would like to be intimate with you and cuddle first. What I feel is lacking right now is more communication. So that I know we ultimately want the same thing. Generally speaking. But right now, I don't want children. Right now, I just want to be together with you. Do you ever plan on starting a family?
o **Man:** Definitely. It is an important topic. I find having children, having own children, really nice. But a concrete "Desire"? Now? No. It's too early.
o **Woman:** If we stay together even more, then I could imagine starting a family. I would definitely like to have children. I could imagine having two. Of course, this is subject to discussion with you; what you imagine.
o **Man:** Two is a beautiful number. Not too much, not too little. One is too little, one is none. But three is one too much.
o **Woman:** Two is an odd number. I think it's great that we're in agreement on that.
o **Man:** We harmonize very well. We are both very open. It feels that if the "Desire" is concrete something very, very beautiful can be created out of it. I have the feeling that the social consensus – what society wants or indirectly suggests – plays a not insignificant role. Is that also for you the case, "Woman"? I just have the feeling, my wish is not quite clean. I need a house, two children and a dog – and then the purpose of life is fulfilled. There is a family image in society of the ideal family.
o **Woman:** I don't feel it for now. I would like to spend a little more time with you now. Are we getting along well together? And would that be a good foundation for you, for me? If we have a good foundation and things work out well for us, then having a "Desire" is definitely good.

47

- **Man:** It feels mostly right, but there is some little essence in it that bothers me, it doesn't feel 100% clean. Shall we ask the "Desire"? "Desire", what do you feel?
- **Desire:** So, I think you both are totally cool. I find you funny and cool. I wouldn't mind if you stayed the way you are if you were to become my parents. At least I can say that much. So, you are not too old for me, and you are not too young. You are just right as you are. When you mentioned societal expectations, I briefly thought that also plays a role. Somehow, I don't know why, I appear too early in this vision. I would rather have you enjoy yourselves without me being there. Otherwise, I feel like a voyeur, like a peeping Tom. But involuntarily. I don't want to eavesdrop. It doesn't feel right to me.
- **Woman:** I agree with "Desire". I also have the impression that you are a little early. If I didn't call you, the "Man" didn't call you, who called you?
- **Man:** The social idea of how to be, which always wants to dictate something.
- **Desire:** I don't like the social idea.
- **Woman:** So, if this social pressure is there, I don't care what others think. Whether they say you have three or two or six children.
- **Man:** I feel a bit inhibited by that, to really feel the "Desire" properly. From the heart, to feel it truly.
- **Desire:** That sounds so exhausting! Earlier, I liked you better. Although you were extremely embarrassing, you were better before. It was funnier and more relaxed. Now it's getting so serious.
- **Man:** As soon as you're 2, 3 years together, you're going to become 30, or are engaged – the question immediately comes.
- **Desire:** Behhhh! I could vomit.
- **Man:** Maybe it's just none of their business?
- **Desire:** Oh, thank you!!!
- **Man:** Maybe it's none of their business? Whether we want two children, whether we want ten, whether we don't want any. The question is of no interest to anyone.
- **Desire:** Exactly!!! Neither of you should even get into the victim mentality. Who cares?

- **Woman:** You, "Man," have more trouble with it than I am. I don't care.
- **Desire:** This goes differently. With you, "Man," it's asked or implied differently than it is with the "Woman".
- **Man:** The topic is not very present among men. They don't talk about it. It runs in the background.
- **Desire:** Something's going on. I can feel it. But I notice that as soon as something comes from the outside and you deal with it, then you both become serious and mature. Then you're both not as cool as before.
- **Woman:** Yes, then we are not so harmonious and not so loving.

*As soon as "Man" hears this, he immediately becomes humorous again, and the playfulness between them comes back.*

- **Woman:** We have such a harmonious relationship, everything is fine, a sip of wine...
- **Desire:** As cool as you guys are, the desire for children is close by. You don't have to work for that. It happens in a flash, quick as a wink.
- **Woman:** And I can plan that exactly. We'll do it and then, bam, the child is there. We're not stupid, the two of us. We check everything. I feel comfortable with the "Man". We can have fun, discuss. I have my feminine side. He has his masculine side.
- **Man:** I feel very well now. I feel very well as a man.
- **Woman:** We don't have any problems.
- **Man:** May I ask a question, "Desire"? What would happen that you say, yes, now is the time! This feels right to me. I am welcome now!
- **Desire:** It's up to you. But I am close. I don't need to travel through Siberia to reach you. If you're in your mid-20s, late 20s – from there. And you just have to be cool, funny, and nice. And you're not dumb. And I find the way you interact with each other totally cool. Because you are so cool, I like coming over. Then you just have to make sure that I don't accidentally slip up. Because then I'll say, »So, now I don't feel like waiting. I want to come now.« That can happen. Because if I find you so cool, then I'm on tenterhooks all the time.

- ○ **Man:** Then you find a way.
- ○ **Desire:** And then I think: Better today than tomorrow.
- ○ **Woman:** The more you talk, "Desire", the more I have a desire to be with "Man".

A very refreshing, humorous work where everyone gets along very well and there is a lot of laughter. It shows that there is nothing inherently opposed to the desire for children when a man and a woman harmonize well: attraction, humor, playful ease, communication, being on the same wavelength, romance, love, sex, and time. If a woman is in touch with herself and her femininity, and the man is in touch with himself and his masculinity, then there is nothing standing in the way of the desire for children. However, a definite disruptive factor is the societal perception. Even the "Desire" was frowned upon.

## 2.2 CONCEPTION

*General-encounter (4 words)*
*egg-cell – sperm – father – Mother*

What was so easy and playful in the previous work on the desire for children is here the exact opposite. Both, man and woman, carry so many of their own issues that the space for the most natural thing in the world, engaging playfully in a relationship and conceiving a child, suddenly becomes very tight.

The image emerges of a man who has no idea how to create emotional closeness with his wife. And the image of a woman who is very skeptical towards men and requires a lot of attention herself. Both lack their own maternal bond and the beautiful experience of truly being allowed to be a child. And because they were not allowed to play as children, it is also not possible for them to playfully engage in a relationship as adults.

However, sperm and egg show us how a relationship is actually meant to be, what nature has intended for us! The wonder of life itself, to honor, to love, and above all, to live. This work is a lesson on how far we have strayed from our inner and outer nature.

50

*"egg-cell" is singing and moving, being full of joy! She is singing a song, her song, to attract "sperm" in a playful, beautiful way. "sperm" is totally mesmerized by "egg-cell", by her whole being and her beauty. They have a mesmerizing conversation adoring each other. You can literally see nature's beauty unfold in front of our eyes. Until...*

o **egg-cell:** Psychology is not working. Biology isn't working either. I think you have to talk, "Mother" and "father". What do you want?
o **father:** I mean, "Mother" is written with a capital "M", my "f" is small. To be honest with you, I would rather like to be in the state of you two, "egg-cell" and "sperm", and relive it once more.
o **Mother:** This is also what I feel. There is a mother missing. There is a lot of experience that I don't have. I don't feel ready. I feel like a little girl who needs the mother.

**father**
»I even can't say that it's my mother that I need. It is this positive experience that I need. I am a bit jealous. I haven't experienced playing. Like small kids play with each other. And I am also a small kid being left out. And you, "egg-cell" and "sperm", you play. And I would like to play as well. To experience what you have. I was not allowed to play. Bit by bit it was cut. Your side is playful and our side is more serious. It is about the senses. You just enjoy your senses! Like she said, you touch and smell. And I carry intelligence, "father". I carry your intelligence. It's nice.«

**egg-cell**
»I want to try things and touch and talk and experience and smell. There could be a lot of magic with "sperm". It's not fun all by myself. I want to play with "sperm" too. "sperm" has a lot of cool ideas. It is exciting. It is the opposite of boring.« ["egg-cell" starts humming]

o **egg-cell:** I am intelligent too, by the way.
o **sperm:** I would like to discover more of that. I feel, I have something you don't have. It's amazing. It's so simple.

51

- **Mother:** I like to watch you both because you are so cute. I feel that I have the power to create or not. To make this decision. But I am still in a state…
- **egg-cell:** It looks like you have too much work in the kitchen. But now is the schedule for LOVE.
- **Mother:** At the moment, I refuse to have babies. I don't want to have a baby.
- **sperm:** But your mother didn't refuse you. Therefore, you are here.
- **Mother:** My mother? Excuse me. I interrupted you. Please go on.
- **sperm:** I feel honored when "Mother" talks to me like that! Oh, "egg-cell", did you hear that? Oh, that's the biggest blessing for me. Oh, "Mother" said, »please go on«. Could you imagine what could happen!? [excitingly raising his arms and laughing!] I am saying: »Dearest "Mother", honorable "Mother", I want to bow to you.«
- **egg-cell:** Yes! That's how it's done, "sperm"! Show them. Honor me! I need to be honored. That makes me alive.
- **sperm:** I do the deepest reverence. I was just humbly saying, respectfully, that your mother didn't refuse you. She said yes to you. So, it's my very humble feeling that we can also say yes to something new. »Dearest "Mother". Most beautiful, most respectful…« [laughing]
- **egg-cell** [smiling]: You are laughing but that's totally adequate for me, you know.
- **sperm** [laughs]: I am laughing out of joy.

**father**

»Oh my gosh. We don't have fun anymore, "Mother" and I! We forgot how it is to have fun! Everything is so serious. We are not yet mother and father. But it is on the horizon. But we are already far too serious. And then the woman is not attractive anymore. Gosh! We need some education! I have no idea how it works! My mind is blank. I have no idea. What do you mean by "starting small and talking"?«

**egg-cell**

»You two think if we have children, it's a lot of work and there would be no fun anymore. But I have a different feeling. We can have fun,

52

right? I mean we can play first. And then produce a child. First, it's about smelling and trying and kissing and laughing.«

**Mother**
»I don't take myself seriously. I could laugh with "egg-cell" and "sperm". It was fun. But I still feel like a little girl, not ready to become a mother.«

- o **sperm:** Maybe you massage her a bit? Her shoulders? Small massage like this?
- o **egg-cell:** Listen to "sperm", "father"! Listen to "sperm". You've got the intelligence inside of you. And I've got the intelligence of "Mother".
- o **father:** Oh! I am totally afraid of touching a woman! Oh, my God! I am afraid of touching her!
- o **Mother:** I don't know if I want to be touched by "father". I don't feel comfortable. To be touched by a man.
- o **father:** That's a pity now.

*"egg-cell" is caressing her arm which totally freaks out the "father".*

- o **Mother:** I even don't find him attractive. So...
- o **father:** Loosen up woman. Don't be so uptight. Don't be so much in your head.
- o **Mother:** Yes, that's true. But I don't want to have babies. I think, perhaps, this is why we don't have fun anymore. Because you don't find me attractive.
- o **father:** No. I have the impression, I am just together with a head. Who always thinks. And that's not attractive. Definitely not.

**egg-cell**
»Well, "father", I think you are pretty demanding now. I think it's understandable that "Mother" is scared of having children because it is a lot of work. And it's going to change everything. I mean, I am a natural wonder! And the "father" is demanding! That's not going to do anything to us. Okay, bye, bye. If he can't see the wonder that we are, there is no chance.«

o **father:** No, I don't understand it. I think like a boy in that perspective. Because for me, it has no implications.
o **Mother:** I feel supported by "egg-cell". This gives me more confidence. I don't think it's true that I am only in my head. And I don't feel welcomed with all of myself. If he is more attracted to his "sperm" than to me, then I don't want to make this wonder happen.
o **egg-cell:** I am with you. I feel that he doesn't take responsibility. He is not interested in: How do I open her up, how do I collaborate? He is not interested in us. So, we don't have a chance. So, I am not going to be with him.
o **father:** Yes, I demand it from the woman. Because I don't know how it works.
o **egg-cell:** And that doesn't work.
o **Mother:** I feel now that…. You told us that you feel like a boy. And then I get into the role of the mother, you know. And I have the feeling that you are searching perhaps for the mother?
o **father:** True. But also, for this happiness state.
o **Mother:** I am a mother. I don't have to become one. I am already a mother for the "father".
o **egg-cell:** But then we can't have sex.
o **Mother:** No. We can't have sex and make babies.
o **egg-cell:** I want a connection.

**sperm**
»Me too. I mean, you have this intelligence. You just have to remember. You may talk with your father or you talk with male friends. They will remind you. They will give you tips. You just have to discover it in yourself. You have this in your cells. It's in you. Its male knowledge…«

**father**
»For me, there are two things: One, women are kind of aliens. They are from a different planet. I don't know what to do with them. It is not that they are not interesting. I am afraid of touching them. And second, when you say "talk to male friends or father" – we don't really talk.«

o **sperm:** Come on! Men talk to each other.

54

o **father:** But not the things I really like to ask. The stuff I am a bit ashamed to ask.

*"egg-cell" is moving her hands through her long hair, doing a pony tail.*

o **sperm:** Look at how she is doing her hair! Oh my gosh! Oh, my beauty! I am just captured. Look "father"! Even teenagers talk about this. How you go to girls, how you communicate… I mean, come on! It's cool. Remember these years!
o **Mother:** My "egg-cells" are cool! They all know how to do it. They know how it works.
o **father:** "egg-cells" looks like a goddess. Really…
o **egg-cell:** That's a good start, "father"! That's a good start.
o **sperm:** Tell her! »Tell her…« There was a song![20] Find the song and sing it to her. Put on some music. Drink a glass of wine…
o **egg-cell:** Just tell me how beautiful I am.
o **sperm:** Yeah, that's it. That's it.

*"egg-cell" is singing the song »Miracle of Love«[21]. while caressing her face.*

o **sperm:** That's it! All my attention goes to her. All my attention. There is life. There is a pulse.
o **egg-cell:** Uuhhh, the temperature is rising. I don't know if you noticed.
o **sperm:** Its warm. Connection is warm.
o **Mother:** I am so fascinated watching you. But I feel so disconnected. Going to my head, when "sperm" was talking to "father": "father" has to do IoPT [= Identity-oriented Psychotrauma Theory

---

[20] »Tell her about it« is a song by the American singer and pianist Billy Joel. It was one of my favorite songs when I was young. Funnily, it was released in July 1983, the month of my birthday when I turned 13 years old.

[21] And there is more singing :) Makes me laugh while writing it… »Miracle of love« by the fantastic British pop duo Eurythmics. The song was released November 1986, when I was 16 years old. By the way: »There Must Be an Angel« was my favorite song.

/ Therapy]. And me also! Perhaps we can come together. I am missing my own mother.

o **egg-cell:** "sperm" and I, we don't need IoPT. We are connected to our nature.

*"egg-cell" is singing: »I love you, "sperm"! I want to be with you!«*

o **sperm:** I love you, my most beautiful "egg-cell". I cannot tell how exciting, how beautiful… You are the one! You make all the sense of my life. You make the world beautiful. All because of you.
o **egg-cell:** Thank you! It gives me goosebumps. Everything you say gives me goosebumps. That connects us.
o **sperm:** I want to shout YES to you. A big YES. Yes. Yes.
o **egg-cell:** YEEES. I shout it back to you. YEES. Come on. LOVE ME! See how beautiful I am.
o **father:** I don't wish for IoPT but I wish for an "egg-cell /sperm"–TV. To just watch you. I will close my video function and just watch and listen to you.

*"father" closes his monitor function and so does "Mother".[22]*

o **egg-cell:** These people are crazy! We are not existing without them, you know. The energy is totally turned off; immediately. I don't know what they are thinking but this not going to work.
o **sperm:** I think these people are really troubled. I wish they can find the necessary help. They forgot what is most essential: to enjoy, to play, to connect. We cannot exist on our own without them. They have to do something. This is not life! This is not life what they do.

*"egg-cell" starts to sing and tease again.*

• **sperm:** We cannot come together. They don't build bridges. They don't open new ways. They don't discover.

---

[22] Side note: See what happens next when people, especially men, try to watch life through their screens. This is a step further in replacing our natural playfulness through technology. We can still monitor us. But that's all.

56

- **egg-cell:** That's true. And we need them to build the bridges between us. We are kind of the energy.

*"father" and "Mother" are instantly switching on their cameras.*
.

o **sperm:** Did you meet your father? Not yet? You have to meet him.
o **father:** I don't know where he is, actually.
o **Mother:** You know, you are totally right. You are full of life and that is troubling for me. Because I can't handle it.
o **egg-cell:** It scares your, right? It doesn't scare me. I feel natural and alive.
o **father:** Now I understand it. I forgot what "sperm" is – and you, "Mother"… Let's not use that word!
o **egg-cell:** Woman.
o **father:** Man and woman, exactly. That would be better. "Woman", you forgot to be like "egg-cell". That's what we are missing. And this is what we are searching. I am completely like a small boy coming into my teenage years and I don't know what to do.
o **egg-cell:** The energy! "sperm" is very courageous and very open and full of life and full of fun and daring. That gives me goosebumps. I am very open and fun and very interested. And I am beautiful. And I really need him to see how beautiful we are.

*Everyone decides and agrees to change names: From "father" to "man" and from "Mother" to "woman".*

o **egg-cell:** We don't need to have babies right away. We are just moving towards each other. That is attraction. Having fun. Getting a feeling for it.
o **man:** Ahhh!!! Okay. Again, "sperm", you need to teach me. How do I do it? I forgot again.
o **sperm:** You just look at the "woman". You feel good in yourself. You have it all. You have it all.
o **man:** But she looks so skeptical. I am afraid to get near her!
o **egg-cell:** "woman", smile!

57

- **woman:** I realize that you, "egg-cell", you drive me on. It is your spirit that drives me on going to the "man". And kissing. We do it only to have a baby. That turns me off. I am stuck. I don't want it. I want to be a woman and have fun with the "man".
- **egg-cell:** Yeah, me too. I want to have fun.
- **woman:** No, you want to go to the "sperm" and have babies.
- **egg-cell:** No, I don't want to have babies. I want to have fun. Because it feels great. It gives me energy. When I see "man", ah, that's interesting! He is totally different than me. It's all vibration in the egg-cell. It is not fertilization. Its vibration!
- **woman:** I feel that vibration.

*"egg-cell" starts to sing again. This time it's the song »Good vibrations«!*[23]

- **sperm:** Yeah! Take her to the dance. To the dinner. And just dance.
- **egg-cell:** Now I am telling you the secret, "man": Just tell her how beautiful she is. All the time.
- **woman:** No. You got me in trouble!
- **sperm:** Nothing happened yet. What trouble? I don't do anything.
- **egg-cell:** I just vibrate. When he said let's go, I started to vibrate.
- **woman:** The "man" is making trouble. Not the "sperm".
- **man:** I think, I now get it. I also had in my mind, it's all about babies. Badabum badabam. But no. No. Okay...
- **egg-cell:** Connection. It is all about connection and vibration!
- **man:** Ah, okay! Okay, "woman", let's go for a dance. Where do you like to go?
- **sperm:** Yes! That's it! You do it well.
- **man:** You like to go for Salsa? Or a Walz or Cha-cha or Tango or Kizomba? Or free dancing? Or Rock and Roll?
- **egg-cell:** Outside. I want to dance outside.
- **man:** That sounds great. Maybe I drink a beer to get my courage up a little bit...

---

[23] Now we move into the 1990s: »Good vibrations« is a song by the American group Marky Mark and the Funky Bunch. It was released 1991, again in July (Hello! This can't be a coincidence!). The catchy hook »good vibrations« was sung by Loleatta Holloway. Now, I am 21 years old and guess who danced like crazy to this song?

- **woman:** I don't want to dance. Let's go for dinner.
- **sperm:** That's great.
- **man:** Really? But then we just sit? We don't do anything.
- **sperm:** No, no, no! Just say when and where. What kind of dinner? Let her choose. Just follow her.
- **man:** Okay… It is not that I should be deciding? I thought I should be deciding.
- **sperm:** No, no, no. Let her decide!
- **egg-cell:** Dancing is very courageous. We need time. We are women. And we need to check first, when we go for dinner, if you really feel and see us how beautiful we are. We need to have that security first. Make that experience first.
- **man:** Can I see your body? Can I see the body of the "woman"?
- **sperm:** Oh, not like that!
- **woman:** That's why I don't go dancing. Because I want to see if we are mentally connected.
- **egg-cell:** We are subjects, "man". We are subjects! We are not objects! Sorry, forget it. You will never go to dance with any of us. If you check our bodies first. We need connection! We want to be seen.
- **sperm:** Yes. Talk. Talk! »How are you?«
- **man:** But that's so boring!
- **egg-cell:** Well, you are boring! Who is boring here? This is not boring at all! Come on, show me how much fun you are and how much you like me!
- **sperm:** Make jokes. Make her laugh.
- **man:** Oh! The first thing which comes to my mind is making jokes about her breasts.
- **sperm:** Oh no, no, no, no!!!! Oh, my God. No, no, no, no.
- **woman:** I am half way out here, you know?
- **egg-cell:** Yes. Same here.
- **sperm:** That was a glitch.
- **woman:** I am looking for another "man" who is also a man inside. Not only written "man".
- **man:** Oh, my God. Okay. When it comes to women, my picture is really just: body and breasts and ass.
- **woman:** Wow! This is horrible.

- **man:** Did I say it out loud right now?
- **egg-cell:** No chance. If you don't see me as a subject, I will not vibrate. No chance.
- **man:** "sperm", teach me please!
- **sperm:** Tell her what you like about her. And also, about some inspiring women in history. That women can be so important and they also have a saying. They also have an impact in history, in politics, in science... There were important women. Talk to her. What does she think about the future? What kind of future she wants? Talk to her like that.
- **man:** The first thing I thought: Was there any woman of importance in history?
- **egg-cell:** Oh!!!!!
- **sperm:** Oh, my God! Oh, my God! Look. No, no, no, no. You need to educate yourself a bit. Educate yourself a bit. Which women does she admire? What are you her role models? And do you also admire the same feminine role models? It's very important.
- **egg-cell:** Yeah. Who do you admire? What women do you admire? And why?
- **sperm**: Let's say (Angela) Merkel was kind of okay.

*"man" making the gesture of vomiting.*

- **sperm:** I mean. Start from somewhere. She did well.
- **man:** Let's take Cleopatra. She was beautiful, wasn't she?
- **sperm:** It is not about beauty right now. Intelligence. Strength. Power.

*"man" is rolling his eyes. Looking skeptical all the time.*

- **egg-cell:** Holly shit. This is never going to happen! I don't know how.
- **woman:** I know how. I like "sperm". And also, the spirit of "sperm". The engagement. But I can tell you, I am total shocked. We are in the 21st century and the spirit of the "man" thinking of a woman is catastrophic.

- **man:** As you say this… I am very basic. I have very basic thoughts about women. Really.
- **woman:** I didn't want to say it but the word is Neanderthal… We are in the Stone Age. I can tell you, it's not a mystery: I want to be seen like a human being. That's all.
- **egg-cell:** No, I want to be seen as a WONDERFUL human being. As a wonderful woman. I am full of wonders. I want to be seen as a wonderful woman.
- **woman:** Yeah. You are right. I want to be seen a woman.
- **egg-cell:** If he can't manage to see that than there is no chance. Then we are going to die like the dinosaurs. I am not going to have children with this kind of guy. No, no, no. I want to be wonderful. And I see that "sperm" is so wonderful. Very different of me but also so wonderful.
- **man:** Okay, okay. Let me try. Okay. "woman", what kind of women do you feel inspired by?
- **egg-cell:** By me! By me!
- **woman:** Yes. I am thinking if there is a woman… But actually, by me and my "egg-cell".
- **sperm:** Oh wonderful! Oh, for me that's perfect. You say: »Your unique. You are a really a different kind of "woman". I want to know you better. I want to know, listen to you more and more!«
- **man:** It is actually true! I never heard such a response before! Tell me more.
- **egg-cell:** I tell you, I am wonderful! I have so many ideas. And my body reacts to what people say.
- **sperm:** You are courageous, "man"! Go on, go on!
- **man:** Can you explain more what you are proud of when you think about yourself?
- **woman:** I don't have to be inspired by other women because everything is inside me. I am still a woman, a human being.
- **egg-cell:** I am intelligent. That's what I am proud of. My body is so intelligent you won't believe it.
- **woman:** Yes. That's what I like. I like that I can create the wonder of life. That feels good.
- **egg-cell:** And I vibrate. I vibrate if somebody sees how beautiful I am.

61

- **sperm:** So wonderful. Perfect. [smiling]
- **woman:** I like being a woman because it feels good.
- **man:** Wow…. Where or when do you feel most being a woman?
- **woman:** Always. I don't know if I am getting the question.
- **man:** Maybe something concrete… What do you love to do? When you feel really joyful? Is that good, "sperm"? Are these questions okay?
- **sperm:** Yeah, it's okay. You can ask it.
- **woman:** I like your engagement, "sperm" and "man". But you don't have to ask me all these questions. I only want you to be a man.
- **man:** I was thinking, maybe you would say you love to dance or to cook. Or to sing. Maybe, I would like to join you?
- **woman:** Yes, I like all that stuff. But it comes naturally. I feel it and you feel it.
- **man:** When you say that, I feel a bit insecure; if I may say that.
- **sperm:** Don't say this. You can ask: »Is there anything I can do as a man for you? It will be my pleasure to do something for you.«
- **man:** Is there anything I can do for you as a man? Would be a pleasure.
- **sperm:** And say yes to anything she says. If she asks for repair, say yes. If she asks for dinner, say yes. Okay?
- **man:** I need some alcohol….
- **egg-cell:** I like that he is courageous but I just really want to play and laugh. I really need him to be more courageous. "man", you know, when you asked me »when do you feel like a woman«, I can ask you: »When do you feel like a man?« Because I feel my vibration when you say: »Wow, you are beautiful!« And you are not just saying it but I can feel it. That you admire me. Yeah, that's a great feeling. Then I become alive. And then I ask you, when do you feel alive? When is your body vibrating? Or maybe, it's not vibration in a man? I don't know. When is your body activated?
- **man:** I would like to take you out. I would like to take you out and… I am not yet sure, I have to think about it. Can I surprise you with something? I would like to take my time to do something really beautiful together.
- **woman:** Oh, I like that! For sure we can do it.

62

- **man:** And I made up my mind. You then get some clues and hints, so that you have the right clothes on. That you don't feel uncomfortable. I would like to take you out to surprise you. Would you like to do something in the afternoon together?
- **woman:** Why not in the evening and dinner?
- **man:** I would like to see you in daylight.
- **woman** [laughing]: Okay. Yes.
- **sperm:** Agree with her. She said yes. Okay, okay.
- **egg-cell:** I am afraid he takes me out boxing or so. To a boxing event or cock fight event.
- **man:** No. I am not interested in this.
- **egg-cell:** Because I need something where I feel nice. A little Margarita cocktail maybe, some music. Nice lights. Like a good atmosphere where we can talk.
- **man:** I would like to move a little bit. Nothing stationary. So that we can enjoy each other.
- **woman:** I like it when the "man" takes some initiative and surprises me. But I think, I hope, he is not messing it up.
- **man:** I think, I wouldn't mess it up. Nothing fancy or spectacular. But something more… which creates more a nice, comfortable, warm feeling.
- **egg-cell:** That's nice. And if he fucks it up, we can run away. We have our own two feet. And we can just run. But I have a good feeling that he knows who we are and what we want.
- **man:** What type of food do you like?
- **woman:** I am open. We can go Italian. I don't know. Surprise me.
- **egg-cell:** But not Sushi! I like warm more than cold.
- **man:** The first thing which came to my mind was also Italian.
- **woman:** Ah, that's nice.
- **man:** And I know a very, very nice small, very small restaurant with some delicious homemade Italian food.
- **egg-cell:** That sounds nice. With a little walk on the river side maybe?
- **man:** I was thinking something like this. I would pick you up at 3 o'clock. Would this be fine for you?
- **woman:** In the morning? I told you that we should go for dinner in the evening, honey. I told you once.

o **man:** Okay, okay. I agree. Okay, I had some other things in mind.
o **woman:** That I realized. And that turns me totally off.
o **man:** At 7 o'clock? I will pick you up at 7 o'clock. Next Saturday?
o **woman:** Fine.

*Now we are coming to the end of this conversation.*

o **egg-cell:** It takes a long time to have babies, doesn't it?
o **woman:** Yes. I feel it's a lot of work.
o **egg-cell:** It takes little steps. I mean, I am still not vibrating. So, I am hoping for vibration on the date.
o **woman:** We really have to teach men being a man. That's the topic.
o **egg-cell:** I don't think we have to teach him but just tell him what we like and don't like, you know. I want him to find me very, very beautiful. And if he just says it, it won't work. Because I can feel it if he sees my beauty. That's what I want.
o **man:** I just had in my mind: I want the "woman" to feel ME instantly... beautiful. Like my mother did. Who always cherished me. And it shouldn't be like... Oh God, "sperm"!
o **sperm:** No, no, you did it very well up to here. I am proud of you. And I like so much when she was smiling. She is so beautiful. Very good, very good.
o **egg-cell:** But how do you see me, "man"? Do you see my beauty or don't you? Does this take a while?
o **man:** I have to un-train myself. I just see the body and what the body is equipped with. I hardly see the rest, to be honest. If you ask me straight away: I feel a bit like a spoiled child. It is strange...
o **woman:** Okay. I thought.... teenagers are like that. Teenager men.
o **man:** But younger teenagers. Not older. A younger teenager.

This is how this general-encounter ended. As you can read and see, "man" and "woman" didn't even make it to the first date. And if you think, this is pure exaggeration and that we are not in such a desolate state, well, you may want to start dating again. This general-encounter is very emblematic of western society as it is today.

64

## 2.3 ARTIFICIAL INSEMINATION (IVF)

*General-Encounter (6 words)*
*Egg-cell – sperm – Mother – Father – Doctor – Long-term effect*

From natural conception to artificial insemination. Whoever thought IVF would be the answer, a blessing, a technological innovation for women to become pregnant, this next encounter will be a wake-up call. Or should I say shock? We don't only understand the wonder of creating life, we are on a path of destroying the nature and wonder that is within all of us. Listen to what "Long-term effect" was saying:

»I can experiment with every type of technology. Crossings, matchings – whatever crazy thing is coming to my mind. And I am really, really crazy. Half-machine, half-man is just at the bottom of my list. Just the bottom of my list! I am crazier than that. And I NEED the "Mother" as the entry door. I have castrated the "Father" anyways already. He is out of the game. He will never ever protect his family.«

o **Egg-cell:** I am feeling quite natural. "sperm", what is happening? I am waiting.
o **sperm:** I don't know where to go. I don't know the direction. When somebody talks, I get stomach aching. I don't know why.
o **Long-term effect:** It is so funny. On my screen, I am between you two: "Egg-cell", you are on my left – and you, "sperm", you are on my right. I could hold up my hand on the left and on the right, just to block you. I am sitting here thinking: »No!«
o **sperm:** When you say »right«... I don't know what is right.
o **Egg-cell:** I feel like a Siren sitting on a stone. Like in a fairy-tale, saying »Hello. I am giving you directions.« I feel like I want to sing so that "sperm" knows the direction on where to go. Here I am. »Hello! Shoobeedoobeedoo.«
o **sperm:** I have nowhere to go. I like it but I am totally insecure.
o **Egg-cell:** That makes me nervous, too. I wish you were more secure.
o **sperm:** Normally, I know the direction but this is not... something is holding me back.

65

- **Doctor:** I wonder if it is about me, because I am observing you. I look at myself and I just have this plain face of watching. I see myself as cruel, looking through a glass or something. I don't have much feelings. I don't feel good. I have a little bit of a stomach ache but I observe you. I watch you. That's all what I am doing. I wonder if this is affecting you, "sperm"?
- **Egg-cell:** Yes, this is affecting me because I don't want that. It is a very intimate moment. Why is he watching?? It doesn't feel good. He is kind of a stalker.
- **Doctor:** I look at myself and I see that I am so uninvolved in a way. Looking through that glass and seeing what you are doing. It is this plain looking and doing my job. But I have a stomach ache, too. And I think I am a male. And what "sperm" is talking about, the physical experience, is a little bit like me.
- **Long-term effect:** I would like to silence all of you. That there is no connection between "Egg-cell" and "sperm" and that no one would be talking. I would like to put my hand over your mouth– on every one of you. Stay silent, don't talk, don't come together.
- **Father:** And there is no connection between "Mother" and me. We are the most far away from each other on the screen. I am in one corner and "Mother" is in the opposite corner.
- **Mother:** I don't recognize anyone here. "Father" and me are drinking, having drinks. He is at a different cocktail party and I am at different cocktail party. I am very busy with my schedule. I have paid for that clinic. So, sort it out. I have things to schedule and attend. Just sort it out.
- **Egg-cell:** I feel like the holly wonder of nature but everybody is working and watching and nobody has respect for me. And then I thought: »Am I inside you, "Mother"?« No, I am not inside you. I am watching you from the outside. What the fuck is happening here?
- **Doctor:** But it is the same for me when I look at you, "Egg-cell". And when you do this, I feel really drawn to it. I really like the energy about it but then I go back to business. As soon as I look at "sperm", I feel like I need to do this. What is happening here?

66

- **Egg-cell:** For me, this is really horrible. I feel no connection, no worshiping of the wonder I am. I feel really raped already. It didn't happen yet but I know it is going to happen.
- **sperm:** I don't have… I am losing my power.
- **Egg-cell:** They are taking your power, too. I want your natural energy and power and security.
- **sperm:** I also want to do my job; in a natural way. But watching "Long-term effect" and "Doctor" … I have also a stomach ache like the "Doctor". What does this mean? Mine or his? I am losing my energy and my faith. I am losing my courage.
- **Doctor:** I was thinking, maybe it is even my sperm? And I see "sperm" as very weak, small. The "Egg-cell" is the strongest part here. But the "sperm" is very weak. Used and abused. And what you just said, I have a stomach ache and you have a stomach ache – I am wondering if I am doing an experiment here using my own sperm?[24]

**Long-term effect**

»If the "Doctor" would use his own sperm? Great! I would love that! The crazier it gets, the happier I am. I am happy with every division which is going on here. If you, "Egg-cell" and "sperm" would get together, it would crush me. But now, I am happy. And if there is another layer of craziness coming in, I am even happier. I am loving it right now! Total disaster. Mission accomplished. I mastered what is not nature. Everything which is artificial or can be manipulated. I love that! I am not pro nature. Let's call it more that way: I don't like if things harmonize with each other. And you and "sperm" where too much in harmony in the beginning. And I don't like that. I am getting happier and happier by the minute. It's amazing! And if "Mother" is having a schedule… perfect! [smiling] Then she is not asking any questions! I can do whatever I want to! It is amazing. I am loving it. I have my own

---

[24] Interestingly, shortly after this work I had watched the series »Frühling« [Spring] in the ZDF Mediathek, which in season 08, episode 03 dealt precisely with the topic of sperm donation. When it turned out after many years that the doctor was the sperm donor… https://www.zdf.de/serien/fruehling/fruehling---das-verlorene-maedchen-100.html

laboratory here. I CAN DO WHATEVER I WANT. It is not control. It is like a game for me. I can do whatever I want and NO ONE IS ASKING ME ANY QUESTIONS. Everyone is distracted and feels miserable. It makes me so happy. It is amazing, really. I feel a bit crazy here, to be honest. Disaster makes me happy!« [laughing out loud]

○ **sperm:** Yes. I feel like I am not inside of me. I feel like a Picasso picture. It is horrible that feeling. I can't start making life with that.
○ **Doctor:** I feel it in my body that what I am doing is wrong. But I always get back to what I have to do here. I think this is what my stomach ache is about. It is not right. But I am anyways doing it. I have to do it.
○ **Long-term effect:** I am more like a master mind employing the "Doctor" who has to do the job! But me, I am the crazy one deciding what to do. What to tweak and whom to manipulate.
○ **Doctor:** Yes, this is right. You are my employer.
○ **Mother:** Well, that "Doctor" seems so likeable to me. I mean, I look more at the "Doctor" than I look at the "Father". [laughing]
○ **Father:** Yes, I am completely whipped out. Completely castrated.
○ **Long-term effect:** You play no role in this game, "Father".

**Egg-cell**
»I don't want a castrated "Father". I want a healthy "Father" and a healthy "sperm". That listens to me when I am singing. And coming naturally my way. But I see this is not reality. I am really frustrated and sad. Because this is not going to make me happy. This is not going to be a base of happiness. This is really sad. All the mystery and natural wonder was such a wonderful feeling. And it is all fucked up.«

○ **Doctor:** And it seems that "Mother" and "Father" are not in relationship. They don't even want a child together. This is why it doesn't work. So, I use my sperm. So, that I can make some money with it.
○ **Long-term effect:** Thumbs up. Oh, fantastic!!
○ **sperm:** Me, as a "sperm", I don't have any connection to that. In the beginning, I have been healthy and I wanted to do my job. But I feel insecure. Like "Egg-cell", now I feel raped by all the

dynamics. And I am much under pressure. I have to find a way out. But there is no way out. I am a little sperm and there is so much pressure on me. Now I feel desperate.

o **Long-term effect:** I almost accomplished my mission. Oh, I am loving my job! I have the feeling, I have more connection to the "Mother". She is a bit as crazy as I am. I can tell her EVERY-THING! SHE BELIEVES ME ANYTHING!

o **Egg-cell:** Working and functioning is always more important than a child! It's really crazy!

o **Long-term effect:** Of course. Of course! What are you dreaming of?

o **Egg-cell:** It is not a dream. Usually, nature is a reality. But now it's destroyed.

o **Long-term effect:** Who cares about nature?? Wonder, nature. Disgusting!

o **Egg-cell:** I feel that you are capable. I can feel that and it is really sad. Because I want the wonder and I want the melody. There is a song in me. There is music in me.

o **Long-term effect:** I am almost vomiting.

**Mother**

»Wonder is technology and all these inventions. And saving time. And going to Mars. And building colonies on Mars. That is the wonder. What wonder are you fucking talking about? Our children will be living in the colonies on Mars. What are you talking about? Wonder, wonder, wonder?«

o **Long-term effect:** THANK YOU! Maybe I can build a little bit of technology inside the child? Don't you think that would be awesome? I am pretty sure the "Doctor" will do it. Or there will be another doctor.

o **Egg-cell:** I really don't want this. It is like the meaning of life has been …

o **Long-term effect:** … yes, destroyed.

o **Egg-cell:** War on the meaning of life. Nothing makes sense anymore.

o **Long-term effect:** Oh, for me it makes total sense.

- o **Egg-cell:** All happiness is killed.
- o **Long-term effect:** Yeah. Yes. That's my goal.

**Doctor**

»And I know it is wrong what I am doing. But I can't step out of it. I don't know if it is about my personal security or something. But I have the feeling I cannot step out. It would be destroying my own life. Or I would be excluded or I would fail. There is something about the consequences. And nobody would care if I'd step out of it. That would be my problem. I would be alone if I would step out.«

**Mother**

»I can hire many other doctors. You are all tools. Very easily changeable. No power at all. No assertiveness. To make sense, you need to be different than previous generations. Like the primitive people, breading in caves with very primitive ways. Each generation is more and more intelligent. More and more advanced. This is what makes sense. This is what makes us different.«

**Egg-cell**

»I rather want all humans to die. And I want this race to not go to Mars or to be with this "Mother". I don't want to live like that. Because this doesn't make sense. You are so stupid! I am not primitive! I am the wonder of nature. I am so complex and you are calling me primitive! This is what makes me puke right now. For me, it is the worst that the "Mother" is so disconnected from nature and from the wisdom. That is so crazy to say that I am primitive.«

**Long-term effect**

»I've done a fantastic job with the "Mother"! I am so happy! So happy! I could even marry her. Amazing! I love it. Because when I have this free pass I CAN DO ANYHTING! ANYTHING I WANT TO. Like a mega maniac. I can experiment with every type of technology. Crossings, matchings – whatever crazy thing is coming to my mind. And I am really, really crazy. Half-machine, half-man is just at the bottom of my list. Just the bottom of my list! I am crazier than that. And I NEED the "Mother" as the entry door. I have castrated the "Father" anyways already. He is out of the game. He will never ever protect his family. Never ever. I did a good job! What should I say? I could really congratulate myself. You see, I am separating you, "Egg-cell", from "sperm" all the time. I am separating you both.«

o **Egg-cell:** Crazy. Life doesn't make sense anymore.
o **sperm:** It doesn't make sense because we can't make children like this.
o **Egg-cell:** Well, we can make children – but without happiness. Without the wonder. Without making sense. Just functional.
o **sperm:** I want to tell you that I gave up. This "Long-term effect" turns out like something with intention.

**Long-term effect**
»I WILL DO ANYTHING TO SEPARATE THEM FROM EACH OTHER! Everyone is so easily distracted and believes everything they hear or read. So simple! It is almost too simple. You know, in former times, you had to do this in hidden sites, facilities, laboratories. These days, pfftt, you can do it almost in the open! Under the umbrella of »technology and future«. Isn't this awesome? This is just the first step. If I could get rid of you, all of you, that of course would be the best thing! You don't need a "Father", a "Mother", an "Egg-cell" or a "sperm". Or a "Doctor". Robots could do this as well. UNLIMITED POSSIBILITES! Welcome to the new world. And then, one day, I don't need to protect but I can raise up my hands and then I am like God.«

**Mother**
»Well, eggs in laboratories and sperms would soon be also produced artificially in laboratories. We are in the 21st century. Come on! Be a bit open minded. Open your mind. This is what is exciting! Imagine, imagine! There is the song…«[25]

---

[25] Reference to John Lennon's song »Imagine« from 1971, published in his album which had the same title. https://www.johnlennon.com/music/albums/imagine/

o **Doctor:** The separation with the dash between "Long" and "term"… The only solution is that "Mother" and "Father" would come to terms with each other. So that they can make babies.

**Mother**
»All the new ideas in science and technology have been received with resistance in all human history. Come on! Just look at the history. We are improving. That is science. You cannot stand in the way for a long time. You just agree. You cannot stop that. Mars is also nature! It is cosmic nature. For the first time in human history, we are opening up to the nature in cosmos. You are the star dust! Isn't this exciting?! Why doing IVF? Another step to experiment and to be courageous. Why not to come? We have all these possibilities. Why not to do it? You just use the opportunities. Don't make it so complex.«

o **Long-term effect:** I don't know why you are all so sad. It is a moment of happiness right now.
o **Doctor:** I find it interesting that my whole body says no to this. But I still can't act to step out.
o **Long-term effect:** You will never. I know that. Once you step into this machine and you are a wheel, you can never leave it.
o **Doctor:** It is so strange. I look at myself and I don't even feel fully human myself. I already feel like I am a mixture of something artificial. I can't see myself as a natural product anymore.
o **Long-term effect:** I feel, when I look at you, that you have been drugged or something. Like under medication or so. You don't clearly see or think or feel anymore. Which is perfect for me.
o **Doctor:** I can feel the aching, too, in my whole belly. Something is not right.
o **Egg-cell:** What happened to you, "Mother"? You are just a head. What happened to your feelings and your body? You are just a head without a body. You are just dreaming. You are just thinking.

**Mother**
»It is like dreaming. That is what fulfills me. This is what makes sense. Be different. Why to repeat my mother, my grandmother? Everything changes so speedily in our times. Of course, I will be dreaming. I have

72

these abilities, mental abilities. Of course, I will be using them. Animals cannot dream. I imagine, I dream, I design. I design!! I design my future with all the details I want. I can set it up as I want. I also set up timings, you see. It is under control in my schedule.«

- o **Egg-cell:** I see that "Doctor" and "sperm" are starting to feel something but there is no feeling in your body.
- o **Mother:** I feel excited about what is coming.
- o **Egg-cell:** When I look at you, I see a raped woman. I see raped women.

**Long-term effect**
»No! I told her that she can have a baby. But why does she need a man? She can do anything she wants whenever she wants. I told her so. Isn't this awesome? That is the first step. Independent. Professional.«

- o **Doctor:** What do you think or feel "Mother" when you look at "Father"?
- o **Long-term effect:** Loser!
- o **Mother:** What about the money that I paid you? Or losing your position? This is not your job to ask me such question. Like everyone knowing their place. I always hire the right people for my projects.
- o **Doctor:** I think I get in touch with me being a child. Asking my mother if she loves my dad. And she says it is not your business. It really hurts. I am so disconnected from my mother and my father right now. It is not my business. Just be a child and don't say anything… No questions. Just take it how it is…

*There is silence for a long time.*

- o **Egg-cell:** Love is missing here.

**Mother**
»Look, don't be so stupid! It is much better to not get too attached to men. You know why? They leave you pregnant! They go. They can do anything. They don't take responsibility. You have to deal with the

73

consequences. So, keep strong! What's wrong with you? You have all the technology, so use it! I have plan A, I have plan B, I have plan C. Love is confusing. So, don't follow it. One moment it is here and one moment it is gone. One moment you love and one moment you hate. I mean, you cannot depend on such emotions. Technology is always giving. In the sense of love cannot. Technology is always 100% efficient. Secure. Warranty. WARRANTY, WARRANTY, WARRANTY! I want warranty in life!«

o **Egg-cell:** Life without love doesn't make sense at all. Even if it is full of plans. I don't want that life, really. I don't. I am out.

o **sperm:** I am totally confused. But I am split. I connected somehow to "Doctor" and I have such empathy for him. But when "Mother" is speaking… There are two sides I cannot get together. Feelings are not confusing but technology is confusing me. Because I am out of nature, I can feel it. Nature is my origin.

o **Mother:** You sound so innocent and you expect me to believe you?? Look, I know exactly what happens when you are in my belly. I know this very well. I researched, I studied it. And this is why I have my plan A, B, C. If this bastard there would leave me one day, I made all my backups. You are very innocent until you are in me, right!?

**Doctor**

»If my mother and my father don't love each other, they cannot love me. I feel it. This is very painful. My mother doesn't love my father at all. My father isn't here. I feel no father. I think, I realized why I am doing this job. This is all I know. It is my experience as a child. My parents can't love each other. Then they can't love me. This is what I am doing here, too. I do what happened to me. I am doing this but my body is clearly in pain about it. Because it is my story. It has something to do with my early life.«

o **Egg-cell:** It is cold there. There is just hate. It is steel. Bang. Bang.

o **Mother:** It is cold because it is a laboratory. When you go home, Mr. "Doctor", you put on a song about love and you listen to it.

74

With a glass of wine. But when you work it is about results, it is about methodology.

o **Long-term effect:** You are telling the story and the "Father" left. Technology will save you. Trust in technology. It is always there. At the fingertip of your hand. Trust the technology...

o **Mother:** If there is no "Father", technology can protect us. We will put cameras all around.

o **sperm:** I don't need a father. I am complete. I don't have the longing towards "Father" or "Mother". There are no feelings about it. I am here and I want to live. Everything is here. I want to do my nature-job.

o **Doctor:** If we would be in one room, I would take you on my lab. For some reason I have the feeling you belong to me. You are almost like a young part of me and I want to take you back. I don't know if it makes sense but this is how I feel.

o **sperm:** Yeah, it makes sense. That is also how I feel. I feel like an origin, a feeling, a primal feeling.

o **Doctor:** Yeah. And right now, I feel the pain but I feel connected to you. I do something right if I take you back in my lab and take you back to me.

o **Egg-cell:** I feel very disconnected from you, "sperm" and "Doctor". What is the harmony about? I feel like dead. My nature has gone. I feel totally destroyed and oppressed. And you are blah blah blah. This is really strange.

o **Long-term effect:** I think I need to launch a campaign. There is too much harmony going on here.

o **Doctor:** "Egg-cell", I hear what you are saying but I think for me, I come out of a very deep disconnection. I am now connecting with "sperm". I got in touch with a very young part of me, a very early pain. And know, I could have the kind of courage to do the right thing. I know that "sperm" belongs in a way to me. I am doing something out of love. Before that I had the feeling, I am doing something wrong here. But right now, I have the feeling I am doing something without admiration from outside. I see you, "Egg-cell". I feel that this is my start.

- **Egg-cell:** I want you to know that I need worshiping. Not like submission but worshipping. And I need awe. And I need longing. And I need security. And I need someone who wants to hear my song.
- **Doctor:** And I had that at the beginning. I could hear it. I felt really attracted to it but I suppressed it. I just did my job because I was so disconnected. But with the connection to "sperm", this is the way. This is how I can stay connected with my own feelings. That it is okay. That I am not wrong. That I am not under a bridge in poverty if I am doing the right thing. "sperm" is very young and small. I think it takes time.
- **sperm:** I can also feel it. When you speak, "Doctor", I feel like growing. I felt very small all the time before. I am still insecure because I have also something in my back. A long-term effect maybe from the "Mother", from the "Father". It is not clear. But I also heard the music, "Egg-cell" singing, and I wanted to start singing the music. I can hear you. But something pulled me back because of the tensions. I want to go to "Egg-cell" but I am still not free. I am confused. I feel like I am in a sterile vacuum. It feels very awkward. Everybody is looking at me. I have to do something. I am not in my environment I used to. In the womb? It feels dead. There is no life. It feels like life is very compressed and under pressure. I feel very awkward. There can't be life in a vacuum.
- **Doctor:** You wouldn't come together unless you are forced to do it in this environment...
- **sperm:** It would work. But it is without soul and without life.
- **Long-term effect:** What are you having right now? Therapy session or what? Then I have to interfere again. What type of bullshit is this now? "Mother", what do you think?

**Mother:**
»I was thinking that maybe after 20, 30 years, there would be the opportunity to modify the "Egg-cell" and "sperm". That they don't produce such silly ideas. You just modify with a quality that you want to reproduce. Just imagine. You select what you imprint.«

- **Long-term effect:** That is a good idea! Let's see if we can take the emotions out of this.

76

- **Mother:** Just a waste of time.
- **Doctor:** "Father", what are you thinking?
- **Long-term effect:** Is the "Doctor" now a therapist? That I don't like. I think we have to do something about the so-called therapists. That they don't do therapy. To get rid of the stupid therapists. I think that should be my next goal. What do you think?
- **Mother:** I never need therapy. That's bullshit. Just apply science. And I am excited that after democracy they talk about technocracy. It is on the way, it is on the way.

**Egg-cell**

»I feel there is going to be two separate kind of people: You, "Long-term effect" and "Mother" – the cold people. And the natural people. And I am going to go to the natural people with the psychologists. It is like a decision to go to that kind of people and be those kinds of people. It is going to be wonderful with the therapist and the natural people. I can feel my wisdom and I can feel that you will be very unhappy. Very megalomaniacal. And it is going to be a cold world and you will be talking a lot. And I will have to deal with defamations and everything. I will not listen. I will be in my crowd of people. This is what I feel. There are feelings on this side. We are interested in loving and feeling. And they are interested in technology and not feeling. I don't want to have to do with those people, really. And it is not going to work long-term, that artificial stuff. I can feel that. Because I am the base of life.«

- **Doctor:** I will quit my job.
- **Long-term effect:** Yeah, but I will do my part to discredit them! Too much happiness on that side, you know?
- **sperm:** I can feel that too. You can't disconnect us, me, from "Egg-cell". And you can't put me in something like cotton wool or frozen state. The original feeling is not going away. I know where I come from and what I am.
- **Egg-cell:** I will find the places with love and feelings. I will kind of build my own society. I will connect with people who can feel.
- **Doctor:** This helps me to step out, to take action, to quit. It is really important that I don't feel alone.
- **Father:** I am not existing.

- **Egg-cell:** Ah, okay. Yeah, for this "Mother" you are not existing. I can see that.
- **Mother:** It is proven that you can derive a chromosome only from the egg. And men are not needed for reproduction. That is possible. Feminine has it all. Men are not needed. That is achievable. Scientifically. I don't have all the details but you can find it on the internet.
- **Egg-cell:** I mean, I don't want to have anything to do with what "Mother" says. I want "sperm", I want men because I need men for love. I don't care about chromosomes and technology and all that. I want nature. I want life. And I want love and feelings. And all the chaotic non-controllable stuff. That is interesting for me. And the music. Everything can go wrong within music but it is really fun to try. Sometimes it is chaotic, sometimes it is crazy but this is interesting. That is life. That stuff doesn't feel like life.
- **Long-term effect:** That is the goal: No life.
- **sperm:** I would like to listen to your music, "Egg-cell". I would like to listen to the music.
- **Egg-cell:** But I think we have to go somewhere else. I can't sing my music with "Mother" and "Long-term effect". With these people, I can't. With you, "sperm", and "Doctor" I could sing. So, we have to go somewhere else, I think.
- **Mother:** Look, you research a bit in German philosophy and human history. The most exciting thing humanity can reach is how to conquer life. When you conquer life, you conquer death. We are at the last point of evolution! Nothing can be more exciting. That is the real life! Life with a big L. Life forever.

*"Long-term effect" is clapping its hands and giving the thumbs up.*

- **Long-term effect:** I did a marvelous job. I am so proud of myself.
- **Mother:** Invincible life.
- **Egg-cell:** She is crazy.
- **sperm:** Yeah. But we need "Mother". We need a woman who becomes a mother.
- **Mother:** "Doctor", it is high time to finish your job! It starts to suck really. I mean, if you quit at this stage or take any of my "sperm"

or "Egg-cell" I will sue you! You will pay me a very high compensation. And I will ruin your career and life. So, finish that! Now!

o **Doctor:** That is exactly why I was doing this job. Out of fear. Why I didn't quit was exactly that fear. But it feels like it doesn't matter to me anymore. I will do what feels right. It doesn't scare me anymore. I see clearly that you are my mother. I see in you my own mother and this is why I got here.

o **Mother** [laughing]: You are the type of people who need therapists! I will ask the clinic for replacement. People sometimes can be really weird.

## 2.4 SMOKING

*Self-encounter (Woman, Poland, 3 words)*
*Polish: palenie -Ja – oddychać*
*English: smoking– I – breathe*

Some background information from the women herself which she shared during her self-encounter:

»My mother was controlling, my father was controlling. They were very good at that. When I was a child, I remember that I had all the time the problem with breathing. Even now, when we started the process, I can't breathe properly. And also, my daughter has this symptom. My mother coughed a lot because of smoking. Early in the morning, she had a big cough. We also coughed a lot because of our illness.
My mother was 30 when she got me. I am the second child. My sister is 1 year and 2 months older than me. Previous encounters have shown that I wasn't wanted.
My mother started to smoke when she was 15 and she smoked all her life. My father smoked occasionally, sometimes regularly. There was a time when it felt natural when they smoked at home. And I remember that I hated it when there were parties. Because my mother's birthday was on October 15 and my fathers on October 16, so they partied together. There was a lot of smoke and yellow curtains. My mother had Parkinson's. One of the researches said that smoking helps with this

disease. It was natural that she smoked all the time. My mother died 2,5 years ago and my father is still alive.«

As it turns out in this work, smoking – just like religion – is a protective function or a distraction to avoid seeing trans-generational trauma. The smoke blinds you, clouds everything around you so that you don't recognize the truth behind it.

**Ja (I)**
»I am holding it there. But I can't fully breathe. It is tight. I am all the time busy with that. I can't open my eyes. It is toxic. I am getting it in because I have nostrils but then I feel how toxic it is and then I stop it. And getting it out in order to not poisoning myself. I don't have any idea about my surroundings. I am so busy with this process. It burns, from my eye to my cheek, and I have to resist it. The toxicity is also in my throat. I feel it also a bit in my esophagus. Very bitter, a sharp bitterness. Heavy toxic gas. I feel very small. I have no orientation where I am. I am very much dependent on my surrounding. I could be in the womb but I can't connect with anything. I am in a constant struggle. I see you and I am with you and I totally understand your feelings and struggles. I experience the same. I don't feel safe. There is no safety. I am expecting the next toxification. I am in a state of "what is coming next to resist?".«

**oddychać (breathe)**
»At the beginning, I felt a strong energy of hate and aggression. I feel good when I have power. And I feel like I really want to control "palenie" (smoking). How dare she goes away, out of my sight? When "Ja" (I) was speaking, I dissociated. When she talked about the feeling in her nose, I got a lot of fluid down my throat. It is difficult to swallow. There is something in me which is really curious to know what we swallowed. It doesn't feel like smoke to me. It feels like a gloopy toxin. You were asked how you felt as a child… I could really sense how hard it was for you to answer this question. I could connect very strongly with this question. It is a good question to ask me. My sense was that every time my parents put a cigarette in their mouth, they forgot about me. Some switch went off and I felt like being left there. Like I didn't

exist. The smoking switched something in their brain and then there was no chance to connect. This hope and expectation – always waiting for something – but also the hope to be seen. But as soon as this cigarette got lit on, there was no chance. There is a sense of hopelessness. I really like that you hear me. I see something shifting in your energy.«

**palenie (smoking)**
»I came in with a sense of panic. I felt my throat being very tight. I can't take breathe from my belly. There is tension in my head. I feel overwhelmed and dysregulated. I was going back and forth. Can't stay here. I am not feeling safe, our parents are not safe, but they are my environment.«

**Ja (I)**
»When "oddychać" (breathe) was talking, I felt that she is that small vital energy which I still manage to protect in my belly. Which keeps me alive. But it's very tight. It cannot expand. I am not given anything. I feel in a kind of environment where I am totally dependent. You cannot ask why we are not safe. It is because I cannot get anything in! And I am not sure I will manage to make it. I cannot make it without taking in! I am in a deprived state. Much worse than deprivation. I do not how to manage to keep the small area of inner aliveness in my belly.

The intensity of being toxified is now less and I open my mouth. Because that is the only way. Still I don't feel nourished. But these sounds – do they come from you? They feel good for me. I don't know what you are doing. I am not sure of anything. I am in a suspended state waiting for something to come. Like being rejected or being wanted. In that in-between state.«

*The woman responds: »Inside of me, I have this question whether to live or not. Sometimes I want to live and sometimes I don't want to live.«*

**palenie (smoking)**
»I want you to live. I love you very much. Move, so that you sense that you are alive. I am clear; I want us to live. I want to and we can do this. I know it's hard. You have us. Things will get easier.«

*We are bringing the mother in, "mama".*

o **oddychać (breathe):** When "Ja" (I) said that I am a part of her, I feel that I am getting some clarity. And I know, I feel connected to "Ja" (I) and I know she wants me. If you go into the symptoms, the stress and the fear, you drag me in. And I don't want to be dragged in. I breath because I breath naturally. The anger that I feel is because I deserve to exist. And there is no question about that in this resonance. When I look at you now, I see you being five years old. I am here and you have to choose. I am breath and life.

o **Ja (I):** I am in a suspended state. You've said very clearly »sometimes I want to live and sometimes I don't«. The way I feel is different: Someone outside of me doesn't want me to live. Sometimes I am toxified and sometimes I can get a bit input which still sustains me here. And that is so confusing. I also heard "oddychać" (breathe). It is in my nature to stay. It is in my nature to take in and to be. As I said this, for the first time, I took a full breath for a moment. It is still very difficult but something slightly changed. Should I be hopeless? I am on the edge of giving up.

o **mama:** Since coming in I feel a pressure on my chest. Constantly being busy not feeling. When "Ja" (I) is talking, it is annoying. I am focused on "palenie" (smoking). I am not interested in you. My only connection is "Ja" (I) and "palenie" (smoking).

o **oddychać (breathe):** I am life. You went to your mother first. I felt a lot of sadness when you chose to go to her first. I have to be in competition with her. I am also beginning to get on the edge of getting pissed off by you. I am here! It is your choice! I could turn in on you if you don't choose me.

o **Mama:** I am getting angry if "oddychać" (breathe) is talking like that.

o **palenie (smoking):** I agree with the mother. She was too much. I don't feel at ease with her. I don't have a sense of myself with her. I wish you could feel the aliveness that I have. I want to support you and "Ja" (I).

*»"oddychać (breathe)" sounded like she would be conditioning us. I wanted all of us to be on the same page together and not against each*

*other. I want to live. I want you to want to live. And I want to support "Ja (I)". And maybe as long as she continues to breathe, I can support her with the heaviness and the state that she is in.«*

o **Ja (I):** You thanked "oddychać" (breathe)? Did you thank me, struggling here for you? What did "Mama" do for you? Either you check me out with your hopelessness or take a decision!!! I don't want your suffering! You like your pain! I don't like it.

*»I want to thank my mother for giving me life. I lived in a religious family. Especially from my mothers' side. I spent a lot of time in church as a child and as a teenager. I attended a lot of groups.«*

*We included a "?" in order to dig deeper.*

**?**

»I can breathe but I am rocking back and forward all the time. What is this? I was thinking about… Turkey… In some religious type of form where they go back and forth, back and forth all the time. What is happening in your family? To which extent were they religious? Do they go into a kind of trance when they are in this religious state? It is very stressful here. I feel like "palenie" (smoking) is here to cover up something in order that you don't see beyond the smoke. There is something mad here. There is something behind that fucking smoke! It is me. I am there. I don't know why "oddychać" (breathe) is blurred, why "Ja" (I) is pulling down her head. You are also covering it up. You don't like to see it either. You keep yourself in that limbo state of "do I want to live or not" because there is a bigger mess on the other side! I am not sure if you really want to see it. Here, no one is talking about anything of deep importance. It is driving me mad! You have to take deep, deep breaths, because you have to go – through that smoke – on the other side. It has something to do with oppression.«

*»One thing which is coming up for me: In the first or second self-encounter in Warsaw, what showed up was that religion is part of my life. There was a priest. Something happened with my mother and the priest. Maybe sexual abuse or something?«*

?

»It is bigger than this! I do not know but something happened with your mother. It is like generational shit. If you stay a victim, you will never uncover anything from your family. Everything will stay behind the smoke. It is like a blur. No one sees anything, no one says anything. But if you decide to step out of this victimhood and take deep breaths, then the smoke will go away. Then you will take one step after the other. And it is important to take one step after the other because there is so much shit on the other side.«

*»Just today I thought about my daughters first communion.«*

?

»I couldn't care less. I couldn't care less about the first communion! There is a mix between religion and something else. It is all intertwined. It is a total nightmare. Forget about everything you know and you have been taught. I am having the impression that religion is blurring your mind as well. It is also like smoke. It never lets you see clearly. And for me that is the decision to be taken. And then your life will change. I know that. Because you cannot live with such a big load on your back. It is weighing you down! It is suppressing you! Everyone in your family lived like that. One generation after the other. Everyone! No one ever lived. You do not know what life is. And it will go on forever if no one is stopping it. It is a conscious decision you have to take.«

o **palenie (smoking):** I like what you are sharing, "?". It is exactly how I felt in the beginning. The stress is overwhelming. I feel like I am also a strong resource. I don't know why things are stuck here.
o **?:** I need everyone to wake up. I know you have a lot of energy, "palenie" (smoking). I can feel it. I can feel your energy. And it is like a very nice energy, a nice power.
o **palenie (smoking):** But nobody is taking it in. There is no one to direct it to. I have all this energy, waiting for a place to go.

**?**

»I need all of you. I need "Ja" (I), I need "oddychać" (breathe), I need "palenie" (smoking). She has such a great energy. She needs a direction. For me, we are repeating the same old patterns like generations before. And this is a waste of life and a waste of energy. This is the reason why your life is so heavy. Because it was always like this. I feel such a burden on my back. It is hurting like crazy. And me, I clearly know, I do not want to carry this with me. I do not want to live the same life. Just bending over, working for someone else. Almost like a slave. I hate it. I fucking hate it! Like I would be in a movie and I can tune into every women's generation. Same shit!! I am tired. Tired of this one! Of whatever religion it was! Smoke it is – what women are supposed to do and not to do. Smoke! I hate it! And I am waiting for your signal – and the others – to wake up so that we can finally embark on this train. And take it step by step.«

**Ja (I)**

»I liked everything that "?" has been saying. That made me raise up again. I don't feel you want me. I don't feel you choose me. You are so interested in the mess, the communion. I don't feel you are interested in your "oddychać" (breathe). You don't give us any strength. And without your decision it is not possible. Decide where you invest in! Where you invest your will in! Do you decide in favor of the communion and attending these groups in church and suffering like a good Christian? This is a decision! Then go with it. Weep. Maybe God will hear you. Then choose this lifestyle. But then I want to be checked out. This is my right! Is it too much? A space of welcome? Please. I want to be nourished. Do you like to see me, to connect with me, to rejoice?«

*»I forgot about joy of life. I forgot about you. I am so sorry for that. I want to be with you. I want to hug you. I want to welcome you.«*

o **Ja (I):** I understand that it is a process. But you, you remember these words. That's the deal.

85

**?**

»I have a wish for Christmas: Let's end the suffering. It doesn't have to be this big and dramatic. I do not want to live the life of previous generations! No! I want live without the burden of this shit. Without suffering and oppression and denial – and what else is in the package. No! It is like you are standing in front of the communion but you are standing in line of the suffering! "Oh, please give me some suffering. Please, dear God, give me some more suffering." Give me a break! Sorry! Are you crazy? No way! By the way: Live is not about suffering. Even if someone told you. That is not true! Simply not true! Marketing bullshit. Keeps you small and in fear. Oh, I hate it. I hate it!«

**oddychać (breath)**

»You like to hear from me? Funny, I have to ask. Clearly you are not going to ask me. I am the physicality of what makes you exist. For me it's clear: Breathe and you exist. Then I will begin to trust you. Then I can grow and grow into "I". I love her. I was waiting in this hopeless state. There is no saving. There is just breathing now. Nothing is going to save us. Somehow in the womb we took the choice. And I see your face different now and I like that. It is not so pitiful. It is wider and more open and expressed.«

Epilogue

Who would have thought that smoking can literally disguise things and deeds? In this case, trauma suffered over generations. The "?" showed the way out of this misery. More than a question mark, the "?" was an exclamation mark. And what did the I, the "Ja", say at the end?

»I am looking at you. It will take some time. But I feel and I can stay. So good to see you smiling. Once you have me and the others, you can do anything and go anywhere. But first, you need to have us. To have yourself. I am not against anything. But first have us and then you can have choices. When you are smiling, I am relaxing. It would be a pity to be unhappy with such a beautiful face. Having everything but not having yourself. We are here for each other. If the outside is negative, we don't have to be there. We have our space.«

86

## 2.5 BREECH BIRTH

*General-encounter (3 words)*
*child – mother – doctor*

There are many different reasons why a baby lies in a breech position – medically speaking, this is now referred to as breech presentation. The German AOK health insurance company's health magazine has written about this:[26]

»In 50 percent of cases, experts cannot clearly explain why the child remains in this position. Sometimes it is due to a rare heart-shaped form of the uterus or the position of the placenta. Occasionally, benign tumors (fibroids) are behind it. Maternity nurses and midwives also report that sometimes the baby does not want to or cannot turn for a good reason, for example because the umbilical cord is very short.«

Four possible options for a birth are listed:
1. »spontaneous labor on your own
2. the "external delivery" by a specialist doctor
3. spontaneous delivery in the breech position by specially qualified obstetricians and midwives
4. planned caesarean section«

**mother**
»Are we talking about birth? I have no connection. An idea comes to my mind: If the "child" comes out with the feet first, it will be easier to pull the "child" out and then it would be over much faster. Wouldn't it? It feels like I want to get it done fast, so that I can get go ahead minding my business. I don't care. I even didn't think about the arms. I have zero connection to being pregnant. Actually, to anything.

I was just thinking about my husband: I would like to continue enjoying my life with him. And I want you, "doctor" – or doctors and

---

[26] AOK Gesundheitsmagazin Online, »Vier Optionen bei Beckenendlage des Babys« [AOK Health Magazine Online, »Four options for a baby in a breech presentation«] from October 23, 2023, https://www.aok.de/pk/magazin/familie/geburt/beckenendlage-vor-der-geburt/

87

everyone in the hospital – to do it fast. I could be the type of woman who leaves the "child" at home and goes for a dance with my husband. And we dance all night. And I don't even think a minute about the "child". I just want to enjoy my life while I am still young.

And I am a bit annoyed by the lack of support from the "doctor", to be honest. They are not helpful either. I have a very demanding attitude when I go into the hospital. And funnily, I don't want to have any operation.

I am not available for you, "child". I am just looking at the "doctor". For me, it's like taking my car to the garage and they fix it and I wait and then it works again and then I can use it. Or like going to the supermarket. I go in, I buy stuff and then I go out. And I expect the same procedure in the hospital. And now I am getting angry because I thought things would work differently. I am demanding IT to get out of me! I am not saying "he" or "she" to the "child"; I am saying "it". And IT should get out of my body. If I could, I would push it. I would start pushing and pressing the upper part of my belly. Push it and press it down. I don't like being pregnant and I don't like giving birth. I am very hard and annoyed. And the "doctor" waits for an emergency. Well, he can have an emergency.«

**child**
»I feel really desperate. If I could speak, I would tell you to fuck off. But I can't speak. I can't do this on my own. I am too little. It is excruciating. Stop saying that! Oh, God! It makes my whole body freeze! What about me? What about me?? Am I visible? I need help. Otherwise I am gonna die. I need my "mother" to engage with me. I need my mom. I need my mommy to recognize that I am in distress. And I need someone to be gentle with me. She doesn't want to help me! But it is an emergency for me! This is serious for me. I need my "mother". I need mommy. I need somebody to help me! I am gonna die!«

**doktor**
»My option as a doctor is that this is very dangerous to pull the "child" at the feet because a child has also arms. It can also get stuck. Now, the birth is a natural process and it has its own time. You cannot speed it up. You cannot pull the "child" out. It's not an object to be pulled out.

88

Does that make sense to you? The doctor here can be just available for emergency situation. If you want a natural birth, I can support natural birth. I am just in a waiting state for the process to start on its own. I will not interfere with the process. If any emergency occurs, I will interfere. I hope, I hope you will not need me. I hope, you will sort it out on your own, "mother". I am educated only to support "mother". And if she is in danger, if her life is in danger, I am educated what to do. I am sorry, I realize now that I am not educated for the "child" part! I don't know what to do here. This is between "mother" and "child". I will leave you at your room. And I will go to my room. And the nurse will inform you, will inform me, if there is any emergency. Usually, I don't go into that type of communication with the patient, with the "mother". You are not in emergency. It is clear that you have breech birth. We told you and we are waiting. I will not converse anymore. This is not my duty.«

*"child" switching off the camera function.*

- **mother:** Let me go on the internet and just check… Let me find some information. So, what do they say? What can I do?
- **doctor:** Babies sometimes are dying. They are reanimated after the birth. There are also such cases. If you want reanimation, I will do it. I am not a healer, I am not a Shaman. I mean sorry.
- **child** [off screen]: I cannot breathe properly. I am afraid.
- **doctor:** Yeah, sorry. That's birth. That's birth. It is not possible to breathe properly during the birth.
- **mother:** It says here C-section. I don't want to have that, to be honest. Means that I can't just walk out of the hospital. Which means I need to stay longer; which I don't want.

**doctor**
»You do all this in order to not face the pain. You are inviting complications and you are inviting emergency. And you are demanding C-section. Even the "child" is afraid to turn into an appropriate position, head looking down. You don't want natural birth. But that comes with the package. You got pregnant. You said okay to be a mother. And now you don't want to deal with it? I am leaving you because this is your

responsibility. This is the consequence of having sex with a man and getting pregnant. Now you deal with the pain of birth, giving birth. That's the result. If you don't face pain, the "child" is facing it in some way and it feels like she is dying. Because it is unbearable for a child. The pain that you can face and process is unbearable for a little creature, for a little baby. Yeah, you do not care at all! I talked to you as a doctor. Now I talk to you as a woman. This is female wisdom. I give it to you and that's all I can do. The more you resist, the more difficult it gets.«

o **child:** I am dying. I can't breathe properly. I am afraid. You are killing me. If no one acts soon I am going to die with the pain and lack of connection.
o **mother:** Let's do a Cesarean section. I am not happy about it but let's do it.
o **doctor:** At this stage you cannot demand a C-section. And also, regulations aren't allowing C-section for a breech birth. Just keep breathing.
o **mother:** I don't feel pregnant at all. I have never dealt with the situation of having a child. During all the pregnancy it never occurred to my mind!
o **doctor:** Where have you been for 9 months? Where have you been? There are so many courses. You could have done some preparation. There are trainings for prenatal times and you do exercises. I mean, I am the last stage, I am the last person you will meet in this process.
o **mother:** During these nine months, I just lived my life; as per usual. I never spent a single thought on, about, in, at… – whatever preposition you want to use – for THAT "child". I mean, if the "child" says it's not doing good…
o **child:** I feel cold. I can't do anything. I am frozen and stiff. I don't know what to do. My cervix is blocked. My limbs are cold. My whole body is stiff. I am going to die because nobody wants me. I need my mommy. I need my Mommy. I need her to work with me. This is not natural. This is hell. I need my mommy. I need my mommy. I need my mommy.
o **mother:** I can only do the minimum.

90

**doctor**

»What doctors do at that stage is to get another cup of coffee. Its night. The mother is screaming or whatever. I have given her a proper amount of tranquilizers or sedatives. That's it. I cannot give you more because your blood pressure will fall at a critical level. So, I leave you with your child. That's your process. I am taking another cup of coffee. This is my night shift. You are not my only case. So, this is your thing to face consequences. Yeah? Coming shortly. The nurse will follow up.«

**child**

»I need my mommy. I need my mommy. I need my mommy. I need my mommy. I need my mommy. I need my mommy. I need my mommy. I need my mommy. I need my mommy. I need my mommy. I need my mommy. I need my mommy. I need my mommy. I need my mommy. I need my mommy. I need my mommy. I need my mommy. I need my mommy. «

**mother**

»I am not at a state of giving birth. Not at all. I need a C-section. I am really getting stressed right now. And I don't want the "child" to die either. I mean, what will the people say about me? I am sorry "child". I will wait for the "doctor". I have no feelings of being pregnant. I have no feeling of giving birth. I am totally disconnected. But I don't want the "child" to die either. Having my belly cut open, I am not sure if this is a great idea either, to be honest. I am a bit more horrified of this option. "child"? Are you there? Do you have the strength to go into the birth process? Okay let's give it a try. Let me start…. Oh, gosh.«

**child**

»I've got so low energy. I don't know. I think there is chance for me if you are trying to engage. Let's see what happens. I don't know what to do. I am incredibly weak. I am really tired. My body has given up.«

*"mother" and "child" go into the birth process, screaming and pressing and moving.*

**doctor**

»Oh, it's a girl! It's a baby girl. And she is healthy! Look at her! [laughing] Welcome little one. Okay, I am leaving you. You are a mother, you are a new mother. We checked, everything is fine. We won't cut the lumbrical cord immediately. Let her just rest. You are fine? How are you? Let me check. The temperature, pulse – the nurse has checked. You are fine. Relax a bit.«

o **child:** I am hungry. My belly hurts.
o **mother:** You are hungry? Okay. Let me give you first my breast. I feel now a little bit guilty, to be honest.
o **child:** I still need my mommy. I want my mommy.
o **mother:** Actually, I have no idea even what that means. I feel a little bit guilty. But I will breastfeed you. Let me take you up.
o **child:** It smells familiar. You smell like my mommy.
o **mother:** I am just starting to question what I did during your pregnancy or when I was pregnant. Was it really the right thing to do?
o **child:** You have been mistaken me with your mom. You need to protect me. Look after me.
o **mother:** I don't understand you.
o **child:** You need to look after me. And protect me. I need to sleep now. I like your voice.
o **mother:** My voice? I like your voice as well. Funnily, the voice is the only thing at the moment that I really can give. It is a little bit difficult with my body. But the voice is okay. As the first step between us.
o **child** [crying]: I am weak. My tummy is aching. Tummy ache!
o **mother:** I suddenly realize that the tummy aching relates to the missing connection between us. I am carrying you. I am carrying you. I am carrying you around.

## 2.6 C-SECTION

*General-encounter (6 words)*
*doctor – mum – child – – midwife – birth – long-term-affect*

Before starting this work, I asked the participants about how their birth process went. The picture that emerged was: two natural births, one woman was stuck but eventually gave birth naturally (although the placenta did not come out on its own), one cesarean section (that was me), one breech birth, and one woman had no information about her birth.

The topic of cesarean sections has so many perspectives that it is impossible to cover them all in a single piece of work. My view had always been in earlier years that a cesarean section is performed when it is a matter of life or death for the mother and/or child. Years ago, I was once part of a self-encounter where a woman blamed herself for giving birth »only« through a cesarean section. However, it became clear in this work that the cesarean section was necessary to save the life of her child.

In the intention of this work, a spelling mistake crept in. However, it turned out during the work that this very spelling mistake contained a lot of wisdom. And this wisdom was much needed, because what was revealed in this work was a mother who was helpless and completely disconnected from her body. A doctor who was only in his head due to his long years of medical training, and a midwife who was not allowed to work from her intuition. And so, the child had to help its mother through birth; instead of the other way around. In the words of the mother, the dilemma of Western societies and our so-called civilized world is revealed:

»I go to school, I do my job… maybe I had a higher education, maybe I even went to university – and now I am stuck here. I don't know what to do! I have to think all the time. I am in a world where I have to work, where there are rules and everything is organized. I am totally disconnected from the origins of being a woman. Because this is not my natural way of living. And in this type of world, I am trying to give birth. I am having this fear because it is my first birth. And now, with birth, I am getting in contact with my womanhood.«

**child**

»I just want to scream "take me out of here!". Take me out immediately. Cannot be worse.«

**mum**

»I am getting a bit nervous here. Just looking at my phone. Thinking, when will it start? I am bit angry when you say, as a "doctor", you don't know what you are supposed to do. You are the reason why I am in the hospital! Sorry, but now I am getting really pissed. Because you tell me all the time how things work and now I am in this.... Ah! I feel so stressed! So stressed. I don't know if I want a child. If I want to give "birth". I don't know anything. And now, I am here in this situation and everyone is tuning out. I have the feeling: Here we go again, again on my own. I just want it to be done. That it's over. That I can go back doing the stuff I need to do. Maybe going back into my job. And I would like to scream. And I am not sure if it's because of "birth" or because I am so angry. I am really disconnected.«

**midwife**

»I feel really sick, so nauseous. So, consumed that I cannot focus on much else. And I have to look away. I cannot be here, really. I have something personal going on. I feel powerless. And I am very nauseous.«

**birth**

»I get headache, pressure on my head. Under stress when the "child" said "get me out here". That put me under pressure. And I don't know what the "doctor" is supposed to do here. And this puts me under stress. I get dragged out. Flouted by anger. Floated by your disconnection.

This is not "birth". This is torture. So much noise, so much noise. The doctors are traumatized as well.«

**doctor**

»I reacted when "child" said "get me out here". An emergency is coming up and that puts me under stress. Even the "midwife" is not 100% here. It is disgusting but it's the truth. I know I should do my job. It is my responsibility to calm down the situation but I am blocked from the inside.«

○ **birth:** Do you want to give birth?
○ **mum:** Not really. I am afraid of it. I just want it to be over. Let's get it done.
○ **child:** I am cold, lying in a tortured posture. I am in an embryo posture extended in an unnatural positioning. It is so weird.
○ **doctor:** I go into the mood of just functioning. And again, I am triggered when "child" is speaking. I read the manual in my mind. Getting into functioning mode.
○ **birth:** I have no idea who "doctor" is. Who is that? I need my mother.
○ **midwife:** When "child" was going into this position, I felt that I should know how to help. But actually, I don't know much.
○ **birth:** For me, the person who should know doesn't want to know. And it's horrible.
○ **mum:** I would love to disagree with "birth" but you are right. And I am startled here: I know I have a "doctor" who doesn't know.
○ **doctor:** Okay, I want to check on the baby, on the "child". That's my focus. The "child", "child", "child".
○ **birth:** I want to say: Leave them alone. Leave them alone!
○ **mum:** Oh!!! I am not important at all! It is okay that you are focusing on the "child". Absolutely okay. But who is focusing on me??
○ **midwife:** I notice this distance to "mum" as well. There is no connection. I always look at "doctor" and "child". That's my single focus. There is such a big gap. I have no idea how to deal with "mum". I don't know what is going on. I am not capable of that.
○ **mum:** Oh God, help me!

- **doctor:** I cannot relate to the mothers' pain and feelings. And that is overwhelming me. That makes me so helpless. And I look at "child" and the machines. I go through my manual of what I have learned. But the knowledge, the skills are not coming out of my body. There is no feeling involved. And I cannot relate, I cannot feel your pain. I cannot.
- **mum:** Of course! How can you transport pain through a book?? Oh, I am stuck! There is something in me which doesn't want to give birth. And there is something in me who wants to. There is something in me which has no connection to myself. And "birth" is so right! Oh gosh!

*"birth" is leaving.*

- **doctor:** "birth" is gone. We need a C-section! That is the emergency!
- **midwife:** I don't know what to do. I just wait for this to be over myself. I don't know even why I am here, why I am doing this.
- **child:** My body resonates with the word »emergency«. It is very urgent. It couldn't be worse.
- **mum:** Oh, my God! I feel like in a slaughter house somehow. Being violated. I am so stuck. It's terrible. I don't want that, I don't want… oh gosh!
- **midwife:** There is completely helplessness. It is an emergency but I feel absolutely incapable of doing anything. I cannot act. I just look. And I realize how horrible that is. I am not emotionally attached either. I am also disconnected from myself.
- **mum:** Oh, I am so afraid. I didn't know how afraid I am!! I know "birth" wants me to engage but I am so afraid! I am so stuck! I don't know what to do. Oh gosh. I can't. Oh gosh! No one told me this!

**long-term affect**

»The exit was blocked and now I am looking at "mum" to decide if she wants a C-section. I am totally disconnected. I can't even talk. But I see what is happening here. I am somehow connected with "child".

96

Stuck in the birth position. I feel the stress to the "doctor". I am very stressed now that the "doctor" is not aware of the long-term effect of the C-section. It affects me. There is no hope anymore. "mum" can't give natural birth because her vagina is blocked. The vagina is traumatized. "mum" is completely traumatized.«

**doctor**

»In this situation, there is no thought of a "long-term affect". It is an emergency situation and we need an emergency solution here. And now I feel like I am getting more into my duty. Me supporting the "mum" in a natural way is not possible. But now that we are talking about C-section, I become confident. Like the machine would be running. Now I can command. Now we do this and that and that and that. I only have the schedule in my mind. This is how we have been taught. This is how we do it. No discussion. Because now, it is all about the manual. Step 1, 2, 3, 4, 5. I am not responding to "mum", not responding to the "child". Just following the book, following the guidelines. I feel like we are preparing the steps for the C-section. At the very, very back of my mind there is the question: Why is "mum" asking us to check how the "child" is? She should know it. How can we know? The "child" is not insight us. But this is just one thought and I continue to operate the machines here.«

**mum**

»I couldn't hear either what "long-term affect" was saying. I am now handing over everything to you, "doctor". Do whatever you need to do. I am starting to feel numb. As there is no help for me, no support, to bring you, "child", in a natural way into the life. I am okay with the C-section. But I agree with "long-term affect" that it has an impact the "doctor" doesn't see. But I am handing everything over. I feel crippled. My organs are not organic. It is about the complete disconnection of being a woman and what this entails and encompasses. And then this type of machinery which is going on... And it is really devastating for me to realize it only now. And now it is too late for me to change anything. I feel like being rolled on a hospital bed into the slaughter house. At least save the "child". Has anyone checked if "child" is still alive?

Please check. Please. Please do something. "Doctor, please do something." Oh gosh, I am afraid of giving birth. I am afraid of C-section. I am afraid of everything. And I just realize it right now. I didn't know it before. And I have no connection to my "child". It is all happening in my head. There is little to nothing happening in my body.«

**child**

»I am shutting down. I also can also not understand and hear well "long-term affect". It is like a metallic voice. Someone talking from the TV. The "doctors" voice sounds differently. I am collapsing, I am shutting down. I cannot bear that anymore. I stopped breathing and it is more like inner respiration. Like my movements are about to stop.«

**midwife**

»When "doctor" was talking about functioning and not having competence, I realized that I was more in my body. However, it was overwritten by all this teachings and education and that system I am working in. I don't have the allowance and the freedom to go with my own intuition. I had to adjust to the construct I am working in. I feel so powerless. I don't even know what I know anymore. It is almost as if everything is taken away from me with this book, with this guideline the "doctor" was talking about. I am not allowed to do anything anyways that comes to me naturally. Like I have only a little cherry stone of intuition in me.

I feel hopeful again. Okay, I did something right. The "mum" felt heard. So, if "mum" is now connecting with "birth", maybe this is helpful. Maybe something could change for the "child". I want to bring "birth" in and help "birth" and "child" to connect. I sense that you, "mum", think that you are not able to give birth. But you can. This is the most natural thing in the world. You can do this.«

**mum**

»Do the C-section at least. I couldn't bear if "child" is dying. It takes so long. I just know that you, "doctor" and "midwife", you can't give me what I need. And I don't know what I need. My head is full of fear!

98

I am stiffing my body. My head is exploding because of fear. I need emotional contact. I don't get any emotional contact to anyone. And it is stressing me out!

I don't know why am I so afraid? Now things are coming to my mind [crying]: I go to school, I do my job… maybe I had a higher education, maybe I even went to university – and now I am stuck here. I don't know what to do! I have to think all the time. I am in a world where I have to work, where there are rules and everything is organized. I am totally disconnected from the origins of being a woman. Because this is not my natural way of living. And in this type of world, I am trying to give birth. I am having this fear because it is my first birth. And now I am getting in contact with my womanhood.«

**child**

»"birth" is like my voice. I don't have a voice anymore. Just have an image of floating in that fluid space. And it's difficult to understand if that flesh is still alive or dead or suspended in that fluid. I don't feel anymore. I don't feel connected at all. Therefore, I want to move somewhere else. Maybe arms will be holding me. I don't feel connected to a human being. Maybe I am in a pool? Maybe I am in space? No connection, no connection.«

*We are bringing in "C-Section".*

o **child:** The moment I saw "C-section" I was startled! I feel very cold. It is quite difficult to orient. I feel like I am in a glass. In an aquarium. For the first time, someone is watching me, seeing me.
o **C-Section:** I feel you, "child". The only way to breath is to split open. I see "child" and it feels like I want to connect with her but it is really impossible to connect. Because I am just a big whole that allows her to breath.
o **mum:** I am happy, "C-section" that you are here. I had a different image of you.

- **C-Section:** You are being cut in two. I am a big slit in your belly. And that is the reason "child" can breathe. We can't think about happiness. Please look at "child" and see her. Please!
- **mum:** I see her but I don't feel her. I am like paralyzed right now.
- **C-Section:** I am just feeling split open. It feels like, the word »paralyzed« feels real. I think this goes far and beyond dissociation.
- **mum:** Now I have the feeling like something would kick in. Medication or something? Drugs? I can barely keep my consciousness.
- **C-Section:** This was done for "child" but it doesn't help "child".
- **child:** I agree. We have no terms yet for that kind of experience. We don't have words yet in our terminology. Like you said, it is beyond dissociation.
- **mum:** Now that you say it, I feel a connection to you. It is absolutely true. I feel like I or we, I don't know, you and me, it is like a betrayal that we had to experience. I am still knocked out here in my head. I hardly feel anything aside of the fact that something is wrong here. Something is wrong.
- **child:** I am like a flesh. You cut an animal and it is not totally dead. There are still some nerves. And my body is making these small startles.
- **mum:** I am not sure if it's true but I have the feeling that we are both victims.
- **C-section:** It is not natural. It feels dangerous. I feel like I am still split between "birth" and "C-section". They are both here.
- **mum:** "child", I am ... oh gosh. What have I done? What have I done?
- **long-term affect:** I feel cold and I can't get out. I think I am stuck in the belly where I am.
- **child:** I feel like a flesh being cut out of something. Maybe I am waste after an operation? I am not sure if I will go to the basket or somewhere else. Maybe, I am a tumor. Am I a tumor? I feel like a tumor. I need to sense it that I can stay. And I can sense only through connection. Still I don't feel connection. I just see "C-section".
- **mum:** Oh gosh. What have I done! Please, please stay, "child"! I want to try. I start to realize what I have done. I want to try to

connect to you. I want to try to connect with me. To do it together. You are fully right: There are no words of what was happening.

o **child:** I don't realize I have a body. I feel I am part of cut-off from something else. I see my future in "long-term affect". Behind the thick glass. Not being heard. Not being understood. And life is passing by. That is my future.

o **mum:** You are able to express what I am not able to see and feel. Same here. And with you, with your birth, I start to realize it. And I have, not that I can promise anything, but I want to get a connection to you.

o **child:** I was hoping to be held. But it didn't happen. When being held, I would sense where I am. I would sense my physical limitation. That was not given.

o **mum:** I need to learn how to hold you. I realize that I didn't built up a connection with you when I was pregnant with you.

o **C-section:** It is interesting when you say that "mum", I feel like I need to go. I have no purpose here. But I feel very stuck and in touch with you.

o **mum:** It is also very difficult for me. I have no idea what to do. The only thing I can say, "child", is that I like to get into contact with you. Although I feel really numb and dump and useless.

**child**

»I hear that and I feel being squeezed in a hug. I didn't have this transition. I didn't have this process of being squeezed through a birth channel. Usually, you're squeezed and released. Push, squeeze and release. Push, squeeze and release. don't feel like I am in the body. I am floating around. I don't know my limits. There is no question to defend my limits for my future. It may sound weird but this birthing process, through the birth channel, is like hugging the child and releasing.

I hug you. It is so nice having you. And I release you out. This is your body. Each time I hug you, I make you sense. I hug you and then I let you go a bit more. I hug you and I give you also your body and let you take your body and move forward. Moving also forward in life. Moving through the birth channel. Hugged, squeezed. And then released.

It is a bit like that and I am just sensing what I missed. Like with animals: The cat would press her kitties, massage each other. That's why they are doing that. I am totally missing that. "long-term affect" is closing the eyes. You cannot face that. There are no resources to face that. I cannot think of any replacement for that. Just close your eyes and shut down. This is not birth. I am not born. I am not feeling anything. This room is a void of the womb.

An image came like I am hugged a lot. Being hugged, being hold in the hug for quite some time. Maybe being hugged by the blankets somehow. There would be my unconsciousness looking for things or people hugging me? But the opposite can be: being hugged by something or someone. Maybe searching for it. Sometimes trees have these spaces where you can move into the tree. I want that kind of space. I want to stay in a tree for a long time. That kind of strange things would attract me in life. When people are moving through very tiny tunnels, from tinny tunnels into caves, big caves. You move through a tinny tunnel and then you arrive in a big cave. These kinds of experiences. There is some kind of excitement.

I am an extension where you load your trauma, "mum", upon me. I don't have my own being. I am not given it. I am reloaded, reprogrammed with your trauma that you don't want to face. I don't have a body, I don't have my life. Lost in caves. Lost in the body of trees. That's the problem. Big glass, aquarium. Window watching life passing by. Maybe I die in a tunnel? Chimneys are also like tunnels. I could have a permanent job like Santa Claus bringing gifts through chimneys…«


**mum**

»And I realize now that I don't know what hugs are. I will try to hug you. The more you speak, "child", the more I am starting to feel you. Trying to find a way of reliving and reconnecting. I am standing here listening in awe. But I am disconnected from it. I only see it through your eyes. Maybe I realize one day that I have to do something. "child", for me you are the only window to what life really is and what it means. I am angry because I believed the stuff which I was told. I bought so much into the unnatural concept of what it is to having a child and to

102

be giving birth. It is just so unnatural. And it has nothing to do with real life. Like the "doctor" was saying, me too, I was learning or reading a manual. I am only in my head, from the neck upwards. The rest has no connection to the body and what it means to be a woman.«

**child**

»I want to play games where there are tunnels. Play games where you are at the end of a tunnel. Trains go through the tunnel. And also, I want to play this with you. And hear stories about tunnels. Can you live in a tunnel? And also, how other beings, animals and people in stories, they make it through the tunnels. What is the name of the animal called who does tunnels? Mole? Maybe you play games with me, "mum", and you press me with pillows? But you need to know how much to press. You will put them on my face and you know how much to press. I will start to make all these sounds, voices, which are stored in my flesh. It will not be a voice of love or connection but an expression of what is being stored. You will need to find a way. I am looking at "long-term affect" when I am talking. You will squeeze me to the point where I will be AHHH! This will be a bit strange. I will not be like a normal child making normal sounds of noise. That tension is an attempt to connect. Like a physical treatment in form of plays and games. And the feet, they press feet like this. You hold them and you don't not let me go. I will try to escape from your hug. But no, you will not let me go. And there will be some kind of fight. You will press my toes. And I will try to escape.[27] [laughing] And strange sounds will come out of me. I will not be the loveliest child. I need to give up all this ugly stuff that I was storing. Yes, that could be a starting point. I will not be a very lovely child because nothing was lovely about me being here. I will not be a nice child. I will be hitting back. Breaking some things in the kitchen. Breaking some vases from time to time. And I want my right to not be a nice child.«

---

[27] Actually, there are methods which exactly support and facilitate these kinds of physical games and interactions. As one example only, I want to point to the work of Franz Renggli in Switzerland.

**long-term affect**

»I am still in the belly, waiting to being born. When I hear you talking, I don't know if I am traumatized, but a part of me is dreaming of an open vagina. A mother who has open legs and wants to really give birth. I think, I am the traumatized part. And when you play games, using my power, I become powerless. I am waiting for somebody to help me out, to release me! But I can't do it. I will be pinching, pinching very hard. I am not sure of the outcome and if this can be treated really.«

Epilogue

As we can see here, it is not enough just to physically relive birth through play. Why? Because when we experience a trauma, we split into different parts. The traumatized parts remain stuck in the age at which the trauma occurred. In this case, that is the womb and birth. We need theories and methods, such as the »Intention Method« as part of the Identity-oriented Psychotrauma Theory (IoPT), that are able to connect with such early splits. Otherwise, we are doomed to repeat the missing connection throughout our lives, and the feeling of not being seen and not being heard will go on and on.

## 2.7 NATURAL BIRTH

*General-encounter (6 words)*
*German: Liebe – Natürlich –Baby – Frau – Mann – Geburt*
*English: Love – Natural – Baby – Woman – Man – Birth*

I had hoped to learn more about natural birth through this work. However, what was revealed instead was the lack of love - the absence of love between man and woman, who themselves did not experience real affection in their childhood. This lack of love not only hinders the natural birthing process but also leads to identity issues, disorientation, role conflicts, unmet expectations, and a distance from the unborn child. How can a natural, loving birth be possible under these circumstances?

**Baby**

»I am disoriented. When my mom looks at me, I get really hot. I think I'm still in my mother's womb. I realize, I'm in a waiting position, waiting for it to start right away. I'm not quite ready to be born yet. With the disharmony between "Man" and "Woman", I don't feel like coming out at all.

That woke me up when my mom talked about anger. I felt the anger, too. What mom says scares me to death. I can feel the pressure and the expectations. And I'm asking myself why I was conceived at all, if not out of love? I like the "Man", but I'm connected to mom. I want to know who my dad is.

I get a really queasy, sinking feeling in my stomach. I have very clear expectations. I'm on my way, I have needs, but there's no room for me. I am completely dissociated. The only way to survive is to identify with mom. Role reversal.

Mom is totally needy herself. I feel like I have to look after my mom. I need a mom who is there for me. I need a mom who sees me and takes care of me. I have no connection to my mom at all. Mom is so confused. I'm also scared of my mom. I can feel that my mom is hurt. That can't be resolved right now.

I'm being carried by love. And that's why I'm doing all this now. There's pressure to be born. But I love you, mom, and that's why I'm doing this for you now. There's no other way now. Birth is here. It just has to go on. To go through the gate.«

**Man**

»Something is constantly expected of me and somehow I feel like I'm alone here. When "Love" speaks, my heart opens. Can't really see the beauty in "Baby". It all feels confusing. I have the feeling that there are more and more expectations, people and opinions. And then the "Baby" disappears too! I have the feeling that no matter what I say,

105

what I do, it's all wrong. And the fact that the "Baby" is disappearing is just tearing my heart apart.«

[Towards "Baby"] »All I can say is that I truly love you. My heart beats faster when I say that. Right now, I can't do more than try to give as much love to the "Baby" as I can.

I'm not doing well right now. And it saddens me that I am portrayed as some kind of opponent. I feel rejection. My question to you, "Woman", what help do you expect from me?«

**Woman**

»I am tight. I find stability with "Love". And with "Man"? I have no connection to "Man". Somehow everything feels wrong. I'm constantly trying to get in touch with "Man". Sometimes the "Man" seemed very absent and that made me feel insecure. But I feel a connection to a person I love so much. But not with the "Man".

[Towards "Man"] I find it so difficult to connect with you, "Man". There's a wall between us. I expect you to support me and stand behind me, not beside me. It hurts me that the focus is always on my flaws. Can I ask you something? Do you want to be a father?

[How was the relationship with your fahter?] Peace, joy, and seemingly perfect on the outside. But when it really mattered, he wasn't there. I am afraid of having a "Man" who isn't a good father.

I somehow feel a fear emerging now, a fear of pain. I don't know what will come. Somewhere, I know what being a mother is like, but somehow I have no idea. I'm afraid of going through birth alone.«

**Natural**

»I feel very confused. The first look was at the mom. I need mom for the natural "Birth" and not a "Woman". I also looked at "Baby". And dad just randomly. Are you a mom? I almost don't dare to say it out loud, but I miss the dad! It seems to me that there are old issues between you, mom, and your "Man". Has the "Love" disappeared? What happened there? During your conversation, I got really involved.«

**Birth**

»I have palpitations. I feel like I have to keep an eye on everyone. It's exciting. We all have to work together somehow. I really want a natural birth. We don't need a doctor for that either. I want us to make it together. That we come out with love. Maybe a "loving birth"? Yes, that would be nice. And I totally understand the pain. If I were in the room, I wish we could come together. That the pain wasn't yours alone. That we could go through it together. It's like a gate for me. I can go through it.«

**Love**

»I am very, very fond of the "Man" and the "Woman" and the "Baby". It's about the love between "Man" and "Woman". And the thought has arisen: But what if the love isn't that great or isn't there at all? And we have to wait? Then the "Baby" dies. But I really can't build up love. I can't reach the "Man" with my love! That you can find each other. Everything happens too quickly. It makes me really sad what the "Baby" said. It's important to be honest with the "Baby". But what I do notice: Mom is doing her best. She's doing her very best. I am completely focused on you, "Baby".«

*The "Man" talks about love, but he can't show it. "Woman" and "Love" feel this very clearly. Since "Love" cannot reach the "Man", she finally focuses entirely on the "Woman" and the "Baby". The "Woman" now also focuses on the "Baby". The "Baby" is about to be born.*

o **Birth:** It's okay. We are all injured. We all have our injuries. The chaos is there. It's all part of it. This is our birth.
o **Baby:** You mean, this is all natural? I have a stomach ache and I think, "Love", can it also happen without mom? And I realize, I need mom. I am facing birth. I notice, it scares me. And I am excited. There is a lot of pressure here. The "Love" is all with me. Okay, I have to somehow deal with this. That's how it feels.
o **Birt:** Mom and "Baby" – I ask you to look inside your body. Where is your head? In mommy's womb? In front of the gate? Well, I

realize I'm getting ready to give birth and I'm scared. The exit is blocked.

o **Love:** I'll catch you with my hands, "Baby".

o **Baby:** I have the feeling that someone is pressing on my stomach. Could that be? I'm not out yet. Could it be that the cervix hasn't opened yet? Well, I'm ready. I can feel it. As if I'm in a waiting position.

o **Woman:** I can only give as much as my body gives me.


## 2. 8 BREASTFEEDING (Self-encounter)

*Self-encounter (2 words)*
*German: Ich – stillen*
*English: I – breastfeeding*

There are already a variety of studies on the topic of breastfeeding, and more studies are constantly being produced, even though it has been undisputed for decades that breastfeeding has a positive impact on both the child and the mother, both in the short term and the long term, both physically and mentally. The international research initiative »Becoming Breastfeeding Friendly«, which is part of the Sustainable Development Goals until 2030, is one of the latest research projects. Based on a model developed by the Yale School of Public Health.[28]

The German Federal Ministry of Food and Agriculture is part of this global research effort and has summarized the results for Germany from their long-term study on the health of children and adolescents

---

[28] Bundesgesundheitsblatt, »Das internationale Forschungsvorhaben Becoming Breastfeeding Friendly. Untersuchung von Rahmenbedingungen zur Stillförderung.« [»The international research project Becoming Breastfeeding Friendly. Investigation of framework conditions for the promotion of breastfeeding.«]
https://link.springer.com/article/10.1007/s00103-018-2784-1

(KiGGS, second survey (2009 – 2012)[29]) in their 2018 fact sheet as follows:[30]:

»Current breastfeeding rates for the 2012 – 2016 birth cohorts in Germany show that Two thirds of mothers (68%) exclusively breastfeed their child after birth. After 2 months it is still 57%, after 4 months 40% and after 6 months 13%.«

I want to show two aspects of the topic of breastfeeding here, which are not quantitatively measurable. Firstly, my own self-encounter, because I was not breastfed. I was born via C-section and my mother, according to her, tried to breastfeed me, but it didn't work out.

In the second work, a general encounter, we look at a completely different aspect of breastfeeding. Why is the most natural thing in the world, breastfeeding, even interrupted? Why don't all mothers breastfeed for at least six months? What forces are at work here?

But let's take a look at my work first.

### Ich (I)

»I'm glad that "stillen" (breastfeeding) is a resonator. It gives me a feeling of something like trust. "stillen" (breastfeeding) is unknown to me. I'm a bit afraid to touch the unknown. The resonator is familiar to me. I want to do a good job, but I don't have the confidence. There is an urge to be good. I'm not afraid, I'm not nervous, I'm still fine, but I'm hesitant. I like to look at "stillen" (breastfeeding). And I can look really good at you too, Natalie. I actually find it quite cozy. «

*»It's interesting that you talk about the unknown. I'm positive about it now. But I felt the unknown when I was breastfeeding my children. It*

---

[29] Bundeszentrale für gesundheitliche Aufklärung, [Federal Center for Health Education] kindergesundheit-info.de, https://www.kindergesundheit-info.de/fachkraefte/grundlagen/daten-und-fakten/kiggs-studie/
[30] Bundesanstalt für Landwirtschaft und Ernährung, »So wird Deutschland stillfreundlich!«, [Federal Agency for Agriculture and Food, »How to make Germany breastfeeding-friendly!«], fact sheet from 2019, https://www.gesund-ins-leben.de/fileadmin/resources/import/pdf/bbf_faktenblatt_ergebnisse.pdf

*gave me a lot of question marks. I'm super grateful that you're both here.«*

**stillen (breastfeeding)**

»It was very nice to hear the "I". I was touched when I heard it. I am touched to be here and at the same time it gives a different feeling. I am in my thoughts. I don't know what it is yet. It's more of a physical feeling.«

*»When I look at you, I want to caress you. You're even smaller than me. Like a little girl. It's almost like I'm your mother. Being connected to me like a mother. Because there was no one to support me as a small child. I have the inner image of being in the hospital. I take myself into another room. I have the feeling that I'm not safe with my mother. Almost like a spiritual experience. I would go there, pick you up and save me.«*

- o **Ich (I):** Me, too. I feel a deep sadness coming up here.
- o **stillen (breastfeeding):** What I remembered was: I was too small to do that. So small.
- o **Ich (I):** Why? But I know you're right.

*»It was dangerous to be with my mother. Part of me thinks it's a shame that I wasn't breastfed. But another part thinks it's okay. Safer.«*

- o **stillen (breastfeeding):** It's actually not okay. No. It's not okay. My head might say yes, but my body immediately said it's not okay. My body says no! It's not okay!
- o **Ich (I):** I get a distance from both of you. Dizziness in my head. I have "stillen" (breastfeeding), but I don't understand anything.

*»Let me explain: My mother tried to suffocate me when I was born. With a pillow on my face. It's far too dangerous.«*

110

- **stillen (breastfeeding):** Exactly. I wanted to say that you weren't wanted. I don't know in what way.

*»Thank you for the confirmation. I feel it now. Like an inner survival program kicking in. Being too close to her is not good for me. I understand the body's reaction, which is a natural reaction, but my mind goes into hyper reaction: be careful!«*

- **stillen (breastfeeding):** There is the wish of being breastfed. I see breasts in front of me.
- **Ich (I):** I am confused now. Who are you? It is bizarre. Which position are you taking?
- **stillen (breastfeeding):** I am not the mother. This is what I can say. I am a part of Natalie.
- **Ich (I):** I have no feelings at all. No emotions at all. What is that?
- **stillen (breastfeeding):** I am not a what. I am not an object. Makes me really uncomfortable. I am very clear on what we are. I want a mom who breastfeeds me. I don't want to be treated like an object. I have needs and this is my need. Now I am getting angry. I want to get this need fulfilled and it's about breastfeeding. I have this need! It makes me angry!
- **Ich (I):** »I am not an object« is looping in my head. It is going around and around and around in my head.
- **stillen (breastfeeding):** Big or little breasts, there is a fucking need! It is normal to have this need fulfilled! It is so normal! Whatever breast is in front of me! It is not about the size of the breasts. I need mama! I need the love. I am getting angry.

*»Object would be too much as you can treat objects a certain way. It would be better for her if I would not exist at all. That is the truth. And that makes me angry. And I fully agree with "stillen" (breastfeeding). For me, it feels great to express this anger. It feels great that you express the anger.«*

111

o **Ich (I):** I'm glad to hear that. I'm proud to see that part. It's so strong.
o **stillen (breastfeeding):** I am so freaking angry! It is so normal, natural to get angry about it. Can you please express it?

*»I AM SO ANGRY THAT MY MOTHER DIDN'T BREASTFED ME. MY MOTHER IS REJECTING ME. NOTHING. ZERO. NO LOVE. NOTHING. ZERO.«*

o **stillen (breastfeeding):** You need that body to body. Feeling the warmth of the body of my mother.
o **Ich (I):** Do you mind saying the sentence in German language?

*»ICH BIN SO WÜTEND, DASS ES KEIN STILLEN GAB UND GIBT: ICH HÄTTE ES MIR SO SEHR GEWÜNSCHT, WILLKOMMEN ZU SEIN, IN DEN ARM GENOMMEN ZU WERDEN. Und dann einfach diese Ruhe, diese Nähe zu spüren. Einfach mal zur Ruhe zu kommen und nicht immer kämpfen zu müssen. Selbst ums Essen noch kämpfen zu müssen. Sondern einfach nur da sein und beschützt werden und in den Arm genommen zu werden.« [I AM SO ANGRY THAT THERE WAS AND IS NO BREASTFEEDING: I WOULD HAVE LOVED SO MUCH TO BE WELCOMED, TO BE EMBRACED. And then just to feel this peace, this closeness. Just to calm down and not have to fight all the time. Even having to fight for food. Just to be there and be protected and hugged.]*

o **Ich (I):** There is no distance with you anymore. Now I feel close to you again.
o **stillen (breastfeeding):** Feeling the tenderness and warmth of the skin. This is what I am feeling. Body to body.
o **Ich (I):** I can hold myself now. The silence is so wonderful. The heat, the body temperature. So protective.
o **stillen (breastfeeding):** It is not about the words. It is about the skin contact. I am safe. I am feeling the warmth.

## 2.9 BREASTFEEDING (General-Encounter)

*General-encounter (3 words)*
*Englisch: Breast – Feeding – Child*

»The most problematic thing, the biggest threat for me would be if the mother has a connection with the "Child" and the "Child" has a connection with the mother. This would be the biggest threat on earth! No weapon poses a bigger threat than this connection! And I am doing EVERYTHING to disturb it! Everything!! And women don't realize it. They are so entranced in the illusion of a happy family, a beautiful family. There are different types of people who create this side of the illusion. I am more the operational, hospital, doctor side. There are others who take care of the pictures of the illusion, like cinema and movies. Magazines also play a big role.«

**Child**

»I hear you. At the same time, I am so focused on what is going on in my body that I can't focus on anything else. I am so hungry!! I literally needed to take something into my mouth, my fingers. Just to suck at something. It is so organic. So deep, inside me. I cannot control it. I need to be fed. I need food. I am not looking for somebody to give me food. Nobody will come. I am trying to eat myself. I don't have any other choice. To suck, to feel the saltiness of my fingers. I need food. I need food. I need food. No food – no life. I am starting to die. I desperately need food. I am two entities: One part is devastated to die and the other part is still focusing on you – "Feeding" and "Breast" – and having to take care of you. I am becoming the mother for my mother.«

**Breast**

»I only see the mouth of the "Child". It is the only focus. And I don't want to offer my breast. My breast is very full and it is growing. But something inside of me is saying that you are sucking my soul out through my breast. And then I will be without soul, without life,

113

without anything. And I face this emptiness. So sad to say this. Because in my mind, there is the beautiful picture of the mother, the feeding breast of the mother, the children. I love this picture! But it is so far from me. It is not real.«

**Feeding**

»I am just looking at you, "Child". I feel like I am kind of trapped in the middle. Hearing "the soul being sucked out" is like a nightmare. In my throat, it's too narrow to breath properly or get something in or out. I cannot even imagine solid food. It needs to be soft and liquid. I don't know what I am, who I am or to whom I belong. I am totally lost. I have hands, I am playing with my hands but cannot reach anything. If you say, "Child", you want to eat something, maybe I could reach an apple or banana? But I can't. It's very devastating. It's a bit sad here. There is no food. It is like being put into a room and being left there. For hours maybe. I don't know. What are breasts? What is their function? What do they do?«

o  **Breast:** I don't want to breastfeed because I want to have this breastfeeding from my mother.
o  **Feeding:** Ah, you want to be fed by your mother?
o  **Breast:** Yes! I don't have this feeling been satisfied by my mother.
o  **Child:** I have some bread with Hummus. I want to offer it to you. Even though I am so devastated, I have the feeling I need to feed you. I cannot put it in my mouth but I am willing to give it to you.

**Feeding**

»Me, personally, I am so happy that you have something to eat. I think, it would be perfect if you would eat a yoghurt. It has the right consistency. Even if it would be strawberry yoghurt. But here, me as "Feeding", I cannot think of eating. I can't even eat. I am so blocked. I am so happy, "Child", if you eat. And I like it when you do it with your fingers. I even like it when you lick your finger. Oh! This is so satisfying for me! No spoon, no nothing!

114

As if the action of breastfeeding is not there to satisfy the "Child" but the mother! To comfort her. To bring her calmness. To get in touch. To have some soft skin on her. It is the other way around. Arg!«

**Breast**

»I am more relaxed as "Child" said she would be feeding me. I feel more and more relaxed.«

o **Child:** Because if I am not creating this connection I will die. So, I need to create this somehow in her.
o **Feeding:** So, while she is feeding you, in essence, you are not feeding yourself. You are feeding her. But what do you then take inside of you?
o **Child:** Only the saltness of her fingers.
o **Feeding:** And her smell. Of her skin.
o **Breast:** It is totally true. I feel like a shell. Because this baby brings me comfort. Oh, my God!

**Feeding**

»It is really like reading a story backwards. Watching a movie from the end. And then you go to the next generation. It is a repetition. But its backwards! Oh gosh. This is a sad connection! It is not a happy one. It is full of burden. I even can't cry. Everything is stuck inside of me and I cannot release any of these emotions. They are stuck in the body. But this is not how it's supposed to be. It's supposed to be for the "Child" and not the other way around. Oh Lord, what a mess! "Breast" is a body part, "Feeding" is an action. What is this all about then? It's like I am questioning the meaning of life. The purpose of life. If the start is so heavy, so delusional... Hopefully I am not drinking poison – that was the first memory when she said »the "Child" is sucking the soul out of me.« That's devastating. My God. I had the picture like you were given away to someone to breastfeed you. In my head, it's like I am going through alternatives. Like I am searching across the globe if there is an alternative way. Is it everywhere like this? Who could give it? Another person? Another woman? The bottle? I am searching like an emergency doctor or nurse. Okay, what can we do now? But funnily, I don't see anyone. There is no one with me. I don't know where I am. I am so alone. I don't know to whom I belong. Who am I? Do you love your "Child"? Why do you have the "Child"?«

o **Breast:** I have to think about it. It is not a natural question for me. I have this need. And I have this illusion, this picture, that this family is so beautiful, so bright. But in reality… it is not so.
o **Child:** These illusions are poison for me. I am fighting to breath and live while trying to keep my mother alive. It is becoming too much. Only way of dealing with it is to sleep. For hours and hours. In order to not see the reality of mother. I have the feeling, in my mouth, of something poisonous.
o **Breast:** I feel my shoulders carry the world. It is so, so heavy.
o **Feeding:** But which world do you carry?
o **Child:** World full of illusions. Nothing is true. And nothing is ours. When I am saying this, I start to transform myself into the mother for my mother. That's the feeling.

*In order to get deeper, we have added the word "Illusion" which was mentioned several times.*

**Illusion**

»Okay. I feel a bit more masculine here. Now, mother, you do this, and the other. And by the way – hurry up! Hurry up, because the next one is coming. Don't take your time. Can you please do it faster? Don't cry. Don't ask. Faster! I feel like the hospital, a doctor, male. Kind of institutionalized. Taking over what is supposed to be an intimate relationship between the "Child" and the mother. Breaking it down like an assembly chain. Like in a fabric. And I have my eye on you, "Breast". I am all over you. I am like an eagle over you. You have to do certain things! Don't ask. Don't talk. Especially don't ask! I even don't want to hear you talking. All this blah blah blah.

I also could take the "Child" now, almost quickly lift it up, put it somewhere else, put it down. I do not care. Because there is a process

116

which has to be fulfilled. "Breast", you do everything I tell you. You don't have your own will. It's like you put your mind and body completely into my space. Even your life! You completely shifted it to me. You don't even have to enter my hospital. Once you get a small dose of me, you are mine. I can do whatever I want with you!

And I will completely cut the connection between you and your "Child". First of all, I cut the connection between you and your body. There is no way you should have a connection to your "Child". No way. It is not allowed. That would be dangerous for me. And my power. That is my worry: To stay in power, not to lose it.

It's a heavy job. And then I would like to give you drugs. So that you don't feel anything anymore. Some injections. And I tell you: "You have depressions, you are a bad mother, you can't take care of the child." I put so much stress on you, mother. For sure, she can't feed you, "Child". The milk is not coming out properly.

It is a complete messed-up world. I am the man. I do everything in order to prevent any connection whatsoever. I don't know if there ever was one? I don't know. But I do my best to create a lot of friction. I have this inner restlessness in me to constantly create friction: With theories, with findings, with tests, with medicine, with new injections, with new hospitals... I am pushing women out. There should be no women at all! Just men, ideally. Because then we can create more and more frictions. Then we can create more and more operations, more and more injections, more and more medication, more and more psychological areas, drawers you can push someone in; like depression.

I don't even see children. My only intention is to create friction. Like a wheel that keeps on turning faster and faster and faster. Ideally, that every connection is being broken. With every woman around the globe. The most problematic thing, the biggest threat for me would be if the mother has a connection with the "Child" and the "Child" has a connection with the mother. This would be the biggest threat on earth. No weapon poses a bigger threat than this connection!! And I am doing EVERYTHING to disturb it! Everything! And women don't realize it. They are so entranced in the illusion of a happy family, a beautiful family.

117

There are different types of people who create this side of the illusion. I am more the operational, hospital, doctor side. There are others who take care of the pictures of the illusion, like cinema and movies. Magazines also play a big role.«

**Child**

»This sounds so creepy! Crazy world. I felt like I am one with the mother. I am not me. I cannot distinguish between us. I am looking at my tummy. It's my tummy but at the same time my mother's. I am so interwoven. What is she thinking, feeling? But when "Illusions" started to talk, it felt for me that "Illusions" talked the truth. And I allowed myself to eat without shame. Something was released in that moment. I felt nourished. I am just looking at my food now. I don't have any connection to "Breast" and "Illusions". The feeling of the food, it felt so good. I am not sure who am I. Who am I? Only thing that matters is the food. But not sure what kind of food is this.

When I hear you, "Breast", talking I want to run away. I am not looking at you as a resource to eat, to be alive. I try to find other ways. Let me escape of you two. It is too much. I don't want to be related to both of you. If I want to have a chance, I need to push everything aside.«

**Breast**

»Ah! This is your purpose. Power. I feel now more released. I want to fight you; for the "Child". "Child", I want to take you in my arms. I feel more adult now. I understand what "Child" said. Maybe I don't look at you like my "Child"? Maybe like some resource to satisfy me on some kind of level? This helps me to see you. I take this "Child" like a salvation to feel myself loved by my mom.«

**Feeding**

»Boah...For the first time, I can see both of you. For the first time, I can see your breasts. And I have the impression that you, "Child", are bigger right now. I feel a bit calmer. Could I be a bridge? I have a little bit from the mother and the "Child". There is a heavy weight on my

118

chest. But for the first time I have HOPE right now. That there could be again a connection when you, "Child", get a little bit older. To realize also who was introjecting all the time. I feel now more like a link. Whatever you like to do, whatever you like to discover, I would be there.

Constantly eating, fighting, sleeping – maybe that is the reason why we are all eating constantly. It is never enough. From the beginning to the end the cycle continuous.

I have the feeling as if we would need a lot of quietness. I was just thinking about the first days, when you come home. For the mother, there is the household, there is the husband and maybe another child. There is so much going on. There is never stillness: Looking at each other, touching each other without intention. With no agenda. Just being there as long as you want to. It doesn't matter if there is a bed or not. It doesn't matter at all. It is just about the mother and the "Child". Because with a house, with a lot of comfort, you always have to do something and its distracting the bonding process. Simple is better. Simple cloths, simple touch… Just simply waking up, feeding, and simply going to sleep. Very simple. We have this craving in this world, these unfed needs.«

o **Child:** For me, the separation of my mother, the illusion, helped me to eat but when you appeared again, I realized I cannot feed myself. My mother wants me only for her benefit. That is the reason I need a male to get me out of this madness or create the separation from my mother. Separation has its benefits. To discover who am I. Because my mother doesn't want me. And now my breast is hurting. Ouch! I feel quite lost. I notice cycles of tiredness, fight for food, eating, and again tiredness and really trying to not die. It is ongoing. 1 year, 2 years, 3 years, etc. When you are talking, "Feeding", I feel the warmth. It is like a dripping.

o **Breast:** I am sad now. I realize now that I am incapable of being a real mother for my children. I am cold. I don't have anything good to give to this "Child". I look at you and you have a face that touches me. For the first time, I realize it is my baby, from my belly.

119

I don't know how to protect you. But I feel that I love you. This is a kind of enigma.

o **Child:** Mmm…. sounds exactly what I need.

**Feeding**

»Actually, me too. If I put myself in the shoes of the mother it's like I don't see you at all. I can't see anything and anyone at all. As if the eyes would now start to work properly again. And the touch and the smell. And when you sleep, "Child", I can see the movements of your eyes, your body, your breath. It is like the best movie on this planet. It's wonderful. Like you would be inviting me into your universe. Enough would be enough. Enough would then really be enough. And it doesn't matter how big the breasts of the mother are. It is always the right mixture. The right food. And it is nurturing, and healthy. And then you do not have to worry.«

o **Child:** I hear you. The feeling it creates while listening to your voice… I could sleep in a restful state. I am fed through your voice when I hear you.

o **Breast:** How did we lose the power of the simple things? There are so many rules to do something in this way and that time. This natural way is living inside of us but we lost it completely. We lost the capability to listen to it.

## 2.10 CURSE

*Genera-encounter (4 words)*
*mother – father – child – curse*

An old-fashioned word, but I wanted to know what kind of curse a child is. What was brought to the surface in this work were aspects I had never expected: parents who hit their children, no safety for children in the family, men who see a curse in women. This creates the breeding ground for mass child deaths, pedophilia, rape, suffering, and misery. In short: trauma spanning generations, fertile ground for the unspeakable. In order to even survive this, people must divide themselves multiple times and dissociate permanently. The consequences and divisions penetrate deep into the innermost parts of our personality and identity. Psychological jargon clouds truths further and caps the unspeakable. And so, with this work, we approach the essential questions of humanity: What is good and what is evil?

»He is lying also for you, "mother". When he said pedophilia, pedophiles are people who are actually quite much liked in their social circles. They know how to not show it. They are very likable, sympathetic and even having some social prestige. No one would recognize them. They are joking like that, they are making people laugh.«

Those who are wondering what the cause of personality disorders could be or in part also of dissociative amnesia should carefully read this work.

### father

»You are the curse, "mother". All of you. All you women. You are a curse. Sub-species. All vaginas. I got bloody toys around me and its irritating the fuck out of me! I don't want to see these toys. I don't want to see the color.«

### mother

»You are drinking your tea and then just say pleasantly "you are all a curse" or what?! And who says that I am a woman? I don't feel it. I am not a woman. I am not a mother. Come on! Now I have to identify with a vagina or what? I wanted to create some drama here and now everyone is laughing. That really annoys me.«

**curse**

»For me it's true. I am a curse. But you are not a woman. You are a mother. There is a difference between woman and mother. But it's another story if you are one. I want to find out why I am here. I focused on "father". I see that nothing is like it seems.«

**child** [smiles, laughs uncontrollably]

»Actually, I like that type of "father"! He seems like coming from the pub. In a good mood. And greeting everyone at home. My attention is also completely on the "father" but I don't feel a connection to him. For me, he is very charismatic.«

○ **mother:** And I would like to beat you up, "curse". But now, as everyone is laughing, I even can't beat you up. Annoying. For me, you are the child, "curse", and I really like to beat you up. And I don't have much else going on in my life, to be honest.

○ **father:** Are you my mother? Because she used to beat me up.

○ **mother:** Could be. He definitely has more humor than I have. Everyone likes him because he is so funny. I am so bored. I need some drama in my life. And I think beating up a child, yeah, is okay. So, what?

○ **curse:** I can't even feel the fear towards "mother". I am very confused that I am a child because "child" is also there. I feel that I am somehow identified with "father".

○ **mother:** The moment you talk, I would like to beat you, "curse". I would really like to beat you up!

○ **father:** I totally identify with "curse". I am the curse! It's all within.

○ **curse:** That makes sense. But this is weird because I feel like a woman. And that's confusing me. If you are identified with me...

○ **father:** Because you are my curse! I am a curse to women and you are a curse to me.

○ **mother:** I don't want to be a woman! I want to be a man! Men can beat. And I can then beat as well.

**father**

»I don't feel violent. I feel overly sexualized. But I do get off on the fact that "mother" is quite violent. And that does kind of intimidate me a little bit. I don't particularly like it. But there is absolutely no way I would admit it. Because I am a man. And I take what's mine. And I see you, to a certain extent, as my mother. I don't see as our child's mother.

I feel now drawn to "child". The minute you said you are identified with my mother, I look at "child". Because she could love me. She could take care of me. She could take care of my needs. I know this feels very uncomfortable. I have to admit it. I almost feel a strong sense of cigarette, tabaco and whiskey.

I feel quite confident you, "mother", won't protect "child". Because I was never protected. And that is what the curse of male to female is: There is no protection. The man can do whatever he wants. But as a boy, you can do whatever you want to me.«


**child**

»I still only see the "father". And when he focuses on me, it is very unpleasant. And I don't like to feel more mature than my age. But I don't feel that the "mother" is present.«


**curse**

»I can feel that there is a lot of anger. There is so much anger! But superficially, I am calm. I am staring at the "father" and I am angry. I am angry at men.«


o **father:** I depersonalized it. I have now granted everyone to be an adult. It's not me that's dangerous. It's all adults who are dangerous.
o **curse:** All men.
o **father:** Or their mothers.
o **curse:** I am the female curse. It's not about the mother.
o **father:** I feel like I am riddled with institutional misogyny and pedophilia. There is no nice way of putting it.

- **curse:** And I am here because I want revenge. I want it for all women, for everybody...
- **father:** Shit. I feel you are a total narcissist, "curse". "curse" is making it up; she is hysterical, she is a liar. It is bizarre. I am not even remotely bothered. I want you to shut up.
- **curse:** There is something very confusing. I am protecting the "child" but it makes it even worse. Because you go on with the circle of violence. It is going on and on if I am here.
- **father:** I feel it is institutional. I feel I could reach out to another man – and another man would endorse what I do, make it all over again. And it would be all okay.
- **mother:** What has the church to do with it? Because I suddenly hear quires singing... For some bizarre reason, I think now more as a woman. I could have been cursed as well. For some reason, I don't see you anymore as the "child" I would like to beat up. What's going on here?
- **father:** I am a pathological liar.
- **mother:** But if I married to a pathological liar, who am I then?
- **father:** You are an enabler. You let me do what I want. Cheers.
- **mother:** That's true. Oh, shoot, that's true. That is true!
- **child:** He is lying also for you, "mother". When he said pedophilia, pedophiles are people who actually quite much liked in their social circles. They know how to not to show it. They are very likable, sympathetic and even having some social prestige. No one would recognize them. They are joking like that, they are making people laugh. Like in the beginning. It is exactly like that.


**father**

»"child" got it. I feel pathological. I feel like I have been given and I am entitled to a lot of power. And I can use it to manipulate things. Like I did with you. I manipulate anything and anyone. Its systemic. I don't know any different. This is something that I was taught how to do. This was done to me. I think this is normal. This is how it is. This is what men do. This is not A MAN. This is what MEN do. I could reach out to another man who would go: "Ha! This is what we do, and this is how we deal with it." I get a level of comfort of the fact that you,

124

"mother", are complicit in it. Because I could blame you for every-thing.«

- o **mother:** And I am the other side of the cover-up. It's true. We need each other. To do the unspeakable. Beating and abusing. And it is also part of the deal to blame me.
- o **father:** And "curse" hints at this. And starts to get angry. And that's when I start to call her hysterical and all of that. Immediately made her the problem. Because I have the power to do this.
- o **mother:** Mental asylums and so on.
- o **child:** I want now "curse" to help me. Because I don't have anyone else to help me. I feel a bit trapped. I do understand. But still, in this set-up, I am the trapped one. I am looking at the "curse" now.
- o **curse:** Why am I here? The "mother" is complicit of the "father", now I don't know where I belong to.
- o **mother:** That's good. If you don't know where it comes from, you will never be able to solve it. Very good. If I would give it a medical term, I would say ….
- o **father:** … identity disorder.
- o **mother:** Dissociative amnesia. But personality disorder is also not bad.
- o **father:** I feel like dissociative identity disorder. I feel like for me, I am so far down the line of dissociation, it's my identity. I identify with dissociation. Almost like psychopathy a little bit. I believe to-tally, in my head, that my actions are allowed, they can be whatever they want. And the minute a woman has any kind of… Even a child… If it's a boy or a girl is irrelevant. The minute its smaller than me, younger than me, I can dominate it. And I know I can. I can manipulate it. Because I am deeply dissociated and traumatized myself.
- o **mother:** And when you talk about personality disorder, I think this is what I have. But its mixed with something else on top.
- o **father:** Yeah, but you have to be slightly softer than me. You can't be as hard as me.
- o **mother:** I do more the beating stuff. This is more my thing. I am more an expert when it comes to beating. And belittling. »You are worth nothing. Useless piece of shit.« These types of things. And I

125

don't feel anything. Nothing! Nothing!! I don't even have a memory of being a child myself.

o **father:** When you say »shut your mouth«, I kind of get dominant. Shut your mouth up! A kind of frenzy internally that I am trying to push down. And I don't want to get near.

o **curse:** I am very old. As old as human nature. And I recognize that now, in the present, I am called psychological terms. In the past, people called me curse.

o **mother:** These days, there are more fancy words. Which is great because you are being covered up once more.

o **father:** Adds to the confusion.

o **mother:** Yeah. And plays into our hands. Which is quite fine for me, to be honest.

o **curse:** I don't feel like a human being. It feels like an energy.

o **mother:** Do you have an idea where you come from? Where it all started?

o **father:** For me its generations. She is a generational curse. She is young forever. And that's why she felt like a part of me.

o **curse:** That's also confusing. Because you are calling me nasty names. You have been very mean to me. It is confusing. It feels it's something about power.

o **father:** It is interesting. I am afraid of "child" in a way. She has a lot of power and she doesn't know it yet.

o **mother:** She has the power to see things clearly. This is what my impression is. I am not looking at her at all.


**child**

»I feel so said because I am losing my "father" which I used to love so much in the beginning. I was feeling so lucky in the beginning, as a child, to have such a "father". He was my hero. I am losing all my trust to anyone whom I meet later. Because you can never know what is behind a person when you live with someone like that. You can never trust. It's also so much what can be done to me but it feels more I can never be able to trust a man, a woman. Its hellish. I cannot trust live. That's the curse. You stand between life and me. And you are not help-ing.«


126

- **curse:** I am identified with "father". When he says he can manage that, I feel he can't. My heart is aching. I am the curse of the "father". I am your curse, you know. Physical illness and heart attacks. When you behave like this, you will not have a good life. And you will die early.
- **father:** Now you sound like my mom. She is my curse! She was my curse. So, I am to call you mother.
- **curse:** Call me what you want. I am always here. Call me karma. Call me resonance. Call me mother. Whatever you want. This is what happens when you behave like this.
- **mother:** I think you need an injection, "father".
- **father:** I become really young now. And I gladly take the injection. I look at the "mother". Yeah, do it. Put me out of the misery. That's cyanide.
- **curse:** What kind of injection is it?
- **mother:** I don't know. But it's a very good one. It is a kind of vaccination but older. What is the oldest injection? [now searching the internet] Oh, interesting! Look at this: »Forms of intravenous injection and infusion are clearly documented in the 1650s. Sir Christopher Wren used a syringe made of animal bladder fixed to a goose quill to inject wine and opium into the veins of dogs.«[31] Opium sounds quite nice, actually. Morphine, opium. Not too bad actually. I have the feeling, I am transforming into a kind of medical nurse. Doing it for the doctors. When you put people under drugs you can make them do anything.
- **father:** I am still going backwards. A police man just went by my window, down the road. And my whole body froze. I feel really little. About 3, 4 years old and I want to be put out of my misery.

*We are taking it the "mother of the father" (grandmother).*

- **father:** I am shit scared of her. You are the psychopath.

---

[31] National Library of Medicine: Norn S, Kruse PR, Kruse E. Traek af injektionens historie [On the history of injection]. Dan Medicinhist Arbog. 2006;34:104-13. Danish. PMID: 17526154. https://pubmed.ncbi.nlm.nih.gov/17526154/

**mother of the father**

»I don't feel anything. I feel like an avatar. No life, no meaning. Like I would be put here on earth and that's it. Maybe I give birth to children, but there is no feeling involved in it. If one dies, okay. Again. Again a child dies. Again. Better not to feel. Giving birth to the next one. I am not killing babies. They get a cold, you don't have medicine, you don't have enough clothes. Then they die. We are poor. We don't have a lot to eat. My husband, he can't control himself. So, I am pregnant all the time. He needs sex and then there comes another baby. That's the reason you see me as a curse, because you want to have a connection. But I can't. I just want to die. But I would never kill myself. So, I wait. And that's it.

10, 15 children. Who cares? I am not allowed to complain. I am just allowed to endure. Better not to think about anything. I got so used to it that I got numb. Keep on working, getting children – that's it. That's life. Just working, surviving, dying. There is no meaning associated to life. It's better to die. Puts an end to my misery. I am cursed as well. Life is hell. Ask your father, son. Why does he constantly hump on me? Why do I constantly have to give birth to children? Why? If you have the 15$^{th}$ child, the 16$^{th}$ child. Be happy that you are not a woman. Being a woman is a curse. Being pregnant is a curse. Ask your father. Don't put all the rage on me. Ask your father. Why is he not here?«

o **curse:** This is also a curse when you feel nothing.
o **mother of the father:** It is also a curse when you see your children die. I can't love, I can't live. I can only work and see children die. Everything inside of me is dead.
o **father:** You have to want me.
o **mother of the father:** Doesn't work anymore. I am dead inside.
o **father:** I want to raw! I feel rage inside. I see her as a killer.
o **curse:** "mother" and "father" and grandmother are dead inside. This is why babies die. "mother" and "father" are perpetrators. By not taking responsibility of their life. Being a woman is a curse. But in this case, it's about rape and it's about sexuality.
o **father:** I get older now and I start on the trajectory that this is bullshit. You created me from rape. You can't neglect me from rape.

128

And telling me, I can't defend myself as an adult. And I am the by-product of rape. And who takes care for me? Who looks after me? Who loves me? Who nurtures me? Who protects me? Who doesn't rape me?? And around and around it goes.

o **mother of the father:** We were poor. No one cared about us. We were disposable. We just had to work. All the time. Under the poorest conditions you cannot even imagine. I am very bitter. I don't want this life. This is hell. You cannot even imagine how it was at that time. Absolutely awful and brutal. A life was worth nothing. NOTHING.

o **father:** And I resonate with exactly the same thing. I don't want this hell. Because I have to become a perpetrator. Because this is what a curse is. I have no choice! I don't know how to feel and think. I don't know how to feel anything.

o **mother of the father:** It's the first thing we agree upon. Because I don't know either. If there would have been drugs at that time, I would have numbed myself constantly. Constantly. I would have been a drug addict.

o **father:** I think I should kill myself. I have the strongest need to just die.

o **curse:** I can feel what your mother says. It is a curse being a woman and getting pregnant all the time. And I think it's about sex. The consequences of being pregnant. That's what is the curse about.

o **mother of the father:** When you said that "curse", I think what is also a curse is not being able to cry. Crying would be a relief. And I am not able to cry. Because I am suppressing every single emotion.

o **father:** It is extreme! I mean it is extreme! On some level I believe I am dead.

o **mother of the father:** Yes. We are dead. Dead men and women walking.


**father**

»I believe violence helps me feel. I want to start hurting myself, scratching my skin. Want to take a knife. Now I look at "child" as somebody who can save me. It is like a desperate cycle. I can take care of "child" and "child" can take care of me. And maybe I can feel something.«

**mother of the father**

»I think "curse" is right. We are both cursed, men and women. Previous generations. For us, there is no way out, no help. The only hope is for "child", the new generation, to do things differently. But we, we are doomed. Hopefully she will find something. We can't help. We don't know either. We don't know better. I feel so disposable. Like waste you put in a bin. I really wish for "child"… that you have a different life than we had. Different for you than it was for me. Really. If there is something you could change for yourself, I would be happy. Well, I can't feel happiness but it would be good.«

o **child** [crying a bit]: I feel better. But I feel I have to find it all on my own. No one to show it. But hearing this is very important. It's crucial.
o **curse:** I can feel tears.
o **child:** Yeah, me too a bit, when grandmother told me nice things I felt emotions.
o **mother of the father:** There is such a vicious cycle of abuse and being abused, of dying and killing. Of working to death. Of starving. Drinking. Freezing to death. I wish none, not even an enemy, to feel what I had to go through. So, "child", there is no need for you to look backwards. I want her to go on and never, never ever to look back.
o **father:** I am made of you and "father" and it didn't work for me. It is not true. We have to tell the truth! There is a certain level of relief with sex. Its small. But it's there. But I need to drink to do it. I couldn't have contact sober.
o **curse:** I can feel it also. It is important that men start to feel. I think this is the solution.

130

**father**

»I want to feel. I don't know how to do it. But if I have sex or drink or… I am just desperate. And then the generational loop kicks in: This is what men do, and they can't feel, and this is how we handle it, this is what we do, we don't talk about it, we don't verbalize it, we don't say anything. Because there isn't this loving mother, this loving space, a wanted space. So, I drink and I do this. And I feel and I become violent. Desperate attempt to feel ANYTHING. Because the torture of everything is massive. It's a curse, a curse. Because what I want is my Mommy. All I want is protection. What I want is love. What I want is connection. I want to feel safe.«


**mother of the father**

»Everything you just said doesn't exist in this world. Safety doesn't exist either. Nothing exists. I feel like we are all being cursed. You are put on this earth, this is your curse. The minute you have to live under such brutal and harsh conditions, you can only survive if you diminish your emotions. And then everything is possible. If one keeps on blaming the other, there is no good coming out of it. I am not a cow. Even cows don't produce so many baby cows like me.«


o **father:** Particularly if you are being put on this from rape. The minute you are being unwanted, the curse of being unwanted is boom! And it's interesting: I don't know how to do that. Apart from absenting from sex. I have absolutely no knowledge of that. Because I have been told nothing. And I don't know the instructions.
o **curse:** The only way out is to feel. I feel sadness of what's going on. I can feel the sadness here.
o **mother of the father:** And for me, as a woman, the first thing which has to stop is having so many children! It is unbearable. Unbearable. It is torture for your body. Torture!


Epilogue

The division between man and woman, man and woman, parents and children is extremely deep. Moreover, the conflict between men and women, who accuse each other, does not help either. Words or psychological categorizations hinder and even block any conversation or search for the cause. It is unbearable what the generations before us had to endure: people were used like cattle, like objects. In a brutal way. No protection, no security, and 24-hour work. The only level of warmth was intimacy. A heatwave, but then the temperature drops like hyperthermia. And with alcohol, it drops even further.

Children are trapped in this environment and this game. Only the grandmother was affirming, talking directly to the child. A small ray of hope, a conversation that made a difference. The child knew: She has to care for herself. Because there is no unfolding possible with these parents. It has nothing to rely on. Because the most important thing is missing: security.

That means: Every generation must decide whether it wants to stop this multi-generational curse, i.e. trauma. Healing begins with feeling these transgenerational wounds. This path requires a lot of courage and inner strength.

# 3. FAMILY

## 3.1 ADOPTION

*General-encounter (2 words)*
*Child – Adoption*

On this evening, we were only two. Initially, I remained in the role of companion before I myself actively engaged in the resonance of the word "Adoption." As the work progressed, an unfathomable pain emerged, originating from the natural bond being severed between mother and child. Be it out of necessity, violence, or profit motives. This primal pain reverberates audibly throughout the cosmos and echoes within every woman, every mother, every child across the globe. Similar to the song of whales, the psychological and physical pain travels thousands of kilometers. Myths and stories have been recounting this pain, this collective wound for millennia. Yet, we no longer hear it. Moreover, we do not shy away from continuing to tear apart the bond of body and heart between mother and child under the guise of mercy and turning it into a business model. This resonance work narrates the depth of the trauma and the collective guilt that lies within.

**Child** [in complete entanglement with the mother]
»I can't tell you how I'm feeling at all. I feel dizzy, lightheaded. Am I pregnant? Am I identified with the mother? I am sad. The pain of her not wanting me. I am completely identified with the mother who turns away from what she did, giving me up for adoption. I place one hand protectively over my heart and the other over my stomach. I am completely torn. I am identified with the mother who lets herself be torn to give up the child. My mind wants to leave and my body wants to go to the child. I have pain, stomach pains. I don't want to see all of this, I don't want to admit what I'm doing. Now, I believe, the child is being born. I am extremely sad. The baby dissolves in my imagination. It is gone, it is not there.«

*»Is there a reason why you gave the child away?«*

»Everything starts to vibrate in my uterus, in my stomach. I want nothing to do with this pregnancy, with this birth. My abdomen, my womb are traumatized. Yes, something very terrible happened to me. After I've told this, shame wells up within me. I am aware of what I am doing, but I actually want to hide it from myself. I feel ashamed that I gave away my child. I am guilty towards my baby. I can't even feel the pain, because it would tear me apart. I am doing exactly the same thing my mom did to me. She also gave me away.

I am surprised because I think, am I a mother? But actually, am I not the child? My mother didn't physically give me away, but she emotionally abandoned me. Gave me away, discarded me. She was always absent. And that's what I'm doing with my baby. I am giving it away. It's becoming clear to me right now. [cries] I am a mother physically, but there is nothing! There is no baby. I would like to breastfeed my baby right now. I am desperate.«

*»I feel an incredible empathy for you. Like an absolute understanding of what you're going through as a mother.«*

»That comforts me in a way. It touches me. And I could start crying now. Okay, that takes a little weight off me. I find it really beautiful that you, as a woman, can empathize with that. That you have so much compassion that you can understand why I did that. Because I fear that people in society might think that I am such a heartless person. I can't even grasp the extent of it. The only thing I think is that the extent of my traumas led me to act that way.«

*»A picture comes to my mind: Actually, if a woman decides or has the idea to release a child for adoption, then a circle of other women, many women, should be around you who are there for you. So that you are not alone. So that the child is not released for adoption. Like a protective, nurturing circle, soft and warm and cozy, that is there quietly, calmly, without many words, like a hug, helping.«*

»What you're saying sounds really nice. It would have been nice. I'm completely on my own. And I don't have a female plan at all to support me, to help me.«

»I realize that this is also a collective wound for the rest of us women, that needs to be healed. It's almost like a stab in the heart when women are not with their children. And children not with their mothers!!«

»All women who have to give their baby away. Yes, that happens to me too. I would never have done that either if I wasn't in this situation. My whole body was turned towards the other body. My body doesn't want that at all. I had to completely split off from myself to be able to do that.«

»In all those moments when something was done to you, in all those moments of the most intense trauma – you were always alone. There are no choices. It's as if the mommy's body – the baby's too – is screaming. They both cry for each other. And the baby screams loudly and the mother's body screams silently. Just like calves that are separated from their mothers. That cry... It's incredible. I can just see whales... As if all mammals scream! And just as the echo of whales can travel for miles underwater, so can the cry of the mother, the body. The baby hears it. For kilometers, thousands of kilometers. Like when the whale cries out into space. There is so much pain. The universe hears how much pain there is. Does no one hear it? The scream? I have to hold my heart. It's unbearable. To separate a child from its mother – just like a mammal, just like a young animal from its mother – this pain is incomprehensible! That's what's getting to me: that it's just as bad for animals to lose their babies. It's in our primal genes. Absolutely existential. It also has to do with primal love. This deep connection to the earth. The cry goes out into the cosmos.«

»That is what distinguishes mammals from others. That we are so attached to our children and children to us.«

135

»It arises through the process of growing up in someone else's body. No matter how many months and no matter how the mammal is born. A foal can walk in a very short time, but it is different for humans. It's as if the cosmos is almost singing and rejoicing with every process. It is such a miracle that cannot be described in words! It's actually a creation of love. One should sing and dance. And it goes beyond what happens here on Earth. I can't grasp how immense it is. I really have to hold my heart.

Every process, every movement, every change is an explosion of miracles. You can break it down into atoms and yet not understand a single one of them! Not a single one of them can I cognitively grasp. Forget about science. Life cannot be cognitively grasped. You could philosophize and sing about each atom for more than a thousand years, but you still wouldn't comprehend it. Actually, I should hold the baby up high with outstretched arms so that everyone can see. Like during the christening. You really have to symbolize this coming together.

It also feels as if the other planets are a family. This dimension is almost unbearable. If we manage to achieve this reunion again, to bring it about, then a portal would explode. From the Earth out into the cosmos. It surpasses all capacities I have here, but I have to say it: As if there was a push coming out of the Earth. And the whole cosmos is watching us! Like an intergalactic midwife. The other planets are watching us and asking, "So? How are you doing, Earth? How are you doing in your process of pregnancy?" This is insane. It's almost unbearable. It's surpassing all synapses in my head right now. I really have to hold my heart.

First, the baby – the newborn baby and the mother – both must come back together. That is so essential. There is indeed an urgency. I don't know if they have drifted apart or been torn apart – but there is a high urgency. That needs to be corrected. Every minimal aspect of pregnancy is a miracle. An explosion of wonders in every process of mother and child. That is the gift of the cosmos. That is the gift of the universe. It's actually deep love. Unbelievable. It's as if the planets, like parents, are looking down, setting the frame, and protecting us. An incredibly delicate process of this development. And everyone is involved. Supportive, protective, lovingly there.«

136

*Since the child was so entangled with his biological mother, we changed the word to "mother". I myself went into the resonance with the word "baby".*

- o **Mother:** I am crying and I am humbled, such a beautiful idea that the cosmos is watching. How every step of development and everything has a meaning, that every word is taken up, is important, is significant. It shows itself in every life to come.
- o **Baby:** Like every plant that grows. As if we don't even see what's buzzing and moving around there. The colors, the life. How it swings and dances and rejoices and sings and is harmonious. I lack human words for it. Suddenly I see the plants. As if they speak to us in every phase of growth. Even the animals. Everything has a specific sequence, a dance. It is so rhythmic. I don't have to feel guilty when I eat plants. No calorie counting. This one-dimensional thinking... And then we think, wow, we have discovered the meaning of life or the meaning of the universe. Meanwhile, you're only at a single-celled level. Everything is so narrowly conceived. How can one be so far off the mark! Unbelievable. I have no idea how it is meant to be thought. But how can one be so far off course?
- o **Mother:** Totally! I can really go there, the whole universe is flirting and swinging and so full of life and we try... That we are able to give birth to life is the expression of this miracle, but because we live in a traumatized society... It makes me sad that we don't see this, how we deal with it on earth. [cries] As if these were two different dimensions, I'm just wondering why this is in adoption?
- o **Baby:** Maybe adoption also has something to do with adaptation? Perhaps we should adopt our original purpose? It occurs to me: »You always want an explanation. It's too big for you to wrap your heads around. Finally learn to simply feel this wonder without always wanting to immediately... You always want to categorize it right away. Always try to make it fit right away.«
- o **Mother:** I am also a traumatized mother who gave up her child, and that is the height of traumatization to give up one's own child. The whole universe works to make mother and child belong together.

137

o **Baby:** Oh, it's good for me if you say that. If we felt as it really is meant, in all depth, the pain would tear us apart.
o **Mother:** I am also torn, I am not able to give my child away without breaking me; it is simply not in us. Now this pain appears.

**Baby**

»I feel like I am so, so small in the mother's womb. Like a crustaccan. I have such a curved posture. And I have to armor myself just like a crustacean, curling up into myself. Outside is the shell and inside it's soft. And I protect this softness. I just want to escape! And protect, protect, protect. I hardly feel any emotion, contact here. I hold onto my heart. There is heaviness here, there is burden, here is weight. I am waiting so much for a word from you. I don't know how to free myself from this armor. How I can ever really live.«

o **Mother:** I'm not well, I am totally resigned, my head hurts, it's hard to see you in this state. I have to take myself totally back so as not to approach you.
o **Baby:** But I'm so longing for it, I feel like we're both going to die, I suddenly have the smell of spaghetti in my nose. Spaghetti and tomato sauce, like someone is giving me a plate of spaghetti, as if I wake up thinking: Ah! Eat! I would like to eat something now. »Children, come and have dinner.«
o **Mother:** Miracoli.[32]
o **Baby:** That's what I was thinking! Now the Miracoli advertisement could come, with the motto: »Get out of your trauma! Eat something!«
o **Mother:** Do you think that distracts from the trauma?
o **Baby:** Sure, I'm like a kid eating spaghetti with tomato sauce and some minced meat.
o **Mother:** Hey, you have a right to your childhood! And you also have a right to a mom.

---

[32] That's what I was thinking! Now the Miracoli advertisement could come, with the motto: »Get out of your trauma! Eat something!« https://www.miracoli.de/

138

- **Baby**: We have a fucking right to family! How twisted and whatever they are! Yes, then the dad is sometimes stupid. He also has a right to be funny and have a spleen sometimes.
- **Mother:** Even if he hurts us?

**Baby**

» No. That's not possible. But if everyone had the right to be as quirky as they are, no one would even think of hurting someone. I'm getting really hot right now. I damn well want a plate of spaghetti with tomato sauce and a little minced meat on top! And then I'll mess myself up nicely. Forget about being healthy. My head is about to explode. I want to have a normal childhood without someone telling me that the world is ending right away. In this family, I can't eat meat, and in the next one, I only get meat. I damn well want a childhood!

I just made a jump from the crustacean to the spaghetti. Now I am a child. I damn well have the right to have the adult crap kept away from me. Mom and dad are there. My goodness, they are a bit daft, but nothing happens to me. I have a family, I argue with my siblings, I'm not an only child – and it's still loving. That's what I want. And sometimes I get it too.

Then some crap happens again. Then the parents are always at work. Or dad's not there. I don't want that. I want this commercial now. Like the happy Miracoli family. And behind it comes the detergent advertisement telling me how to get the stain out. And then we siblings fight. Yes, I feel like this was in the 1970s, 1980s. Maybe more in the 1970s? There's always something great in every era. But then you forget what was good. You should actually take that along to the next decade. For example, school is shittier now than back then. I know that instinctively. But I also know instinctively that there are a few things that are better now with mom and dad. That's what I want.

And I just realized, I made another jump. I'm now about 8 to 10 years old. I want to have humor and lightness. And that everyone can be who they are. Interestingly, I'm not adopted. As if I'm speaking for all children. I want to have my original family. I want nothing to do with adoption. Maybe I'm dreaming myself into a family? But it's totally real to me. I want to have that. In my imagination, I have a family, you and dad, and I have two more siblings.«

- o **Mother**: I have a stomach ache, I'm still in the desolate, sad state of separation, I'm still not feeling well. But I can tell you that we are not together, it is unbearable; I am somewhere in the basement, in a dark room. I am really cold and it is dark.
- o **Baby:** If you say that, I'll have to pull out and go into my Miracoli ad. But if you say how you are, then my Miracoli ad shakes. Then I don't know anymore: Do I really live in another world or do I just imagine it? I can't judge that. I'm too young for that.

**Mother**

»My relinquished child, I am trying to make a connection. And then I think, I am so happy that my baby is doing well. And then shame arises, that I am burdening my child. I still feel a connection. I am sorry that I wanted to make a connection. But I can't quite let go yet. My body has adjusted to having a child. But there isn't one. My body grieves for my child! It's as if the body had prepared to become a mother with all its senses. I shared my body with another being for nine months. It's what the body is made for. And then it will no longer fulfill its purpose. It can't breastfeed the baby. It's as if the body is crying. I am mourning. I feel empty. There is emptiness and heaviness. I don't feel dead, but rather numb. I feel a loss in every single cell. It's as if I am fading away. I did it consciously, voluntarily, involuntarily, or forcibly, but I gave it up. It's a decision I made. I have to live with it.

I am the perpetrator against myself. There is a desperation that I am completely working against my nature. Because I decided something with my mind. I don't know if that's schizophrenic, but it's so paradoxical, ambivalent, contradictory. I find it comforting that you have such gentle words and so much understanding and compassion. That helps me. But I am much harsher on myself. I wonder if I can ever forgive myself. I realize that this is a very important realization for a mother who wonders whether she should give her child up for adoption or not. For me, it's too late. I gave my child away. I have to live with the consequences for a lifetime. We live in Western civilization. There are

140

many women like me who are alone. Left alone in shock. With the pregnancy.

The patriarchy emerges. We, as women, have to embark on this journey ourselves. In the patriarchy, it is not anticipated for women to support each other. But there is a connection because we are women. Because every woman carries so much wisdom within herself. Wow! That's beautiful. It's a language we all speak. On a small scale as well as on a larger scale. No matter where we are in the world, being a woman means the same thing. How wonderful it would be if all women in the world united and connected! How wonderful it would be if all women around the world, on the same day, did the same thing or contemplated what we are currently discussing. That would be a fantastic idea. What energy that would be! I am still cold, but I no longer feel so alone. Knowing that there are so many other women in the world in a similar situation is somewhat comforting.

Through the compassion you have shown me - as a woman - it has shown me that I can take on the blame. Perhaps, due to circumstances, I couldn't even make a decision. Being together and talking about it with you as a woman, representing as a woman, helps process this wound. Perhaps even to heal it. It is completely therapeutic and nurturing. I understand that we need community. There are many women in the world who feel this. Who are so disconnected.

Then the next wound emerges. I find it good that it's just the two of us. I sense the longing for it. Because we lived in clans, because we raised the children together. We are so disconnected from how we originally lived. And then I feel the trauma. It's also about pacing. There is a yearning for depth and the fear of showing vulnerability and being hurt again. Perhaps right now it can only happen on a small scale.«

Epilogue

We were now at the end of this work when suddenly these thoughts came to me:

»In the body, a transformation occurs when new life emerges. The memory of it cannot be erased because the new life and the body, both

141

*of them, have attuned to each other, have spoken with each other. Like two ensouled bodies that come into contact, into resonance, singing. Like a new melody that is created and emerges. Something new must be thought. We cannot speak for the men. We only speak for ourselves, women.*

*This community of women is incredibly important for us. Compassion, slowness, a connectedness to life, connectedness to the Earth. Like sisters. Independent of age and skin color, nationality or religion. It is important that this extends across generations and beyond all so-called boundaries. None can do it alone. It requires the entire community of women.*

*It is local, it is regional, it is national, but it is also continental and global. Nothing excludes the other. I need the community with me locally and worldwide. And from the large, it becomes small again. It is like inhaling and exhaling, like an organism. Everything is connected. And when one travels, she finds a local group again.*

*We have so many similar fears, so many similar worries, so many similar thoughts, doubts, joys. And you always have someone local who is wise. Or who has something beautiful to share. A woman in distress, in fear, desperate - how beautiful it would be to say, "Hey, I am in contact with another group of women, maybe they know something?" A network of community. Unassuming, no fuss. If I feel the need to speak with a woman who grew up in the Amazon, I can do so. Or if I dream at night of an indigenous woman, I can connect with her through this women's network. Over Chinese food, I can connect with a woman from China. Then I can share the experiences with my local group.*

*Perhaps then you invite some women. "Hey, come visit us!" And even if we just think of the women we really like, or send a very loving hug or a kiss. That's a beautiful feeling.«*

## 3.2 DIVORCE

*Self-encounter (Woman, Romania, 2 words)*
*Romanian: Eu – divort*
*English: I – divorce*

»My Mom had a divorce but she still stayed with my father. I want to know why she did divorce my father. Maybe she caught my father abusing me? She denies it. Memories are coming back and I am shocked and I am not sure if it's true. I am stuck. It's painful. If my mother caught my father sexually abusing me, why did she decide to take him back? I cannot believe it. Am I entangled with my mother? She doesn't want to face anything. She didn't want to take responsibility for anything and now I don't want to take responsibility for anything. I don't know how to deal with this. She is saying: "No, you are mad, you are the crazy one." Am I really crazy? I don't want to believe her and I want to believe her. It's a big conflict.«

**Eu (I)**

»I am at a loss of words. It is difficult to look at "divort" (divorce). I am keeping my eyes down. I want to look out of the window, at the trees. Looking outside is a distraction. Perhaps I just go out and see if the bird would like to have some company. It is interesting because I make up this story, so that I don't have to feel what is happening within me.«

**divort (divorce)**

»I somehow feel important. And I even thought: Why do you start from your "Eu (I)"? You should have started with me. But at the same time, I don't want to interact within the room. I don't want to deal with anything. Just leave me alone. I don't want to face anything. I can talk as the mother. I can talk as "divort (divorce)". I can talk as your part. It is confusing. I don't know how to fix it and I don't know what to do. I just want to sleep and close my eyes. It feels too much to face it.«

143

*»It feels like a betrayal. There is so much anger. Its stuck in my throat. The marriage of my parents was horrible. There was a lot of violence, sexual abuse, madness. I was four years old when one night my father came home drunk. He smashed all the windows of the house. My grandparents were still living with us. He bit my grandfather in the cheek.*

*My mother denied to divorce. "He is the father of my children." There was a lot of beating, running from home. Police. He was abusing my mother. At one point she tried to go with him to the psychiatrist. He had this psychotic moment: "You tried to poison me! You tried to kill me!"*

*With the last encounters ,what came up was that he started to abuse me when I was four years old. But I am also entangled with my mother's trauma. It is a nightmare in my head and body. I found out this week that my mothers' grandfather was abusing children as well. Incest is transgenerational. I found out that he sexually abused my cousin as well. I found out that my grand grandfather was a pedophile as well. My aunt was abused and probably my mother as well. And I remember that my cousin said: "I was 14 years old when the uncle [i.e. my father] touched me." And she talked to my mother, but my mother was angry and denied it. BTW: My cousin and my mother have the same name.*

*There are fractures of memories. Memories that I was in the room, I was out of my body, and my mother went into the room and said: "What are you doing? Let the child alone." Aunt and mom, they discussed it together. From November until now everything came up. And I remember, my mother said: "Don't tell anybody. The shame will kill us."«*

## Eu (I)

»When you talk about the transgenerational abuse, I became interested. There is unbearable sadness here. I really want to cry. It is good to say that. And there is a part of me which wants to slow everything down. It is too much. I feel confused in my head. What do I need to do? I feel sadness and shock. I need you to see me in my sadness and my shock. A feel a tingling down my leg and my teeth begin to chatter. I feel so cold. I feel it in my body. It helps when you are quiet and you can be with me. There are words which want to come out, but I just need to be with this feeling. So that my brain can stay calm. When I am breathing, I can hear the fighting and the screaming.«

»Now I feel sad. It is like I am creating space in my body. Step by step. [crying] My mommy doesn't love me. My mommy doesn't love me! As a child, I wanted to grow up fast, fast, fast, and get a job and get away.«

## Eu (I)

»I feel about seven years old. I want to grow up very quickly. I have the feeling that when I will be old, I can go. And I know it's bad what is happening, and they are bad people. Good people don't do bad things. I know that. I know what bad things are, because I've seen my father doing bad things to my mother. The father is doing bad things to her when they are alone. Bad things that she doesn't want to. There is a split in my eye. In my left eye. I don't want to see what is happening. It is like a consensus.«

»I remember. She didn't want to suck his penis. She scratched him. He shouted at her. "Why did you want to do this?!" She didn't want to touch his penis. My mother was disgusted. And I was hearing that from the other room. He was drunk and she was fighting him. A child shouldn't go through that. It was hell.«

## Eu (I)

»It feels so confusing. What is normal? I have to figure out what's normal and what's right and what isn't right. It is a lot for my young brain. I feel so isolated. Its consuming my brain with everything that is happening. I want to do well at school. I want to do my homework but how can you do your homework?

Now I feel a little older. Maybe around 13. I can see the reality. This anger, this madness, this fucking craziness. This house! Am I the only one who is sane or insane? Other girls are talking about getting their period. Three or four more years and I will get some freedom.

145

Then I will build my own life. I don't care if they die. If they die, they die. I want something other than what I experienced. It actually feels good to say this to you. I am feeling like I am getting more empowered, like I am growing up inside.«

**divort (divorce)**

»I am spaced out and I am disconnected. I wanted to take off your headphone when you were telling the story in the family of abuse. I hardly resisted it. I cannot face anything. But I inhaled a point: "It is not my responsibility." I shift between feeling like your family system, at times like your mother, at times like "divort" (divorce) which happened – it is very blurred. No boundaries. No boundaries. Who is who? It is not clear.«

*»When they divorced, I felt so guilty. It is not my fault, not my responsibility. I am not their mother. It is a confusion between not to take the responsibility for them and where is my responsibility.«*

I stepped in saying: »I think it is time to divorce your family.«

*The woman started to cry and to laugh, saying: »Oh, my God!!! It sounds so good. It feels so good in the body. As if something was released.«*

o **Eu (I):** I am still feeling some coldness going through me. It was good to see you relax, breathe. It sounds like it could be a fairy tale. The idea of it. I am wondering how to do this. How to be with me? I am not really connected with »to divorce from my family«. Yes, I know that I can step out of my family, but my family is in me. Even if I don't have contact with them. They are in my DNA. I don't know what to do. It sounds very logical. How to change my experience, what I lived through, what I have experienced?

*»What we can change is how we live our life. This is what we can do. I cannot change anything from the past. I am free to live. Even if I don't know yet how. We can let it sink in. To figure it out.«*

○ **Eu (Ich):** I like that! »Let it sink in.« Let it sink in. Down the body. And not from the body up. Something needs to be connected in me.

*»It feels like I am unreal. I still have the believe that I am not real. That something is not real in me. I still don't believe that I am alive.«*

○ **Eu (Ich):** This makes so much sense to me. Can you say that again, please?

*»It feels that I am not real. But I am real and I am alive. I am not a dream. I am alive and I am living. And I have bones and skin and feelings. I am real. I am not a dream. I am real. I am not a dream. I can live my life. I am real in my life. My life is real. My life is real now. I am real. [looking at her hands] I am real. You are not in a dream, "divort (divorce)", you are real. Your life is not a dream. It is real as it can be. I am not a nightmare.«*

○ **Eu (Ich):** That really helps me. It is making me feel human. Like I have a body. My mother was very traumatized. What was real, growing up, sometimes seemed unreal.

*»Yeah! Like a nightmare, hell. And I was waiting to wake up. I have a sense of dreaming through my life. My gosh. I was having nightmares going to sleep. I am still in the nightmare. How many years do I still have to do that? Living in the nightmare? Nothing seemed real. I am not the nightmare.«*

○ **divort (divorce):** I was opening my eyes a bit more. The sentence I heard is »to divorce your family« felt good for my body. Whose divorce is that? Boundaries are not clear yet. Who is divorcing whom? Still so mixed.

*»Because our mother decided to still stay with the father after they divorced. She also asked me if my father could come back. The responsibility was put on me as a child. It wasn't my decision to make. And I felt guilt for even saying yes. I was angry on myself. Because if I would have said no, the abuse wouldn't have happened. I was just a child. I was supposed to be protected. They were supposed to take responsibility and protect me. It was their mess! It was their madness and not mine! [crying] She threw me to the wolfs! Again, and again, and again. It was so heartful. I was so longing that they would see me, protect me and love me. I just wanted them as parents.«*

o **Eu (I):** I feel so proud of how resilient you are. Keep breathing, keep breathing, keep breathing. I have nothing more to say than keep breathing. And keep your feet on the ground.

## 3.3 SPLIT OFF

*Self-encounter (Woman, Romania, 3 words)*
*German: Wieso – ich – abspalten*
*English: Why – I – split off*

The woman wants to know why she has felt so disconnected since her childhood? She was born in Romania, raised there, and came to Germany as a teenager with her family. Who would have thought that this work could lead into the depths of gender identity and femininity?

»This is always my theme: Am I feminine, am I masculine? I always wanted to be more on the masculine side. I wanted to please. I wanted to please my dad. And I fell more into the masculine. I also took on the male role for my mother. My father was only there physically, not mentally. Not so much physically either. I played his role and was the man for my mother. I went very much into the masculine to please and

148

fulfill the male image. And I rejected my femininity. There, one is in danger, is weak. One must always expose oneself to danger.«

**ich (i)**
» I am pregnant. I think I am identified with mom. The initial impulse was joy; then fear emerged. It clouded my joy. There are doubts. I am truly scared. I have the baby in my arms. I assume it's an identification because I believe you don't have children yet. I also feel very heavy and strained. I don't feel at all. I feel like I am completely identified with Mom. I can hardly breathe as well. It's all pressing. The entire belly, the whole space here, the entire body... it's very exhausting, very heavy. Now, as you ask me, I somehow feel the baby moving. And that's giving me a headache. It still feels very small. It seems to have little feet. Maybe in the $4^{th}$ or $5^{th}$ month? I don't know. I'm in pain. The question of whether I want to get rid of it, there is complete confusion. My lower abdomen hurts.«

**Wieso (Why)**
»Deep sadness, feeling of heaviness. No more strength left. You want to cry, but it's almost impossible. And to some extent, there's also a fighting anger to survive. But it's overshadowed by the feeling of sadness.«

**abgespalten (split off)**
»I had to read several times at the beginning that I am split off. I do that or I am that - split off - so that I remain in clarity. I have to be very careful here that the truth is spoken here. I see the "ich" (i) and "Wieso" (Why) quite blurry as well. That's why it's important that I stay in clarity and pay attention to what you say. I am hyper-aware. What I noticed in between is that sometimes I struggle to breathe. There is bad air here. And at times I smelled something chemical in my nose and on my tongue. It started with the smell of Patex and then nail polish remover. They're always there for a very short time. Then I smell and taste them. And then I have to focus on breathing again. And then I notice that I can breathe well, but around me there is really bad air. It's very uncomfortable.«

**ich (i)**

»Yes, well, I'm not doing badly. I think it's good that you're addressing me. This confusion, that I am so identified with Mom, is really getting to me. I listened attentively. What "abgespalten" (split off) said really interested me. I am so glad she is here because I am so confused. And I wondered if she can tell me where I... if I have not spoken the truth somewhere or where I am not speaking the truth. And the chemical smell, that immediately resonated with me. The right thigh, the right leg, and eventually the left side... the lower area resonated with that. And I wondered what that is. And then that foot-kick came out of my stomach again when the baby made itself known. Was there maybe an anesthetic needle? Medication? I'm not sure. When the "Wieso" (Why) came up, I started to stroke and protect my stomach. And I had my left hand on the heart center. I listened attentively and wondered what part that is. And I wondered why the "Wieso" (Why) is a man.«

**Wieso (Why)**

»I can't say anything about the topic of man. Actually, I would say I am genderless here. Rather relatively small, in the process of emerging. Definitely like a growing child, but preoccupied with survival. Very unclear about the situation and who one is. I think I am not in the world. I am in the womb. One is there, but not accepted as one would originally need to be. And one does not yet have the strength to speak up and resist influences.«

**abgespalten (split off)**

»I believe that everyone is speaking the truth right now. It was like that in the beginning: I need to maintain clarity; probably for all parts. The "Wieso" (Why) confuses me a little, and I have to pay close attention to what he says. And I had the thought of a twin a few times in between. But I immediately pushed that away. No, I don't want to think about that right now. I want to focus on what the 'I' said. Is it about medications? I got really hot. That triggered me a lot. It takes a lot of effort for me to always stay clear.«

150

**ich (i)**

»I can totally relate to that. I think I need the "abgespalten" (split-off). I believe I need the separation, because I feel so confused. That's why I'm glad the "abgespalten" (split-off) is there. But it's also very exhausting. The medication also resonates with me. I would like to know what happened there. And regarding the "Wieso" (Why), I also wondered if it's a twin. On one hand, I feel a connection to the "Wieso" (Why). What it said also makes sense. Then also a twin moment emerged. And I wonder if the medications have to do with the confusion? That I am so intensely identified with mom, that I feel like I'm not even there. I can't feel myself at all. Where I do feel myself is in the stomach, the kick, the sign of life. It's as if someone kicks me out of the stomach. That's the only time I feel like that's me.«

○ **abgespalten (split off):** So, I have the feeling that when I look at the "ich" (i) intensively, then I see all the ancestors. As if I see not only one face, but the face stands for many.

○ **ich (i):** That's how I feel, I feel occupied, and it makes me sad, I really find it a bit scary. I am cold and it makes me shiver, and I feel myself under pressure. There is also a despair and I can not do anything.

○ **Wieso (Why):** I have gained clarity, especially from the feeling: you feel like you are under medication, so calm, you want to be but can't. The feeling of sadness is still there, but I have gained a sense of clarity for my own condition. That you are immobilized and that you can't do anything.

**abgespalten (split off)**

»When you say that you can't do anything, the image that comes to mind for me is that in the "ich" (i), many images are superimposed. And all the images show a person. And all the people have no self, have no personality. I really don't know how to explain this. The photos can be stacked one after the other. Then sometimes there's something young, sometimes old; but it's all the same. There is nowhere a self, a personality. Someone who animates that. You could also look at this in an album. "Look here, here's the mother, then the grandmother, then the great-grandmother." Those are images. And they don't really come to life.«

o **ich (i):** That makes me very upset and sad right now because I realize that this is true.
o **abgespalten (split off):** I know that this is a women's issue, that women are not allowed to have an identity. That women are used like dolls, get a job and do it. I think that's been the case for many generations, and this is not the subject of the "ich" (i), but a woman-theme behind it.

*»I unfortunately don't know much about the time in Romania. In fact, I know very little until my birth or thereafter. Nothing was ever told. Not even about how the pregnancy was. My birthday is in January, and I only know that it was cold then. But in general, the role of women, yes, submissive of course. Women have no say. For example, my mother, after I was three months old, went back to work. That was common in communism. And then I grew up with my grandparents, with my grandma. My grandma was in the war, in captivity in Russia. I would say that women are partly submissive and partly strong. Very strong and they do a lot. But still, women are not worth much. That's how I would summarize it, I think.«*

**abgespalten (split off)**
»By the way, I feel completely different with you. I wouldn't see you in that role. I see you as alive. Just now, you said that women are not valued as much. For me, it's more like: They play a role and remain invisible. They are not seen. You are something completely different to me. It's as if you haven't continued down this path or aligned yourself in that way. That's how it feels.«

o **ich (i):** I feel a lot of fear and worry. I was wondering when your mom found out you were a girl? It came to me that the mother is afraid that you will be the same as her. Fear and worry about you as a woman.

*We add her mother because of the extreme entanglement.*

152

**Mama (Mom)**

»Oh, I'm having huge problems staying present. It's like I'm struggling to maintain presence, to stay here at all. I always have to shake my head in disbelief that I manage to do this. At the same time, I have huge difficulty in opening my eyes. It's a strange feeling. So, I am so absorbed in whatever I have there. I also feel like: Pregnancy just happens. There's no thought or desire. I can't explain it properly. I am there and at the same time, not there. But I have to fight to be present. It's not that I don't want to see. It's more like I can't see. I am in distress! Like a struggle for survival. It feels so existential. But don't ask me what or how or why. I have given birth to two children, but nothing is happening in my body. I don't perceive anything. And I don't even realize that I'm pregnant. I don't realize that it's being born. I don't realize anything at all! Forget identity! I don't even have a concept of being human! I am so far removed. You could go back thousands of years to the inception of humanity. I can't even say, this is my body, yet. Because I don't know what a body is. What is it? The word? The concept? The matter? Nothing. It's like going back in evolution to the origin. Or to the origins. It's like my mind is blank. Oh, my stomach hurts!«

**abgespalten (split)**

»So, I have to be very careful that you don't leave, because otherwise the baby won't be born! I feel like it's my responsibility for the mom to stay here so the baby can be born. But I don't know how I can help you in your distress. Except that I sit here attentively and make sure you don't leave.«

○ **Mama (Mom):** Correct. How should I describe such a feeling? How should I formulate something like that? You'd better get on with it. And I'll disappear into some corner.
○ **abgespalten (split off):** I'm coming with you to the corner. I can't allow you to leave. You have a task here. And you have to fulfill it. There's no baby without you! I have no idea how this is supposed to work. All I know is that you have to stay here and you have to fulfill your task. Just like everyone else before you has done somehow. I don't know how.

- **Mama (mom):** Exactly. »How, I don't know.« Exactly. You know, theories are based on something. They have some basis. They have a foundation. But there's nothing here!!
- **ich (i):** I'm here. And I'm just now realizing why I'm so identified with "Mama" (Mom). So that I can survive this. I think I also kept making myself noticed so that "Mama" (Mom) would even notice that I was there. Otherwise she wouldn't have noticed us at all. I made sure that we could be born. Whatever.
- **Mama (Mom):** I think that's right. It's like on the screen here: I have obstetricians on the left and right.

**Wieso (Why)**

»Actually, as an emerging child in the mother's womb, one feels something. One is somehow here, no need to worry about not coming into the world, but nobody really cares. As you said, you're "cut off". It's like with the pictures in a book. Actually, worse. You're there, yet not really there. You are not seen. And when "Mama" (Mom) came in, there was a glimmer of joy and movement. But then again, not really. A certain hopelessness. Worse than death. At least that would be a decision. Similar to being "abgeschnitten" (cut off), where you have to ensure that "Mama" (Mom) doesn't leave. That would at least be a decision. This way, it's difficult. You don't have the strength. You are actually like numb.«

**Mama (Mom)**

»Yes, that's right. That's how I feel too. That is much worse. I almost feel like you are giving me something like... I always struggle for words. I can't find the words. When you always speak of "one", that confuses me. As if I were an "it". At the same time, "one" [which also means in German "man"] resonates with it as well. That stresses me out a bit. Unbelievable. I feel exposed. Like amnesia. Like a mix of amnesia, non-existent, an "it", a ghost. It is almost unbearable. When I hear you, it's as if you're grounding me bit by bit. I see no nature. I see no colors. I see no people. It's like I'm going back in evolution. But without people. There was the earth, dinosaurs, plants. It is almost unbearable.«

**ich (i)**

»I see nothing, I know nothing. I am still an embryo. I am still developing. I see "Mama" (Mom) very clearly as my mom. An adult who is in front of me. And I have a lot of fighting to do. I actually have real problems distinguishing myself from "Mama" (Mom). I have to use all my energy to stay alive. To get through the pregnancy. For "Mama" (Mom) to bring me into the world. There is no room for me at all. When "Mama" (Mom) came in, I felt sick and nauseous. And then I felt like I was completely paralyzed. I am in a vacuum. There is nothing. It's hard to describe. And I'm hungry and cold. I have very basic needs, but I am completely frozen. I can only sit here and endure this vacuum. I can't do anything here. And I don't hear anything either. It's completely silent around me. I don't even feel like... I imagine amniotic fluid or something, but there is nothing here.«

o  **Mama (Mom):** It's so strange. When I hear the "ich" (i), I can only be there in the first place through the resonance with it. I'm still nothing, but at least I can breathe more right now. But everything she said is true.

o  **abgespalten (split off):** One always concentrates on what is important and everything else is black and white in the background. The non-living images are discarded. And one concentrates on the now so that things can continue. So that it can go on, so that boys can be born.

o  **Wieso (Why):** I feel alive and angry. Just as the "ich" (i) has spoken. Destructive anger. Anger at the "ich" (i). It was very difficult when they talked about the embryo. There is an anger that is destructive. That's when you have the best kind of liveliness.

o  **ich (i):** Are you angry with me? Why? Why?

o  **Wieso (Why):** I think the image of the twin sums it up quite well. I don't need a twin. I am the one. There is no one else.

o  **ich (i):** But I don't see you as a twin at all. I see you as a living part of us. As a healthy one. As a feeling that has somehow saved itself. In the guise of a man. That you can be there as a man. You are the healthy feeling and I wonder why you are angry with me. I also sense that something has happened. "Mama" (Mom) found out I

155

was a girl in the third month. I'm also getting a real headache. Because I'm trying to understand.

o **Mama (Mom):** Women are just birthing machines. I don't know either. There is something, but I can't say anything. I don't know anything.

*I ask: »Should you have been a boy?«*

*The woman replies: »Yes. My knowledge is that it was only clear what I was at birth. And then there was the disappointment, at least for my father.«*

o **ich (i):** Now, I can't tell you if your "Mama" (Mom) knew this beforehand, but did she have any fears?

o **abgespalten (split off):** I believe that it is a fact: that women are not authorized or that women are not wanted. That it should rather be men. Only men are entitled. That's how it feels. As if "one" or the world determines it.

**ich (i)**
»Yes, it's true that it comes from the outside. I feel that "Mama" (Mom) actually wants it to be a boy because she is afraid it might be a girl. "Hopefully it will be a boy." Then there's the added factor of the centuries-old notion that women are worthless. That's what I grew up with. But I also feel that I am a woman. I am a woman and I would have liked to live my life as a woman. It all resonates with me. I don't want my daughter to have to go through that as well.«

o **abgespalten (split off):** The country needs soldiers. The wish does not come from "Mama" (Mom), but from society or something similar.

o **ich (i):** I feel the whole burden of society in my body. Having to be different from who I am.

o **abgespalten (split off):** I am so sorry to see you, because I would like you to be in your power. For you to confidently say that you are there. That would be my wish. For you not to be a victim, but to be strong in yourself.

- **ich (i):** I would be happy about that too, but at the moment, I feel overwhelmed by expectations. I can't even sit properly. My whole system is out of balance because I am not allowed to live my sexuality, my identity at all. Everything is so crooked and skewed. I really don't know how to free myself from this.
- **abgespalten (split off):** Now I'm facing the same situation with you as with my "Mama" (Mom). I would like to support you, I'm staying here, and I don't know what I can do.

»I can resonate very well with the "ich" (i). This has always been my theme: Am I feminine, am I masculine? I always wanted to be more masculine. I wanted to please. I wanted to please my dad. And I fell more into the masculine. I also took on the male role for my mother. My father was only physically there, not mentally. Not so much physically either. I played his role. And I was the man for my mother. I delved a lot into the masculine to please and fulfill the male image. And I rejected my femininity. Now my path is to accept myself and my femininity. What role should I play to meet the expectations that I also feel from the outside? To be accepted, without putting myself in danger? That's where one is in danger, one is weak. That's how I feel about it.«

- **abgespalten (split off):** I can identify with that. But I don't think I'm weak. No. I am not weak.

**ich (i)**

»This has just been very good for me, what you said. When you talked to Natalie, that had an impact on me. When you say it directly, I feel the need to get in touch with you. I see you very clearly and distinctly. I have you very much in my view. But at the moment you spoke to me, I realized that I am afraid to make contact. Then I immediately looked to "Warum" (Why). I feel that there is a danger there. I feel that it is dangerous to contact you. It does me so much good that you are so honest. I can breathe calmly. When you talked about your father, I immediately went into such a high alert. That confused me. There is something there. The confusion, the danger that comes from this male figure. But I can't tell you what it is.«

157

- **abgespalten (split off):** I can confirm that. So, the "Wieso" (Why) is so present that I can't connect with you. And I know that I belong to you. The connection is as if cut off.
- **Wieso (Why):** On the one hand, one is in the wrong body. And on the other hand, one is practically the parents' wish. The parents' wish to have a boy.

**ich (i)**
»Yes! And there's the confusion! Now I also know what "Wieso" (Why) is. That is a concept. It is in the mind. It is a wish, an idea, a concept. And it is not reality. I see "Wieso" (Why) as a mental instance in us that tells us we are in the wrong body. And there I see the distortion. Because we are exactly right. We are in the right body! But the perception of us is wrong. And we have adopted that. I believe "Wieso" (Why) is a survival strategy. That we were able to survive. That it is dangerous to be a woman. It's exactly like that. I have to say again: We are not in the wrong body! That is really important to me! We are right! The concept of us is wrong.«

- **Wieso (Why):** And that is very strong. When you speak, it makes me very angry. And a destructive rage arises. One has to separate it.
- **abgespalten (split off):** On one hand, it makes me so angry that the "ich" (i) has so much understanding. On the other hand, I am fascinated by your wisdom. It's very ambivalent. My wish is that you don't belittle yourself. You always have so much understanding. And that's what I admire on one hand. On the other hand, it annoys me that you belittle yourself so much.

Epilogue
The theme of "split off" led deeply into the topic of sexual identity and femininity in this work. Children unconsciously adopt the desires of their parents, which are in turn shaped by societal norms. But behind this are generations of traumatized parents. This leads to massive confusion. Therefore, a warning to all who advocate for gender transformations: There is a great risk of becoming perpetrators themselves. Mothers, fathers, medical professionals, psychologists, etc. Those who

are not internally reflective, who have not dealt with their own traumas, or who submit to the dictates of profit-seeking, become perpetrators and accomplices to their own and others' children. A guilt that they and generations after will have to bear.

# 4. Childcare and Support Facility

Since the 1990s, i.e. shortly after reunification, childcare in state daycare facilities in Germany has steadily developed from family care to state care. The Bavarian law on the education, upbringing and care of children in kindergartens, other daycare facilities and in daycare (Bayerisches Kinderbildungs- und -betreuungsgesetz – BayKiBiG) defines the following terms:[33]

»Child day care facilities are non-school day facilities for the regular education, upbringing and care of children. These are crèches, kindergartens, after-school care centers and houses for children.« (...)

(2) »Regular education, upbringing and care within the meaning of para. 1 sentence 1 requires that the majority of children attend the child day care facility for an average of at least 20 hours per week over a period of at least one month.«

The following steps have been enshrined in law in Germany with a legal entitlement:

o 1996: Kindergarten (children from 3 to 6 years)
o 2008: Expansion of child daycare
o Since 2013: Daycare centers (children from 1 to 3 years)
o Planned: from 2026 to 2030 - Primary school with all-day care (children from 6 to approx. 10 years)

While these services already exist in some federal states, the Federal Ministry for Family Affairs, Senior Citizens, Women and Youth aims to expand them throughout Germany.

---

[33] Bayern.Recht, Bayerische Staatskanzlei, »Bayerisches Gesetz zur Bildung, Erziehung und Betreuung von Kindern in Kindergärten, anderen Kindertageseinrichtungen und in Tagespflege« [Bavarian State Chancellery, »Bavarian law on the education, upbringing and care of children in kindergartens, other day-care facilities and in day care«], https://www.gesetze-bayern.de/Content/Document/BayKiBiG-2

»The aim of all efforts at the time was to create a more child-friendly society. In order to make this possible and to give women an incentive to have children, the legal entitlement was enshrined in law.«[34]

The German government talks about the benefits of »being able to better combine family and career«, »improved educational and participation opportunities«, »individual support«, »motivation and self-esteem«, »equal opportunities" and »equal opportunities«.[35] All parties of all political persuasions were and are involved.

It is interesting that the topic of mother-child bonding, especially in the first three years, is ignored in discussions and legislation, despite the results of studies worldwide. The information sheet of the »Zukunft CH«[36] foundation has briefly summarized some of the most important studies and their results. Here are a few quotes:

»Educator Erja Rusanen (University of Helsinki) reports after 40 years of group education in Finland: The risks of these children's lack of bonding skills are ignored, although statistics show a massive increase in aggression, behavioral problems and depression among young people. The Swedish natural scientist Christian Sörlie Ekström reports that the lack of attachment development and parental education in children between the ages of six months and three to four years leads to a lack of stress management, which manifests itself in antisocial behavior, among other things. Depression in girls has increased by 1000 percent in the past 20 years, anxiety disorders by 250 percent.«

---

[34] Die Tageszeitung (taz online), »Kein Platz im Kindergarten bis 1999« [»No place in kindergarten until 1999] from February 4, 1995, https://taz.de/Kein-Platz-im-Kindergarten-bis-1999/!1522012/

[35] Bundesministerium für Familie, Senioren, Frauen und Jugend, »Die Entwicklung des Ganztagsförderungsgesetzes« [Federal Ministry for Family Affairs, Senior Citizens, Women and Youth, »The development of the all-day support act«], https://www.recht-auf-ganztag.de/gb/politik/ganztagsfoerderungsgesetz

[36] Stiftung Zukunft CH, »Krippenbetreuung aus wissenschaftlicher Sicht« (PDF) [»Crèche care from a scientific perspective«], https://www.google.com/url?sa=t&source=web&rct=j&opi=89978449&url=https://www.zukunft-ch.ch/wp-content/uploads/2016/05/Zukunft-CH-Infoblatt-Kinderkrippen.pdf&ved=2ahUKEwiToYX5nq6IAxW0_rsIHRvnH-doQFnoECBQQAQ&usg=AOvVaw093Mf1FpUf7uLTWFf4Ma5W

## 4.1 DAY CARE CENTER

*General-encounter (3 words)*
*Child – Parents – Day Care*

How does a child under three years old feels when they are cared for by others? What about the bond between a child and their mother when the child doesn't see their parents, especially their mother, in the morning or even all day? When a career takes precedence over one's own child? What are the long-term consequences for the child? What is revealed in this work is alarming: lack of contact, lack of relationships, and panic attacks. But the worst thing is the loss of creativity. You may go through life, but you no longer feel it.

o **Child** [smiling]: I want to go into your arms. Stay in your arms. I feel so far away. It's not enough for me.
o **Parents:** No. That's business. I'm just looking at "Day Care". So, what do we do now, "Day Care"? Give me some options, please.
o **Day Care:** I see the "Child" and that's enough. That's all I do. And that's quite a lot of work.
o **Parents:** I am in agreement when you say »you see it and that is enough«. I am okay with that. Fully okay.
o **Child** [smiling]: I need warmth.

**Parents**
»Not me! Sorry. I am thankful that "Day Care" is doing the work. I don't really have an attachment. I don't even want to discuss anything. I just like to hand "Child" over. And that's it. I even don't want to know how much work you have, "Day Care", as long as IT is delivered. I have to emphasize the word "it". As long as "it" is delivered back to me in a proper and well-mannered state. Meaning, diapers exchanged and clothes with no stains. Proper, clean clothes. That's it.«

o **Day Care:** This is how "IT" will be.
o **Parents:** Great.
o **Day Care:** But you will discover other things over time.
o **Parents:** Not interested. I don't want to discover anything.

- o **Day Care:** I know, I know. But he is showing it even now. I would look at it. You don't have to.
- o **Parents:** I just thought you said »he«. And I was… Really? What? Is it a boy? I don't want even to know the gender. Call it an »it«, please.
- o **Day Care:** In the contract, we will shortly mention it as »it«. No name, no gender.
- o **Parents:** Thank you. If it would have a gender… I am starting to cough! Then I would need to deal with »IT«. Oh, I don't want to. No. And the less IT talks, the better. It is just between you and me, "Day Care", and that's it.
- o **Day Care:** We have some methods for that. We will train accordingly.
- o **Parents:** I even don't want to know. Because if there is something, I can at least say: »Oh, I didn't know! I wasn't aware of it.« So, don't tell me. It's better like this.
- o **Day Care:** The state is also responsible.
- o **Parents:** Great relief! If the state does everything, awesome. Awesome! Another layer in between. Perfect. I am more interested in doing things which are of real importance. Where I can go back to work.
- o **Day Care:** You can go when you want. I will stay with it.

**Child**

»It is so heavy on my back. I am really small and I don't speak. But I wait for someone to come. I feel, I don't want to have an embrace. No hug. I stay in silence. It is too heavy. I feel so alone. Outside and inside alone. I am agitated. I feel that I am one or two years old. I don't do a lot of things. Time passes slowly. If I stay five hours like this it's crazy. It makes me crazy.«

**Day Care**

»We simply wait. It is a waiting space. I wait for you and you wait for someone.«

**Parents**

»Sorry, I am just checking my mobile phone. I can't find the time. When is it time to pick it up again? When the "Child" is sick, can it still stay with you? I don't really want to deal with it. But it is a necessity to have children.«

*"parents" left and are now coming back.*

o **Parents:** Okay, I am back again. Everything okay?
o **Day Care:** Of course. Everything is always okay here.
o **Parents:** Ah, you are the best. You are the best. Thank you. I don't want to take IT home, to be honest with you, but okay. I will take IT home.
o **Day Care:** Yeah, we have to close. But we are always happy to see you again and this lovely "Child". It was such a pleasure playing with him. It.
o **Parents:** Thank you, thank you, thank you. I had so much at work today, I can't tell you! I had so much important stuff to do. It was awesome.
o **Day Care:** This is why day cares make lives of important people like you easier.

**Parents**

»Yes. And BTW, I don't know why I am sharing this with you. Calling it IT is very important for me, because I am also an "it". I don't know any more if I am mother, father, woman, man. I have no idea. So, thank you very much. Sorry, I am a bit stressed. I have to leave now. I don't have so much time to talk to you. Bye! "Child" come on!«

o **Child** [smiling]: I am so happy! I am so happy!
o **Parents:** Oh gosh!
o **Child:** "Parents" don't like me.
o **Parents:** I don't want see any happiness. I don't want to see happy faces. I just want to see working faces. Please, I mean, really, I have so many important things to do!

**Day Care**

»They develop really well here. And they use mobile phones much earlier than other children who stay all day long at home. Because there is more interaction with the world, with other children. The most modern methods of raising a "Child". The most recent update. Our day care is certified and the certificates are updated every year.«

**Parents**

»Whatever you say. I am fine with everything you say. You are the expert. Sorry, I need to run again. I have something very important to do. Listen, I am just telling you that so no one hears it. Actually, I don't care. I couldn't care less. Even if you don't have certificates. It's good that you have it on paper. But I am happy that "Child" is not playing. Oh gosh! Playing! There is another word for it…. What do they do with scissors? When you do something, building something? Let me check my phone… Here: Creativity!! See, I need to cough even when only saying that word. Let me drink something. Ah, drinking helps a bit. Of course, it is only water! Only water. I am just drinking water. See? Only water. I am not drinking. No, no, no. Do you have children, "Day Care"? I mean, on your own? I never wanted to have children. But you have to. «

o **Day Care:** Leave it to us. It is our job to care. You don't care at all. We care for everything. Just take them to sleep. We need to have a closing time. Every institution has it.
o **Parents** [whispering]: Just a question, I have issues sleeping sometimes. Do you have an advice or any sleeping pills? Just let me try one or two?
o **Day Care:** For sleeping? Well, I guess it is because you are too active during the day. Well, to tell you also in between us, we know how to silence these toddlers. But if you have to much activities, then you will have sleeping problems. I personally don't. It is so silent here and there is not so much going on. Well, we keep some sleeping pills but they are effective only for children.
o **Parents** [wondering]: This would be a good idea as well. But this is just a thought. Sorry. Sorry! Didn't want to say it out loud.

165

*Throughout the work, there are always longer, silent phases.*

- **Parents:** "Child" really gives me stress. I am stressed at work. And I am constantly in stress. But thank God, you are used to play on your own.
- **Child:** Yeah. I am playing on my own. And I am taking things I wrote. It was important for me and I didn't do anything with the things I wrote.
- **Parents:** Oh, writing doesn't sound good to me! I don't like that. For some reason, I want you to grow up quickly. And that's it.
- **Child:** To be busy like my mother and my father.
- **Parents:** Yeah, yeah. When you say that, it is the first time I can look at you. That sounds good. Keeping us constantly busy. Busy, busy, busy. Busy or strangely active. Sometimes, I don't get enough air when I am busy. Then I have to slow down. And technology is PERFECT. Perfect! Gives me distractions. Keeps you busy. Perfect. I was just thinking about children. Ah!!! What type of a concept, children!? Oh, my God! This modern world has to function. Thank God, you are picking up your new iPhone. Thank God!

*We were adding in another word which is "Long-Term Effect".*

- **Long-Term Effect:** Hi, "Child". Oh, you are not a child anymore. How old are you? You look so sad.
- **Child:** 14. I am really sad. I am really sad inside. And I feel, I don't want to look at you. I don't want to look at anyone. Just at things, just at objects. I feel a lot of weight on my shoulders.
- **Long-Term Effect:** They disappointed you, your "Parents", didn't they?

**Child**

»Yes. I have so much to give. Remember, when "Parents" said »let's go, child«, I was so happy. It is still in my head, this image. I don't want to talk and stay here. It is like I am not alive. I am alive but I don't feel it. It is so weird. And I feel that time is passing. I am getting older.

166

I am not 14 anymore. Maybe 17, 18, 20 years and it's the same. Inside, it's the same.

I miss "Day Care". It was so little but at least it was something. I am waiting for this little attention from someone. I feel I am not alive! I don't know how to breath. I don't want to kill myself but I am not alive. Why do I miss "Day Care" so much? I miss her! Even if she didn't give me anything. I am shocked. Since how long are we like this? 14 years? 40 years?«

**Long-Term Effect**

»There is no connection, no attachment, no nothing between you and "Parents". And I can only observe it if I take all the emotions out of myself. Better not to feel. It is too little to live and too much to die. Even me, when you showed me your scissor with the pink color, seriously, I almost got anxiety! It is so strange! I could get a panic attack right now only when I see the scissors and the color! It is not because it is a scissor but it is a reminder of life. And that gives me already anxiety or a panic attack! Seriously. I mean, if you put this layer which is in front of us, away, I don't know if I could cope with it. Ah, I react the same as "Parents" did! And closeness? No, no, no. I don't want anyone to come close to me. No, no, no, no. Yeah, you can live together, be a couple but please with a distance. Please, please, keep a distance. We have our stuff, they have their stuff. Don't mix it. No, no. I can't bare closeness! No, no, no, no. At least,

"Day Care" looked at you. The others even didn't do that. I don't want to be looked at, really. Not so much talking, not so much laughing. And I don't want to commit. I don't want commitments, like marrying or so. Children? No. I don't want to commit to a job. I don't want to commit to people. I don't want to commit to certain brands. I don't care which clothes I am wearing.«

○ **Child:** Now I want to cry seeing you. I don't know why. I see you older. Like many years passed.
○ **Day Care:** That touches me a bit, seeing you crying. I don't feel like crying. Are you doing okay? I am a bit surprised. It is not usual that you visit back day care. Usually, you don't send postcards to a

day care. I could only give two drops of tears. I cannot give more. But I see you and hear you. Okay.

o **Child** [crying]: I want to hug you! I miss hugging.
o **Day Care:** I don't know how to hug. You are triggering my stuff. No one told me… I cannot do that. I don't remember a hug. That would be too much.

**Long-Term Effect**

»It was good that you talked to "Day Care" because I was too afraid. When I see you two, I feel like… the term is "hospitalism". You give children nutrition and a physical home but when there are no hugs… Now, as "Day Care" is here, I feel like being deprived of something. I have more energy than before. You can cry but I can't. And I was thinking also of "Parents". Are we just a job? Oh, I need that group of people you were talking about. You know, to heal together. I have that hope for the first time.«

**Child**

»It's not about me, it's about her, "Day Care": She couldn't receive my love and she didn't give me love. I am healing myself. I had a thought about inviting more people who speak English to do it with us. Because it is a great opportunity to help ourselves, heal ourselves. And I want more friends. I want them to be my friends. Everybody is a friend but it's not true. They are not my friends. I like them but I don't know them. I didn't receive a lot. And I see that I have love inside of me. It's hidden but it's here.«

168

## 4.2 DAY CARE CENTER IN THE GDR

*General-encounter (5 words)*
*children – Father – Mother – Day Care – GDR*

In the former German Democratic Republic (GDR) there was comprehensive childcare. During my research I found a large number of facilities.[37]

o   Infants under 3 years of age:
    ▪   Infant homes (from 0 to 3 years, mainly children of single mothers)
    ▪   Day nurseries (from 6 a.m. to 6 p.m.)
        ▪   Weekly crèches (up to 3 years. From Monday morning to Friday evening)
o   Infants from 3 years of age:
    ▪   Children weekly homes (from 3 years to school entry. The entire week; also overnight)
    ▪   Harvest kindergartens (during the summer and fall months)
    ▪   Kindergartens
o   School: Pre-school homes & after-school care centers

The historian Felix Berth has delved into the history of infant homes in both East and West Germany. In an interview, he explained:[38]

»At that time, there was the belief that infants are little tyrants. They must be disciplined, must be harshly enforced to eat every three hours, sleep regularly, and change diapers on time. If that is the prevailing conviction, then of course one can say, okay, an infant home is suitable for that purpose. Today we would say: It's a disaster. (...) The youngest ones lay in cots with bars, often 20 in one room. The slightly older ones, who could move a bit, were called sliders and were all in another

---

[37] I cannot guarantee the completeness or correct naming.
[38] Taz, »Historiker über Säuglingsheime, „Jeder wusste, dass es sie gibt"« [»Historian on infant homes, "Everyone knew they existed"«] from April 4, 2023, https://taz.de/Historiker-ueber-Saeuglingsheime/!5922970/

room. There was no active engagement, no playtime with these children. Often they would stand or sit around, making those typical body movements, a rocking of the head or upper body, which we know as hospitalism.«

Regarding the weekly cribs, this is how it was:

»On Monday morning they were brought by their mom, only picked up on Friday evening – this was the reality for thousands of young children in the GDR. No mention was made of the negative effects on the development of these "week children". (...) However, it had already been known for a long time through various studies that "the children in weekly daycares and also in orphanages exhibit special behavioral issues and that it is not actually an optimal environment for children to develop."«[39]

In Dresden[40], the largest weekly daycare had up to 90 children. Everything was documented, everything was scheduled; meals were always served at specific times. It was reported that the children were sometimes restrained in their beds so they wouldn't get out. This was because due to staff shortages, it was not possible to supervise all the children for 10 to 12 hours during the night.

»The doctor, social hygienist, and nursery researcher Eva Schmidt-Kolmer researched in the German Democratic Republic (DDR) in two studies the development of children in the first three years of life regarding the influence of various forms of care: day nursery, weekly nursery, and long-term residential care. (...) A large number of respondents described feelings of loss that accompany them throughout their lives, as well as feelings of guilt for not being right and for

---

[39] Deutschlandfunk Kultur, »Kinderbetreuung ohne Eltern – Das schwierige Erbe der Wochenkrippen in der DDR« [Childcare without parents - The difficult legacy of weekly crèches in the GDR] from March 15, 2023, https://www.deutschlandfunkkultur.de/wochenkrippen-ddr-kinderbetreuung-kunsthalle-rostock-100.html

[40] Wochenkinder in der DDR, Forschung: »Fall Dresden«, Studie der Sozialwissenschaftlerin Heike Liebsch [Weekly children in the GDR, research: »The Case of Dresden«, study by social scientist Heike Liebsch] http://wochenkinder.de/fall-dresden/

fundamentally doing something wrong in relationship problems. Many of them reported repeated difficulties in feeling a sense of belonging to a group and a fundamental feeling of being different.«[41, 42]

Especially in socialist and communist countries, the state-sponsored care of children from a young age is already part of the political narrative. In 2008, the book by Agathe Israel and Ingrid Kerz-Rühling »Krippenkinder aus der DDR: Frühe Kindheitser-fahrungen und ihre Folgen für die Persönlichkeit und Gesundheit« [Nursery children from the GDR: Early childhood experiences and their consequences for personality and health] was published, which they wrote together with East German psychoanalysts. In an interview with Deutschlandfunk radio, Ms. Israel summed it up[43]:

»It was about the "education towards the socialist personality", starting with a deficit model: Children are becoming adults, everything they do not yet know is understood as a deficiency. Secondly, children are almost infinitely malleable. This is the "tabula rasa" model, meaning they are "empty" and need to be "filled". Thirdly, it was based on a model of collectivization; children must acquire an adjusted, rational-conscious, and socially obliging behavior.«

One is left speechless in the face of such measures. How could it have come to this? What are the origins of this hostile view towards children? The next work will show that it was never about the children. Never. The mother-child bond was deliberately disrupted to create a

---

[41] Bundeszentrale für politische Bildung, Deutschland Archiv, »Wochenkrippen und Kinderwochenheime in der DDR« [Federal Agency for Civic Education, Germany Archive, »Weekly crèches and children's weekly homes in the GDR«] from January 19, 2018, https://www.bpb.de/themen/deutschlandarchiv/262920/wochenkrippen-und-kinderwochenheime-in-der-ddr/

[42] University Greifswald, »Das wissenschaftliche Werk Eva Schmidt-Kolmers (25.06.1913 – 29.08.1991) unter besonderer Berücksichtigung ihrer Beiträge zum Kinder- und Jugendgesundheitsschutz in der DDR« [»The scientific work of Eva Schmidt-Kolmer (25.06.1913 - 29.08.1991) with special consideration of her contributions to child and youth health protection in the GDR«] https://epub.ub.uni-greifswald.de/frontdoor/index/index/docId/217

[43] Deutschlandfunk, »Krippenkinder aus der DDR« [Crèche children from the GDR] from February 2, 2009, https://www.deutschlandfunk.de/krippenkinder-aus-der-ddr-100.html

model of domination, power, and commerce. Behind closed doors, then anything is possible.

- o **Mother:** I'm so stressed, you can't imagine. All I can see is what I have to do. I can hardly think about my child. Oh God, there's something else! How am I going to manage that now? I'm fully occupied with work, coordinating appointments and things like that.
- o **Day Care:** So, in my picture there is a hand reaching for the mother. That's intentionally done. That's how it feels. You're doing exactly what you should. That's good. I am fully focused on the "Mother". The rest is just decoration. I'm not interested in that.
- o **Mother:** That creeps me out now. How do you know that? Did that come from you? Now I'm completely confused.
- o **Day Care:** No, that didn't come from me. But I know that.
- o **children:** I have slept. I feel like I have been shut down. Eyes closed and in a state of rest. I heard a cough that completely stressed me out. I am focused outwardly on mom and am totally stressed. I don't even know what "child care" is. This is somehow scaring me right now.
- o **Mother:** Have I experienced "Day Care" myself? I am cut off from "children". I don't know if I'm cut off from myself or from everything. If there was a connection to the child at some point, it's cut off now.

**Father**

»I will just say something briefly because I'm actually not even here. I am neither a father, nor a husband, nor anything else. I am somehow put there. I work as well. I have nothing to do with anything. I have no connection to the "Mother". We are also not a couple. I don't know the child, I don't know the "Mother". Whether I am here or not, it doesn't matter at all. I could be a bedside lamp right now or a newspaper stand. What I hear the loudest is the "Day Care". Like an authority. That's all. There is nothing else to say. "Day Care", you are an institution and automatically have the authority.«

- **Day Care:** So, I am an institution, but am I the authority? No. I am innocent.
- **Mother:** Something is wrong. They've got you doing something. Or do you want that yourself?
- **Day Care:** No. I am responsible for what I was created for. I'm not there to make sure the child is well. I'm here to make sure everything runs smoothly.
- **Mother:** That the industry is running. The "Dather" looks so foolish that I almost have to laugh out loud. Yes, you are forgettable. Now, I've really looked at "children." There, I feel that the child is really suffering. I don't realize it's my child, but rather that it's a child. That child is doing very poorly.
- **children:** I feel cold. And I wonder why "children" is spelled with a small letter. I am indeed a human being. When it comes to "children", I feel replaceable. Like I am one of many. I am a child and represent all children.
- **Day Care:** Those who are unimportant. You can also receive a number. It's good that you don't have a name and are spelled with a small letter.
- **Mother:** I notice that this already touches me. My gaze is on you, "children". I want to change something. I know "Day Care". I also have experience there...
- **Day Care:** No, no! Now, I'll make sure you don't go off course, "Mother". I have to make sure you function. I'll report you! Maybe we didn't do a good job with you? Maybe we need to make improvements there?
- **Father:** I believe you did a good job with me. I don't feel anything anymore. I don't perceive anything anymore. I don't care about anything. One must not take on responsibility.
- **Mother:** I am thinking about what I could do. Here, in my chest, it hurts a lot.
- **Day Care:** So, I'm reporting you! It's not my job to look after the "children". My job is to look after the "Mother". It worked, right?
- **chilren:** I'm completely frozen when "Day Care" said she will contact the mom. I'm really scared of "Day Care". I have body sensations when "Day Care" talks. I have body memories. But since she said she will contact you, I'm completely frozen.

**Day Care**

»Yes, that's also a means of pressure for "children". I wash my hands of it. I've done my job. I reported it. Maybe we could build up some social pressure? I just denounce. And help, in case a few names are needed. The work is so stress-free!«

**GDR**

»We'll take care of the "Mother" at some point. Hasn't worked properly, I'd say. They need to be brought in for an appointment. Giving a shot wouldn't be bad. Vaccination or something like that. I'm afraid she's a bit resistant, somewhat rebellious. But at some point, someone from the population will get scared, huh! That can be resolved very quickly. Like you said: a little something in the food, a small shot. Oh, whatever is available. We always try something different. They don't even notice! That's why I don't understand why 'mother' looks so horrified. It makes life completely stress-free. Everyone has their place. Everyone has their task. Everything works like clockwork. The neighbors are just coming over. It's important to know who the neighbors are. So that peer pressure is built up by the neighbors. ""Mother", are you coming over? At such and such time on such and such day you have to appear." I am here completely relaxed and happy. It's going quite well. I don't have to worry. The "children" are already subdued anyway. We didn't assign you for the "children", "Day Care". You're not qualified for that. Well, who really wants to take care of "children"??? [laughs] Honestly! We have much better things to do!«

**children**

»I somehow have a connection to the "Mother". I was more awake then. But since she doesn't talk at all anymore, I am not there anymore.«

**Mother**

»If I wasn't so intimidated and didn't feel so alone, I would kill all of you, both of you. It was stupid that I said that, but I can't go back! They

174

are destroying the "children" and manipulating us. Now I have given it to you!« [laughs and drinks from a bottle]

## GDR

»One can put something in the bottle. Let them have the nice, colorful thing there. Then we will put something in it, or else she will become an alcoholic. What do you think, how quickly the reputation drops. You can't even look that fast. I'm going back to work. Let me know if something should happen again. It's really astonishing how WELL this is going. You know what? If things go too well, we could almost take on orders from abroad. You can even do experiments on people... What does experimenting on people mean... That sounds so negative. Let's put it this way: You can try something out. As long as the "children" are being produced, that's good. As long as there is offspring, that's fine.«

o **Day Care:** So stress-free here. I'm almost a little bored.
o **GDR:** We'll do it in a way that she becomes an alcoholic, the "Mother". It's a good plan if she slides into alcoholism. We will manage that.
o **Day Care:** I find that exciting now. Can we create something like that?
o **GDR:** Yes. And then we'll see what that does to the "children". And then you can play that back to me. We can even set up cameras. And then we have live material when a client comes from the so-called Western industrialized countries...
o **Day Care:** Let's see what it takes to turn someone into an alcoholic, to drive them crazy. Then we can separate the families.
o **GDR:** That's great. The interesting thing is that all the assignments and ideas come from over there. They don't come from us at all. Those who claim democracy as their banner, they are already criminals. Well, I have to say, we didn't come up with this.
o **Day Care:** Really? I thought you guys were going to do that.
o **GDR:** No, I can't remember that coming from us. But we will be contacted. We don't even have to do marketing for it; or whatever it's called today.

175

o **Day Care:** Oh, I thought it was a great idea on its own.
o **GDR:** Yeah, well, at the beginning, a little bit, I have to admit that. We came fresh out of the 1930s. That's where we continued a bit.
o **Day Care:** 1933, I don't really want to talk about that.
o **GDR:** I mean, we were still experimenting back then. But I have to say, the other way is much more stress-free. Much more stress-free.
o **Day Care:** Well, no one finds out about that either.
o **GDR:** Exactly! Because no one can trace back. Whenever we did something before, there was always the risk that it could come to light eventually. But with that other thing, who would even suspect?
o **Day Care:** I wash my hands of it.


**children**

»I notice that a fainting spell is spreading here. Nothing is working anymore. Complete helplessness. I can't stand your talk anymore. I can't stand the talk anymore.«


**GDR**

»There are no records! They are all with the original recipient. We don't keep anything. We're not interested in it. All original recordings are with the original client. And so, no one can trace anything back. No one can blame me! It's such a stress-free life! I don't fear going to bed. And the material gets destroyed. All good. And if I want something to laugh at, someone sends me a study that has been published. Then I think to myself: "Oh, look at what they've made out of it!"«


o **Day Care:** Actually, it's good as it is. It's really an easy job here.
o **GDR:** And if you have an idea, I'm totally open to it.
o **Day Care:** Yes, sometimes I come up with something. Depending on whether I like the person or not, then I can come up with something good.
o **GDR:** Right. I'll write that down. And then someone says, "Hey, I need a study here in the daycare center in blah blah blah." And I say, "Hey, someone had a great idea. What do you think? We

already thought about this and that." "Oh, yes, good idea." And then you can do that.

- o **Day Care:** Do you know what's within my power? It's within my power to further denounce the immediate surroundings. I have that under control.
- o **GDR:** That is really important. That way, we also know what is happening where. Look, "children" is asleep again. Did you give it sleeping pills or medication again? Great.
- o **Day Care:** That's probably what you do with "children" who have been there for a long time.
- o **GDR:** That's what I thought too. Then it's not so bad that they stay there for so long. They would totally freak out somewhere else, but it works for us.
- o **Day Care:** I have my people who work for me. I gather that and pass it on to you in a bundled way. But it's very simple and very chill. It doesn't cause any stress.
- o **GDR:** We are definitely on the relaxed side. And then, a state official comes to visit again. And during the visit, we discuss what they might need.
- o **Day Care:** Oh, then you give me instructions on how I... That requires quite a bit of effort. It shouldn't happen too often because then it's stressful. I don't like that. Those darn kids don't handle it well.
- o **GDR:** That becomes routine very quickly. From what I can see, you really have them under control.
- o **Day Care:** I have that. But sometimes you also have to show lively "children". It's stressful. How do I get them to be lively?
- o **GDR:** Then just leave out the medication for a bit. Temporarily. It'll be fine.
- o **Day Care:** But then I don't know if they will function correctly. I think it's expected of me to know exactly what the dosages are. That stresses me out a bit. I want to please. When someone comes, I want to show exactly what you want to see. I am striving to make you happy.
- o **GDR:** Hey, I am very satisfied with you. I'm not worried about that. Let's pat ourselves on the back for doing a great job. I'll try to keep you in a good mood with some treats.

- **Day Care:** When visitors come, do women also come along? I only see men.
- **GDR:** Mostly men. But usually no one really comes to observe. The video recordings are enough. And you can set up the cameras openly. They are highly satisfied that we are doing this. When they see that, they will be jumping with excitement. Then you can tell them everything.
- **Day Care:** I notice that it's more modern now. I've been around for a long time and there used to be inspections more frequently. I had to function well, had to show my best sides. Yes, that always stressed me out. But I don't feel that way today.
- **GDR:** Well, I'm still stuck in the old times. I don't understand why there had to be a new era. The old times were great, weren't they?
- **Day Care:** It's better now. We have better opportunities.
- **GDR:** It's even easier now? Respect! Respect. Looks like we laid a good foundation.
- **Day Care:** It's been going on for a long time. It's not just since the GDR existed. It's older than that.
- **GDR:** My memory only goes back to around 1900.
- **Day Care:** Yes, I would say the same thing too when I see the men in their suits. Instead of a daycare center, maybe it was once a children's hospital?
- **GDR:** Ah! Children's hospital is also great. I immediately feel happy when I hear about a children's hospital! Ah, just hearing the word makes my heart rejoice! That was a beautiful time! It makes me feel nostalgic.
- **Day Care:** There was still discipline and order back then.
- **GDR:** You could still go into the rooms in the evening. Oh! That really brings me to life. It was a beautiful time! It had a bit of a Wild West atmosphere.
- **Mother:** Who else is going to work for you if you keep destroying everything? I can't do anything anymore. I'm not stupid. I hear everything and I see everything.
- **Day Care:** What did she say? Is she getting a bit rowdy again?

*"Mother" is switching off.*

178

**GDR**

»Hey, she shouldn't go. This can't be happening! But look, she has left her "children" behind. We know what happens when mothers abandon their children. The consequences. Yes, then a child might die. So, what? Why was there even a reunification? Why didn't they just leave things as they were?«

**Mother**

»Either I kill or I throw a bomb. I did not realize why I gave away my child. At first, I thought I had to do it. I was in a functional state. And then I was switched off. No bond developed for my child. Only compassion for many children is still there. But it was boiling inside. Can I seek allies? But I also felt isolated. When I was switched off, I don't know if I killed myself or went into hiding. That it had to end? There was no way out.«

**Father**

»I am completely switched off. Men are turned off first. Then it is easier to approach the mothers. Then you can disturb the mother-child contact.«

**children**

»I was sedated, but I was mentally present. I was in a twilight state, lost in my thoughts. When spoken to, I was very attentive. I wanted to be with Mama the whole time. I realized how dependent I am on her. "Day Care" and "GDR" were unfamiliar to me, but I had something to do with them. When "GDR" said, "I'm going then", I had hope. But when "GDR" didn't actually leave, that was terrible.«

Epilogue

Just a few days later, I coincidentally read this article on STERN online[44]: »"She cried and cried in her sleep": Kindergarten director

---

[44] STERN online, »"Sie weinte und weinte im Schlaf": Kita-Leitung verabreichte Kindern Melatonin-Gummibärchen.« [»"She cried and cried in her sleep": Kindergarten

gave children melatonin gummy bears.« In the USA, more than 4000 children have already ended up in the emergency room. There have also been deaths for years as a study[45] from the University of Oxford shows.

»More and more children are being given melatonin gummy bears to sleep better. With devastating consequences: nightmares and anxiety sweat are just some of the symptoms that can occur. In the USA, a daycare center director is now facing court for sedating children with the sleep medication.«

## 4.3 KINDERGARTEN (Self-encounter)

*Self-Encounter (Woman, Germany, 3 words)*
*German: Ich –Tochter – rausreißen*
*English: I –Daughter – tear out*

It's about a mother in her late thirties and her 4-year-old daughter. After a long time abroad, in the USA, she moved back to Germany when her daughter was two years old. There are conflicts in the kindergarten, and the woman considered changing the kindergarten. The current kindergarten is in a different city, so she commutes about 8 km every day. The new kindergarten would be in her hometown. A mix of being overwhelmed, feeling guilty, and an incredible inner turmoil that she cannot grasp or explain prevents her from making a decision.

»At this point, I get emotional because it's so hard for me to get her out of there. I don't know if I have the ability to bear the pain," she said, starting to cry.

---

director gave children melatonin gummy bears.«] from February 8, 2024, https://www.stern.de/gesundheit/fall-in-den-usa--kita-leitung-verabreichte-kindern-melatonin-gummibaerchen-34440950.html

[45] Oxford Academic, Journal of Analytical Toxicology, »Melatonin Supplementation in Undertermined Pediatric Deaths« [Melatonin-Supplementierung bei ungeklärten pädiatrischen Todesfällen] vom 27. Mai 2022, https://academic.oup.com/jat/article/46/8/808/6593956?login=false

180

In this work, it is immediately evident that it's not about the kindergarten, but rather about old fears and traumatic experiences from her own childhood in the first three years of her life. She has no recollection of the first phase of her life until about the age of four. What she does know is that her mother had an accident when she was four months old. Therefore, the woman was given to her godmother as a baby for a month. When she was six months old, her mother became pregnant again and had to rest a lot. This led her to her godmother for a second time. Her brother was born when she was 15 months old. Her parents had a total of five children.

The picture that emerges is that of a large family, marked by Catholicism, coldness, loss, attachment trauma, and unspoken family secrets in which she is still deeply entangled. Her father's family is extremely religious and very large with 10 siblings (two of whom have passed away).

»This theme of death also runs through my mother's and grandmother's family. I have also lost my older sister. There is so much darkness and so much violence and so much illusion. It's a real clan. They call themselves that too. My father was the patriarch, my grandmother the matriarch. Everything revolved around the family and the family business.«

The daughter mirrors the emotional world of her mother. In her, the woman actually sees herself, her own pain, her abandonment, her distress, and her struggle to survive as a child. When her daughter was three months old, her family came to visit. »I arrived from the airport and she was in a panic in my arms when she saw my father. A three-month-old baby! And she still reacts that way to him today. She is filled with panic when she sees him.« After over 10 years in the USA, she moved back to Germany with her family when her daughter was about two years old, close to her parents. »I felt like I wanted to come back when my daughter was born.«

*"Daughter" grabs a blanket, wraps it around her shoulders, covering half of her face.*

**Daughter**

»The attention is too much on me at the moment. If possible, I would like to go further away from here, so that I would only be a small dot. Something is not right. It could be dangerous. I am not in a safe environment. What or who it is, I do not know. But it is better for me to hide or not be visible. And I don't have much contact with you. I wonder if I have good contacts at all. I need help.

No, it's not about the kindergarten and those taking care of the children. You're not listening to what I'm saying. It's as if you are in a completely different universe and I have no contact with you. I look around trying to find a clue, but there's nothing. It is much, much older. Like a play being replayed. It's like a memory of something old that happened in the family. I have no connection to the present. I may be physically present, but the rest... I'm stuck in something old. It's so difficult for me because I feel like it would happen to me as well.

I can't distinguish what you are and what I am. It's crushing. I'm also afraid of the godmother. Just the word alone is intense! The English word is better. Because "Patentante", the German word, sounds too neutral. The English word, "godmother", embodies the fear of "oh, my God". This word hits the nail on the head. And religion is a part of it. It's huge. It's so old and has such enormous power. I can't escape it.«

**Ich (I)**

»My attention is focused on my "Tochter" (Daughter). I can't understand what's going on. I can only see her clearly. I could be as old as you. I hear every sentence. Somehow, I feel it on a different level. Every piece of information was like yes, that is true. No doubt.«

**rausreißen (tear out)**

»When I entered into the resonance, I felt a deep sense of despair and disorientation. It was crushing. I felt like I was in a different world. I didn't recognize anything. I was in a state of overwhelm and didn't

182

know where to turn for help. And when you connected with the "Ich" (I) and with your daughter, these questions arose: "Who am I? Am I a part of you?" It felt like I was an energy or holding onto an energy. And that put me in a state of dissociation. It felt like I couldn't speak or move. I could barely survive in this state.

Who doesn't like you? I had the feeling of being a small part of you, and I was in great danger because something happened to us when we were little. Maybe 2, 3, 4 years old. And we found ourselves in a similar situation of desperation. This unspoken fear. We feel that something happened to us. Who didn't like us and what happened to us? And when you said "dad and I". Whose dad? Our dad? Has something happened to our dad? Has something happened to us? Has something happened to our family when we were not yet four years old? Why were we so frightened? And I have no one to protect me or us. That is such a deep fear. It feels like we have been abandoned since then and all this time! Am I dead here? I don't know if I'm alive or dead. Until I was three years old, I wasn't aware if I was alive or dead or whatever. I feel like I am lost somewhere... We survived!«

**Daughter**

»When you say clan, and family and the business... oh... I feel so much more than that. It's overwhelming! And you now live near your father? Oh, my God! Oh, shit. Oh, my God!!! Geez... that gives me back pain. It's okay if you don't want to live in the USA, but not back to your parents! Oh, God! That's the problem! Not the Kindergarten. That's how I reacted to your father and now you bring me close to him? That's too much for me. Oh, holy shit!

I don't feel like you would suffocate me. But I feel like I can't distinguish between my mother and myself. It's like one. The "Ich" (I), me at this age – I have exactly the same feelings as you at this age.«

**rausreißen (tear out)**

»Why do we live near him? I feel like I am literally embracing my "Tochter" (Daughter) and sitting on top of her. I cover her. I crush her. That she is an expression of me because I lack the words. And she

183

responds through her body. And because I am still in a state where I do not know if I am dead or alive. All the energy and what happened to us, what happened to me until I was three years old. I am on top of my "Tochter" (Daughter) because she is the ONLY person who responds to me. She could even be my reference point. Is she my mother or who? Because she sees me. It feels so strange. All the trauma I had until the age of three can be seen from here. My daughter is the only one who sees me, who feels me, and who is aware of me.

Now I feel like a little, a proper little part of you, stuck between four months and three years. Now I have clarity about who I am. But still, we have feelings! And you have named them, what happened there. And the fear you talked about...

I have wondered, if my mother wasn't there, who took care of us while she took care of our brother? Was my father there? And how was he actually there? I feel like a little sinner who must constantly be punished. And something happened when I didn't listen. Do you remember that time, how did our father treat us? Was he violent? Did he punish us in some way?«

»My father worked a lot. My father has a way... even now towards me, I am now 38 years old... when he sees me, he grabs my head and gives me kisses. From both sides. Or he does it by grabbing me by the neck.«

o  **rausreißen (tear out):** It feels like a duality. In this caress, there is something suffocating. Like a control... Something is wrong. It is so confusing, so confusing for the part that is stuck. Does he love me? But in his love, he suffocates me in a way. I am very confused about love. What is love?

»I can't remember him ever hitting me or anything like that. But I can tell you – what has stayed in my memory about my older sister, who is already deceased – when she didn't want to go to church at the age of 15, he dragged her down the stairs by her hair to make her go to church. I can only imagine what else he did when we were younger.«

184

**Daughter**

»There is something dark here. And it's good that you don't have those memories. It's better to start with the feelings first. I don't even know where to begin with your parents. Should I focus on the father or the mother? Whichever way I turn my head, it's yuck...! If only I could vomit it up... But it's not possible. The truth must not come to the surface. It's a big no-go. In this family, they stuff everything inside. Whatever may have happened, they bury it.«

*»I actually want to vomit it out. I generally have trouble throwing up. I don't even have fever. I never really get sick. That stuff never comes out. One of my father's siblings died after birth. She was a twin. And to this day, no one knows how she died. Supposedly, a nurse went to my grandmother and said she slipped from her hands. My father says something like that. But no one really knows. And my mother, who was a good Christian, his mother was a good Christian, forgave her immediately. It's a strange story. And that's just one example.«*

○ **rausreißen (tear out):** I don't know if she was happy that the child was no longer alive. That's why she forgave so quickly! And when you say that: Someone also wants us dead. And there is a lot of abuse. I don't have the strength to talk about it yet, I'm not ready, but there is a lot of abuse of all kinds. That's why I'm not allowed to talk about it. It's dangerous. There is a criminal energy here, my God. So many fake news and confusion. I don't know what to believe.

*»I have a mother for whom death is a constant companion. There is death and abuse everywhere. For generations. So, it goes both ways. It breaks my heart that all my hard work of the last four years... and my daughter still carries my crap with her, you know. That in itself is devastating.« [crying]*

185

## Ich (I)

»I hear every sentence and I'm here, but it's not my time to show myself. It's the time of "rausreißen" (tear out). Because it comes before me. I'm not fully born yet. But still, I'm here. And cognitively, I feel very clear. And I even feel a certain compassion for you, but I can't do much yet.

### rausreißen (tear out)

»In our family, a murder was committed, and it was covered up. It was not recognized as a murder. I am between four months and three years old and I am greatly afraid that the same thing could happen to me. They will take me out of the family and I will also be covered up. I cannot regulate myself. It is so immense. And the way I was treated at that age, like a ping pong. Mother, father, godmother... Will she kill me? And everyone will say: "Thank goodness, she's dead. We will forgive our godmother." I feel like I am constantly in danger. I am not aware of it. And I really want to connect with you, but I don't know if that's possible. I hope you don't want me to die either. I will not kill you. And I hope you won't kill me either. If you don't want your parents, does that mean you don't want me? That is confusing to me. Because if you don't want to see me, that means, oh my God, that means I'm still stuck in this place, all alone! And that leads to loneliness. I don't know what to do with these feelings! They are there and I am overwhelmed and frightened. And I have no reference point.

But at least I have hope because you have these feelings. And I am waiting for you. I love your eyes. I love that you see me! I feel less lonely when you look at me. I want to feel safe. Being in your family doesn't seem safe. That scares me very much. I cannot understand why we are here. Not necessarily in Germany, but why are we so close to them?«

*»I was much further away in the USA, but I didn't have to look at things in the USA either. That's what I've learned so far. Things are now so obvious that I have to see them. To feel them and be in touch with them.«*

186

- **rausreißen (tear out):** And that's a smart move. It's very important that you say that to me. I am not in a state of total fear now. Oh, so you have a strategy. It's not about confronting the parents, it's about us leaving the illusions. And seeing things as they are. I feel a little safer now than before. Finally, I can see a reference point. That gives me even more hope that you're taking care of yourself.
- **Ich (I):** I haven't changed much, but I'm looking again at "rausreißen" (tear out) and feel positive. When talking to her, it feels right.

**Daughter**

»The biggest hope is security. That I am in a safe place. And that you sort out whatever this strange thing from the past is. Those are the two things. Because that is the only way, the only hope – at least for us – to have some kind of life. In a way, I know that I can rely on you. But on the other hand, I am so entangled with you. It's unbelievable how entangled I am. And by the way: I don't need grandparents. I don't need the concept of grandparents. I'm not interested in concepts, but in real people.«

## 4.4 SCHOOL (VOICE OF THE BOOK)

*Self-encounter (1 word, i.e. one intention)*
*Voice of the book*

Using the Intention Method, one can truly delve into any topic, and so in November 2023, I wanted to give my book the opportunity to express itself. I never would have imagined that the topic of school would come up. More specifically, the beginning of elementary school.

For those who are interested in the topic of education and schools, and for those who have listened to speeches by Sir Ken Robinson or heard the insights of Gerald Hüther, Arno and André Stern, they will find some ideas echoed – and even more. But let's see what my book has to say. My questions or statements are written in italics.

»I don't understand what you are trying to do but I feel what you really want is to play. And you don't know how to do it. That is why there is some playfulness in the air but not knowing how to connect. And I feel that it has something to do with my voice being taken. «

» "Voice being taken" that resonates with me is: I never had a voice.«

»Huh! Oh! Yeah! Now I feel some gathering and going straight up when we come to that point. I am adjusting. But now I feel like a child starting school and having to adjust and to sit properly. I put my hands very properly on my knees. I know where my handkerchief is. Everything is very properly adjusted. And I am proper. No playfulness. Yeah, and I am checking a bit if I am secure of course.«

»When we had to go to school, did we lose the connection even further?«

»Well, for me, that is not a place to be playful. Not at all. I heard about German discipline but I don't know if it is something like that. But it is quite something! It is very strict.«

»When I look at you, I have the impression it is like a jump from childhood to adulthood. The need to sit, be still, just look to the front, no talking, just listening. Obeying, doing the things which are requested from you. Or is there still playfulness in you? Did I see a smile?«

»I am squeezing my lips again. Sounds would come out of my mouth. For me, voice is sounds. Voice is not talking. And I remember moments, when I could make these sounds. [laughing] But I have to hold myself. I don't understand what's happening. What is this place? I suddenly found myself here. There was not any transition where you slowly get used to school. It was like – sit! That's all. I am posing because that's what's proper. And I don't process so much.«

»What would you rather like to do?«

»Oh! For example: I want to look around. Yeah. But I am cautious about it because, you know, there is an appropriate way to do things and a not appropriate way to do things. But when you asked, I really wanted to start looking around. Yeah! I noticed that there are others like me. I am not alone. Then I see…, ohoh…, the others are also suffering. And I felt a bit funny. I felt like giggling. I should not show it.

So, I am still squeezing my lips. And squeezing is also in my lower part of my body. Up and also down. No breathing at all. I didn't have any transition. Like children would get to know each other in their own way, in their own timing. Not like adults. But here, there is no transition. We were just put in our spots. That's it. That feels so weird.

And the moment I start looking around, I could maybe burst. And suddenly all the class bursts into laughter. Everyone knows this is so silly. What the hell is going on? And what comes to my mind, sometimes people sit in a circle. This is more an organic set-up. In a circle you see everyone's face. Adult or children. There is still some… you can talk with your expression. But I don't know what is that? I have never been in such…«

»… military environment.«

»Yeah. It feels cold. Nothing moves. Now I feel also how resilient I am. Standing like that for a long time, not everyone can do it! I am not even getting tired. [laughing] I am also quite resilient. I don't even know how I do it. I don't know for how long this lasted. Nothing is coming from outside. Nothing that sparkles something in me. Nothing.«

»What would you do? Looking around you said. What else?«

»I would simply move. My feet. I am rolling my ankles of my left foot and that feels good. But there is also a thought, that this is noticed. Each movement is somehow spotted. There is a Big Eye watching me. I like this movement but there are so many eyes around. I can't do something like that. [slouches] It is about the body. When you asked me, what would you like to do, I don't even have anything in my mind. Even saying "I want to go home", no, there is not even that concept.

What is that place? I want my attention back for myself. My attention is taken from me. I want it back. This is what I want. And then some time maybe. And now I can look at you a bit.«

»So, let me know if I see this correctly: When you have the attention on yourself, your body, you know exactly what you want and want to do?«

»I don't have any agenda in my mind. I just feel that somehow. My attention is not mine anymore when I am nailed there. And that's also why I am also not in my body. I don't have my body. Invisible, like you tie an animal – a donkey or dog, in order for it not to escape – you tie them to a rope. An invisible something. And it's 100% taken from me. And when I have it back, I don't need too much. No hunger or thirst. I am okay. I am back in my body and I am okay. Oh, yeah!« [touching her body]

»I have now an adult question. Adults say: "You have to go to school to learn something". What do you think about that?«

»What I experience is that I am not processing anything. Learning is downloading knowledge. There was not even a bleep of learning here. It doesn't make sense. What am I supposed to learn? Do I have to learn something? No. Nothing. I cannot relate to the question. When I am in my body, I am whole. I have everything. I am not in need or lacking anything. I feel like a child at the first day or days or first few months at school.«

»I have another adult question. What is then the target of sending children to school?«

»Somehow, I know a bit about it. With my child intelligence I know a bit. The mother, or my care givers, they will be resting when I am at school. [laughing] And I want them to be well. So, I disappear for a while. Because as children grow, they become louder. Louder and louder and louder. When you are a toddler, well, you still make some noise but it is not so loud. But imagine, when you are 6 years old, 7, 8, 9, 10. Oh! The noise can be even louder and louder. And teenagers!

Uhhh! Impossible to bear! Having teenagers all the day at home! No, no! No one can bear it. Believe me, no one can bear it. That's why they send us here so we are somehow compressed. Why does the word asylum come to me? We are not coocoo but for their mentality we are. So, we need to be treated or tamed. Because it is too much. They not only want but they don't know how to deal with it.

I am also not very angry with them. I feel how difficult it is for them. Parents, I still have some love. This is how much they can do. We bear it. Ah, when I say this, I exhale. Having my breath. That's why we are laughing at teachers and adults. In the background. We are sensing the real set-up behind that kind of organization. We haven't lost all this intelligence of being fully alive, you know!

Sorry, I should not shout. We need to learn how to keep our volume proper. [squeezing her lips] That's why we like music being loud. Like rap. Because we decrease our volume but there is still volume pushing from the inside. It wants to come out! Hey, hey. [moving her hands like in rap music] Like this. As you grow, it becomes louder and louder. You cannot hold it. Where to put it? Where to put so much energy? Maybe the children which dedicate themselves to sports, they are a bit more balanced. But others? Very difficult!

»That's the reason I like to dance. And listen to music.«

»Yeah, yeah, yeah. Dance is also very good. I like dance. I like these moments when it is about creativity. Painting, colors. I have an image when we are painting, we come together somehow in a group on different tables. With 3, 4, 5 groups, small groups. Everyone is painting together on a big cartoon. And then we start to knowing each other better. We are still not interacting very openly but still exchanging in a careful manner. I like group work.«

»Could you think – again a stupid adult question – about a way for children and their parents to interact differently? Is there an alternative for school?«

»For example, exploring at home. Exploring whatever subject, I may be interested in. And having guidance somehow from someone. It can

191

be someone from the family or it could be someone volunteering to guide me when I am exploring.

But, I would say, I could go to an institution. But not every day, every morning, from 8 to 4. No! My main place is my home. I really breathe now deeply when I express what would be better for me. Very interesting. Maybe just two hours a day? Or even twice a week. But depending on my feelings. Could be different for everyone. Flexibility is important. Like more in an organic way. If something attracts me in this institution, I would come more often! Oh, that teacher, it feels so good being around her, in her atmosphere. Some people, they are just like a role model. Like someone in the movies. And then I go by myself. And I say: "Oh, I want to spend more time with that person." And then I come more often!

And then time comes when home is not so much interesting and I start spending more hours here than at home. Smoothly and organically. I am given the time and choice; and softness.

Softness is so important. Because it was rigid and so sudden. I am the owner of that process. This is my process. This is my process of growth and exploring. I still want to call it exploring; not learning. I don't know why. And every child can be different. For me, I don't want to stay all the time at home and all my childhood at home. And when I say that, on some days, I don't feel like going to school, I want this to be heard and to be acknowledged.«

»And it is your decision and not the school's decision.«

»Exactly! What a good, nice thing this would be! I would like to grow like this, really. Yes.«

»And the subjects, too. Or the topics, the themes, you can decide them.«

»I can feel attracted or not, I would say. I want to feel it. I am not so much in my brain yet. I have curiosity. I want some time. I want to dive into a subject. I am mostly feeling and sensing rather than deciding. It feels very different for my body! Oh! Yeah. For me, this is what life is.

I really like colors. How colorful it could be. Playfulness. I would feel new spaces with these qualities. And also, in my life, I would find

192

and go to spaces where I could resonate and feel with these qualities. This is what spaces are for. I don't want spaces who mold me. I want to give something to the space. Yeah. For me. That's my world. This is how I feel.

And my music can be softer. It can still be loud, that's okay. I will not aim to irritate others with my music.«

»Go with the flow. Do you have any wish for the book, for my book?«

»Any book or any creation, I would say creation... It is not production, it is a creation. It would be an extension of that kind of resonation and connection with these original qualities of ourselves. And then it comes out as something to offer, to share. Like children, they find something exciting, beautiful. [laughing] For them it's natural to share it. It is like that overflow. This is the energy. This is what "book" would mean for me. Because there are many ways of writing. Seriously. It is a matter of choice, of course. I want to enjoy myself first. Each step. If I don't enjoy, I would question it. Am I in the correct tune? Maybe I need to go a few steps back in order to remember something.

There is also no rush. I have all the time. Like children: They have all the time! Who cares? This is what I would say. Then, when people would read this kind of book, they would lose sense of time. Time flew – like in a different time zone. There are such books.«

»What you said about school... this is exactly what my daughter told me lately.«

»Because you gave her space to express her own truth. Not every child can tell this to their mother.«

## 4. 5 SCHOOL SUPPORT

*Self-encounter (Woman, Germany, 2 words)*
*School Assistant – Boy*

»More and more integration aids for children and adolescents with mental disabilities,« as stated in the 2021 press release from the Federal Statistical Office for Germany.[46]

»The mental and social problems of children and adolescents are playing an increasingly significant role – not only since the outbreak of the COVID-19 pandemic. In 2019, providers of child and youth welfare granted around 109,200 integration aids for children and adolescents with mental disabilities. According to the Federal Statistical Office (Destatis) on the International Day of Disability on May 5th, this was 156% more than ten years earlier when the number of integration aids was around 42,600. These aids are intended to facilitate the participation of children and adolescents who are affected or threatened by mental disabilities in social life. This can happen, for example, through counseling and therapy services, as well as through school support and integration assistance. The latter has gained importance in the school environment, which may be a reason for the increase in the aids granted. Due to the time period covered by the data, there is no information available on short-term COVID-19 effects.

**Common reasons are psychological stress and developmental abnormalities.**
Integration aids were initiated for a variety of reasons, with the most common being emotional problems or developmental abnormalities in 2019 (41%), including issues such as anxiety, suicidal tendencies, or developmental delays. In 30% of cases, integration aids were granted due to school or job-related problems, such as ADHD, hyperactivity,

---

[46] Statistisches Bundesamt, Pressemitteilung Nr. N 027, »Immer mehr Eingliederungshilfen für Kinder und Jugendliche mit seelischer Behinderung« [Federal Statistical Office, Press Release No. N 027, »Increasing Number of Support Services for Children and Adolescents with Mental Disabilities.«] from May 4, 2021, https://www.destatis.de/DE/Presse/Pressemitteilungen/2021/05/PD21_N027_221.html

or truancy. Social behavior abnormalities such as isolation, drug use, or aggressive behavior motivated the use of integration aids in 16% of cases.

**Nearly three-quarters of those affected are boys**
Almost half (48%) of the support was utilized by children aged between 9 and 13, which is around the transition phase to secondary school. Almost three out of four affected individuals are boys (73%), with the percentage slightly increasing over ten years (2009: 70%). On average, a support duration lasted just under two years (23 months).«

In Germany, there are various criteria for school assistance. In Bavaria, for Munich and Augsburg, six basic requirements are mentioned[47]:
o »ADHD
o Autism
o Auditory perception disorders
o Concentration difficulties
o Physical limitations requiring support
o in general, when the child's behavior at school still necessitates assistance.«

The woman here worked as a school support worker in two grade levels for over a year. The boy, a teenager, had been diagnosed with Autism Spectrum Disorder. A diagnosis that both the teachers and she herself increasingly doubted over time. While the boy settled well at school, she, the teachers, and the school administration worked very well together, conversations with the parents were extremely nerve-wracking. The experience was so unsettling that years later the woman had to sort through her thoughts and feelings again in order to finally close the chapter on the matter.

What is revealed in this work is disturbing: The child is not at the center at all. It finds itself helpless in the face of the problems of the parents and actions of the institutions, the school, the organization, and

---

[47] Schulbegleitung Bayern, »Schulbegleitung München & Augsburg« [School Assistance in Bavaria, »School Assistance in Munich & Augsburg«] https://schulbegleitung.bayern/Voraussetzungen/

the youth welfare office. No one wants to acknowledge that the child is just a carrier of symptoms. Can there be genuine help in this way at all?

**School Support**

»That makes me really dull. Everything freezes instantly with me. What was alive before – I had felt really alive in my body – now shrinks. Especially in my stomach. As if I have rocks in my stomach. I feel a bit helpless. There are so many things at once in my head that don't fit together, that cannot be sorted out. I'm confused because I can't focus on any one thread. It's like ten people talking to me and I don't know how to bring it all together. Parents, school, youth welfare office, the organization... It's very difficult because each stands alone. Everyone says something different, everyone has a different opinion, and there is no consensus. And what's clearly in the foreground now: It's not good for the child. That's completely out of focus. I can't even focus on the child.

I think I also don't want to do anything wrong. So much is being put on me. I can't be authentic there. I put myself way back. It's not just that I'm not fair to myself, but I betray myself! So, I make myself much smaller than I am. I know I could do it well, but I don't have the chance amongst all the external factors to show my qualities. But apparently, those qualities are not even desired!

I feel the resistance that's coming. Not even desired by the parents??? What's that about? I thought now that the parents want something good for their child. But right now, I don't believe that. They should realize that the main cause probably lies with them!

And let me tell you, I don't want this anymore. I know what I'm capable of, and I don't want to do this kind of work. Because then, I'm not achieving anything.«

*The woman is crying. »I can't get the image out of my head: It's like in a boxing ring – I'm lying there and getting another hit. I don't understand it at all. Why do I have to fight and defend myself?"«*

»I'll tell you what I think: You were not properly prepared for what awaited you. And then they could do whatever they wanted with you.

196

You didn't take your place properly and then they certainly determined and pushed you where they wanted you to go.

And as a school support, I also notice that this never works! The interests are too different. It feels like someone is writing the contracts or laying out a concept. And that doesn't work. It can't work at all!

Who sets the guidelines? Many foolish people! Everyone thinks they know it all. There's no competence! There are too many interests. And then they mix it all in a pot and say, "It'll be fine." "Look, we're doing something great. Look at what we can offer." And in reality, it's garbage! It's a pseudo... like a label they can adorn themselves with. "Let's paint a pretty flower on it. Look, everything is so green, everything is so beautiful."

The principal also has very little competence. He should be familiar with children's emotions! That doesn't seem to be the case. But there is a competence that is not quite audible. Was there a school psychologist in the school? Someone is standing there on the left, all alone, but they get overruled. The principal, however, is standing right in front of me, and there are several people in the background who are in charge.

"School support", I'm just reading that. It's more like holding hands without much ambition. I don't even see the child. You couldn't really see him at the beginning, and now, in this context, he's not even there. There are only adults standing here. And it's all about their egos or what they think. It's not about the child. I would place the child somewhere in the middle. But it doesn't. I take the child by the hand and make sure nothing happens to him. That's actually the role. The ambition is not very profound.«

**Boy**

»I am completely withdrawn, have pulled myself out of my body all the way back. No, as a boy, I do not speak. I do not share what is inside me. I feel like my identity has been stolen. I feel too small to be able to place or understand it. I cannot. So, I have retreated shamefully within myself. I cannot handle questioning adults, but I also do not agree with what they attribute to me or say about me. But I cannot place it. So, I become numb. I let everything happen to me. There is not much dialogue inside, because it is determined from the outside anyway. I am just there to endure and suffer everything, like a container.

197

I do not expect any help from you. Even if I notice that you are interested. I do not expect help from adults in general. I have given up on that already. I have shut down everything that could be. Whether parents arguing or hitting me. I have made my body numb, so that I cannot even say what actually happened.

You are not the first one who is sad. I think I have experienced that many times. That's why I cannot react properly. It could be that some have tried to help me and have failed. And that did not make it better. Not at all. Maybe even worse. I do not expect help.

I have a lot of anger! Suppressed anger in my stomach. Also, anger in my fingers, in my fists. I am like a volcano inside. It is all bottled up in there. I do not know if I have acted it out. It is definitely inside me. It is against mom. Dad is disappearing right now. He is not great either. But I think mom is worse. Are there siblings? I am angry with them too. I feel like I own nothing. Others always decide about my things. Maybe my sister takes something from me? And she always gets it right. But I have resigned to that. Still, I am very, very angry. But I feel like I keep everything inside. I am not sure if I really lash out.

Hopefully I do not enter puberty! I would have liked to stop that. And if it comes, then it comes over me.«


## 4.6 SYSTEM DISRUPTOR

*Self-encounter (Man, Germany, 3 words)*
*German:Ich – Jugendamt – Systemsprenger*
*English: I – Youth Welfare Office – System disruptor*


This is the work of a social worker who is managing a youth welfare facility in Bavaria. Throughout his career, he has repeatedly dealt with difficult adolescents. In 2024, a so-called "System disruptor" was supposed to be assigned to his facility. The teenager had committed over 70 offenses per week up to that point. The question was: Can he say no and not accept the youth? Background: His facility was new and at that time did not have enough staff or suitable premises. So, he defended his decision to the best of his knowledge and conscience to his superiors and to the youth welfare office. Nevertheless, he struggled with internal conflicts because he could not help the youth and because he opposed the authorities.

What was revealed in the work: Why choose a social profession? What is really at stake here? Do our institutions – a such as the youth welfare office – truly care about the well-being of children? Do children really matter to our society? Which system is truly being disrupted here? And why is there no bond between mother and child? What does the "Systemsprenger" (System disruptor) say:

»I have never received what I needed from the outside. One part is that I have felt guilty. And another image: So much has been owed to me from the outside. They have become responsible for me.«

# I

»Breathing is difficult for me. And I am disturbed by "Systemsprenger" (System disruptor) and "Jugendamt" (Youth Welfare Office). My whole stomach turns. As if something is physically twisting. It goes into the prenatal area. When you talked about the "Systemsprenger" (System disruptor), I felt overwhelmed. I saw parallels with you. I am not confused, I do not feel anger, but I feel sick and tired. I felt a stab in the heart and a heaviness. I react physically. I agree with what the "Systemsprenger" (System disruptor) says. It is difficult for me to express this. I also wonder if there is a way to bypass the "Jugendamt" (Youth Welfare Office)? I feel like all the attention is on the "Jugendamt" (Youth Welfare Office). I cannot decide anything at all.

I don't know what you want from the "Jugendamt" (Youth Welfare Office). I see heart written on it, but the "Jugendamt" (Youth Welfare Office) makes it clear, there is no heart in it. I feel helpless. Your behavior is most similar to the "Jugendamt" (Youth Welfare Office). Should one kick up a fuss? I don't feel anger, I feel helplessness. No matter how many times you ask if I feel anger. I feel a little manipulated by you right now. It's a leading question. You want to guide me somewhere I am not. It feels like you want to moderate me. I wish you would try to understand me. You are doing the same thing that was done to you. I feel completely like an object right now. I'm not doing well.

When you talked about the "Systemsprenger" (System disruptor), I withered away, collapsed in upon myself. I need you to notice me. I need you to see me. I am completely alone now. You don't understand me at all. You look at me as if I were an alien.«

### Systemsprenger (System disruptor)

»As I came into the resonance, my eyes felt heavy. I wasn't turned out, but I started staring into space. And then a deep sadness arose. But when you started talking about yourself, my interest piqued. I saw you as a lifeline. The "Jugendamt" (Youth Welfare Office) was not even on my radar. They are so occupied with paperwork. When the "Ich" (I) started talking about its desires, I thought to myself: "I need someone who is not confused." You were grounded and talking about yourself. There was someone who might be able to help me... But I need someone on the outside who is well-connected with themselves.

Because there is a sense of hopelessness within me. Nobody likes me, nobody has a place for me, and I don't know what to do or could do. I don't want to keep talking because I don't know how it affects me. But I believe that I can speak for myself and that you are interested. That is good for me.

I have developed compassion for you, where you are stuck inside. The authority lies with the "Jugendamt" (Youth Welfare Office). If you offer me something, I would even like to support you! I have developed a very warm connection with you. I thought we could form an alliance. And I will pull myself together for that. For us. So that we can bypass the "Youth Welfare Office".

It seems to me that you need help, that you are seeking help so that you can express your anger, your realistic perception. They should deal with us. I am so close to you. For the reason that it is my only chance. For you as well. For all of us, somehow. I can confide in you. If you're struggling with yourself a bit... And still, that fits. I am still very much involved. Why do I feel asked and seen by you?

200

The second image emerged as if it were my mom. And it gave me chills and made me even colder.«

**Youth Welfare Office**

»I've been aimlessly wandering back and forth from the beginning, sorting papers randomly. It's difficult, difficult. All this talk is really getting on my nerves. The whole personal talk and how you're feeling. I don't want to hear that at all. I have zero interest in that. So, if you talk to me from your management position, okay, then you get a time slot. But then it has to be done. I have no interest in children. Children interest me ZERO. I just want things to be taken care of. I'm nervous, I'm agitated, I'm bossy, I'm controlling. Nothing interests me here.

They could diagnose me as well. And ADHD would be the least of it. I have an attention span of one minute. Then I would have to go away again, have to do something. Right now, I could only uncontrollably, illogically, disorganizedly move papers from one corner to another. In between, I have the urge, the compulsion...

No one was there for me either. You just have to make it, right? In English, they would say, "Get over it. Get over it!" Where's the problem? You won't get any solutions from me, no plan. There's nothing from me. Zero. It's like going into the institution and saying to someone sitting in the padded cell, "Decide now!" Who decides here?

""Jugendamt" (Youth Welfare Office) has no heart" – that's the first sentence I can relate to. I am really off track! The system of youth welfare has something crazy and anti-youth about it. It's unbearable here. It's completely insane. It's just exceeding all limits here. I'm looking down at the child right now: It's just a poor, scared child. Where is the problem? But I'm the one with issues! Creepy, creepy. I need help. I really need help!«

*»I know what it's like to be alone, that sad feeling... Well, "know" is the wrong term. I believe that the "Ich" (I) is right on this one: The feeling of sadness is so far away.«*

201

### Ich (I)

»I understand that you are cut off from it. But I would like to clarify two things: I feel male. I am you. I am not confused. Never have been from the beginning. This is a projection. I am very clear about my feelings. I understand that you are cut off from it, because I believe that it started very early. I sense that in the prenatal realm. In the mother's womb. What I also feel: I have a very clear connection to myself and my feelings. And I would like you to find access to me as well. But I can't do anything. You have to perceive me. You have to listen to me. And you have to also understand and be aware of me. My heart hurts. I feel so isolated when I talk about it. I think I somehow even perceive myself as being bad to some extent. What do you say to that, "Systemsprenger" (System disruptor)?«

### Systemsprenger (System disruptor)

»What comes to mind now – when I feel the powerlessness within me and the distress I was in, which still exists within me and around me – there is anger. But that is not the solution either. It only leads to more pain, loneliness, and feeling abandoned. Then the thought was: "But that makes me angry." Maybe not when I am a small child, but when I am older, as a teenager, I simply do things that really go too far or hurt. As an attempt at balance. I never got what I needed from the outside. Part of it is that I felt guilty. And another image: I have been left with so much debt from the outside. They have become indebted to me.«

### Ich (I)

»Exactly. They have twisted that. It really makes me feel good that you articulate that. It lightens me and somehow and I can breathe better. I also resonate with the word guilt. And somehow, they have burdened me with that. They have made themselves guilty towards us and twisted that. I now feel sadness and would like to cry, but I can't. I feel like I can't cry because you [addressing the man] have a total resemblance to the "Jugendamt" (Youth Welfare Office). I don't dare to cry because you are here.«

*»Sadness is familiar, but crying is impossible. I disconnect from that and have no connection to it. No matter how shitty the situation may be, I don't allow that. Not even within the feelings of helplessness. That's why I know about it, the inability. Purely verbally. Emotionally, there is no connection. Because they are two different topics. One is about a child, prenatal, and the other is about adulthood.«*

- o **Systemsprenger (System disruptor):** You can't allow it. You are afraid.
- o **Ich (I):** The only thing is desperation. Somehow, I notice there is helplessness again. A despair that spreads.

*»Then the head comes back. The helplessness that is unbearable. Then I get angry again. I was a well-behaved child. In kindergarten, I was also on my own. There used to be no preschool, no preparation. So, I could play undisturbed. Nowadays I would be in a normal kindergarten... With my behavior, I would have challenged the educators.*

*Academically, I blew up the topics: I didn't really fit into the normal regular school system. In 3rd grade, I had the recommendation to go to a special school. But my educated parents didn't want to do that. An intelligence diagnosis was made. There I was found to have an IQ of 100 and once an IQ of 70. Because I no longer felt like painting the pictures and therefore only made scribbles and said to myself, "You can all go to hell". The result: "We can't say what IQ he has." I then went to a private school."*

*But the feeling of helplessness as a child – I started speaking late – it makes me angry. It makes me angry at the "Ich" (I) sitting there. And that's a problem. The "Ich" (I), in the suffering, in this helplessness and confusion, makes me angry because it reminds me too much of my mother and my grandmother. And I can't have that.«*

## Ich (I)

»Well, I don't know who is confused, but it's not me. I'm also a bit speechless right now, hearing how you talk about me. It's pretty heavy that you're talking about me in the third person. You have no idea who

I am. I have listened to you very attentively. I am by your side. But I am also devalued and judged. And what's more: I could explain to you what that is.«

»Interesting, this dynamic. That's why you have such a connection to "Systemsprenger" (System disruptor). Because you also shattered the system of your parents. I experienced feelings of sadness with my mother. They made me so angry. Terrible.«

o **Ich (I):** You get angry to avoid feeling powerless. Out of that powerlessness and desperation, a thought arose that I perceive myself as evil. That's why you don't want anything to do with me anymore. Maybe I also have the conviction that I am evil because you don't want anything to do with me.

o **Systemsprenger (System disruptor):** But they always say that to us! Everyone who is dissatisfied and overwhelmed with us as we are. I can't even call them mom and dad... the people around me. Hope is the last thing to die in me.

o **Ich (I):** You know, I feel what your parents did to you. And you're doing that to me. You fight against me all the time. You deny my truth. And that's what your parents did to you. That's why I see myself as evil. Everything I am is not allowed to be. The only way I was allowed to exist was to be evil. I am not allowed to exist. And if I am there, I am evil.

o **Systemsprenger (System disruptor):** Because you just sit and wait for something to happen outside. What should happen outside? You want something.

»With being not wanted... one can do something with that. That it was an accident. My sister is seven years older. "I have a daughter and I want a son" – such a plan did not exist. My father was practically never there because he was a workaholic and worked himself into the grave.«

204

We have added the word "man" (one) because the man struggles to speak in the first person. Also, addressing his parts is very impersonal and rational.

- **Ich (I):** I found it good that there was a bit of space given there. Something happened there. I am in the mother's womb... completely frozen in the mother's womb.
- **man (one):** The only reference I have is to you, "Ich" (I). My mouth is very dry. I can't quench the thirst at all. My back is burning, the upper back. I have to hold my jaw. It's like you're keeping me alive; somehow. But there is nothing here. Somehow there is nothing here.
- **Ich (I):** Aren't you getting enough to drink?
- **man (one):** I feel like I haven't drunk anything for days. Is there no food or drink coming in? My whole palate hurts. I can hardly speak. It hurts so much. I only orient myself to you, "Ich" (I). If you were gone, I wouldn't exist. So, these back pains, this burning, feels like an open, burning wound.
- **Ich (I):** I have been holding a band on my pants for a while. I stroke along there. It makes sense what "man" (one) is telling. It's like an umbilical cord. As if I want to establish a connection.
- **Systemsprenger (System disruptor):** That might have been my own story. The second image I have is that you were not taken care of. Unconsciously.
- **man (one):** Not unconscious, but very conscious. The word "man" (one) is actually wrong. It should actually be "it". An object. When it gets personal, then you give it a name, or you say "he" or "she". But here there is nothing.
- **Systemsprenger (System disruptor):** And there is a threshold where one wants to kill IT.
- **man (one):** I only know that it is so. It's about what happened to me during... I can't even say the word »pregnancy«. I am so disconnected from everything. I can't even say that I am in a belly. It feels so empty. This image keeps coming back to me: I see myself like a cowboy walking through the Sierra Nevada. Like in the desert. And the vultures are already circling above. And they are ready if we

don't make it. It sounds as if someone else had said to me, "Oh, man." „Oh, man!"[48]

o **Ich (I):** I think our parents thought about killing us, but didn't do it.

o **man (one):** Or didn't manage. It's not entirely clear which option. I am currently leaning towards »didn't manage«.

o **Ich (I):** Hasn't mama drunk enough?

o **man (one):** I can't even relate to the word »mom«. You, "Ich" (I), you make me feel good. And it makes me feel good that "System crasher" is here.

o **Systemsprenger (System disruptor):** As a system crasher, I have so much to bear myself. But a part of what I feel or represent belongs to you as well. As if I were a youthful, childish part. From the part of the general wishes that you also take steps with yourself. I also feel very connected and compassionate. And it's okay that you hold on to the "Ich" (I) so tightly. It just hurts me that you're fighting for your life and no one is helping. They're just waiting for you to die.

o **man (one):** Yes. Exactly. But I'm not dying. I'm like the cowboy in the desert. I keep going, even if the sun burns my skin. Always on. Always on. Always on.

o **Ich (I):** You're the system crasher. You survived. You had to endure a lot from the beginning. I think it's really nice that you're here, "one".

o **man (one):** It's weird, I'm thinking right now, I have three friends for the first time.

o **Systemsprenger (System disruptor):** I also feel such joy. And such love. I almost don't dare to say it. The three of us. You need time.


Epilogue

Who or what then disrupts a system? In 2019, the film "System disruptor" by Nora Fingscheidt[49] was released in Germany. It is a frequently

---

[48] German wordplay: "man" means "one". But in German, it is almost similar to the word "Mann" (= man).

[49] Die offizielle Seite des Films »Systemsprenger« [The official site of the movie »System Crasher«] https://systemsprenger-film.de/

awarded, stirring, and extremely controversial social drama depicting an overwhelmed mother, an absent father, and their 9-year-old daughter. The girl Benni has uncontrollable tantrums that also escalate physically. A journey of suffering begins through all institutions: special education, foster parents, homes, psychiatric care, living group, police, youth welfare office.

Fingscheidt wanted to raise a societal understanding for severely traumatized children and therefore conducted intensive research for over five years. »In relation to reality, we even toned it down in parts,« said Nora Fingscheidt in an interview with the Frankfurter Rundschau.[50]

»However, during my research, I quickly realized that certain aspects of childhood are suppressed in our society. Many people are not aware of the fact that every major city has a child psychiatry department that is usually overcrowded and has a waiting list. Or that there are still children's homes today, which are now just called something else like residential groups, separated from the general discussion about upbringing.«

Professor Dr. Franz Ruppert wrote in a 2020 commentary on this film[51]:

»The child and youth welfare system portrayed in the film, however, does not understand the core of Benni's problem – her futile attempts to bond with her traumatized mother or being deeply emotionally entangled with her. This system is trapped in an unsolvable contradiction. On one hand, it separates children like Benni from their mothers under the argument of endangering the child's welfare, and on the other hand, it is caught in the ideology that every mother fundamentally loves her

---

[50] Frankfurter Rundschau, »Nora Fingscheidt: „Ich war selbst ein wildes Kind"« [»Nora Fingscheidt: "I was a wild child myself"«] from September 27, 2019, https://www.fr.de/kultur/tv-kino/nora-fingscheidt-ich-selbst-wildes-kind-13046197.html

[51] Prof. Franz Ruppert website, article »Systemsprenger« [»System disruptor«] published 2020, https://www.franz-ruppert.de/aktuelles/86-systemspreinger

child and that a mother is irreplaceable for the child by anyone else. The system has no concept for the fact that women who have been traumatized early on may become mothers biologically but not psychologically, and then they only act as mothers based on their trauma survival strategies. Instead, they hope that mothers will one day undergo a change of heart and then handle their child's upbringing well.

Because all patience with such traumatized mothers does not work, children like Benni become the test subjects of creative ideas of psychiatrists, social workers, and educators. They try out medications meant only for adults after the supposed children's pills have no effect. They conduct heart and brain scans. They organize a three-week adventure stay in a cabin in the woods without electricity and running water. They try a new approach with a foster mother, and so on. The idea to finally send the girl with a male educator for an intensive educational experience in Kenya crowns the pseudo-professional game of trial and error: "We're sending the child to the desert now, because we can't handle it here in Germany." Logically, the child refuses because otherwise it would have no chance anymore, just as it had previously escaped from the various assistance facilities, determined to find its own way back to its mother.

What would be the alternative course of action? Instead of focusing on treating symptoms and relying on pharmacological or behavioral change solutions, the core issue should be addressed: the traumatized attachment of the child to its mother. On one hand, attention needs to be directed towards the mother so that she can come to terms with herself and work through her loss of identity – what I call the "trauma of identity" – along with all its consequences. (...)

For a support system deserving of its name to understand why mothers and their children are mentally fractured and trapped in their trauma survival mechanisms, the helpers themselves would need to be willing to confront their own early traumas and realize their own mental fractures.«

That would be a long journey where no one can hide anymore. Neither the parents, nor the medical professionals, nor the institutions. It would be a journey that goes inward and would require a lot of courage. It would be a path of togetherness. It would be a path that could bring help to everyone.

## 4.7 FOSTER HOME AND YOUTH WELFARE OFFICE

*General-encounter (4 words)*
*Children – Parents – Youth Welfare Office – Foster Home*

How does a child feel when they know they are going to a care facility? And why would parents even place their child in a foster home? This work shows how children are still means to an end today and what happens when traumatized individuals do not address their traumas and pass them on to the next generation. This work also illustrates how traumatizing offices and institutions emerge from a traumatized society worldwide. And how dark their origins are.

**Children**
»Physically, I'm feeling bad. Actually, it's disgusting. When the "Parents" don't talk, I feel better. Then the nausea subsides. If I imagine that I would have to live in a "Foster Home", that would be even worse! With the "Youth Welfare Office", I had hoped for help. It was a slightly better time, but very brief.«

**Parents**
»I am in a multi-layered world of emotions: Okay, there sits my son, who is upset or not behaving as I want him to. I fluctuate between being angry and thinking "not again!" I'm not really interested in him. The child is just my child. I am completely unhappy with my situation. I would like to step back from the responsibility, but I don't know how to do that. I can't just put him in a "Foster Home". What would people say? How does it look from the outside? Have I failed? I am too preoccupied with myself and the physical processes. There is no impulse. I just feel nauseous.«

**Foster Home**

»So, I'm more concerned with the term "Foster Home". I thought to myself: "at home" or "homeland". Then came to mind, "off to home." Now I googled where the word "Foster Home" comes from. Look here, it says, "who invented the umbrella?" Funny, right? I can totally relate to what "Children" say. For me, it's crystal clear that "parents" have no interest in"Children", to put it bluntly. I think the "Youth Welfare Office" and I are both offices. But I'm a bit odd here. I'm reading through the websites because I don't know what a "Foster Home" is. I could read you the Wikipedia entry.[52] The topic is really exciting. So, I believe, I'm slowly getting a clearer picture of what I can do here. Feel free to keep talking.«

**Youth Welfare Office**

»I am totally absorbed within myself. But it's uncomfortable to admit that. I have no connection to "Parents" or "Children". The only connection is to "Foster Home". I am sitting here cross-legged as if I were meditating. I have my right hand in front of my stomach and my left hand in front of my lap. But I can't say why. I also feel a little pregnant. I am ashamed to say this. I do not see myself as child-friendly.«

o **Foster Home** [continues reading the Wikipedia entry]: »From the system of special homes (...), it is known that educational abuse aimed at re-education was applied.« That sounds good here! Don't you think? »suffered injustice« is mentioned here. Sounds good, doesn't it?

o **Parents:** Whaaat??!! Are you completely out of your mind? This can't be real. What should I do? This is creepy. What should I do with my child, damn it?

o **Foster Home:** You don't care.

o **Parents:** But when I hear such horrible things, I also want to have help.

o **Foster Home:** Look, it also says here: »cheap labor«, »physically abused«... Sounds good! »Sexual abuse« is mentioned here. Look

---

[52] Wikipedia, »Heimerziehung«,[»Institutional Care«] https://de.wikipedia.org/wiki/Heimerziehung

210

how extensive it is! I wouldn't have thought it. Nothing is impossible.
o **Youth Welfare Office:** No wonder that "Children" are suffering.

**Children**

»Here is absolutely no impulse at all. I can only say that there is an absolute nausea here, sometimes strong, sometimes less strong. At the beginning, I had hoped to get some kind of help from the "Youth Welfare Office". But actually, I don't even notice the others. And if I had to imagine coming to the "Foster Home" with these ideas now, that would not be good for me at all. It's really difficult. What I find fascinating is that the office says nothing!«

o **Foster Home:** Look at this in Romania: »Conditions in children's and disabled homes«, »bad conditions«... »Forced labor« in Switzerland... Look at this in South Korea! »Homeless, dissidents, and children are being locked up, abused, and killed.« This is insane!
o **Parents:** They are working together. This is highly criminal! Look at their faces! This is unbelievable! Unbelievably bad.
o **Foster Home:** I don't see it. It's not that bad. Here! »Adoption system«. It's getting more and more. Goodness. »Developmental disorders«. Wunderful! »Attachment issues«!
o **Parents:** They can be abused. I don't see any connection to "Children".
o **Foster Home:** You are in good company
o **Parents** [desperate]: No. I want to.
o **Children:** Also interesting: I don't relate to the "Parents".
o **Foster Home:** We don't either. To anyone.
o **Parents:** It wasn't established. Where does that leave us? Now I'm thinking: What has actually happened to me?
o **Foster Home:** Oh, look here! "regularly treated with medication and sedated"! In Schleswig-Holstein. Oh no, that was just a study; nationwide. Isn't that nice!
o **Children:** The fact is, I can understand that. This is unbearable. Something needs to change. I would pull out all the stops so that they are pushed to their limits in their work.

o **Parents:** I have now entered a childish state because I can no longer bear what the "Foster Home" is saying. The one from the "Youth Welfare Office" smiles so smugly, it's unbelievable. As if they're going to come get me and do goodness knows what to me or pass me on. I want this to stop! I want to get out of there! Please, please, who can help us with that?

o **Foster Home:** I wouldn't take that so seriously. Just try it out! Just give it a try, right? Nothing is impossible. Oh! »Forced sterilization« in Switzerland! Look, another point! There are so many ideas out there! And this is just one article. Oh, how great. Does this work for infants too?!

o **Children:** I'm feeling better now, actually, but I've left the child's level. I find it interesting that the "Youth Welfare Office" doesn't say anything at all. When it should actually be about me.

o **Foster Home:** Haha, that was a joke! I can laugh about the fact that it's about you now. It's already a funny evening...

o **Jugendamt:** I wanted to say something earlier, but "Parents" and "Foster Home" are... "Foster Home" already speaks for myself.

*"Foster Home" nods and laughs.*

o **Children:** But I am sitting here! I am stuck in this "Foster Home"!

o **Foster Home:** You are just a file. But nothing more.

o **Youth Welfare Office:** I am so preoccupied with myself. And as was mentioned earlier, also apathetic. I smile friendly, but deep down, "Foster Home" speaks to what is going on here.

o **Foster Home:** Exactly. I need to come up with a plan first. So far, I don't have a plan. But when I come up with a plan, then... You won't do anything anyway, "Youth Welfare Office". You are just from the office. Isn't that wonderful. I don't understand the concern of "Parents" and "Children".

o **Parents:** I remembered my childhood and completely collapsed within myself, with no possibility in any direction. Shaken and turned off.

212

**Youth Welfare Office**

»I have no sympathy for the "Parents" in this situation. I think the "Parents" probably didn't want the child anyway. So, I don't understand why they are worried at all? It's not about the child. You could have thought about all of this much earlier. I'm not going to let you, "Parents", silence me! If you want to know – you probably don't want to know, but I'll tell you anyway: Behind my friendly facade, I am really angry. And I have dark thoughts. What the "Foster Home" conveys, there is a lot of anger and hatred towards the "Children". They shouldn't even exist in the first place. And if they are there, they only have a right to exist if they comply with everything. It's really dark. Let me show you my true face here... I am totally friendly to you and keep you in a position of dependency the whole time. I would have continued to smile and let the "Foster Home" take care of everything. And you would have hoped that I would do something. And I would have sat there, smiling.«

**Children**

»This is unbearable. It makes me feel so sick. The children are being forced into an adult role.«

**Parents**

»I cannot get out of my childhood shock. And for a moment, I entertained the idea of freeing my child from prison. But I am so realistic that I know that's not possible at all. And I don't know how to reconcile myself with my experiences and responsibilities. It's very difficult. I still want to live. It's a catastrophe. «

# 5. BODY

## 5.1 RAPE – AND IT HAPPENS EVERY DAY

»It is much easier to place blame firmly on a sexually perverse foreign man abusing innocent children that it is to look at a situation where the sexual abuse of children is endemic and has become normalized, and indeed, institutionalized.«[53]

Sexual abuse, sexualized violence against children knows no boundaries, no nationality, no religion. In Germany, since 2016, there has been an "Independent Commission for the Processing of Sexual Child Abuse" that not only examines the acts in the Federal Republic of Germany but also in the former GDR. Currently (as of December 5, 2024), there are 782 written reports and 2,042 confidential hearings; the trend is increasing.[54] Here is an excerpt from the study »Sexueller Kindesmissbrauch in organisierten und rituellen Gewaltstrukturen« [»Sexual Child Abuse in Organized and Ritual Violence Structures«] from April 2021:

»According to study participants, the experiences of individuals affected by TRA started early, on average at the age of 3. On average, it took the survivors more than 24 years before they disclosed to another person what had happened to them; often, long-existing amnesias for the violence experienced were also reported. 65% of respondents named members of the family of origin as perpetrators, more than half

---

[53] Thailand Institute of Justice (TIJ), Women and children Empowerment Programme, 163rd International Training Course (PDF), »Violence against Children in Southeast Asia: the case of child sex tourism in Thailand, Lao PDR and Cambodia«, https://www.google.com/url?sa=t&source=web&rct=j&opi=89978449&url=https://www.unafei.or.jp/publications/pdf/RS_No100/No100_VE_Sita_3.pdf&ved=2ahUKEwi0pJL_s8mHAxXyxgIHHe0lNVwQFnoECDEQAQ&usg=AOvVaw0BBlPJX6cxuZvVv5Eg2QME

[54] Unabhängige Kommission zur Aufarbeitung Sexuellen Kindesmissbrauchs [Independent Commission for the Investigation of Sexual Child Abuse] https://www.aufarbeitungskommission.de/

confirmed that TRA had occurred in the family in the previous generation, and 58% involved relatives. A wide range of violent experiences were reported. Severe sexual exploitation in childhood (known as child prostitution) occurred particularly frequently, with 67% of respondents, and 65% experienced abuse through pornography (known as child pornography). A third of participants also reported forced prostitution in adulthood, with over 24% becoming victims of human trafficking. More than half of the participants (65%) indicated that ideological indoctrination by the perpetrators occurred, giving a seeming sense to the violence. Involvement in satanic groups was specifically mentioned most frequently at 49%; religious sects were less frequently reported at 19%, as were racist, right-wing extremist, and fascist groups each at 12%. The reported experiences of violence were severe and recurring. Violence included not only repeated rape by multiple perpetrators (85%) but also near-death experiences (86%) and forced violence against others (68%).

Psychological Symptoms and Care Situation

More than 91% of the survey participants confirmed that as a result of early life biographical and repeated violence, dissociative personality aspects have emerged. More than half stated that the dissociative personality aspects were deliberately generated by perpetrators through the use of violence. Accordingly, Complex Post-Traumatic Stress Disorder (CPTSD) (85%) and Dissociative Identity Disorder (DID; 84%) were frequently diagnosed over the course of their lives. The evaluation of the two questionnaires at the end of the study regarding acute symptom burden of the participants confirmed a high severity of symptoms related to Post-Traumatic Stress Disorder and somatoform (body-related) dissociation.«

Rape, sexual abuse, mistreatment, sexualized violence, sexual traumatizations – while the wording is still being turned over and over, deafeningly loud silence prevails around the causes. We settle for ludicrously mild sentences and discuss financial compensation. Why aren't such institutions or networks dismantled? Why aren't offenders locked up for life? And why is German media coverage often cold and distant?

Why do we keep talking about young men and young women when they are actually children, adolescents? Why is there no lasting outcry, no protests on our streets?

I have decided not to do a dedicated work on this topic, but rather let articles, studies, and lectures from around the world speak. The screams and the pain are deafening.

**Berliner Morgenpost, Germany, from April 2009**
**»Haftstrafe für Kindesmissbrauch«**
**[Prison sentence for child abuse]**
https://www.morgenpost.de/printarchiv/berlin/article103845026/
Haftstrafe-fuer-Kindesmissbrauch.html

»Because he sexually abused two children and a teenager a total of 25 times over several years, the Berliner Harald W. must spend three and a half years behind bars. Additionally, this verdict means the end of his career for the 45-year-old, as W. is – or was – a police officer.«

**Kinderschutz [Child Protection], Switzerland**
**»Sexualisierte Gewalt«**
**[Sexualized Violence]**
https://www.kinderschutz.ch/sexualisierte-gewalt

»Sexualized violence leaves deep scars on a person. An assault usually has traumatic consequences for the entire life. (...) For affected children, it is generally difficult to talk about an act. They often feel responsible themselves. Studies show that only a fraction of children report a sexual assault to the police. Additionally, affected children often have to confide in someone multiple times before receiving help. (...) According to the Penal Code, any sexual act with, at, or on children under 16 years of age is punishable. It does not matter whether the child consented to the sexual act. Nevertheless, in Switzerland, around one in seven children experiences at least one instance of sexualized violence with physical contact by adults or older children. The extent of the assaults in the virtual space is even greater. Perpetrators come from various social backgrounds. (...) No child can protect themselves from sexual assaults without help. The prevention of sexualized violence is a task for society as a whole.«

**»The Dancing Boys of Afghanistan«, movie from 2010**

https://www.pbs.org/wgbh/frontline/documentary/dancingboys/transcript/? (Transcript)

»Najibullah had returned to investigate reports Afghan boys are vulnerable to being sexually abused by powerful men who have brought back an ancient practice. Banned under the Taliban and still illegal under Afghan law, it's called bacha bazi. Translation, "boy play". (…) The DVDs show Afghan boys dressed in women's clothing, dancing before audiences made up entirely of men. The boys are street orphans or boys bought from poor parents in the countryside. It's common knowledge in this world that after the dancing, these boys are often sold to the highest bidder or shared among powerful men for sex. (…) "I go to every province to have happiness and pleasure with boys. I want to have a boys' party. I really like to watch. Some boys are no good for dancing, but they can be used for other purposes. (…) I mean for sodomy and other sexual activities."«


**SBS News, Australien, from April 2015**

**»Horrific abuse at Queensland orphanage«**

https://www.sbs.com.au/news/article/horrific-abuse-at-queensland-orphanage/d5cdsjktx

»Sobbing uncontrollably at times, Ms Adams told the hearing in Rockhampton she was punched, slapped, pulled by her hair and on one occasion flogged with a skipping rope so forcefully she struggled to walk for days. Boys who tried to run away from Neerkol were publicly flogged with horse whips and those who wet the bed were forced to stand with the soiled sheets draped over their heads. (…) "No amount of money can ever give back my childhood, my loss of confidence, my lack of formal education, my dignity, my self-esteem and self-worth," Ms Adams said. About 4000 children passed through what was known as St Joseph's Orphanage between 1885 and 1978. Earlier, a 67-year-old woman who worked at Neerkol said Bishop Heenan had been originally dismissive of her claims she was raped more than 100 times by parish priest Reginald Durham, who is now dead, from when she was 11. "After each time I was sexually abused, I had to go to confession to him and confess my sin of impurity," the woman, identified as AYB told the hearing. Father Durham was in 1999 sentenced to 18 months prison for indecently dealing with the woman but many more serious charges involving her and other complainants were discontinued.«

**The World, USA, from Dezember 2015**
»Half a million kids survived Romania's 'slaughterhouses of souls.'
Now they want justice.«

https://theworld.org/stories/2015/12/28/half-million-kids-survived-romanias-slaughter-houses-souls-will-they-ever-heal

»The group is pushing Romanian authorities to admit to, and apologize for, the hunger, cold, beatings, sexual abuse and lack of care suffered by an estimated 500,000 children in the country's dismal orphanages before the end of the Cold War. (…) In 1989, Codruta Burda was an educator in Sancrai in central Romania. She cared for around 25 orphans who were then 3 to 4 years old. Some were evaluated as mentally disabled, though that diagnosis was often incorrect. "But because they were not stimulated, they couldn't walk, they couldn't talk. You had to feed them, " Burda said. (…) "I saw beatings every day," Burda said. "I cannot even remember how many beatings I've seen." (…) Orphanage employees who didn't hit children were considered weak. So corporal punishment was encouraged. (…) An estimated 100,000 Romanian children were in orphanages at the end of 1989, when communism ended. The high number is linked to the pro-family policies pursued by former dictator Nicolae Ceausescu. In 1966, the regime banned abortions and contraceptives to keep the population from shrinking after World War II. From 1967 to 1971, Romania's population increased by more than 6 percent. (…) Children born in the last 20 years of communism were nicknamed "decretei," meaning "children of the decree." Many were unwanted, especially when the Romanian economy was contracting in the 1970s and 1980s amid Ceausescu's inept management. (…) "We were moved like boxes," said Balan, a former official in the youth and sports ministry who founded another nonprofit, Drawing Your Own Future, which helps orphans in the somewhat improved system today. "The difference was that we were screaming, but it wasn't a big difference. We were boxes with voices." (…) "They were inhuman," he said. "Stalls where children, babies, were treated like farm animals. No, I am wrong — at least the animals felt brave enough to make a noise." Even after the revolution, the Romanian authorities

218

continued to deny the existence of the orphanages. "Anyone in authority denied, denied and denied even more. It was appalling," Graham said. But foreign journalists like Graham forced officials to acknowledge the tragedy unfolding under their noses. Western newspapers and television programs showcased a so-called "recovery and rehabilitation center for the disabled" in Cighid on the Hungarian border that resembled a concentration camp. The child's gulag, as it and other orphanages became known, housed around 100 children rocking back and forth alone in the dark. Most were naked, nothing but skin and bones, their legs crossed. Half died each year, usually before the age of 3, making space for others to occupy their beds. (…) In February 2010, then-British Prime Minister Gordon Brown apologized for his country's role in a "misguided" child migration program that deported around 150,000 poor British children, some orphans, to Commonwealth countries between the 1920s and 1960s. It was cheaper to care for these children in their new countries. Many of the children were sent, usually without the consent of parents, to "the harshest of conditions, neglect and abuse in the often cold and brutal institutions which received them. These children were robbed of their childhood, the most precious years of their life," Brown said. "We are truly sorry." (…) "When Romania joined the EU, it agreed to dissolve the institutions and completely respect the rights of children," he said. "It never respected its commitments: There are still around 100 big centers with over 100 children. Their rights were never fully respected, and their chances to be socially integrated are very low."«

**Report on trafficking girls and women under**

**the mullahs' regime in Iran, from January 2015**

https://wncri.org/2015/01/31/report-on-human-trafficking-under-the-mullahs-rule-in-iran/

»Hamshahri state-run newspaper had also reported at the time that the cost for each girl between the ages of 8 – 12 is $300 – $800. (…)

On August 20, 2004, a social affairs expert, Susan Bahari announced, "Some time ago, 54 Iranian children were sold to some merchants in a market similar to a slave market in Dubai." (News database reported by Radio Farda) (…)

According to the head of Iran's Interpol bureau, the sex-slave trade is one of the most profitable activities in Iran today, at times conducted with the knowledge and participation of the ruling fundamentalists. Government officials themselves are involved in buying, selling, and sexually abusing women and young girls. He added, "After the 2003 earthquake in Bam, traffickers abducted female orphans and brought them to Tehran, where they were sold to Iranian and foreigner merchants."

The Association Defending Victims of Violence issued a report in 2003 and wrote, "Every month 45 Iranian girls between the ages of 16 – 26 are only sold to the rich in Karachi." (…)

Young children are sometimes among these victims. They are held in secret places until they reach the right age and are then sold in the Middle East and India. (…)

In its 2010 Annual Report, the Women's Freedom Forum wrote: "During the last eight years human trafficking has had a dramatic increase in Iran. According to some estimates, there has been a 600 percent increase in prostitution in recent years. The average age of prostitution has dropped to 16 and girls as young as 10-years-old are being sold. In many cases which have been reported, government officials are involved in heading prostitution rings and trafficking rings."«

**CBC News, Kanada, from November 2016**

»**Open secret: Sexual abuse haunts children in Indigenous communities**«

https://www.cbc.ca/news/indigenous/indigenous-sexual-assault-1.3839141

»Freda Ens says she was a baby when her birth mother sold her for a bottle of beer. The buyer was an unrelated man she would later call "Grandfather". Her earliest memories include being sexually molested by a number of men in his extended family. (…) Child sexual abuse is a disturbing reality in many of Canada's First Nations, Métis and Inuit communities, research is beginning to show. Extensive interviews with social scientists, Indigenous leaders and victims undertaken over the past few months by The Canadian Press show that the prevalence of sexual abuse in some communities is shockingly high. And only now are prominent Indigenous leaders speaking out publicly for the first time about the need for communities to take a hard look. It's a painful legacy connected to almost 120 years of government-sponsored, church-run residential schools, where Aboriginal leaders say many native children were physically and sexually molested by clergy and other staff. The abused in turn became abusers, creating a cycle of childhood sexual violation that has spread in ever-expanding ripples from one generation to the next. Within Indigenous society, the knowledge that children are being molested is often an open secret — but one to which few are willing to give voice. Instead, they dance around the words, talking instead about child welfare, bullying, substance abuse, intergenerational trauma and community conflict. (…) Intergenerational sexual abuse is one key reason behind widespread substance abuse, a form of self-medication that helps both victims and perpetrators push down their emotional pain and bury their shame (…).«

**Organized Crime and Corruption Reporting Project, OCCRP, from April 2020**
**»Europe Cracks Down on Global Paedophile Ring«**

https://www.occrp.org/en/news/europe-cracks-down-on-global-paedophile-ring

»Federal police in Belgium said on Tuesday that a court in Brussels had convicted four men in "one of the largest cases of sexual abuse of minors ever known," with authorities cooperating on investigations into further suspects across no less than 44 countries worldwide. The probe began in 2015 after one of the men was caught taking photos of children playing naked on a beach in Belgium. His arrest led police to another suspect in the town of Wetteren in East Flanders, where they discovered more than 15 terabytes of child abuse images. The database reportedly contained more than nine million pictures and videos. Police described the quantity of images and footage as "unprecedented," with mostly male victims all under the age of 13, and some as young as just a few months old. (…) It added that being exposed to such "disgusting images and messages on a daily basis" was hard even for veteran investigators. (…) Child Focus, which acted as a civil party in the trial on behalf of the unidentified victims, criticised the "exceptional softness" of the indictment.«

221

**Frankfurter Allgemeine Zeitung, Germany, in June 2020**

**»Wie Berlin 30 Jahre lang Kinder an Pädophile vermittelte«**

**[How Berlin placed children with pedophiles for 30 years]**

https://www.faz.net/aktuell/politik/inland/wie-berlin-30-jahre-lang-kinder-an-paedo-phile-vermittelte-16817390.html

»The sex researcher Helmut Kentler placed street children in the care of criminals. It seemed to benefit both sides: the children were off the streets, and the men were no longer conspicuous because they abused them within their own four walls. It sounds like it's from a horror thriller, but it was a bitter reality in Berlin over thirty years: the so-called Kentler Experiment. The controversial sex researcher Helmut Kentler, against whom there was never any legal action, deliberately arranged for children and adolescents to be placed with pedophile foster fathers in the 1970s. He was firmly convinced that "sexual contacts between children and adults are not harmful." Foundlings and street children from West Berlin were thus placed under the care of mostly single foster fathers, many of whom had prior convictions for sexual abuse.«

**Unabhängige Beauftragte für Fragen des sexuellen Kindesmissbrauchs**

**[Independent Commissioner for Child Sexual Abuse Issues]**

**Germany, in January 2021**

**»Kindeswohl hat höchste Priorität«**

**[Child welfare is of the utmost importance]**

https://beauftragter-missbrauch.de/presse/meldungen/detail/roerig-zur-vorstellung-pks-2019 (the site is not available anymore)

»At the end of January, I also spoke about the deafening silence that still surrounds us when it comes to sexual violence against girls and boys in politics and society. I explicitly did not have in mind the abuse cases in Staufen, Lügde, or Bergisch-Gladbach, but rather the many thousands of cases that are not reported and do not become scandals, occurring in mass numbers and invisibly among us. (...) Sexual abuse is a pandemic, a chronic crisis in Germany and worldwide, a universal problem, always was and still is.«

222

**Deutschlandfunk Kultur, Germany, in June 2021**

**»Im Keller vergewaltigt«**

**[Raped in the basement]**

https://www.deutschlandfunkkultur.de/missbrauch-in-bayerischen-heimen-im-keller-vergewaltigt-100.html

»According to a study, one third of the children in Bavarian homes were sexually abused from 1949 to 1975. Many cases have been known for a long time. However, the process of dealing with this issue is slow, and the victims are waiting for justice. "You feel disgusted by yourself, that's why you also have immense problems entering into relationships. For example, I couldn't stand it when my foster mother hugged me; I would immediately push her away. Today I know why." (...) But many of the most severely abused children in institutions were afraid to speak out, he says: "They don't speak up out of shame about what happened. And I said: I don't care anymore, this needs to be made public because these institutions should now pay for these abuses or be held accountable." (...) The Munich "Institute for Practical Research and Project Consulting" has examined the situation of former children in Bavarian institutions. In surveys, one third now report having experienced sexualized violence in care – in most cases by the care staff, such as educators, clergy, or caretakers - people who were supposed to protect them. (...) Here was Villa Maffei, where "difficult to discipline" children were placed – as it was officially called. "The institution was surrounded by barbed wire and tall walls, as if it was dealing with dangerous individuals. Think about it: children between the ages of six and 14. There are children who, when they left Fieldafing for further education, experienced further sexual abuse: being sold again, being abused again. The idea of the network was my motivation to delve deeper into the situation of children in care."«

**National Library of Medicine (NIH)**

**»Prevalence of child maltreatment in India and its association with gender, urbanization and policy: a rapid review and meta-analysis protocol«**

www.ncbi.nlm.nih.gov

»In India, home to 19% of the world's children, it is estimated every second child is exposed to sexual abuse and violence. The Indian National Crimes Records Bureau (NCRB) reports a child is sexually

223

abused every 15 min and 53% of children report abuse by a parent, relative or school teacher. The prevalence of child sexual abuse (CSA) in high-income countries is 20% for females and 8% for males but in India, the estimates vary between 4%-66% for females and 4%-57% for males. (…) The greater economic hardship in areas like urban slums, the greater the likelihood and severity of child maltreatment.«

**THE CONVERSATION, UK, in May 2022**
**»Jimmy Savile: how the Netflix documentary fails to**
**address the role institutions play in abuse«**

https://theconversation.com/jimmy-savile-how-the-netflix-documentary-fails-to-address-the-role-institutions-play-in-abuse-181383

»Jimmy Savile was one of the UK's most serious serial sexual predators. Over several decades the television personality groomed and abused up to 1,000 boys and girls in TV studios as well as patients at NHS hospitals across Britain. That he was able to do so without being apprehended, even being knighted in 1990, is the subject of a new Netflix documentary series by Rowan Deacon. (…) Jimmy Savile: A British Horror Story presents its subject as a fame-hungry manipulator who, through his carefully cultivated relationships with British elites, was able to abuse and intimidate his victims, evade justice and fool the nation. But despite its high production values and impressive use of archival material, it leaves key parts of the scandal under-examined. (…) But, as our research shows, he was not alone in constructing his image. Like the official inquiries after Savile's death, the documentary fails to capture the pivotal role Britain's core institutions played in producing his "untouchable" celebrity icon mask. Validation from the BBC was crucial to Savile becoming a celebrity personality. And the corporation's support continued to underpin his charmed career. As the BBC's biggest star, he was embedded across numerous primetime BBC radio and television programmes and afforded a direct line to the inner circle of programme makers. (…) It was for this charitable work, more than his celebrity achievements, that Savile was made OBE in 1972. He was subsequently knighted, by both the Queen and the Pope, in 1990. (…) By then, the BBC, the NHS, the Department of Education and Science (as it was called in the early 1990s), the state, the church, the monarchy, the military and the nation were all involved in his

224

collective validation. (...) By marginalising the empowering role of institutions in Savile's crimes, both the Netflix documentary and official inquiries ultimately preserve the reputations of those institutions, and absolve key individuals of responsibility.«

**The Sound of Freedom Foundation, USA, in January 2023**
**»Human Trafficking Reference«**
https://soundfreedomfoundation.org/trafficking/

»According to Professional Investigator magazine (January/February 2023), Kym Kurey, Strategic Account Manager at Vital4 defines human trafficking as "modern day slavery; the recruitment, harboring, transportation, provision, or obtaining of a person for the purposes of a commercial sex act (or forced labor), in which the commercial sex act is induced by force, fraud, or coercion, or if the person induced to such an act has not attained 18 years of age." "12-14 years old is the average age of entry into sex trafficking. Shamefully, the United States ranks in the top three countries where human and sex trafficking occur, according to the World Population Review's Child Trafficking by Country 2022 map."«

**CRIN – Child Rights International Network, in March 2023**
**»Latin American countries ranked on child sexual**
**violence prevention and response«**
https://home.crin.org/readlistenwatch/stories/oosi-latin-america

»Brazil is Latin America's best-performing country in preventing and responding to child sexual exploitation and abuse, while Argentina is the lowest ranked, according to a new report released today by Economist Impact comparing the laws and policies of nine countries in the region, the launch of which CRIN coordinated. (...) The research is part of the Out of the Shadows Index (OOSI), which is the first global assessment of how countries worldwide are addressing sexual violence against children. It covers 60 countries, home to around 85 percent of the world's children.«

**ZEIT Online, Germany, inJune 2023**

**»SOS-Kinderdorf vertuscht laut Bericht jahrzehntelangen Missbrauch«**

**[According to a report, SOS Children's Village conceals decades-long abuse.]**

https://www.zeit.de/gesellschaft/zeitgeschehen/2023-06/sos-kinderdorf-sexuelle-gewalt-missbrauch

»According to an internal investigation report, the international aid organization SOS Children's Villages has covered up incidents of fraud and sexual violence against children, some resulting in child pregnancies, in their facilities for decades. The organization, as reported by a special commission, has been concealing "serious allegations of abuse" of minors in multiple countries since the 1980s. The report reveals that "scandals were covered up, evidence was destroyed, and employees who raised concerns were intimidated". Published on their website, the report documents "numerous cases of child pregnancies" attributed mainly to rape. Girls were reportedly coerced into "forced abortions" without "verifiable family consent". (...) According to the findings, a major donor in Nepal was granted access to a facility "contrary to the organization's rules", where he abused multiple minors between 2010 and 2014. A "climate of fear" was reported in facilities in Panama. Additionally, the commission found significant wrongdoings in Cambodia, Kenya, Sierra Leone, and Syria. It was noted that the local staff in these places prioritized "protecting the organization" over the interests of the children.«

**Thailand Institute of Justice (TIJ)**

**Women and children Empowerment Programme**

**163rd International Training Course (PDF)**

**»Violence against Children in Southeast Asia: the case**

**of child sex tourism in Thailand, Lao PDR and Cambodia«**

https://www.google.com/url?sa=t&source=web&rct=j&opi=89978449&url=https://www.unafei.or.jp/publica-tions/pdf/RS_No100/No100_VE_Sita_3.pdf&ved=2ahUKEwii_LDz6q6JAxX_gf0HHWRAA04QFnoECBMQAQ&usg=AOvVaw0BBlPJX6cxuZvVv5Eg2QME

o »Violence against Children is more prevalent in lower income countries.

o Child sexual abuse in travel and tourism denotes child sexual abuse by tourists, travelers or foreign residents who commit child sexual

226

abuse in the country or countries in which they are visiting or living.
- o In 2014, fastest growth in sexual exploitation of children by foreigners.
- o Traditional Destinations: Thailand and The Philippines.
- o Emerging Destinations: Cambodia, Lao PDR, Myanmar and Vietnam.
- o Offenders: Male from another Southeast Asian country or East Asian countries (Japan, China, South Korea).
- o Children at Risk: Stateless children, refugees, indigenous children, ethnic minority groups, children working close to tourists.
- o Impacts and Consequences: A rise of webcam-based child sex tourism due to the advancement of information technologies. Many survivors have substance abuse problems as means to cope with their pain. Survivors have increased suicidal thoughts and tendencies.
- o Common Points of Access:
  - Establishment-based prostitution: Bars, Karaoke Venues, Beer Gardens, Massage Parlors that operate as brothels.
  - Direct/facilitated solicitation of vulnerable children living/working in public places popular among tourists such as beaches and market places.
  - Access may even be facilitated by those in child contact roles such as schools and orphanages who target children from broken homes.
  - Thailand: (…) Travel agencies and hotel operators are the main facilitators. Children are bought from their parents and forced into Thailand sex trade.
  - Flawed Justice Processes for Victims: State justice systems often inaccessible & inhospitable to child victims of sexual violence. Corruption in certain factions of the police leads to the tipping off of owners of brothels and sex clubs in exchange for bribes. State judicial systems often fail to monitor an restrict the movement of accused exploiters in the pretrial period. (…)«

**Bundeskriminalamt, Germany, in July 2024**

**[Federal Criminal Police Office]**

**»Im Fokus: Bundeslagebild Sexualdelikte zum Nachteil von**

**Kindern und Jugendlichen 2023«**

**[Focus: National Situation Report on Sexual Offenses against**

**Children and Adolescents 2023]**

https://www.bka.de/DE/AktuelleInformationen/StatistikenLagebilder/Lagebilder/SexualdelikteznvKindernuJugendlichen/2023/BLBSexualdelikte_2023_node.html

»In 2023, the police once again observed an increase in sexual offenses against children and adolescents. The numbers continue to remain at a very high level - they have more than tripled in the past five years. In many cases, the internet is a central tool used in the crimes, such as when offenders establish contact with minors through social networks. Additionally, the internet itself can become the scene of the crime, for example, in cases of abuse shared through internet live streams. (...)

**Sexual abuse of minors**

Since the criminal law reform in 2021, sexual abuse of children is now covered as a separate criminal law norm. There were 11,900 suspects registered, of which 94.0 percent were male. In total, in the year 2023, 18,497 victims of sexual abuse of children were registered. The proportion of female victims was 75.6 percent, while the proportion of male victims was 24.4 percent. (...)

**Sexual abuse of adolescents**

The number of victims increased by 5.5 percent to 1,277 adolescents. The majority of the victims were 78.0 percent female and 22.0 percent male. Also, in nearly 60.0 percent of cases, there was a pre-existing relationship with the suspect. (...)

**Portrayals of child and adolescent abuse**

The number of these cases has been steadily increasing in recent years, reaching a new record high in the reporting year with 45,191 cases (+7.4 percent) involving 37,464 suspects (+2.9 percent). The most common cases involved the distribution of child pornography content and the possession or procurement of child pornography content. (...) The Federal Criminal Police Office (BKA) receives hundreds of reports daily from the National Center for Missing and Exploited Children (NCMEC). In 2023, around 180,300 tips were received, an

228

increase of 32.0 percent compared to the previous year. (...) Since 2019, the cases of production, distribution, acquisition, and possession of youth pornographic content have been steadily increasing. In 2023, they reached a record high with 8,851 cases, showing an increase of about 30.0 percent compared to the previous year. (...)«

## CHURCH INSTITUTIONS

Religious institutions, regardless of the country and faith denomination, have a centuries-long history of abuse. Like a blood-red thread, violence, excesses, and a lust for murder run through all instances and leave behind suffering and misery. Entire regions are soaked in blood. Whether physical, psychological, or sexual abuse, there appear to be no boundaries. Hand in hand with other parts of society, up to the highest levels of judiciary and politics, these actions are perpetuated and tabooed to this day.

»Since the publication of the abuse reports, especially in the archdioceses of Cologne as well as Munich and Freising, the discussion about strengthening state responsibility in dealing with sexual abuse of children, particularly in the context of the church, has fully erupted. (...) It is rightly stated time and again that it should not be left solely to the churches to address the massive acts of sexual violence against children and adolescents committed within their areas of responsibility. Churches may not handle concealment, denial, and their own failures on their own.«[55]

---

[55] Unabhängiger Beauftragter für Fragen des sexuellen Kindesmissbrauchs, Positionspapier 2022 »Staatliche Verantwortungsübernahme und Aufarbeitung von sexuellem Kindesmissbrauch – Bilanz und Ausblick« [Independent Commissioner for Child Sexual Abuse Issues, Position Paper 2022 »State Responsibility and Addressing Child Sexual Abuse - Review and Outlook«] https://beauftragte-missbrauch.de/fileadmin/Content/pdf/Pressemitteilungen/2022/PM-02-16/Positionspapier_2022_Staatliche_Verantwortungsuebernahme_bei_Aufarbeitung_Missbrauch.pdf

**Willems, Helmut; Ferring, Dieter – Springer Verlag, in December 2013**

**Buch »Macht und Missbrauch in Institutionen«**

**[Book, Power and Abuse in Institutions]**

https://zentralbuchhandlung.de/shop/i/macht-und-missbrauch-in-institutionen-9783658042967-8818.html

»While the public debate on sexual abuse largely focuses on the question of possible compensations for the victims, there remain a number of open questions for the scientific discussion. This concerns the search for the causes and organizational risk factors for the occurrence of such abuse cases, as well as the identification of suitable measures for prevention and intervention. The anthology addresses not only the abuse of children and adolescents but also emphasizes the issue of power and abuse of power in different institutional contexts (such as in caregiving relationships, nursing homes, prisons, etc.).«

**mdr, Germany, in March 2018**

**»Katholische Kirche legt Missbrauchsstudie vor«**

**[Catholic Church presents abuse study]**

https://www.mdr.de/religion/bischofskonferenz-stellt-studie-zu-missbrauch-in-katholischer-kirche-vor-102.html

»The lead scientist of the study, Harald Dreßing, lamented a lack of willingness for transparency in large parts of the Catholic Church when presenting the results. The extent of sexual abuse of children and adolescents, as well as "the handling of the responsible parties", had "shaken" the researchers, Dreßing said. He emphasized that the issue of abuse is by no means over. "The risk persists", said the forensic psychiatrist, who works at the Central Institute for Mental Health in Mannheim. Dreßing stressed, "Our study results suggest that there have been and still are structures in the Catholic Church that can foster sexual abuse." Reasons for this are the abuse of clerical power, the obligation of priests to celibacy, and an internally "problematic approach" to the topic of sexuality, especially homosexuality. (...) According to their own statements, the researchers examined more than 38,000 personnel files and case records of the 27 dioceses from 1946 to 2014. They found indications of allegations of sexual abuse of minors for 1,670 clerics of the Catholic Church. This corresponds to 4.4 percent of all clerics. "We have to assume a significantly larger dark

230

field," said Dreßing. (...) The accused could be linked to 3,677 children and adolescents who were sexually abused. 62.8 percent of the victims were male, 34.9 percent were female, and 2.3 percent did not have gender information available. At the time of the first sexual abuse, 51.6 percent of the victims were a maxiMom of 13 years old, 25.8 percent were 14 years and older, with the average age being 12 years. (...) The abuse triggered both health and social problems for the victims. Victims often suffered from depression, anxiety, sleep and eating disorders, post-traumatic symptoms, suicidal or self-injurious behavior, as well as alcohol and drug consumption. In social terms, the victims frequently had issues with education, career, relationships, and partnerships.«

**Ceylon Today, Sri Lanka, in April 2023**
**»Breaking the silence on child abuse at temples«**
https://ceylontoday.lk/2023/04/29/breaking-the-silence-on-child-abuse-at-temples/

»Although the abuse faced by children, who are in the care of adults, has come to light, child abuse in religious institutions hardly makes it to the headlines. When someone dares to speak about children, who are subject to abuse in temples, many are offended that reporting such incidents brings the religion to disrepute. Society chooses to remain silent regarding the lives of novice monks (samaneras) who are also children. (…)

In many cases, these abuses have been carried out by senior monks or teachers who were entrusted with the care and education of young novice monks. The abuses have included molestation, rape, and other forms of sexual exploitation, often perpetrated against children.

One of the reasons for the prevalence of these abuses is the lack of accountability and oversight within the monastic community. Many monks and teachers are revered and respected figures in Sri Lankan society, and as a result, their actions may go unquestioned or unreported.

Additionally, there is often a culture of silence and shame surrounding sexual abuse, which can make it difficult for victims to come forward and report their experiences. Many victims may feel that they will not be believed or that they will be blamed for the abuse.«

**Rolling Stone, in July 2023**

**»Sinead O'Connor's 'SNL' Protest Was 'Monumental'**

**for Church Sex Abuse Survivors«**

https://www.rollingstone.com/music/music-features/sinead-oconnor-catholic-church-abuse-legacy-1234797102/

»More than three decades after the singer ripped up a picture of the pope to protest child abuse, history has proven her right. (…) In 1992, after Sinéad O'Connor ripped apart a photo of Pope John Paul II (…) on protest of the Catholic church ignoring child abuse, (…). "A lot of us had to grow up with that photo of John Paul," says Peter Isely, who is a survivor of a priest's sexual assault and is a cofounding member of the organization Ending Clergy Abuse. "Kids were raped and sexually assaulted in rectories and churches with that photo in the room, looking down upon us in complete silence." (…) O'Connor became a global star with hits like "Mandinka" and "Nothing Compares 2 U," she described her own childhood as brutal. She was the third of four children born to John and Marie O'Connor, a working-class Catholic couple from Dublin. Marie physically abused Sinéad and sent her daughter to Ireland's Magdalene Laundries — Catholic-run reform schools for "fallen women" — after Sinéad was expelled from Catholic school and arrested for shoplifting. (…) It was Marie's personal picture of the pope that O'Connor shredded onstage. "(…) In Ireland [when she was growing up], the church would tell her to be a better child, and her mother would just do horrible things to her. And there were instances that would happen where she would see a child being abused by the parents when she was taking her oldest child, Jake, to school, and it would just floor her. Things would trigger her. Her childhood would trigger her."«

**Tagesschau, Germany, in January 2024**

**»1.259 Beschuldigte in der Evangelischen Kirche«**

**[1,259 suspects in the Evangelical Church]**

https://www.tagesschau.de/inland/gesellschaft/missbrauch-evangelische-kirche-106.html

»For decades, there has also been sexualized violence in the Protestant Church. A study now reveals the extent: According to this, at least 1,259 alleged perpetrators have been documented. Probably only the

232

tip of the iceberg. (...) In an extrapolation, which must be viewed with "very great caution" from the perspective of the research team, a total of 9,355 victims would result from an estimated 3,497 accused. (...) In the past, there has been repeated criticism of the slow processing of abuse cases among Protestants. The Cologne constitutional law professor Stephan Rixen criticized the behavior of the EKD and Diakonie. Often, no disciplinary records were even initiated in cases of sexualized violence. It is also "completely absurd that personnel files are not being investigated because upon realistic examination, indications of misconduct can also be found in personnel files," says Rixen, who is a member of the Independent Commission for the Processing of Sexual Child Abuse of the German government.«

**Wikipedia**
**»Catholic Church sexual abuse cases in Ireland«**
https://en.wikipedia.org/wiki/Catholic_Church_sexual_abuse_cases_in_Ireland

»Like the Catholic Church sex abuse cases in the United States and elsewhere, the abuse in Ireland included cases of high-profile, supposedly celibate Catholic clerics involved in illicit heterosexual relations as well as widespread physical abuse of children in the Catholic-run childcare network. In many cases, the abusing priests were moved to other parishes to avoid embarrassment or a scandal, assisted by senior clergy. (...) In the 1990s, a series of television programs publicised allegations of systemic abuse in Ireland's Roman Catholic-run childcare system, primarily in the Reformatory and Industrial Schools. The abuse occurred primarily between the 1930s and 1970s. (...) These programs interviewed adult victims of abuse who provided "testimony of their experiences, they documented Church and State collusion in the operation of these institutions, and they underscored the climate of secrecy and denial that permeated the church response when faced with controversial accusations." (...) The commission found that Catholic priests and nuns had terrorised thousands of boys and girls for decades and that government inspectors had failed to stop the chronic beatings, rapes and humiliation. The report characterised rape and molestation as "endemic" in Irish Catholic church-run Industrial Schools and orphanages.«

# INTERNET AND PORNOGRAPHIE

**Stuttgarter Nachrichten, Germany, inNovember 2022**

**»Boystown: Pädophile wissen, was sie tun«**

**[Boystown: Pedophiles know what they are doing.]**

https://www.stuttgarter-nachrichten.de/inhalt.kinderpornografie-boystown-paedophile-wissen-was-sie-tun.3e4dee23-f091-4a36-9dff-f0d10b46f1ee.html

»Criminals on the Darknet platform Boystown worldwide exchanged child pornography content. In addition to nude images, everyday photos of children also circulated on Boystown, apparently found and copied from the public Instagram or Facebook accounts of unsuspecting parents. Users were occasionally awarded medals for material that was deemed particularly pleasing to pedophiles, as a form of recognition and further incentive. The portal has more than 400,000 user accounts and cannot be found through normal internet search engines. In the virtual shadow realm, pedophiles exchange photos and videos depicting the most severe sexual abuse of children, primarily boys.«

**Statista, worldwide, in October 2023**

**»Online Child Pornography Skyrockets«**

https://www.statista.com/chart/30964/total-number-of-urls-confirmed-as-containing-child-sexual-abuse-imagery/

»The amount of online child sexual abuse has skyrocketed in the past few years, according to the latest annual report of the UK-based NGO and watchdog, the Internet Watch Foundation (IWF). As many as 255,588 URLs were confirmed to contain images or videos of the abuse last year, up from 132,676 URLs in 2019. This rise is partly being linked to the pandemic, when lockdowns meant more people - including younger children - were staying at home and turning online for longer periods of time than before.«

**CNN, USA, inDecember 2023**

**»Hundreds of images of child sexual abuse found in**

**dataset used to train AI image-generating tools«**

https://edition.cnn.com/2023/12/21/tech/child-sexual-abuse-material-ai-training-data/index.html

»More than a thousand images of child sexual abuse material were found in a massive public dataset used to train popular AI image-generating models, Stanford Internet Observatory researchers said in a study published earlier this week. The presence of these images in the training data may make it easier for AI models to create new and realistic AI-generated images of child abuse content, or "deepfake" images of children being exploited.«

**Bundeskriminalamt [Federal Criminal Police Office] Germany, 2024**
**»Cybergrooming«**

https://www.bka.de/DE/UnsereAufgaben/Aufgabenbereiche/Zentralstellen/Kinderpornografie/Cybergrooming/Cybergrooming_node.html

»The term describes the deliberate initiation of sexual contacts with minors over the Internet. The perpetrators engage in chats or online communities pretending to be approximately the same age as children or adolescents or present themselves as understanding adults with similar experiences and interests. They gain the trust of their victims with the aim of manipulating them. In many cases, they convince the children to send explicit self-portraits. The photos are then sometimes used as leverage against the minors to coerce them into further actions. Some perpetrators also aim to meet with the minor victims "offline" and abuse them. In Germany, Cybergrooming is prohibited as a form of child sexual abuse (§ 176 of the Penal Code). Those who harass children and adolescents on the internet with sexual intent can face imprisonment of up to five years.«

**Duisburg, Police North Rhine-Westphalia,**
**Germany, in October 2024**
**»Bundesgebiet: Erfolgreicher Schlag gegen Kindesmissbrauch –**
**Sechs Tatverdächtige in U-Haft«**
**[Federal territory: Successful blow against child abuse –**
**Six suspects in pre-trial detention.]**

https://duisburg.polizei.nrw/241008bundesgebiet

»From September 24th to 28th, 2024, a major operation led by the Police Headquarters in Duisburg took place in six federal states. (…) According to the investigators' evaluations, globally active users in the

235

mid-six-digit range were identified on the platform. (…) The data to be analyzed on just one suspect's computer amounts to 13.5 terabytes. If a photo has an average file size of 4 MB, this corresponds to about 3.4 million photos. (…) North Rhine-Westphalia Minister of Justice, Dr. Benjamin Limbach: "Children suffer their whole lives from these crimes. Fighting child abuse on the internet is therefore a duty for society as a whole. The success of the Duisburg police and the ZAC NRW is a powerful statement. It sends an unmistakable signal to all perpetrators of child abuse: You cannot hide! Not behind four walls, not behind a pseudonym, and not even in the darknet!«

## WAR, ESCAPE, AND DISPLACEMENT

Especially during escape, displacement, and war, the door is wide open for sexual trauma. Often, it is even deliberately used as a weapon of war or to exploit the chaos of war for heinous experiments. Under the guise of humanitarian efforts, escape assistance, and adoptions, human abyss are revealed, causing despair. Children and adults who survive these acts of violence are marked for life. They carry unspeakable physical and psychological burdens every single day and every single night. Those who dare to confront their suffering – bit by bit every day – are among the bravest people I know. They are the true heroes. Because they strive not to walk the same path as their perpetrators who hide behind suits, uniforms, money, and power. A path that is extremely painful and very, very lonely for the victims. The outcome? Uncertain.

**The New York Times, USA, in February 2019**
**»Thousands of Immigrant Children Said They Were**
**Sexually Abused in U.S. Detention Centers, Report Says«**
https://www.nytimes.com/2019/02/27/us/immigrant-children-sexual-abuse.html

»The records, which involve children who had entered the country alone or had been separated from their parents, detailed allegations that adult staff members had harassed and assaulted children, including fondling and kissing minors, watching them as they showered, and

236

raping them. They also included cases of suspected abuse of children by other minors.«

Amnesty International Switzerland, in March 2019
»Jemen – Milizen vergewaltigen Kinder«
[Yemen - Militias rape children]
https://www.amnesty.ch/de/laender/naher-osten-nordafrika/jemen/dok/2019/taiz-vergewaltigung-von-kindern-durch-milizen

»The mother of the boy[56] described the evening when her son came home after the incident. "He came home in the evening and went straight to the bathroom. When he came out, I asked him what was wrong, but he couldn't tell me what had happened. He started crying, and I began to cry too. We sat next to each other for three days and couldn't eat, drink, or sleep... He was scared and in a very bad mental state, and his face was yellowish and pale... He just stared into space. He couldn't sit without pain and didn't go to the bathroom for three days. (...) The doctor said that my son was fine and he wouldn't make a report. I then asked him if he didn't fear God at all."«

Unlimited Hangout, by Whitney Webb, in July 2020
»"Charity" Accused of Sex Abuse Coordinating ID2020's
Pilot Program For Refugee Newborns«
https://unlimitedhangout.com/2020/07/reports/charity-accused-of-sex-abuse-coordinating-id2020s-pilot-program-for-refugee-newborns/

»A biometric identification program backed by the ID2020 alliance will see its new "digital id" program rolled out for refugee newborns in close coordination with a charity tied to Wall Street and prominent Western politicians whose workers have been accused of sexually exploiting refugee children. iRespond, an international non-profit organization that is "dedicated to using biometrics to improve lives through digital identity," has begun piloting a new biometric program for newborns among the predominately Karen refugee population along the Myanmar-Thailand border, a program it soon hopes to "quickly

---

[56] The boy was 16 years old and had even tried to influence the perpetrator. »He told me he wanted to rape me. I started crying... and asked him to imagine I was his son. He got angrier and hit me even harder...«

deploy" at a greater scale and make available to the general global population. The pilot program is being conducted as part of the controversial ID2020 alliance, backed by Microsoft, the GAVI vaccine alliance and the Rockefeller Foundation, and with the International Rescue Committee (IRC), a non-profit organization deeply tied to the Western political elite and Wall Street with a controversial track record of silencing numerous sex abuse and fraud allegations. (…) However, iRespond's CEO, Scott Reid, told Biometric Update that these credentials do "not carry the same weight as a true birth certificate," but asserts that the organization's biometric "birth attestation" program "could leapfrog the traditional barriers to establishing identity." Despite the fact that iRespond's quasi-birth certificates would seemingly serve little purpose in areas where actual birth certificates are readily available, the organization notes that "once the pilot is completed, iRespond is ready to quickly deploy the solution at scale" for mass use around the globe. (…) For instance, it was revealed in 2018 that IRC was one of several U.K.-based charities where "workers [were] alleged to be in sexually exploitative relationships with refugee children" including through "sex-for-food scandals" where "sexual abuse was so endemic that the only way for many refugee families to survive was to allow a teenage girl to be exploited." Reports further alleged that IRC and other charities named in the report, including Save the Children, had known of the egregious abuse for years prior to the allegations being made public and chose not to act.«

**Save the Children International, in 2021**

**»Weapon of War: Sexual violence against children in conflict«**

https://resourcecentre.savethechildren.net/document/weapon-war-sexual-violence-against-children-conflict/

»Globally, 426 million children live in conflict zones today. We estimate that a staggering 72 million of them, or one in six, live 50 kilometres or closer to conflicts where armed groups or forces have perpetrated sexual violence against children during the last year. This report presents the very first quantitative analysis of the risk of sexual violence against children in conflict for the period 1990-2019. Worldwide, people of all genders and all ages experience sexual violence, which is fundamentally rooted in unequal power dynamics. For children, their

238

age and gender play a significant role in their vulnerability, placing adolescent girls at particularly high risk of sexual violence in conflict settings. Our analysis shows that the number of children at risk of sexual violence committed by conflict actors is ten times higher today than in 1990. The number of children at risk fluctuates from one year to another, but the upward trend is very clear. In the most recent years we also see that a bigger share of armed actors who commit sexual violence in conflict also perpetrate it against children. The countries with the highest share of children living in conflict zones with reports of sexual violence perpetrated by conflict actors against children include Colombia (with 24% of all children in the country facing this risk), Iraq (with 49% of all children at risk), Somalia (56%), South Sudan (19%), Syria (48%) and Yemen (83%).«

**Think Global Health, in November 2022**
**»The Devastating Use of Sexual Violence as a Weapon of War«**
https://www.thinkglobalhealth.org/article/devastating-use-sexual-violence-weapon-war

»Rape and other forms of sexual violence have been pervasive in conflicts throughout history. This fall, three UN reports highlight the prevalence of these atrocities in Ukraine, Haiti, and Ethiopia. While the nature of the conflicts in each country differs vastly, the horrifying use of sexual violence to torment civilian populations; punish ethnic, political, or cultural rivals; and assert and maintain control, is present in each case. (…) Victims of sexual violence range in age from four to eighty-years-old. (…) Other documented violence includes gang rape and forcing family members to watch while their children and mothers were sexually assaulted. (…) Conflict-related rape and sexual violence are uniquely challenging to address. Cultural taboos and fear of reprisals make many survivors hesitant to share their trauma, often rendering the abuse they have experienced an "invisible" crime. (…) Jemal Abdella and his wife Tirungo Ambaye say their daughter Zara, 17, was killed by Tigray People's Liberation Front forces for resisting rape.«

I could keep on quoting endlessly now, but there are two fundamentally important questions amidst all this suffering: What are the causes and

239

how can this vicious cycle be interrupted? Dr. Jordan Peterson[57] said very wisely:

»Most people who abuse their children were abused as children. But, most people who were abused as children do not abuse their children. And the reason for that is because if you were abused there's two lessons you can learn from that: One is, identify with the abuser. The other is, don't ever identify. And if this didn't happen, every single family would be abusive to the core very rapidly. And some of the best people I know – and I mean that literally – are people who had childhood so absolutely abysmal that virtually anything they would have done in consequence could have been justified. You know, when they chose not to turn into the predators of others. And that was a choice. And often one that caused them to reevaluate themselves right down to the bottom of their soul.«

## 5.2 NEURODERMATITIS

*Self-encounter (Woman, Germany, 3 words)*
*Boy – Neurodermatitis – ?*

»Neurodermatitis (also known as atopic eczema) is a common, chronic or episodic inflammatory skin condition in which patients tend to have dry skin and eczema. (...) The frequency of the disease varies depending on factors such as climate and age. In sun-deprived Northern Europe, up to 25% of the population is affected, while only about 1% suffer from it on the coasts of Southern Europe. Experts estimate that in Germany, based on health insurance data, the overall prevalence is between 10-15%: Babies and toddlers are the most affected age group, with 23% suffering from it. By school age, only about 8% of children are affected. These numbers show that the condition improves with age for a large portion of patients. However, it is not just a "childhood

---

[57] YouTube Shorts @jordanpetersonrulesforlife »Jordan Peterson on abusive parents«, https://www.youtube.com/shorts/LuCJKP1W_SM

disease", as 2-4% of adults also have atopic dermatitis. (...) The predisposition to atopic dermatitis is hereditary.«[58]

»Within Europe, the figures vary significantly depending on the study. Since 1990, in British and Scandinavian studies, the number of affected school children ranged between 9.7 and 23 percent. A British study on ten-year-olds found that 41 percent of them had experienced eczema at some point. Many children with eczema develop additional allergic conditions over the years, such as asthma, hay fever, or food allergies.«[59]

The son of this woman had neurodermatitis as a young child. Around six months old, he developed severe neurodermatitis with bloody rashes and scratching during the night. This led to a journey of suffering to experts and clinics that lasted for four years until the symptoms slowly improved. The woman was completely overwhelmed by the situation at the time and still carries strong feelings of guilt because she couldn't help her son. However, his suffering had actually been the beginning of her own work on herself.

**Boy**

»I observe and take a look at everything. I feel like I'm between 8 and 12 years. I don't really like that I'm so in the spotlight. I think "Atopic dermatitis" is totally cool. Also, the ants. Because I am a bit stiff here. But I believe that has something to do with Mom. When we are alone, we can handle it. I would love to hit the slopes with "Atopic dermatitis".

---

[58] Gemeinnützige Europäische Stiftung für Allergieforschung (ECARF) from February 2017 [Non-Profit European Foundation for Allergy Research] https://www.e-carf.org/info-portal/erkrankungen/neurodermitis/

[59] Allergie Informationsdienst, »Wie häufig ist Neurodermitis?« [Allergy Information Service, »How common is Neurodermatitis?«] https://www.allergieinformationsdienst.de/krankheitsbilder/neurodermitis/verbreitung

**Neurodermatitis**

»I am generally very restless. I find the boy totally cool. I am around the same age and I have a strong urge to move, which needs to be suppressed. The "?" unsettles me. Had exactly the same feeling as "Boy": It's uncomfortable that you, Mom, don't stop bothering about him. You keep asking the boy so many questions all the time. The "?" sticks to you; but it's not yours! It's in the space. That creates so much uncertainty.«

**?**

»I would be mute, invisible, and wouldn't say anything. I also don't want you or anyone to see me. I am female. The "Neurodermatitis" distracts from something. I am your grandma. With us, it's like Sodom and Gomorrah; like in the Bible. Everyone with everyone. It feels like group sex to me. Like animals, like pigs. Everyone. I mean everyone! Your mother, her mother, father, siblings... The men did that. There were so many. It was so normal for me. I know nothing else. No one noticed.«

**Boy**

»About men... Men are pigs. I have the feeling that my "Neurodermatitis" protects me! Because men are pigs in the women's line. And I am a part of that. And then I have these hands and feet, two things that are very intimate before I undress. And men are pigs. Now that "?" talks so disdainfully about men, it is almost unbearable for me to be a man. Because the men in your family are all pigs. If I am to be relieved, then the pigs must come. It's about the "Neurodermatitis." It protects me!«

**Neurodermatitis**

»Mom, I feel so sorry for you. For me, the thing with the ants and the restlessness... there is a lot of disgust. I want to shake it off of me. I don't want to have anything to do with it.«

*The woman asks her son and "Neurodermatitis" to step into the background. To protect them while she wants to get to the bottom of the causes. Two more words are added: "Men" and "Grandpa" (maternal).*

## ?

»I am the grandma. There are dirty, disgusting hands that touch me. They are on my skin. This hatred for this male world is in every cell of my body. This filth is in every single one of my cells. Men are pigs – and that is putting it mildly. I am without my own will, without my own self. A disposable product, worthless. I don't really live at all.«

## Men

»I am completely sexualized in everything. Women are pure sex objects. And I can only think about sex. I am completely consumed by the sexual act itself. The human, the woman, is completely insignificant. It is very animalistic here. I make no distinction between boys or girls. As soon as one sees the woman in the boy as well, it makes no difference. In my world, there is nothing else. It has always been this way and always will be. The questions you [woman] ask, I don't understand at all. They are questions from the new world.«

## Grandpa

»I find her [referring to grandma or "?"] quite interesting. I think it's great that she is so needy, submissive. It really turns me on. You can't resist anyway. All normal. It's not abuse, right? [addressing the woman] Maybe you also need a real man?«

*The woman is shocked by the story, as she did not know these details before. She says: »But I can act. And I see the truth; even if it is only in part. And men are not swine. Not my son, or anyone else!« As all this misery rises up, her son becomes calmer in response.*

**Boy**

»When you are quiet, without speaking, then I find you to be better. Then I can feel you. Then trust comes.«

Epilogue

The neurodermatitis manifests as a protective function of a multigenerational trauma of sexual abuse within the family. As the woman has had a son – and she herself was abused by her father during her childhood – her son carries the burden of the violence that men in previous generations have inflicted upon women. The bodily symptom of neurodermatitis wanted to draw attention to this! That is why it is so important not to suppress this bodily symptom, but to bring to light the suffering endured, the perpetrators and victims, and all truths. It must be seen, told, felt, whitnessed and acknowledged.

## 5.3 WETTING

*Self-encounter (Man, Germany, 3 words)*
*German: Ich – Windel – Einnässen*
*English: I – Diaper – Wetting*

What happens when a boy is not allowed to be naughty, to try nothing out, to not be allowed to be funny? When liveliness, playfulness, mischief have no place? When one grows up in an extremely repressive, constricting household and must always stand up straight? When one is not allowed to be oneself and is repeatedly told that one is wrong? What if bedwetting starts in the teenage years and continues into adulthood? When there is no room for anger? When as an adult, one still fights against their feelings? And since adolescence, that is, for decades, finds satisfaction in wetting oneself in a diaper?

**Ich (I)**

»I find it really hard to keep my eyes open. I constantly feel like I have to blink. I feel very, very strange. There is some restlessness. But there's also anger. I can't tell you what the anger is directed towards. The anger is destructive. I want to chew on something. Bite down. When I tell you this, it helps me relax a bit.«

**Windel (Diaper)**
»First, I thought, pah! How stupid. What am I even doing here? I don't belong here at all. And when the "Ich" (I) spoke of anger, I thought, wow, this could get interesting! Otherwise, I have no idea what I'm doing here.«

»*I can relate to the anger. As a child, I was always very angry. So impulsive and quite headstrong. I was always someone who went in and out a lot. My parents would then leave the key in the door or leave the door open. That was easier.*«

**Einnässen (Wetting)**
»When the "Ich" (I) started speaking, it felt good to me. And then I could resonate with it. Before, I couldn't manage that. I had this impulse to somehow sway back and forth. But I'm so tight and can't move freely. And when the "Ich" (I) talked about anger, I don't feel it. I feel more back pain. And I have strong needs. I also have to think about breastfeeding. I feel like I have needs that haven't been met. And I'm tired too.«

»*Background info, I had a herniated disc three years ago. And I'm currently experiencing problems again. "Windel" (Diaper), are you bored with everything?*«

○ **Windel (Diaper):** Totally. There's no action here. The anger hasn't been addressed anymore. The rest of the conversation doesn't interest me. It makes me tired.
○ **Ich (I):** I'm also very tired. I only catch half of what "Einnässen" (Wetting) was saying. I sense a heaviness, but I also feel my pelvis. The bladder. I'm super tired. Numb. Exhausted. All the energy that was there at the beginning is completely gone. There's a sense of giving up. Pelvis and bladder, they're keeping me awake. I sense something there that isn't good.

- **Windel (Diaper):** "Ich" (I) and "Einnässen" (Wetting), they don't interest me. But if the diaper were to be properly filled with poop, that would be fun for me. Action, indeed. Let's do it right away!
- **Einnässen (Wetting):** So, I'm a little afraid of "Windel" (Diaper). I'm a bit scared. I resonate with "Ich" (I). I feel this pain in my back. It's very present for me. Actually, I should feel my bladder, but there I feel a numbness. When I speak that out loud, I feel a slight pulling. I have a feeling that the back pain has something to do with anger. Whenever anger is mentioned, I feel the pain in my back.

*»Do you feel tormented by someone?«*

- **Einnässen (Wetting):** It was good for me that you asked the question. Now I see the "Windel" (Diaper) as a small, young part that is bored. The one who tests the limits. I am an even younger part than "Windel" (Diaper). I am a baby.
- **Ich (I):** I fully resonate with "Einnässen" (Wetting). For me, "Windel" (Diaper) is a small, cheeky, playful child who likes to test boundaries. And I don't perceive her as a threat, but rather I appreciate that she tests boundaries. That she has that wild side and her own mind. But I also notice that I always grit my teeth.
- **Windel (Diaper):** Just let all the crap out! Then you'll feel better too! If I had an identity, I would be a jester. Just throw the shit on the table! And suddenly it's fun here. Then you'll feel better too. Then you won't have any back pain!

*»This is actually a parenting issue for me. My parents were like this: One must not stand out, one must be nice, one must watch what one says. One must not voice their opinion everywhere, even though one should bang their fist on the table about certain things.«*

- **Windel (Diaper):** Oh, these nasty words, I would like to use them all. That would be fun. I wouldn't say »pee-pee«, but rather »piss«. Not a little pee in the diaper, but a proper load of shit! That's what the diaper is for!

246

- **Ich (I):** I feel a love for this "Windel" (Diaper). I find it so awesome that this part lives so vividly. There is a feeling I have down in my pelvis. I feel completely inhibited there.
- **Einnässen (Wetting):** No, there is a fear. But I find "Windel" (Diaper) totally cute, what she says. It's enchanting, the way I see her like that. It makes me feel good when the "Ich" (I) talks. And since then, I've been sitting here with my fists on my hips, realizing that there is anger building up. I can't express the anger, and it's taking such a self-aggressive direction.

## Ich (I)

»I totally resonate with that as well. For me, it's here, in the jaw. The tension from the pelvis has moved up to the jaw. It's as if I have words... that mustn't come out. I'm not allowed to say them. Everything tightens up.«

*»It wouldn't have been possible with my parents. Not even as a child. And I started speaking correctly very late. In fact, only when I started school. Before that, it was an artificial language. That's why I can relate to the speaking part. My mother would have gone to a psychiatric clinic if I had spoken the way "Windel" (Diaper) suggested. It wouldn't have been doable. Not even during puberty.«*

## Einnässen (Wetting)

»That's terrible! I feel completely trapped. I find it awful what you are telling me. So, I find it really terrible that this wasn't supposed to happen. It gives me stomachaches. The only thing I could do was wet myself.«

*»As a child, it was not an issue. I was potty-trained by the age of two. I was dry and clean overnight. My parents never talked about it afterwards. There was a minor incident at school, but nothing dramatic. The issue of bedwetting started for me during puberty, at 16. I can't understand why the desire to wet myself is still so prevalent at 40. It became a pleasure. And that hasn't changed until today. Then the diapers came into play. Now, I have a problem because this was not*

*supposed to happen. "Einnässen" (Wetting) and "Windel" (Diaper) were not supposed to be a part of it.«*

o  **Einnässen (Wetting):** About wetting, all I can tell you is that it was the only way I could somehow make myself noticed and communicate: something isn't right here.
o  **Windel (Diaper):** I find it really nice that you said that now. Do you know what I liked the most? That you said, »that became a pleasure.« That makes me happy

*»Although, yes, the pleasure, in puberty, it was related to women who wet themselves. That is a desire that actually scares me. The desire is dangerous for me at that point.«*

o  **Einnässen (Wetting):** I would like to know more about how you feel pleasure.
o  **Ich (I):** I had really intense jaw pain for a long time before you told me that. And I felt like I couldn't speak, I had no words. But when you told me that, it kind of loosened up a bit. And with that dangerous pleasure, there was an instant connection to my pelvis. It feels so trapped. And that shouldn't be. It's also a sexuality issue. And I have to hold something back there. It feels older.

*»I'm only asking because I was born in the 1980s with a cesarean section. Because I was lying upside down in there. You also mentioned sexuality...*

o  **Windel (Diaper):** See, I was already wrong back then. Who says I'm wrong? I don't want anyone to judge me. Who says what is the right way around?
o  **Einnässen (Wetting):** I feel the need. I want to be at my mom's chest. I have a strong need to drink something.
o  **Ich (I):** I feel like I can't let anything out about it. I feel the interaction between the pelvis and jaw and that shouldn't be talked about.
o  **Einnässen (Wetting):** When you asked if we were at birth, I could deny that. I believe I'm at the age where I'm becoming clean. That

248

I grew up very quickly. That maybe I didn't really live out this phase. And I really want to be with my mom. Sorry if I say that again.

o **Ich (I):** I feel so uptight. As if I had to hold back something really bad.

o **Windel (Diaper):** Would you like to really poop in your diaper? And feel how nice and warm and mushy it is? Well, I find it nice.

o **Einnässen (Wetting):** Yes. I feel it right in my stomach, in my bladder, that I have to hold it all back.

o **Ich (I):** I don't even feel it anymore. For me, it's all in my head. I don't want to let it out. I don't want to let it out.

*We are also adding the words "verklemmt" (repressed) and "?" to it.*

**verklemmt (repressed)**

»I am currently experiencing physical sensations. But it's not in my pelvis, it's here [center of my chest]. It feels like someone is pushing into me. Oh! Help! And I'm hunching over in my upper body. I can't breathe! Heavens! It's as if I were lying on the changing table and then... [mimics the motion of a fist pressing down on the infant's chest from above] I am you, I am small, I am a baby, I am lying on the changing table. And then someone comes and forcefully presses down on me here... I can barely catch my breath! I can hardly speak anymore.«

*»I haven't been told anything about a story of violence. What I can remember is that my father tried to put me in the trash can in the basement. And my mother said he's like a tyrant. That affected him greatly and he remembered that, even after his heart attack. What I also know: As a child, I was so headstrong that I had to be locked in my room.«*

o **verklemmt (repressed):** Sure, they don't talk about violence, that's clear! It's logical. You know, I have the feeling that there is violence. I don't know from whom, but there is violence towards me.

o **Einnässen (Wetting):** I believe, "verklemmt" (repressed), that we were subjected to this. That someone tried forcefully to push into our chest. I'm in full alert mode. Frozen. Terrified and trying to calm myself down.

o **Ich (I):** I have my hands folded in front of my genital area. I feel like I need to protect it. No one should touch it. I must protect it.
o **?:** I feel guilty that "repressed" is doing so badly. I am male. What do you know about your grandpa? I feel pretty old.

*»Maternal side or paternal side? I never met my grandfather on my father's side. He died at 50 and was never present. My father didn't know him either. My father grew up as an orphan with his brother and then found out that he had passed away. My father must have also experienced severe violence. Kneeling on wooden logs, he practically grew up in a barn with his brother. I did meet my maternal grandfather. However, he was not present as a man. He was a teacher, I believe a Latin teacher. My grandmother always used to say, "Georg, put your foot down." That was the catchphrase in the family.«*

o **?:** I perceive myself as a man, a bit chubby, a little older, with red cheeks. Holding a bony stick. Like a hunter. A typical manly figure, I would say. I am not kind. I hold very old-fashioned views about men and women. And somehow, I have power. I would like to have someone bold, so that I can give them a good thrashing with the stick. But when you all sit there in suffering, then I cannot exert my power.
o **Ich (I):** Before the "?" came, I had this image of war in my pelvis. Two factions, male, warring against each other. Even with weapons. That something would be at war in the pelvis.

*»I have an association: My grandpa was in Stalingrad and came out on the last plane. He was so injured that they probably didn't need to fly him out, because he was only injured on his finger. From history class, I know he came out on one of the last planes. "Einnässen" (Wetting) has gone completely silent«*

**Einnässen (Wetting)**
»So, I am appalled. When you talked about the first grandpa, I felt a chill down my spine. And with the second grandpa, I completely shut down. Somehow, I'm feeling quite different now. I'm sitting here with

250

my hand protectively over my genital area. And I have to look at the word "Einnässen" (Wetting) the whole time.«

**?**
»I feel like I have the power... If someone were uptight or gay, I would beat it out of their head with my club!! I will ensure law and order. That is, law and order so that no one has a different disposition. I would beat it out of them with my club! I am older than your father. Maybe a grandpa? Like a sturdy man from Bavaria. And I'm telling you, I know the way!"«

o **Ich (I):** I also feel really sick. Like I'm about to puke any moment.
o **verklemmt (repressed):** Just the word »discipline«…

*»No matter where you look in the family, discipline and order were always a topic. It was a topic with my grandma's sister. Also, with my uncle. That would make sense, because he was so corpulent as well«*

o **verklemmt (repressed):** Also, in my body, there is so much experience of violence! As small as I am, but so much violence. With "Ich" (I) and "Einnässen" (Wetting), it's all further down in the body. Very concrete physical violence. It left me speechless when you spoke about the orphanage and father. It all mixes together. There's violence, violence, violence. It's so crazy. Man-to-man violence. Really intense.
o **Einnässen (Wetting):** This violence, this anger that I feel, it's directed at masculinity. It goes into the hips, into the lower area. That makes me think of being gay. Violence against the masculine. Against male love.
o **?:** I tell you, I'll beat you out with the club!
o **Einnässen (Wetting):** There's homophobia. I don't feel gay. I feel like this has nothing to do with me. This is what grandpa experienced. Tell me about the concept of manhood in your family.

*»Driving out with the cudgel, when talking about being gay, or other kinds of sexuality, or other ways, that I can attribute to my parents. The male image was very classic. I would now say: Working until you*

251

*collapse, until death. Not taking much care of others. A kind of patriarchy. As one knows it from the mafia. Care only on a material level.«*

o **verklemmt (repressed):** Well, I'm listening to you with great interest, but I have the feeling that you are avoiding the real issue. It's like you're always skirting around what it's really about. They filled you with all sorts of pseudo stories so that the truth wouldn't surface.
o **?:** And what if I had been gay as a grandpa and wanted to drive that out of others? That I don't want to admit it? That I fight against what I can't allow in myself externally?

*»I could sign that. He was married. He was around 20 years old when he was drafted into the war. He and his wife had met through an advertisement. He was not a man in the traditional sense. And he did not love his wife.«*

**?**

»I act overly masculine and judge in others what is within me. Your parents completely crossed your boundaries the whole time. They used you as an object. Decided for you and didn't perceive you as a human being. And certainly not as a child«

**verklemmt (repressed)**
»Let go of the thinking. Something is coming out and you are like a deflector shield. There is so much there and I am slowly realizing how I am getting into it. Masculinity, sexuality. There is something completely surreal happening in the background. I feel like I am the buffer between "Ich" (I) and "?". The body that takes all this crap, all the stuff. And I have to deal with it. And that drives me nearly insane. Because there is so much violence coming in! Like I have to cushion tons of things. I am just enduring and in distress.«

**Einnässen (Wetting)**
»I am currently stuck on the phrase »Feelings are for gays«. And then the fantasy came up, what did grandpa get up to in the war! I notice very clearly, it's about feelings that shouldn't be there. ""Einnässen"

252

(Wetting) is for girls, and I am doing it now! I'll show you guys!" Rebellion. But when you talked about the "?", that's when the headaches come, that's when the anger comes. Our parents are really crazy! Now I am getting really angry. The anger arises that dad wanted to throw us in the trash can! I feel like garbage. Mom didn't react appropriately. That makes me really angry.«

**Ich (I)**
»I also notice here that I am not quite masculine. And I also notice, as soon as the "?" comes with the stick... I don't even want to hear it properly at first. And that makes me furious. I feel good as not masculine. I want to be soft, playful. I want to show emotions. But then someone comes with the stick and I lose it. I split myself there. I don't even hear what you are saying about this violence. As soon as the violence comes, I disconnect and I am far away in space. I am there with "Einnässen" (Wetting). I also physically sense that. And don't know anymore what I am. I'm not sure if I'm a boy or a girl. More like a tomboy, a feminine man. Who really likes himself the way he is. And this war in the pelvis would also fit in. That these two components are fighting each other.«

# 5.4 TONSILS

*Self-encounter (Woman, Ireland, 3 words)*
*I – want – tonsils*

*»I was born two weeks before a baby died. I was conceived to replace her. Because she was a breach birth and she was always going to die. They were waiting for her to die. My parents were numb. I grew up in a family of numbness and grief. It seems that I put expectations also on myself. When I look at "tonsils", I feel scared. Scared of losing a part of myself. My mother had OCD[60]. It was all about clean and dirty.*

---

[60] OCD = Obsessive-Compulsive Disorder

*Anything which comes out of the body is shameful. I wonder if "tonsils" where told to be dirty.«*

**I**

»I needed to prepare myself. Just to have everything arranged on the table. But then a wave of coldness came. I am shaking. And I am in fear. I want to be present but if I look at "want" and "tonsils", I am losing my connection with what I am feeling. I will not bend my head. I feel abandoned in a way. It was terrifying. I thought I would be dying and nobody was there. All these strangers. I feel a relief when I am telling you about that. When you are talking with me, I feel so happy and less lonely and less scared. I feel warmth when I am looking at you. I am here and available to connect. For a moment I felt seen. Connection is the most precious. I really want to be with you. It was shit but we are not there anymore. Thank God, we are not there anymore!

I am in a child state where I want to play. And finally, maybe, we might have space to do our own things now. But at the same time, I don't want to deny "tonsils" or "want". Because it feels that some parts of us are still blocked there. I am starting to be an adult. It is like up and down. I want to be here as well for you and for them. We are brave. I feel very grateful that we are doing this together. But I don't want to push anything.«

**want**

»I feel... not myself. Your "want" has left you in the hands of the medical care and they know what they are doing. I am looking at a picture of the family over there and I am going to go to my family. Because the medics know what they are doing. This is the "want" of your mother! Of course, it is what your mother wanted.«

**tonsils**

»I am a bit dissociated. I was a bit unclear that the process had begun. I think I might be at the moment of anesthesia. It is a bit blurry. I can feel my tonsils and I can also feel a taste of something. I have no pain or discomfort. I have a kind of blurriness... Was your mother anesthetized when you were born?«

*»Very possibly. She may also have had her tonsils out. I am not sure. She was very ill when she was very young. She told me that she almost died. She got antibiotics that saved her life. Around the same age as me. I remember the anesthetic.«*

**tonsils**

»I am less interested in what happened to your mother. I am more interested what happened to you. In this resonance, I still have my tonsils. This is pre-incision. Even if we were anesthetized it was so traumatic. It is the weirdest experience, both being anesthetized and still having some awareness in your psyche. It is not good. I am not in a very good state. The level of expectation that I have to be different of what I am right now. But this is how I am right now.«

**I**

»It touched me deeply when "tonsils" were telling about the expectations. Even a part of me is expecting to get over it in a way. It was only a moment. What "want" or "tonsils" were saying was true for me. I feel the bitterness, the metal taste in my mouth. This substance is not new for our body. We kind of had it before. Maybe when we were at the process of birth? Maybe mom experienced it as well? It is not new for us. And then when "tonsils" were talking, I literally felt like I am out of my body. And the experience is – am I dying right now? Is this death? Because it is unbearable how they were cutting through a part of me. So much anger arises! If I would have the power, I would want to shake them and shout: "Get out of me! Don't touch me." "So, what if it hurts?" "But it is mine!" It is so painful. The decision is made. It feels like I am dying. At the same time, I have a clear mind that I am not dying. Thank god. I exist. I am alive. And it is in the past. And I am here. And I want to play with "want" and "tonsils".«

**want**

»I can't talk. I am very young. There is no one here. I am playing with my hands. I want to clap. I want ice cream! I want ice cream. I scream! I scream! I want ice cream. I scream. Ice cream! You are not listening to what your "want" wants. Ice cream & I scream. I scream – and ice cream to eat. And no one is listening to what I want! I don't know what age I am. It is a bit fuzzy in my head. I have to figure it out myself. It is a big question and I am afraid I get it wrong. I really don't know what to say because I don't have many words. But I know what ice cream looks like. And I want to scream.«

»I was promised ice cream after. The nurse promised it. Oh, don't worry, you will get ice cream.«

**I**

»Can I punch that nurse!? I don't want the "tonsils" out. I want to shout: "Ahhh!!!! I don't want them out! They are mine! They are mine." And I want ice cream as well and don't want the "tonsils" out! I am so scared. I am so petrified! I want to punch and kick and scream. Ahh!!!! Let's punch the nurse. Let's do something. I can't do it by myself. When you were talking, I felt so alone. We were so alone for so long... Even before that. I feel so sad. They never listen to us. They are doing something to my throat. So, I can't scream. It was so scary. It was always like this with us. They were never there with us. And Mom was never there with us and even before the "tonsils" came out. We were so alone. It's hurting. It is hurting. I want to punch.«

o  **want:** I want my mommy! I want my mommy! I want my mommy. I WANT MY MOMMY. Mommy! I want my mommy.
o  **I:** She is nowhere. Why did she leave me? It is like we don't exist. We were never seen. It is like... are we even alive? Or are we dead like "tonsils"? Where is mommy? She never was here. Even before the "tonsils". Am I to blame? But then, do I exist? I am not dead? I want my mommy. And I want...I am hungry too!
o  **tonsils:** I have to come out of resonance to speak because I am very dissociated. I can hear the distress in "want" and "I". I am not able to feel. I've been noticing, how you speak to your parts and how it feels like there is another part of you who can be softer and warmer to us. It is quite hard to say this to you. Like I said something taboo. I want to see you. There is another demand from you to be different than what I am.
o  **I:** All the time we took care of ourselves, we didn't have anybody to take care of ourselves, to attend our needs. And it brings me so

256

much sadness. But I am happy to see "want". It is the ice cream that I want. I feel I am between this and a deep sadness and the will to shout how painful it is to be so lonely. But I want ice cream. At least a little bit of pleasure. Chocolate. One of my favorites. Can I shout? You will not be scared, "want"? I really want to scream.

o **want:** I want to shout louder but I don't think I am allowed.
o **I:** I am here. Can you see me? Now it feels like I can shout so badly. Can we shout? What stops us to shout? I really want you to shout? You are not afraid if I shout? I want you to shout. Do you really want to shout? I don't want to push anything. But I have this deep need to be released.

**tonsils**
»I don't feel like your mother. I feel like a cut-off of you that is really hard for you to see. When we were born, either we tried to shout and we got muffled or… I am actually wondering when we were able to vocalize. Something happened there.«

»I don't feel a scream in me. I don't feel it. I have been terrified of my mother. I am scared that we really have to defend ourselves that we exist. The level of terror is huge. I have gonne into that place and collapsed.«

o **want:** I am an adult now. I feel my psyche is in my 30s, 40s. I am evolving and evolving. And I feel grounded and connected and I can take in the "I", the younger "I", with a lot of compassion.
o **I:** I know that we are doing a process but I really want to go to the toilette. If it is okay? I am coming back.
o **want:** I feel a lot of fear. I am hoping that "I" will return.
o **I** [returns and smiles]: It feels like the child in me! »I am allowed to feel needs.« I can do whatever I want. I released myself! I have needs. It was so good that I could go to the toilette. It is important to listen to your needs. We can do this. Nobody is stopping us or terrifying us anymore.
o **tonsils:** I have a lot of contact with you. I have so much sense of what you experienced. How difficult it was to "want" and even feel.

There was a big difference when you felt it and said it – puh, here I am! This made a big, big difference.
o **I:** I did a wee and nobody punished me! I am very happy. Was the mother beating us when we had accidents?

**I**

»She was so cruel. I just wanted her to love me. All I was for her was dirt! Not only dirt. When I am looking at "want" and "tonsils", I feel less alone. We can talk about and feel that we can express what we need. I do exist. I have a nose. And two eyes. Look at us, we have glasses! I love this.«

## 5.6 BRUXISM (TEETH GRINDING)

*Self-encounter (Man, Germany, 2 words)*
*I – bruxism (teeth grinding)*

Since his youth, the man has been grinding his teeth. Today, he is in his forties. Especially when he suppresses his anger, he starts grinding his teeth. But the question arises, what else is he holding back? "Bruxism" says tot hat:

»Oh, now I understand something! The moment I show up, you need sleep, change or rest. So, I can be like a slight symptom. Not very dominating but reminding you of something. But it is time to change the attitude. The attitude towards yourself; and then attitude towards others also. Your daughter especially.«

**I**

»I've got a weird feeling in my shoulder blades. I feel quite young but can't quite determine an age at the moment. I start to feel a bit anxiety, feel stuck and I keep forgetting to breath. I am very aware of my environment. Yeah, it feels important to know my environment, to see my environment, to know what's in my environment and to know where things are in my environment. That makes me feel a bit anxious as well. There is a person that stood in the doorway. I think the person male. I am quite small and I am playing or doing something on the floor. When I see that person, I forget to breath and I start to freeze a little bit. I don't know what to do about this presence. I feel like I should be doing something but I don't know what I should be doing. There is a sense of – am I overthinking something? There is a demand and I don't know how to meet the demand. I am too small, I am too young. The demand isn't clear, it isn't explicit. I scan and I check. It is almost like the silence is dangerous. It is like a landmine. This is how it feels. It feels really uncertain. There is something that could change the behavior of this person very quickly. But I don't know what behavior I should solicit in order to maintain or manage this person. I don't want to do this but this is what I have to do.«

**bruxism**
»The first thought was: That will be my show for a while here. [laughing] Now I am watching your "I".«

*»I don't really know if "bruxism" is a part of me, connected to me or something causing danger or making the "I" feel in danger. I want to connect with "I" but also feel responsible for "bruxism". I don't remember a lot from my first years of childhood. My memory starts with my school years. During the first three years of my childhood, I just remember a little bit during the time I was in Kindergarten. Not so much emotional memory but I remember situations. My dad was not available. I needed his help, his support. I felt anxious, anger when I realized that he wasn't there for me. But was he scary? Is he my dad? My granddad? Who is that male person that you are afraid of? Do you feel responsible to make him happy?«*

**I** [via chat-function only]
»He is scary. I feel invisible and can't keep him happy. I feel scared when you talk about dad and grandfather. I feel connected to you. I felt scared when "bruxism" laughed at me. I had to go in order to feel safe. My heart is pounding and I feel really anxious. And I also feel, I don't know how to make "bruxism" happy. This just feels too much for me. So, I stay here to kind of keep myself safe. But I feel connected to you. I feel quite young, like two or three years old. There is a lot of

259

responsibility on a very small child. And I don't know how to do that. I need to know whether "bruxism" is safe for me. And then I can determine whether I can come back.«

**bruxism**
»I am quite patient and I am waiting. I don't have any bad intention. And I don't want to be scary. But I have things to say. And I have a place here. And this is what I am instilling. I was going to say that but then "I" disappeared. I am looking at you and I feel like taking care of you. I am inclined to feel more like a feminine energy rather than masculine.

I am like a condition. I want to give you a message that you have to grow up fast. I have seen your "I". You cannot be so hyper-sensitive like a flower. Be a man! Gather yourself! Be tough! There is no place for so sensitive beings. Come on! What kind of world you are living in!? I feel like a trainer. I am tough. I can be tough. I don't mean harming. I feel like I am doing this for your good. Sometimes trainers are beating their athletes for good. You cannot be weak! You can NOT be weak! Get that! Fast! Clear? Okay. If you convince me, maybe I step back.«

*»Funnily, I remember now how I was talking to my daughter. "She has to grow up fast, taking responsibility, blah blah blah." No time to be a child. Not in the context of sensitivity. So, this must have been something that I have experienced myself when I was very young? Thinking of that age, it feels like a mixture of both parents: My father was also very sensitive. More female than male. Not being available in a sense of taking care, protecting me. And the other, the crazy part, the trainer part, is my Moms' part. There is not space for sensitive men. Basically, I feel very insecure in the communication with "bruxism". I feel a strongly attached to "I". To protect I".*

*My grandfather was potentially abusing my Mom where I was the result of. I didn't know him personally. Maybe I was 2, 2 ½ years when my grandfather died. My parents then moved to a different city. My Mom wanted to forget and leave everything behind that remembered her of the past. I remember my grandfather from a picture. He was a master pastery chef (=Konditormeister), baking cakes in a coffee shop.*

260

*He was always baking things for me. Towards me, he was a loving grandfather. But the role between my mother and grandfather was oppressive. In the sense of, he had power of her or something. I have a picture that I was just looking at two days ago: I am playing a shop owner, and on the one side, down on the floor, my mother is looking at me. And on the other side was my grandfather holding me. I was standing in the middle, playing with the telephone. And I had the feeling that I had the role of communicating between the two.*

*I am in the middle of figuring out who I am and what I need. When my grandfather died, he wasn't available for me anymore and my dad stepped into the role. But could never fulfilled it.«*

**bruxism**

»When you mentioned the way that you were treating your daughter, for a moment, I felt that I could take the role of being your daughter. Now, I feel and I see you in a different way. What you said about your daughter, energetically, it was clear to me. But what you said about mother and grandfather, energetically, it was not so clear. I felt closer to the story of your daughter. I feel smaller now. I am depending on you somehow. I can disappear now but at times I can come back. Do you want me to go?«

**I** [cames back]

»I felt quite scared of you when you spoke to your daughter this way. I felt shocked. In this" I", I don't feel that I could do that because I am so small and young. I feel a little bit safer with "bruxism" now. I actually think that I got a little bit older and I feel a little bit angry. A bit frustrated almost. There is so much! I have to be like this and I have to be like that! Wow! And this is really frustrating. And I am I. I just want to be I! That's it! The rest of it feels too much. I feel connected to you. This is my purpose. And I can do this anywhere. I need you. The rest is a distraction and it is quite overwhelming. I just need you to see that I am here and want me. And yeah, we are sensitive. And this is okay. We are sensitive. And it is absolutely fine!

*»Do you think "bruxism" had a more important role for us when we are younger? Or scared us more when we were younger?«*

- **I:** Yeah! Definitely! I am not mean or cruel. But if I have to become mean and cruel if I am not me. Then I am something else. This doesn't feel like a weakness. I certainly don't feel weak.
- **bruxism:** Oh, now I understand something! The moment I show up, you need sleep, change or rest. So, I can be like a slight symptom. Not very dominating but reminding you of something. But it is time to change the attitude. The attitude towards yourself; and then attitude towards others also. Your daughter especially. I feel a bit softer here.
- **I:** I don't need reminding about my attitude. If I got you that is all I need. I just need a good consistent connection with you. There was an attempt to emulate cruelty. Because this is what we had to do. But this is not where we are now! But it resonates also what "bruxism" said: When we don't take care of ourselves, we merge into that space when we can be cruel to ourselves. And this doesn't feel safe. And we become disconnected.

*»Am I putting some pressure on myself? Probably. I am making good experiences of being gentle, lovely, connected with others. But there is still some pressure – I don't know what this is. This pressure in the shoulder. It got lighter. It is about expressing our needs.«*

**I**

»Definitely. I want to feel safe before I want to say something. It is not always possible. And when I use my voice it has the opposite effect. But it doesn't make it wrong. I am interpreted as weak because I don't speak aggressively or cruel. We are not deliberately upsetting people if we allow other people to upset us. This is the destabilization. I'll give anything up to keep that situation happy! But this is useless. I need to be able to say: "Stop, no, I don't like this, this is not for me, I don't agree." So that I can get where I want to go. It is a privilege that I didn't have. I can stay connected with you when you express your needs, your wants. Let's be honest: We can't negotiate how other people interpret it. That seems a bit nuts to me. Can you say no? Or do you try to be overly nice?

262

*»Sometimes yes, sometimes no. In relationships it is more difficult for me. Because I am often adapting, being in this scanning state, and trying to overlook and foresee everything. And trying to be nice. And when I do something out of my own need, the other person in that relationship is then confronted with their own feeling. And then I try to step back and lower my energy. But that doesn't feel right.«*

**I**

»I don't then feel connected to you when you do that. I am allowed to exist in this world how I am. Unfiltered. I don't need the world to approve of me. I need you to approve of me. Do you then take responsibility when something doesn't work? Thinking it's your fault? So, if they are emotional or triggered by maybe something that we said that is still not ours. It is okay for them to be upset and sad. But what is difficult for me is, when you are trying to convince somebody that they are triggered. Then you go away from me. I don't have to take on board their perspective. I can just see it for what it is and let it be. And I don't have to filter myself. Because it is too much to constantly filter. This is what "bruxism" said. That is your marker.«

I said to the man: *»It is very valuable to recognize that you didn't have a safe environment when you were little. You didn't learn it. You don't know how it works, this interconnection. You try and then you retract. And then you try again. But you never find the right balance for you. And this is when you cringe your teeth. It is also important to recognize: "I do not have the answers." Especially not in my head. "My mind can never produce the answers and I can never learn them from a book." It is about staying in your body. Only there you can feel your "I".«*

*»In the past, I have mostly trusted the thoughts and the connections that I made in my mind. Trying to observe everything. And now I am learning much more to get into my body, and trusting my feelings, listening to them and trusting what my body is telling me. But it is like learning a completely new language without having any books or anybody telling me how this language is being spoken. Learning by doing.«*

263

**I**

»When Natalie says that I feel more relaxed! You need to be in your body so that I can resonate with you. I really feel that. The other thing is – breathing feels very relevant. When you are in your head, I don't breathe properly. And I want to breath. I want to feel my lungs and my belly and in my body. Not temporarily but all the time. And I don't want to control myself. I just want to breath. Just moving naturally. This would feel helpful to me. Just breathing. Breath regularly, deeply. We couldn't fix our parents. We couldn't fix our marriage. We can't fix anyone else. This is our self-care.«

## 5.5 MENSTRUAL CRAMPS

*Generic-encounter (4 words)*
*girl – menstrual – cramps – ?*

Most women are familiar with menstrual cramps. Some experience them during puberty, while others have them throughout their lives and only see them vanish during menopause. Some only feel pain at the beginning of their period, while others suffer from intense pain throughout the entire cycle. I, too, had unbearable menstrual cramps in my youth, spending nights in the bathroom, curled up in pain, repeatedly tormented by intense waves. But why should the most natural thing in the world be accompanied by cramps? Why must so many girls and women suffer during this time?

**menstrual**

»I have something in my throat. Little bit of aching. And I have the impression there is something I can't speak about. When I look at "cramps" there is something which wants to get out but it is not possible. I have the feeling I am in the birth channel. Completely contracted. And I can't breathe. And I am stuck there. Maybe I don't have connections to my feelings? I have the impression, when I look at my picture, I saw the mother in my face. It feels like I would be possessed by something so powerful, dominant that I can't do anything against it. I can only sit here and go through it. It's horrible.«

**cramps**

»I cannot move. When I look at "girl" I feel pain in my back. I don't understand what "menstrual" is saying. I pay attention but I don't understand. I look at "menstrual" and I see her being sad. I feel someone is pushing me and suppressing me. And I feel I like am going down more and more.«

**?**

»Something feels really bad here but I just don't know what it is. I don't feel cramps, I don't feel any problems but I am not getting any air. And I sometimes have difficulties to hear you or to see you. It is like someone would suffocate me. I had a little bit of hope when you, "menstrual", talked about birth – that could be a clue… Everything is just so confusing! Being female doesn't feel good. It's just heavy, it's depressing, its lonely, its checked-out, it is giving up. Hopeless. I mean, shouldn't it be, when you get your period as a girl, shouldn't it be something to celebrate? It is also a period of change, something new. But here it just feels as if life would be over already! And it hasn't even started!«

○ **menstrual:** I have the impression, I have the hope, when I look at "girl" that she solves the problem. Sorry, that I say that but I have the hope that you are the key. I don't think the key is the woman.
○ **girl:** I want to hear stories. I want mothers to tell me stories. How this started and why and when. What happened first? The source of this. It is a weird situation. I have not done anything to deserve this. I didn't do anything. Why does this happen to me?
○ **?:** You are right. There is something missing. Maybe I would call it an initiation process. I have the feeling it is not only that. Curse, the word curse, still resonates with me.

- o **menstrual:** There is no reason why it happened to you. It is because our mother and grandmother and every woman before didn't solve the problem. That's why. That's the reason why we get cramps.
- o **girl:** They were talking about first woman and first man and what they did and how they have been punished. Is it because of that?
- o **?:** You mean Adam and Eve in Paradise?
- o **girl:** Yeah, they ate an apple and Eve, I don't know what she did, she offered an apple. She convinced a man to have this apple. And they were fired out of the heaven. And they have to deal with all that anguish of being on the earth. Isn't it because of this?

*Adding another word, "women".*

**menstrual**

»I also find the question of where it starts very interesting and important; but it is repetitive. I have the feeling like I lost my purpose of who I am. I am "menstrual" and I am something natural. I am because there is no baby on the way. Nature, I am very close to nature. Something rhythmic. But in the stage "women" is, I lost my purpose and power and I don't know any more who I am.«

**girl**

»Nature is playfulness. And when there is menstruation, I cannot play. I cannot enjoy myself.«

**cramps**

»We are disconnected, me and "girl". And I really like "women". I like the colors of "women". It is good for me when "menstrual" is laughing. It is good if she laughs and smiles. I see light.«

**?**

»I feel now a bit better as "women" is here. And hopeful. This is interesting what you said, "cramps": It is the color that I am missing here. The color is the vibrance, life, vibrant life... I have the feeling that life is kind of sucked out of female, woman... of this gender. When you talked about nature, it almost suffocates me. Like nature is suppressed here. The nature of a woman, of a girl, of a female, of this gender is super super suppressed. The natural, nature, has been sucked out of it.«

**women**

»I feel I got cramps. And what comes up is, how is this a problem? It feels normal and we have to get on with it. We have to find an ebon flow with it. But something is irritating me. I could go through the range of emotions very quickly – from anger, to sadness, to frustration, to pain, to cramp. Like a wash machine. And it's interesting that as "women", I come in last. But we need a woman to start it. You need to be a woman to create a girl. I can feel "cramps". It feels like I am on my period. I am drawn to this yellow color here. I am gravitating towards more and more color.«

- ○ **girl:** Who else is bleeding in nature like that? Which animal?
- ○ **women:** I wanna say dogs. Female dogs do it. That's the only animal I can think off. Female dogs who are not muted bleed every three months.
- ○ **girl:** Much better. They are luckier than me.
- ○ **?** [laughs]: Yeah! That's true!

**women**

»We get no compassion for it. We get no love for it. We get no time for it. And it is getting more and more oppressive as I sit here. I can really feel the oppression of being female and having a menstrual cycle. I am not allowed to talk about it. I am meant to endure it instead of loving myself for it. I am not allowed to get angry. I am not allowed to cry. And if I do it, it is inconvenient. I do it on my own. Quietly. I am not allowed to smell differently. I feel like this is work. This is a form of endurance. Because even if I am in a job, I still have to do this around every environment. And they don't want to except that this is even there. And they mock it.

There is a big no! Now I feel like I get the same no from my own mother. My own mother would say no to me discussing my period openly around anyone. Its dirty. And I feel, this [red cloth] doesn't represent my blood; this represents my anger. There is something, when you talk about sexuality, that shifts something. I can meet the same intolerance from women as I can meet from men. My mother would say: "Don't discuss it." If I go to a teacher, a teacher would be like "sh…". There is nowhere I can go where it isn't mocked, ridiculed or dismissed. Or belittled, you know.

And in that, it is interesting, "cramps" start to build up. It is almost like I need to remind myself that this is part of nature. My body, my physical nature. And I need it. But I can't go anywhere with it. I can't support myself. It doesn't feel wrong, it's just feels that "cramps" are something that makes me part of being a woman. Because I see "cramps" as part of child birth as well. It reminds me, okay, I am here. This is part of my femininity. But I can't go anywhere with this reality.«


?

»And we are not even talking about sexuality. Problem is that it has a big impact on the sexuality as well. Everything is just constraint and oppressed and boxed in! Its treated like a secret and not like nature. Nature is sucked out of it. Women took it over from men and from society. I have the impression that this kind of world is going against female nature. I liked you, "cramps". When you were standing, your T-shirt said "the star". And I was thinking, this is what we should be. The star. We should be shining like the stars. And sparkling like stars. But here, we are depressed, in black and white.«


**menstrual**

»I can also feel it. I have goosebumps all over my body. I totally agree with what you said. I have the thought that I want to celebrate my "menstrual". Something like "?" said, like an initiation. To become a woman. To celebrate that I can make babies. It is a wonder! But I have to hide it. I even have to hide it from myself. It is something technical, something functional. And to behave like it is nothing and go on. It is frightening me. I am very cold. It is because it's a man's world. It's a man's world. And it doesn't fit to a woman's needs. And nature. I have the impression that I am a part of the nature and the femininity.«

**cramps**

»I feel like I don't understand everything. And I can't speak like you speak. And I feel like I don't want you to think that someone took something from woman or "women" or "girl". Instead, we are receiving something. For me, it is important that "menstrual" is happy. When you speak, there is this yellow color around your [Zoom] window. I am not bad. I am good. I don't want to be pushed down anymore.«

○ **menstrual:** I totally understand you. The indigenous tribes, they celebrate the menstrual period and to become a woman. That makes me sad because in our countries we are treating women like…
○ **cramps:** When a girl gets her menstrual period, it is like a weight. It shouldn't be like this. Because I like "menstrual" so much! [laughs] For me it is really necessary that you smile and are happy.
○ **menstrual:** I like "cramps" as well. When you speak, I can breathe. When you talk about being happy and smiling, I can see that this is my nature. But I am confused because I can't feel it anymore. It is suppressed.

**girl**

»"cramps" is like a teacher which I simply cannot connect to. And because no one is giving me an answer, I looked at books and researched a bit. And in the religious books they say that you bleed every month because you don't get pregnant. And it's a punishment of not getting pregnant. You are punished as a woman for loosing that potential life. And your uterus is crying with bloody tears of not having a baby! This is what religious people are saying! If you get pregnant, you have cramps when you are giving birth. So, in any case women have "cramps". You don't get it. I will have serious issues with God!«

- **?:** Oh God! [taking her smartphone and hitting her head against it]
- **cramps:** To get pregnant is not a guilt of "menstrual". It is when two people have sex…
- **girl:** You don't understand. In both of these two options I will be in "cramps".
- **menstrual:** I am getting very hot now and I can feel that this is not true. But I don't know what my purpose is. But what religious people are saying is not true.
- **?:** No, definitely not! Oh, I was feeling so good before but that just pulled me back, this religious shit. Sorry to say that.

**women**

»I think we need to burn the books. I feel, when I hear "girl" speak, I feel this is when we start to oppress, to manipulate what a cycle really is. So, when you come into womanhood you are already problematic. Like an indoctrination which comes from somewhere that you have you be taught. It is not about listening to your body. It is not about the taking the natural cycle of your own body. This is a projection of what somebody perceives happening to your body. So, where do I go as a woman if I have this believe that's taught to me as a child? And I am not allowed to follow my body or attract my own natural response in my body?«

- **?:** I was thinking about what you, "girl", said in the beginning. Of Paradise and Adam and Eve. Well, Eve, she is a sinner. Isn't she?
- **girl:** She got punished to have pain when you have children. And when you don't have children, you bleed every month. She is punished heavier than Adam is! This is very important! She is a bigger sinner because she seduced Adam to ate this apple.
- **?:** It is so wrong!! I can feel it in my body! I can't get it out of my mouth/throat! I don't know how to get it out of the system. It's awful!

**menstrual**

»I agree with you. I can connect with this. I don't know where it started but it's a story. I have the picture of the natural people in my mind; all the time. When "women" have their "menstrual" they go for several days on their own, perhaps away from the tribe. And they bleed for themselves. And it's open. There is no tampon. They don't suppress it. They just let it go. Something very natural and free. And they bleed in the sand. They make a whole and bleed and give it to the earth. It's like a ceremony. I get goosebumps when I talk about it. I give it back to earth. And the ceremony is to celebrate the "menstrual". That's what I want to.«

**girl**

»Can I ask a question, "menstrual"? Because I am in the age of questioning everything. And I also studied biology, physiology and I try to understand. It's a human body and it eliminates. We eliminate every day our poo and we pee. This is elimination, right? It's okay. But it's easy. It's not problematic. Menstrual blood is also an elimination process. I am okay with that. But why is it so difficult? And it lasts seven days? It is one quarter of your time, of your life! You have four weeks in a month and one out of these four weeks you are dealing with this elimination? And God, if he wanted, can make it much easier. I am still okay to eliminate blood. Okay. But why is it not compressed like poo for example? Why is it not blood clots compressed and in a different shape and you just once a day? I am okay to eliminate but why it is like torture? Constantly all my attention is there! Seven days! It is hard for me to agree. For me, it is still like a punishment. It is too much. "God, make it easier. I want to bleed but make it easier. As a function, as a physiology. You can do it! Small particle clots, datatatat. Easy." This is my childish mind. Why God cannot be creative, making things easier? That how I think. No one can answer it. I have a problem with God.«

**women**

»As women, it is interesting when you, "?", say it's too often, it's too long. In the context of this world that's is what we can't handle anymore. If you hold it and if you nurture it, does it have to be such a prolonged agony where we are against ourselves? Because if you look at it the other way, your way, everything is against us. Can't it be just a natural state that is gently, compassionately, lovingly, tenderly and made space for? If you falter that into today's world, forget it. It's not going quick enough, it's inconvenient, it's a trouble, it's irritant. I am an irritant to myself. What comes up now if I go down the generations, women tend to be the creatures that preserved the home. There is something of what you said, "menstrual", that made me kind of going "oh, okay". And in this resonance, I feel it's like women against men. Is there a male energy here?«

**?**

»Now I feel again a bit better. But we, as females, are living completely against our nature. And "cramps" are a reminder that we should go back to our nature. It is the way we live, it is the way we dress, it's the way we think, it's the way we work, it's the way we interact. All of that – and more – is against our nature. There should be more playfulness and laughing and enjoying.«

○ **cramps:** I would like to say that every time I see "women" putting on more clothes, I want her to take them off! It is like she is suppressed. She is pushing herself down.
○ **menstrual:** What also comes to my mind is that it takes time. A few days. We are close to nature with our menstrual. Because life is like spring, summer, autumn and winter. This is the cycle of life. And this is what we are going through every month. We create life and life is also going. That's why we are here.
○ **women:** Life should be slower! We preserve our own life if we are gentle with it, don't we? We preserve our femininity. Our purpose is also to preserve life. If we create a baby we still have to produce the milk. We still have to preserve life. We have to take care of

ourselves to be able to keep another human being going. That cycle is equally important.

o **menstrual:** For me it is very important to say that "women" is also listening to me. Listens to her own period and rhythms. I find it very good that we are here together to find a solution.


**?**

»For me, I feel for the first time a connection. A connection between all of us. Because there is no answer coming to us on a silver plate. We really have to find out what it is to be a female. But the way we are living right now is not natural. I think also that it is natural to be sexy. There is nothing to be afraid of. But the current state we are in is: "cramps" wants to get rid of everything and enjoying life and the rest of us, including me, are covering up. And when you say that I have to think about medicine on one side and nutrition on the other side... Then I am going again in this disturbed mode.«


**menstrual**

»Maybe my purpose is to celebrate the circle of life. To remember that I am a part of nature and the circle of life. But now I have the impression my task is to clean something, to get something out. I feel there is a toxicity and I have to clean it out with the menstrual cycle. I can also feel that there is something put over menstrual. It has to do with something dead. And I see dead babies. I don't know what it is.«


**girl**

»That's interesting what you just said! It is almost like a new page, this toxicity. I have to clear it as a menstrual. Maybe that's why it feels so intense and achy because of its toxicity? This is now very interesting. I take it as a subject to explore. If there wouldn't be toxicity, maybe I would feel it in a different way? Like indigenous people? Now I am intrigued. I am curious now. It is an interesting connection: toxicity and problematic menstruation. The religious books, I said it, are saying that ache is dying! There is potential life you are losing! When the chicken makes an egg, it is like... She made an egg! She is very happy!

Because there is life! A small chicken woke up, you know? But when "women" is losing her egg, oh my God!«

o **cramps:** This is the first time I understand what "girl" is saying. It is the first time!
o **girl:** It is about something is dead. That's why the womb is crying. Blood. This is what religious men see.
o **women:** It feels like the cycle of menstrual. If we get stuck in the cycle of the confusion.
o **?:** Can someone go and just slap these people and shut this door, please? All the stuff is loaded, like layers of clothes "women" is wearing. On and on and on and more and more and more.
o **girl:** Seriously, I have a last question because "cramps" said the word "innocence". Something about innocence. So, let's say, I am innocent, I am a virgin and I am having menstrual. And after I have sex, will I have still menstrual? Seriously, I don't know. I don't know whom to trust. And after you give birth to your first child, do you still continue having menstrual? For me, my head is in total limbo. That's how you feel within the first three days of having menstrual. In total limbo. You cannot mentally operate. There is no mental functionality. And when it comes to menstrual that's how I feel. I really ask stupid questions but they are not stupid.
o **menstrual:** I don't know, I feel hot. In the beginning of this encounter I saw me carrying the rape of my mother and grandmother and every woman before; and dead babies. And the women who can't have babies because they are so traumatized. Now everything comes up. And this is what comes through "menstrual". And I can't breathe. I feel so much trauma.
o **girl:** Maybe we are bleeding of all these raped women and children. Oh, I go crazy!
o **cramps:** I want to take "menstrual" and shake her. You are alive! You are alive! And I feel stronger because you are alive. Celebrate to be alive. And I feel that my work, during menstrual, is to remind you that you are alive.
o **menstrual:** I feel that I am carrying all that. I am still alive and I know that my purpose is something different. I have the feeling that

274

I bleed because of all the pain that has been done to a woman. I see your faces but for me it is very important to speak out the truth.

o **girl:** Come on. Do you enjoy bleeding? As a girl I feel, younger people and children are much more honest. Who can enjoy this kind of bleeding? The body enjoys that? I am on my second day of the period and I am in emotional collapse. I lay down for hours.

o **women:** I have met so many women. For some people it is hard, for some people it's painful and for some it's not. For some people it's like nothing and for some it's like: I am going to bed for four days. For some people, they can't go anywhere. There is a whole spectrum. I don't think the way its portrayed in the world, in society, is really helpful. It doesn't help us. Because we are against ourselves. And I hear "menstrual" speak and I really feel connected to her. But what I also want to know if she wants me to help her or not. Because I want to help.

o **menstrual:** I am very glad that you said that. Because now I feel very embarrassed and very alone. For me, maybe the most important thing is to be recognized. To hear what has happened to us.


?

»I feel like I would like to slow down the process between you, "menstrual", and "cramps". Being this joyful nature and how it should be; and then also all the truths between you. It is far too fast. We need this joyful phase in order to be able to look also at the shitty stuff, that you, "menstrual" talked about. But I need more joy; and then a bit of a shitty stuff. And again more joy. If things come up too fast, too quick, I am in an overload status. And then I can't breathe and then I am collapsing and then I would like to shut down everything here. Otherwise it's like being a machine, being in a technological word which keeps on running and running. Higher, higher, faster, faster. And I need color, and I need sun and need slowness. And that we talk is fantastic. But we also need to slow it down.«

# 5.7 ANOREXIA

*General-encounter (4 words)*
*Girl – Mom – Dad – Anorexia*

Who would believe it possible that behind the topic of anorexia lies generational trauma? Crimes committed by institutions against children? The truth could come to light if parents had the courage to face their own past, family history, and traumas. As anorexia so aptly put it:

»It's totally crazy here! I'll tell you one thing: If 'Girl' didn't have me, she would be dead. I'm not the one bringing death, I'm the reason why she's still alive! This is a madhouse! (...) I'm still the healthy one here! I'm still the one with strength, the one who is healthy and clearly sees what's happening here! I want to know now where all this crap comes from!«

**Dad**
»Oh, if no one says anything, I think that's good. Then I can focus on my work. The chit-chat was too much for me anyway. "Mom", you never have a clue. As a mother, you have nothing to say. You should rather take care of your daughter. She's crying. That's your job! So, working from home is not far enough away from you, I have to say honestly. I'd rather go to the office and have nothing to do with this here. I'd rather count my cash. I bring home the money. Where has all the money gone?«

**Mom**
»I am completely confused. I could start arguing with you now, "Dad". I really hate "Dad" right now. I have no capacity, no interest, and no connection to "Girl" at all. You are all the same to me. I have this urge to control "Girl" and "Anorexia". I also find it terrible how you look, "Anorexia".«

276

**Anorexia**

»I am confused. I don't have anorexia, I have stomach pains! I have severe pain in the upper abdomen, below the chest. And I keep coughing. Save yourselves. Oh God. How did I get into this mess here? What does it mean to control? You don't even want us! You take care of everything, "Mom"? We are completely insignificant to you. You are not "Mom" and "Dad"! What are you then?«

**Girl**

»"Anorexia" is the only reference point. I have become completely silent. It hurts my heart. "Dad" is so cold and evil. And "Mom" couldn't care less about me anyway.«

o **Dad:** Also, I don't want anything to do with such a crybaby.
o **Magersucht:** Yeah, "Dad," you would have preferred a boy anyway, right?
o **Dad:** Yeah, I think so. I can't deal with stuff like that. Hiding and crying around. Oh well, "Mom" can take care of that better. So, I blame you for spoiling her like that.
o **Anorexia:** Spoiled? No one gives a damn about us! Whether we're here or not, no one really cares. We could be dead and you would just go on living. Fuck you!
o **Girl:** I'd rather that.
o **Mom:** Well, death just doesn't work at all. What will the neighbors say?
o **Anorexia:** Oh, my God! I have to be careful not to go crazy here in this household!
o **Girl:** It's so bad. I want to hide, but somehow, I keep coming back into view. I do nothing, I don't move. I want to hide. And if this continues, I want to be dead.
o **Mom:** Yes, I have power over you.

*The "Girl" creams and cries under the blanket. Meanwhile, the camera keeps moving from bottom to top and back, zooming in and out on the "Girl".*

o **Anorexia:** This is totally insane here! Let me tell you one thing: If "Girl" didn't have me, she would be dead. I'm not the one bringing death, but I am the reason she's still alive! This place is a madhouse! It's a horror show right now.
o **Girl:** It's good that you always talk, otherwise I would be gone.
o **Mom:** I also feel like a part of me wishes you weren't here.
o **Dad:** There is so much money missing here.
o **Anorexia:** Something crazy is going on here. And I feel like it's multi-generational.
o **Dad:** That has my full attention now.
o **Anorexia:** I'm going to search now because we can't expect anything from you, parents! We have to do it all ourselves! "Girl", is it okay if I do this?
o **Girl:** Yes. Because I am completely paralyzed. I am unable to act and in full panic and paralysis.
o **Mom:** "Girl" is completely under my control, under my spell. "Anorexia", you are the one who can act.
o **Anorexia:** I am still the healthy one here! I am the one with strength, the one who is healthy, who clearly sees what is happening here! I want to know now where all this crap is coming from!
o **Dad:** Well, I am afraid. I hide behind my wife. I feel like a little child.

**Anorexia**
»Fuck you! Sorry, if I say it so bluntly. I still have to do that shit myself! The man who should actually protect his family, he pulls in his cock.«

*Let's include a "?" to go deeper.*

**?**
»I am reminded of the song "Oh, come, little children… Oh, come, one and all."[61] Yes, come on, all little children. „Oh, come, little children,

---

[61] Lyrics, »O Come, Little Children« (Dresden Kreuzchor), https://www.lyrics.com/lyric-lf/1411832/Dresdner+Kreuzchor/Ihr+Kinderlein+kommet . Here are the lyrics of the English version: https://www.fbcradio.org/lyrics/361/o-come-little-children/

oh, come, one and all. Oh, come to the cradle…" I would say euthanasia here. I briefly thought about the concentration camp, but that doesn't quite fit. Yes, I have all power. I take all the children. And then they are dead. Then the camera goes up, then they ascend to heaven. Then the camera goes back down and then I focus on a child again. Look, now I target another child and then it ascends to heaven. "Oh, come, little children, oh, come, one and all." No adult protects the children. They all die. The one who should protect his family, the father, does nothing! That's great. "Oh, come, little children, oh, come, one and all." So, I'm more responsible for killing children. There is always a supply. I would say this is not limited to Germany. You can do this in England too. Everywhere. It has a different cultural hue then. There used to be even more sadistic violence. I'm comparatively harmless here. At least it ends quickly with me.«

**Dad**

»Stop that! I'm getting goosebumps! I'm so scared. I don't know if I can keep my composure. I'm afraid of the almighty power. I feel small. Boys and girls, none are safe. And I'm glad it's happening to you. And I'm hiding.«

**Mom**

»"And see what joy the Father in heaven brings us on this most holy night."[62] This has a sexual component for me. I feel exploited right now. I need to have control over "Girl" to prevent the same thing from happening to her. Who are you?«

**?**

»Someone in your family. You can choose the variants. But for me, the killing of children is institutionalized. And that comes from the past of both of you. Actually, the "Dad" needs to get moving and do something. That should actually be his job to figure out. But he's busy. He doesn't protect his families, and I have free rein as a result. Be as religious as you like. We also have a few people onboard who participate. They even give their blessing. Accomplices. And your poor child has

---

[62] Literal translation from German.

279

to deal with all of this. So, I can only tell you one thing: If you don't pay attention, you won't be able to solve this. You need to look at yourselves, at your families – fathers and mothers, grandfathers and grandmothers – to see what happened.«

o **Dad:** I am cleaning the silver. I polish something from the church.
o **Mom:** Now, for the first time, I feel the need to watch "Girl." I feel like I have been sexually abused. »And see what joy the Father in heaven brings us on this most holy night.« I am stuck in that. And I can't pay attention to anything else.
o **?:** This makes me think of priests. We would need a priest now who can give more information about what they have been up to. But that's not my job. Dad covers his ears.
o **Dad:** I have to protect myself. If I distract myself and don't look, they won't get me. And I don't care if they take "Mom" or "Girl". Just not me. I'm afraid. I can't protect anyone.
o **Anorexia:** I can't believe it! Are you trying to deceive us? I can't believe it!
o **Dad:** You have been caught after all. I made myself invisible. I hid. I got away. And I also know: They don't just take the girls. They also take the boys. I was lucky. Just because I am so clever.
o **Mom:** I am frozen. I collapsed into myself. I am completely traumatized.
o **Anorexia:** I'm not looking at you, "Mom" or mother. I am so shocked that "Dad" doesn't protect us! I can't get that into my head at all.
o **Mom:** He's only busy with money and silver.
o **Anorexia:** …and with his work. Distracts himself.

**Girl**

»I am completely twisted and almost dead. I'm breathing very little. I have to close my eyes. Just stay still. I'm all tense and almost collapsing. Before, I could still hold on to you, "Anorexia". And "Mom" is just as bad as "Dad". I can't differentiate. There's no other way. I can't get out. I'm dying under the covers. I can't survive this. It's so crazy. I'm considering whether I should jump into the water underground and end this. It's so terrible. I have no illusions that things will change. I'm abandoned.«

**Anorexia**
»I'm definitely by your side! I won't leave you alone, I promise. I'm so mad at you, "Dad"! Why don't you protect us? Because those people don't care about their children, others can do whatever they want with the kids!«

**Dad**
»"Girl" is doing it right. As long as she stays quiet and remains thin, she'll be spared. Somehow, she's clever. I'm not interested in her. I was afraid too. I survived. They took the girls. But I was clever. I hid. Buried my head in the sand. Everyone knows it. Everyone knows but does nothing. Now another girl will be taken. That's how it goes. Everyone knows it. You never know when it will happen.

I didn't form a bond with my daughter because I know they'll take her. And if I don't form a bond, then I don't need to protect her. I don't need to care. I can act like nothing's wrong. I can focus on my work. I need to check if I'll get paid when they take "Girl."«

o **Anorexia:** Oh!!!! A mental hospital is like a kindergarten compared to this! Oh my God! I don't want to die. Oh, my God... It just keeps going. Another child, another child. It never stops.
o **Dad:** Looks like a confessional.
o **Anorexia:** The church has a lot to confess.
o **Mom:** Do you think the church is taking the children?
o **Anorexia:** It's definitely involved.
o **Dad:** No one sees through it. Everyone knows. No one does anything. And it's not seen from the outside. That's why everything stays the same.
o **Girl:** Those who deal with themselves... There's hope now. But there's definitely someone who has walked the path of facing their pain.
o **Anorexia:** The problem is that along with the pain comes madness. I'm afraid of madness.

- o **Dad:** The girl is totally in focus. It's as if we're being watched here. No help is coming from outside.
- o **Mom:** The danger comes from outside. Big brother is watching you.
- o **Anorexia:** Strangely, that immediately makes me think of the priesthood. The holy brotherhood.
- o **Dad:** They used to peek through a little hole. But today, they have completely different means.

## 5.8 OBESITY

*Self-encounter (Woman Isle of Man, 3 words)*
*I – contact – fatness*

Who would have thought that behind obesity lies a horrendous family history? A total entanglement of abuse, neglect, ADHD, medication, and suicide!

»When I was seven years old I was slapped with the label of ADHD. And I was medicated. They took me of the medication because it was too extreme. And I can see this in the "I" now: I was constantly moving. I was also heavily abused, physically and sexually and mentally.«

**I**
»I am daydreaming. I have a protein ball in my hand, looking out of the window, daydreaming, eating and drinking. I am enjoying this food and that's it. I don't have much contact with myself. Now I am feeling embarrassed. I feel like I shouldn't be eating, I am feeling under pressure but I guess I am about 5, 6 or 7 years old. This food is really nice and delicious. Is it right, is it wrong, should I eat it? I am being told to do something. I guess I want some time to figure it out. To find my way.«

**contact**
»I am hearing my name being sometimes mentioned. But I am annoyed and I feel tortured a little bit. I don't want to be here. I observe myself.

282

Distracting me with things like looking outside of the window, looking at my mobile phone. I feel nervous or stressed. That [ADHD & abuse] resonates but I don't want to hear and I don't want to remember it. But I like that you talk about it and remember it because that makes me feel like having some kind of contact with you. But I still don't want to remember. I am happy observing for the moment and staying with me.«

**fatness**
»From the beginning I thought of slapping you in the face. I feel like slapping you but not in order to hurt you. I am not negatively towards you. And there is some kind of veil. Covering something, maybe.« [putting the veil over her face]

»*But it wasn't a pillow over your head? Because my mother tried to put a pillow over my head when I was a baby. She tried to smother me.*«

**I**
»I am two and a half years old. I am looking out of the window. I am looking at the sky. I have very little sense of me. I am just passing the time away. There is no one in the room with me. I want to go out and play. There are two ponies.«

»*We lived in the country side. We didn't have two ponies but there were two horses across the road. We had dogs and hens. Is there any reason you can't go out and play?*«

**I**
»I don't know if I am allowed to. I might get into trouble. No. I am curious now. I can see "contact". And "fatness". F….. ATNESS! FFFFFFF….. Father. "fatness". F A THER.«

**contact**
»I am dizzy and annoyed by "I". "I" is completely crazy. I don't want to see and hear "I". And seeing "fatness" doing this thing – it feels for me like I am in a circus, in a completely crazy world. This makes me breathe heavily. I don't have any ideas how to distract myself. It is

good to hear your voice. If I wouldn't hear your voice, I would have left this room. But when I hear you talking to "I" and "fatness", I hear no emotions. I am missing a contact. I am craving for contact with you. I feel observed. They all want something from me. I feel embarrassed. Look at them! They are doing crazy things!«

»*My brother who hung himself in May. We miss him. Probably, I am entangled with him.*«

**I**
»When I hear you say that I become an adult. [crying] There is so much that hasn't got words in here [touching the throat]. It's been like hell for us! My right hand feels dead, a numbness and disconnection. Like somebody else's. It is also around my heart. And I hide this part because my mother… aaaaaahhhhh! Get it out of the throat! It needs to get out. Exhaustion. I am tired of it all. I don't like the cards I have been dealt with. There is a weariness in here. I feel older than I am. Am I dismissed now? I don't like being dismissed.«

»*I was born and my mother tried to smother me with a pillow. And then she let my dad do whatever he wanted when I was 18 months old. He molested me. And then they starved me, for prolonged periods of time. And it went on and on.*« The woman starts to cry, to shout, to cry more and to scream.

**contact**
»I am with you. Now I feel being in touch with you and also being able to see the others. You are getting in touch with yourself made me getting goosebumps. I am now focused on you. And I had the sentence in me "I love you for shouting it all out". I feel love.«

**fatness**
»I stopped doing these distractive things. I really don't feel you have a real relation with me. That is okay. That may take time. I am not something nice for you. But I am your part. You don't want to receive from me at all. It is a possibility to let you know that you can develop some communication with me. If you want. Learning, receiving, whatever.«

284

*»This is accurate. Because as I child, I was heavily ridiculed for my fatness; even though I wasn't fat. I was a baby, a toddler, a child. That was mental. And I started to realize that I kind of rejected that part. That is the reason I don't have contact with it. But I wasn't allowed to have contact with it! «* [crying heavily]

**fatness**
»Say it to me. I want to have contact with you. I am here! Now you are allowed. I give you all the time you need. I am here for you. I don't want anything from you in return. You can just be yourself. You are okay as you are. All the screaming and shouting and swearing is fine for me.«

**I**
»When "fatness" mentioned that you could start to communicate with her, I felt like an opening in my heart. Like a free energy in my heart space.«

**contact**
»I am feeling relieved now because I believe that my job is done. I can just be there without needing to do something because you are being in touch. It is getting easier and more relaxed for me. Wow! I need a moment to take this in. I see you, "fatness". I see you, "I", I see you, "contact".«

## 5.9 ALLERGY

*Self-encounter (Woman, China, 3 words)*
*Allergy – Daughter – Me*

How closely linked a physical issue such as allergy can be with a country of origin and its politics is illustrated by this work of a woman from China. She spent a month in China in the summer of 2023 with her husband and two daughters. Since returning, she has been struggling with severe physical symptoms, and her 8-year-old daughter suddenly developed a horse allergy.

285

I have often seen how deeply politics interferes in families where people come from authoritarian regimes. How it extends its claws and seizes possession of every aspect of life and the body from conception to old age. Peeking behind closed doors reveals fear, terror, indescribable violence, and profound sorrow.

But having experienced the unspeakable, how can one then have children of their own? And if one does have children, how can they possibly build a healthy relationship? Many children absorb all the chaos and react physically. In this case, with outbursts of anger and physically acting out towards the mother.

**Daughter**
»For me, I am surprised that you want to start with me. I am shy. When you asked me, my first impulse was to hide myself. I need protection. I feel uncomfortable with myself. I don't want to be here. I am a little bit ashamed. I can't talk about it at the moment.«

**Allergy** [rocking back and forwards constantly]
»I am really a mixture between a wild horse and a raging bull. I feel like I am the opposite part of "Daughter". She is the shy one, the introverted and I am ready to explode. Boah! I am sitting on a shit load of anger! So much anger, rage. Raging bull. It is really, really difficult to control myself. And now, as I am talking, the rage is building up more and more. Before, I could kind of control it. And you dissociate as always: Drinking tea, yawning, doing whatever you do. Boah!!! I am like a rocket! I am like a rocket READY TO EXPLODE! Oh, my God. If I will become a teenager, be careful. If you think you know my rage and anger – you have no idea!

I don't know in which language to express my anger. It is unbelievable! I am like a cooking pot. But it is more than this. The words can't even describe, no matter which language, how I feel. And now you yawn again?? I can't grab you. I can't grab you! It is like you would glitch between my fingers. I would love you to get into the ring with me. But you are like a ghost. Ahhh!!! It is unbelievable here. It is unbelievable! Now you yawn again! Can't you stop it if I tell you?! Can't you freaking, for heaven's sake, just stop it when I tell you something?!?! Ah!!! I don't have the words, I don't have the language to

286

express my anger. I have nowhere to direct it to. It is like I would try to grab someone [grabbing the air in front of her] – you or dad or someone else – and everyone escapes my fist.«

*»You slapped me. It triggered my rage.«*

**Allergy**
»Did it help? Did it change ANYTHING?? Sorry! I give a shit about triggering! I can't grab anyone. Makes me… ahhhh!!! A volcano without start and end. I am sitting on my anger and rage! Oh, it is unbelievable! And there is no one here! You are here. Now. But you are not here. I am not sure if you understand me. You are always floating somewhere. It drives me mad. Then I try to look at dad. Where is he?! Where the freaking hell is he for heaven's sake? He is also a ghost! It drives me mad! Aaahhhh! I am waiting to become a teenager. To really burst out and explode. I will smash furniture. I will destroy things. I am so much in rage. If it wouldn't hurt that much I would put my head against the wall. So that you all would finally wake up. You are like ghosts! You are not here! It drives me mad! Sorry guys, to both of you, for taking so much time. Ahhh!!!!«

*»You are highly demanding. Ahh…« [The woman is breathing like she would be doing Yoga or attending a spiritual session]*

**Allergy**
»Demanding?! I am not demanding! Why does no one listen?!!! Why is everyone dissociating left and right?? "Ahh", drives me sick! I am giving a shit about you giving attention to someone else! I give a shit about you being so acknowledging and loving. You are not even here! You are not even a full-fledged being. And dad neither. I am so sick and tired. I will smash everything when I get older. I will destroy everything. So that you guys FINALLY WAKE UP! I AM SO TIRED OF IT! ALL OF THIS AH's::: HM's::: I AM SO SICK OF IT! All the same emotions, all on the same level.«

*»I can't come closer to you. When I am there and want to spend with you…«*

**Allergy**
»How can you spend time with me when you are not even here?! On this earth! Where for heaven's sake are you floating? Tell me! You are like an air balloon, floating! You give a shit about me. Be honest. You would be happier if I wouldn't be here. That's the truth. You don't want to be with me. You don't want to spend time with me. I am a burden to you. And the same with dad. You are, he, you, he – it is the same shit. You don't want to live. You don't want to be here. You just float. I am so tired. No, I am not tired. I am building up an enormous amount of energy. Every food I take in is building it up, building up, building up, building up. Like gasoline. Like I am in a gas station. I am fueling up my tank to the absolute maxiMom!«

*»And then you hit.«*

**Allergy**
»Yes. And then I will explode. And then I will smash things. And then I will be full of rage. I will be like an atom bomb. I have the impression you are somewhere in the universe. You want to fly somewhere in your, I don't know, air balloon, rocket ship, universe, star ship… You don't see me, you don't hear me, you don't understand me. I am talking now to "Me" because I think she understands me more. Hi, "Me".«

*"Me" was laughing, giving the thumbs up, showing a heart sign.*

**Me**
»I feel very split. I feel like I have all that rage inside me. It is so hard to just repress it. I am what we are looking at here. And I feel the itchiness on my skin. And when I look at the "Daughter" and what she said about the belly, I was wondering about some pregnancy which was a secret, a secret or shameful pregnancy. And nobody has talked about it. That feels like an ancestor. A trauma of an ancestor. Dead child. It is lifeless. And I feel everything that "Allergy" is feeling. But I have also this cap put on. The cap that I put on the bottle. I am the cap and she, "Allergy", is what's in the bottle. And when I look at you [the women] I see this lifelessness. You are pretending not to have rage.«

*»Me? Not to hear the rage?«*

o **Me:** And now you pretend to not understand.
o **Allergy:** Exactly. You didn't even hear what she said.
o **Me:** That's true. Now I feel the rage in every cell of my body. In my shoulders. I could kill someone. It feels that strong. I feel it on my shoulders. Like being slashed. You know these big knifes, huge swords. Right across my shoulders.

**Allergy**

» I think someone was killed. I am really scared. And you, although you are my mother, I have the feeling you don't understand nothing. As if we would be talking in a foreign language.«

*»Yes. We cannot talk really. I don't understand you.«*
o **Me:** I don't feel you want to.
o **Allergy:** True. True. I wouldn't have been able to express it.
o **Me:** For you to sit there and say »I don't understand you« is like... Seriously? Get a fucking life.

**Daughter**

»Now I am totally checked out. This is too much. I don't feel seen at all. From nobody at the moment. I listened. I gave you the space. I didn't have the impression that I have the space to say something. I am very irritated by "Me" rolling her eyes. I told you, I am very shy. And there is a lot of going on inside of me. But I am getting more and more fearful of what is happening here. I have the connection to you, "Allergy". It was the fear, the anger you expressed. I wanted to laugh... It was familiar. It was confusing. But I was anxious. I have fear to express my anger. I get in resonance with you, when you said, you tried to grab and there is nothing to grab. Everything I am trying to express is going into the vain, it doesn't get somewhere.«

**Allergy**

»What do you want to say, "Daughter"? Because I am a part of you and I don't understand you. I asked you now 2, 3 times to say something and you didn't say anything. It is really confusing for me right now because I am part of you, "Daughter". And my mother has this rage. This is what "Me" expressed so well. But now I feel more connected to "Me" than you, "Daughter". And it is kind of weird. What is happening here right now? I have a stupid question. Can it be that you are younger than me? I am older than you? Am I overwhelming you with all these feelings and knowledge? And forgetting that you are younger than me?«

o **Daughter:** Yes, this sounds true.
o **Allergy:** I want too much of you, too early.
o **Daughter:** I start to see you. But I want to know why you are so angry?

**Allergy**
»Hm… Let me know if it is clear what I am saying. I look at Mom and I look at dad and it is like constantly grabbing the air instead of getting hold of them. I am getting really furious about it. And my Mom is right now here. I can see that she is floating somewhere in the air. And "Me" expressed it so well: My mother has so much rage within her and she doesn't see it. And I – through "Allergy" or hitting her, screaming at them – I want to wake them up. I am shaking my mother. I am trying to shake my father. But how do you shake someone if you can't get hold of them?«

**Daughter**
»I understand now your rage. It is now totally understandable why you are so angry. But I also I think I am a little younger and I can't express myself. I get heartaches that I couldn't land with my mother.«

o **Allergy:** And I have the feeling that I am already more like a teenager. That is the reason I am older. While you are still having this heartache, my body is bursting outwards. And, by the way, I am not sure if you heard it, "Daughter", but "Me" said something important for me. Which has something to do which happened in the past. And over time it gets bigger and bigger and bigger and bigger.

*»I want to say that I really have some stomach pain. I really feel all the fear of all this rage and also the violence...«*

o **Allergy:** »Violence« is a good word.
o **Me:** Somebody is not taking responsibility. And this feels like the snowball you are describing, "Allergy". But also, I am not taking responsibility. To feel anything, to acknowledge, to care enough. And the word »violence« really resonates with me.
o **Allergy:** Uff... I am getting a strange body reaction here! It is dangerous.

*»I am getting chills over my body. I am continue getting this stomach pain. I am very alert.«*

o **Allergy:** It is dangerous. Very dangerous.
o **Me:** They killed babies. Killed babies, slaughtered babies. Like in a slaughter house. Where you slaughter animals. Not killing but slaughtering.

*»Can abortion also mean slaughtering children? Or do you mean it in terms of murdering? Like in a war? Or in the family?«*

o **Me:** Murdering. Yeah, murdering, slaughtering. I see both. I see a grave of dead babies. And I see as it a symbol of girls. Dead girls. They are all girls.

*The woman is now talking about the 1-child-policy in China and the patriarchic culture: »Boys are more worthy than the girls. And there are so many girls that are like being... I don't exactly know in my ancestor lineage if this has happened. But it was common. It often happened in China. Especially in the country side. My primary wounding was that I was born as a girl and not a boy. That causes a lot of guilt and shame. And also, my coping strategy to proof that I am worthy. As worthy as a boy. That has been a predominate topic and wounding in this life.«*

291

**Me**
»There is something about it when you changed into German language. In war, when people changed languages – it was like a cover-up. I feel all that fear now in my body. I feel it everywhere. Especially in my back, shoulders, my arms. Like a baby being grabbed just like that, by the arm, and just slaughtered. Do you have anything in your shoulders?«

*»Yeah, I do have it. I have a lot of problems in my shoulder, neck and back.«*

o **Me:** This is being wrenched. Being lifted by the socket of the shoulder and slashed from behind. I understand now why "Allergy" and "Daughter" … This shame of being girl.
o **Daughter:** I am ashamed of being a girl. I am ashamed… I have to cover up my sexuality. I have to cover up everything that shows that I am a girl.

*»A lot of repair already happened. There is no shame or guilt anymore. I hear "Daughter" but I somehow can't connect with it, understand or relate. I feel like I already let go of this shame or guilt.«*

o **Me:** When you were setting your intention, I had the feeling of shame of sexual abuse. And I was surprised that you didn't use the word »sexual abuse«. Sexual violence.

*»I assumed that happened to my mother; with her stepfather. Who was very, very violent. She was raised by her grandmother because her mother, my grandmother, was not there. And then at the age of 11, she went back to her mother when her mother married the stepfather. This stepfather is a very violent person. He also hit and beat, very violently, towards my grandmother. And he had also affairs. And my mother didn't tell me the details and didn't mention a word of sexual abuse. But this is something I can imagine happening to my mother.*

*This is also something what I have experienced in my life. Not from my father but from authority figures: A teacher in school and later in college and a doctor in the hospital. They misused their power. It was just so disgusting. So disgusting. I've been working on that a long time now. This happened to me as well, this sexual abuse.*

*Only recently, I started to release the anger and resentment and all this rage through other healing modalities. But just recently, I found out there is still so much there. So much, so much anger, rage. And just recently, I kind of recognized officially this #Metoo movement. I didn't really dare to say or relate to it in that moment. I don't want to live my life, the rest of my life in resentment, anger and rage.«*

o **Me:** It feels to me as if you are covering for somebody. You are protecting somebody at the expense of yourself. This is why I asked: Who are you trying to protect right now? What are you not admitting for reasons of loyalty or fear? What about our father?

*»Actually, I didn't experience any sexual abuse or harassment or assault from my father. But violence, yes. He beat me. I got beaten very often. But never, never ever any sexual abuse.«*

o **Me:** See, for me, I am not sure that if we had to write in Webster's dictionary what abuse is. That we might not be able to do this definition very well. We would start to get very particular about how we may choose how to define it. But we wouldn't really know. Because it is confusing. You got beaten?

*»Yeah. Very often. When I got a bad score or didn't obey and follow their rules. When I came back home late or something. When I had my first boyfriend. Lot's happened. I got beaten and shouted and beaten. And I was not allowed to scream. I was not allowed to cry. Towards the outside. I think this makes sense what you are saying: It was covering up. Towards the outside to pretend peaceful and in harmony. Role model family. But inside there is so much, so much fight and conflict.«*

o **Me:** Our father abused us.
o **Daughter:** I can feel it. Everything what you are saying, everything is in my cell. Violence. The abuse. I don't know what happened. But there must have been something going on.

293

**Me**

»I want to say that it is very irritating when you use words like "release" and "letting go". Because there is lack of responsibility of feeling the level of violence that happened in our body. And somehow normalizing that and being convinced. It is not about letting go or surrendering. This is bullshit. It is about feeling the rage. And saying that this happened. And this is how I feel about it. Now I feel like I have spoken truth. It is very helpful to get this out of the shoulders. At a certain age, it is good to release anger like this. That is not a part of you. We were like a rag doll. When you feel the anger and acknowledge the pain of what happened to you, your "Daughter" doesn't have to do that.«

**Allergy**

»It would be better if you would go boxing. And even my father. Because it is not my job to release your anger. Sorry. Why should I do it? I am so mad at all the previous people before me. I even have rage against my ancestors. I am so mad. Because no one takes responsibility. "Me" is beautiful because she tells the truth in your face.«

o **Daughter:** I also want to say something. I don't feel the anger. I am very afraid. I have a lot of fear.
o **Allergy:** Don't worry. You have me.
o **Daughter** [laughing]: That's good. Yeah!
o **Allergy:** I promise you, I will keep it to something that you can cope with.
o **Daughter:** It is too much to feel; everything. I am tired. It takes time to process it.

**Allergy**

»Can I ask you something? Sometimes I am not sure if things are not mixed up within us as well? Sometimes you feel a bit like our mother? So, I wonder if you are really you? Things confuse me sometimes when you speak and I can't get it together. I think, I am also a little bit mixed up with the rage. You know what I would really like to do? You and me, we go in a separate room and sort things out. And they go in a different room and sort things out.«

**Me**

»I would like to say to "Daughter" that I know that she gets the allergies when she isn't breathing. She is breathing just from here. [showing the throat] And everything is getting tighter and tighter here. And in relation what you just said, it feels like a really good thing if "Daughter" and "Allergy" would go – and you just have to face me. If they are not here, you can only face yourself and your pain. You can talk about your "Daughter" but in the end, you have to face me.«

- o **Allergy:** And if you promise me to talk about all the different levels of violence then I am fine. But that you have to promise me. That it is not again being swept under the carpet.
- o **Me:** Yes. That violence it not normal. What I feel is that there is something in your psyche that thinks it is normal. It is not admitting about the violence that happened to us. That's not normal for human beings.

»But it was normal in China in that time. Every time.«

- o **Me:** That is no excuse.
- o **Allergy:** What a horrific picture that this should be normal!
- o **Daughter:** I want to shout it out. It was not normal! I have the impulse to scream. When you said it was normal in China. It was not normal in China or the whole world. As "Me" said: We are all human beings.

»Terrible. I mean, yeah… I was in China this summer. For one month. For the whole one month I was…«

- • **Allergie:** Woah! Oha! Ich will es nicht einmal hören. Ach du meine Güte …. Woah! [beginnt zu husten und schwer zu atmen]

»On the first day…«

- o **Me** [interrupts)]: Why are you continuing? Didn't you hear "Allergy"? It is too much.
- o **Daughter:** You know what I feel? I feel death pain!

*»When I landed I got already so sick. Terrible pain.«*

o **Me:** I really don't think this is fair on our daughter.
o **Daughter:** I am not a part of "Daughter" anymore. I am now a part of my mother. I can feel it. I have the fear of death by being a girl. It is stuck in my breath, you know.
o **Allergy:** It is a nightmare. It is a full-blown nightmare. Everything here. One month. Oh gosh. It is like a death sentence: 1 month!!!

*»I haven't heard anything for a whole month. And it lasted even longer.«* [Tinnitus]

o **Allergy:** Oh gosh. No wonder. Oh!!! I am done. I can't anymore!
o **Me:** You didn't want to hear it. And I feel, I am the only person here taking responsibility. It is all pushed on "Allergy". There is really something here… That you take responsibility. I want to say: *»I keep putting myself in abusive situations.«*.

*»I can say it maybe to the general collective environment in China. To the government. But I cannot say this to this day that I was abused.«*

o **Me:** Going to China for one month is abusing yourself.
o **Daughter/Woman:** I have a question – what about your mother? Did she have babies before you? And why are you here? You are a girl. And what about you? Did you have girls before "Daughter"? These are the questions which are coming up now.

*»Yes, I had. I had two abortions before my daughters were born. Both times where in college. Between 20 and 21 or 22 years of age.*

*I think, my parents, they didn't do the check. They didn't know what kind of gender I have. When my mother gave birth, there was a big disappointment for the family. Because my father was the oldest in his family. And especially my grandparents, they were very much disappointed that my father didn't get a son. And later, I think, I learned from my mother that she was pregnant again but she had to do an abortion or take the child out. Because she had a, not a tumor, but*

296

*something in her uterus. And she had to get a surgery to take this all out. That baby was a son, a boy. And she mentioned it. It was a boy.«*

o  **Me:** The cyst that she had were all the dead babies.
o  **Daughter/Woman:** I feel that I am not allowed to be here. It is about me, you know. I should have been dead. That's why I am not here. I am a part of you. And I am not allowed to be here.
o  **Me:** You didn't finish talking about what happened in college. You were very vague. Why was there no other choice?

*»I was 19, I think, when I got pregnant from my first boyfriend. It happened during the holidays. And it was absolutely taboo. I had such fear. My parents would never, never allow it. Would get furious if they knew I got pregnant. I had the abortion. This abortion act itself was very violent. And I had no one to tell, no one to share. That was the first time. The second time was when I was 21. I got into a relationship with my professor. And back to that time it was taboo because he lived separated but not divorced yet. We came together and I got pregnant. You are right, "Me". I am abusing myself by getting into that kind of situations. And deeply hurting myself.«*

o  **Me:** I feel the confusion lifting from my head. Is this the first time you shared it like this? It is important to me that this is witnessed. That this is fully witnessed.

*»We have done this in the previous healing work but different setting. I carry this guilt with me; with these two abortions. I often think my current two children, two daughters, are these two souls coming back to me. And I really feel guilty. [crying] Duty is also part of it. I still think it wasn't my decision to have a child. My first child was shortly before my mother's 60's birthday. And she said her wish is to have a grandchild. If I want to give her a birthday present?«*

o  **Me:** Now you are speaking the truth.

*»And my "Daughter" came during the phase when my big one was five years old and was saying: "Oh, every child in the Kindergarten and*

297

*everyone else has sisters, has siblings." She wished for a baby sister. After the birth of my child I lost my freedom. Everything is duty. I lost the time together with my husband. I felt like she took my husband away. I think I was jealous about the connection and relationship between my big daughter and my husband. And there was a thought in me, if there is a second child, there would be a little more balance. And then I got pregnant again. I knew that I am still such a kid. And cannot take care of another child. I was already so overwhelmed. Deeply traumatized. I didn't even know that I was so deeply traumatized. But I knew I wasn't really capable of raising a child.«*

o **Me:** Now I understand why "Daughter" has allergies. Because you didn't want her. You didn't even make any kind of decision for yourself. Except one from emotion of jealousy. When we were a child we tried to fight for some kind of power with our parents also.

*»It is such a power play. Also, between my parents. They wanted me to take a side. And I felt a deeper connection with my father. We share some interests. But my mother was very much hurt. It is the same pattern I am carrying now. I feel hurt. I feel neglected when I see my daughters having close relationship with my husband.«*

o **Me:** It is because when I look at you now, I only see an 11-year-old. And she doesn't want an 11-year-old connecting with her. She wants her mother. I see you at 11; sometimes 14 years.
o **Daughter/Woman:** I am a part of you. I am the little girl inside of you. I feel neglected by "Me". I have the impression there is no space for me. I am not recognized.

*»This is also what my daughter keeps complaining. And also my big daughter. But my little one is very, very... she keeps complaining. She is very, very demanding. Keeps talking and also wants to be the center of the family.«*

Natalie: *»Your daughter doesn't want to be in the center. You and your daughter are completely entangled with each other. And the pattern, the violence, and the entanglement, is going on from one generation to*

298

*the the next, to the next. She is revealing the truth. She is a truth warrior. So, you, your family are repeating this pattern. I think, it is time to break this vicious cycle. Because this is not doing you any good or your daughters. Because otherwise they are going to repeat the cycle of abortion, violence, murder. And this is not a good life.«*

**Me**
»As long as I am being given the name "Me" I will never be "I". I will continue in this pattern as "Me" and not "I". I want to be "I". And something changes now. It is the first time I feel my power. I want to know if you have told your daughter about the two other siblings that are no longer here? Because they already know this; their cells. They were in the same womb where these siblings were. And this rage and also not hearing the truth of what happened to you. They need to know. That you made mistakes. what you did, what you did to yourself and why you did it.«

*»No. I didn't tell my daughters. No, not yet. I am not sure if it's for my daughters to hear at this age. If it wouldn't be too much. I think, you remind me of something else. My husband only knows about one of the previous abortions. I will tell him.«*

o   **Me:** It frees up a lot of energy in my heart. I just want to check. Was there a fifth child? Was there a possibility of a fifth? It feels like there were 5.

*»Oh gosh. It is possible. There was no five but it is possible. Shortly after the second abortion, I think, shortly after that – within two months' time – it might be that I got pregnant again. For a month, I didn't have the period. [crying] It reminds me of my grandmother giving birth to three kids. And one of the kids she had to give to her sister because it was not allowed. The biological grandfather who was already put in jail then escaped from jail. And then he came back to my grandmother – mother of my mother – and then they had this child. But it was not possible to raise it as her own child. Because officially my grandfather was still in the jail. And how could she even give birth to a child without the husband being home? Before she died, she told her*

*son, my uncle. But even now we don't talk about that. My mother heard that from her mother before she died that she told her brother. Ah...!«*

o **Me:** More secretes. And when you don't speak the truth you are lying with them. You can't be who you are.

*»That's true. That's true. So many secrets and so much suffering. And also, again this topic of gender. My grandmother, before she died, she told my mother that the cousin is the biological brother of my mother. And she said, I want to have also his name on my grave so that everyone sees that I also have born a boy.«*

o **Me:** Now I understand why there were no boys born to you. It all makes sense.

*[crying] »So much suffering. So much trauma. So much pain. It is unbearable. This is why I had this unbearable pain when I landed in China this summer. I cannot hear anymore with one of my ears. And I had such unbearable pain.«*

Epilogue

So much suffering and so much pain were revealed here that it could almost tear one apart. This self-encounter not only exemplifies China, its educational methods, and the one-child policy, but also many other countries in Asia, as I have experienced repeatedly. The work also serves as an example that moving away from one's homeland does not heal all wounds, but is equally important. Because only through physical distance, in a safe environment, does it even become possible to look at one's wounds and give space to deep emotions. Our soul, our body, and our children show us how far we are in this process with ourselves.

Shortly after this work, I discovered the book "Fact Sheet: One-Child Policy of China" by Dr. Wilfried Korby[63]. I would like to quote

---

[63] Ernst Klett Verlag, »Infoblatt: Ein-Kind-Politik Chinas« (PDF) [»Information sheet: China's One-Child Policy«]
https://www.google.com/url?sa=t&source=web&rct=j&opi=89978449&url=https://

an excerpt from it because we can see here that no research or study can ever delve into such deep layers as this form of work or in the face of our children.

»Elderly Chinese, who typically grew up in large families, often complain about their spoiled single grandchildren – whom they themselves have usually showered with excessive care. Mothers and fathers lament their only children, whom they have given all their love to, but who now behave like "little emperors" and refuse to help with household chores. Teachers have to deal with little egoists who have barely developed social skills in their upbringing so far. All of these are consequences of the one-child policy, which has been controversial since its introduction in 1979. Some saw it as a remedy against the looming overpopulation not only in China but globally. For others, this policy model represented an outgrowth of misogyny and a restriction of individual freedom. What are the facts?«

## 5.10 VACCINATION

*General-encounter (4 words)*
*Baby – Tetanus (vaccination) – Polio (vaccination) – Rotavirus (vaccination)[64]*

Among the participants there were three mothers with adult children. Since we were no longer up to date, we wanted to get an overview of the current vaccination situation. The main point of contact for all vaccinations in Germany is the so-called »GELBE LISTE PHARMAINDEX« [»YELLOW LIST PHARMAINDEX«]. Here, »Ständige Impfkommission« (STIKO) [65] [Standing Vaccination Commission] publishes its recommendations.

---

www.klett.de/alias/1083022&ved=2ahUKEwiHjKS_udaI-AxV_hP0HHaZ3JGgQFnoECBMQAQ&usg=AOvVaw1LlpPnP8q_6fQ0ZRTLwbfn
[64] In the beginning, the words also did not have the addition "vaccination." However, when the work stalled and we couldn't make progress, the addition was added.
[65] Robert Koch Institut (RKI), »Ständige Impfkommission« [»Permanent Vaccination Commission«] https://www.rki.de/DE/Content/Kommissionen/STIKO/stiko_node.html

»Yellow List Online is an online service of Vidal MMI Germany GmbH (Vidal MMI) and provides news, information, and databases for doctors, pharmacists, and other medical professionals. The GELBE LISTE PHARMINDEX is a leading directory of active ingredients, medicines, medical devices, dietetics, dietary supplements, dressings, and cosmetics. Recommended standard vaccinations. It is annually revised and published by the Standing Vaccination Committee. The present vaccination calendar was updated in August 2020.«

| Impfung | Säugling 6 Wochen | Säugling 2 Monate | Säugling 3 Monate | Säugling 4 Monate | Säugling 5-10 Monate | Kleinkind 11* Monate | Kleinkind 12 Monate | Kleinkind 13-14 Monate | Kleinkind 15 Monate | Kleinkind 16-23 Monate |
|---|---|---|---|---|---|---|---|---|---|---|
| Tetanus[b] | | G1 | N | G2 | N | G3[d] | | N | | |
| Diphtherie[b] | | G1 | N | G2 | N | G3[d] | | N | | |
| Keuchusten (Pertussis)[b] | | G1 | N | G2 | N | G3[d] | | N | | |
| Kinderlähmung (Poliomyelitis)[b] | | G1 | N | G2 | N | G3[d] | | N | | |
| Hepatitis B[b] | | G1 | N | G2 | N | G3[d] | | N | | |
| Hib[b] (Haemophilus Influenzae B) | | G1 | N | G2 | N | G3[d] | | N | | |
| Pneumokokken[b] | | G1 | N | G2 | N | G3[d] | | N | | |
| Rotaviren | G1[a] | G2 | (G3) | | | | | | | |
| Meningokokken[c] (Serogruppe B) | | G1 | N | G2 | | N | G3[d] | | N | |
| Meningokokken (Serogruppe C) | | | | | | | G1 | | N | |
| Masern | | | | | | G1 | | N | G2 | N |
| Mumps, Röteln | | | | | | G1 | | N | G2 | N |
| Windpocken (Varizellen) | | | | | | G1 | | N | G2 | N |
| Grippe (Influenza) | | | | | | | | | | |
| HPV (Humanes Papillomvirus) | | | | | | | | | | |
| Herpes Zoster | | | | | | | | | | |
| COVID-19 | | | | | | | | | | |

Source: YELLOW LIST PHARMINDEX
»Impfkalender Babys und Kleinkinder«
[Vaccination Schedule for Babies and Toddlers]
https://www.gelbe-liste.de/impfung/impfkalender

Shortly after this group work, I happened to come across the book by Dr. med. Gerhard Buchwald »Impfen – Das Geschäft mit der Angst« [»Vaccination – The Business of Fear«]. On page 29, there was an overview explaining the vaccine production of nine vaccinations:

302

| Vaccination | Animal species used for vaccine production |
| --- | --- |
| Smallpox | Calves (skin), sheep (skin), rabbits (eye) |
| Tetanus | Horses |
| Rabies | Dogs, sheep, monkeys, rabbits, hamsters, rats, mice chicken eggs, duck eggs |
| Tuberculosis (BDG) | Cows (udder), voles |
| Polio | Monkeys (kidneys and testes) |
| Rubella (German Measles) | Rabbits (kidneys) |
| Measles | Dogs, guinea pigs (kidneys), Japanese quail eggs, chicken embryos |
| Pertussis | Mice |
| Influenza | Chicken embryos |

»Tabelle 1. Quelle: Dittmann, S.: Atypische Verläufe nach Schutzimpfungen,
Johann Ambrosius Barth, Leipzig 1981«
[Table 1. Source: Dittmann, S.: Atypical Courses after Vaccinations,
Johann Ambrosius Barth, Leipzig 1981.]

Further on the page, it can be read:

»Certain vaccines are cultured on the allantois membranes of incubated chicken eggs. Today, the pharmaceutical industry claims to require animals little or not at all for their production. The industry is technically capable of culturing them on "HeLa" cells or "HDC". These are cancer cells but not referred to as such. The name "HeLa" consists of the initials of the name of that woman, Henrietta Lacks, from whom these cancer cells originate. They are also referred to as 'cell lines' to conceal the fact that they are cancer cells. The pharmaceutical industry has no concerns and believes there is no link between this fact and the increase in childhood cancer.«

The future of vaccinations is described on the page of the Vfa, the research-based pharmaceutical companies[66]: »New vaccines are now being developed with genetic material (mRNA, DNA) or vector viruses and already used in at least some countries.«
Let's take a look now at how a baby feels when it's being vaccinated.

---

[66] Vfa, Die forschenden Pharma-Unternehmen, »Entwicklung und Herstellung von Impfstoffen: Die Impfungen der Zukunft« [Vfa, the research-based pharmaceutical companies, »Development and Manufacture of Vaccines: The Vaccinations of the Future«] from September 9, 2020, https://www.vfa.de/de/arzneimittel-for-schung/impfen/impfstoff-herstellung

**Baby**

»I'm just thinking, what are you all doing here with me? I feel a bit confined. Like you want to get next to me or crawl into my skin. I'm trying to protect myself with my blanket. Stay away from me! I don't find it funny, but I can still laugh about it.

I'm looking at "Tetanus" and thinking, eventually I'll become stiff. As I get older, I'll get something that makes me rigid in my body. When "Rotaviruses" speak, I see worms crawling along. Twitching, movements? Exactly, spasms. Then I will eventually become spastic. Or get Tourette's. When I hear "Polio" from you, I think of diabetes, high blood sugar.

Stay away from me! Don't come too close to me! I don't understand this at all. There are no parents here. I don't see them. It's like I've been put or laid in a playpen and you three were placed in there with me. And I don't understand why I have to deal with this. Everything was fine. It's not about my protection either. Because I am protected. And I realize, I still have so much strength as a baby, it doesn't bother me.«

**Tetanus**

»Oops, I am so stiff here. I am completely stiff and tired.«

**Rotaviruses**

»So, I kind of creep under your skin and slowly expand. It's quite eerie. I make twisting movements. Feels very unpleasant. I have something slightly spasmodic here. Everything hurts. I feel somewhat disabled myself. So, I need to Google myself because I don't know what Rotaviruses are... I'm not really dangerous. I am just diarrhea. That is of course unpleasant, but I have no long-term effects. It will pass. Like a flu or a stomach infection. And now I wonder why I am a vaccine. Why do you have to be vaccinated against me? It's a certain control. It's not about the Rotaviruses. I am neither good nor bad. I am a virus that exists.«

**Polio**

»With me, it's quite peculiar. I have something to do with sugar. I only move my eyes, but otherwise, I don't feel anything. Immovable. I only move my eyes when you have spoken. I somehow feel sorry for the "Baby".«

*After not receiving any more information, we added the word "Vaccination" behind each word.*

o **Polio Vaccination:** I have more compassion. I don't want to scare you.
o **Baby:** You are also the one who scares me the least of all. You still have a connection to me.
o **Tetanus Vaccination:** I still feel everything hurting from the cramps, but I am very relaxed. Now you are also interesting.
o **Baby:** What do you want from me?
o **Tetanus Vaccination:** You want something from me!
o **Baby:** Huh? No, no! I want nothing from you.
o **Polio Vaccination:** Are we serving someone? Is someone using us? We can't give ourselves to the "Baby".
o **Rotaviruses Vaccination:** My vaccination is completely unimportant. Since I became the "Vaccination", I feel a sense of power. I don't understand "Tetanus", but "Polio", the empathy – because polio can also be a very tragic disease. Is this vaccination really life-critical?

**Baby**
»Well, I don't really understand the concept of vaccination. But from what I've picked up, it's about my protection in some way. At least, that's what I think. But I don't need anything! There's nothing wrong with me. Or am I incomplete? I'm not unprotected or anything. I just don't understand.«

*"Tetanus Vaccination" laughts.*

o **Tetanus Vaccination:** I come to you... You interest me. That's where I go.
o **Baby:** Yes, I'm most afraid of you! You're a bit suspicious to me. I don't understand anything. Are you possessing me? I don't understand this. Why? Everything is fine, right?

o **Tetanus Vaccination:** As "Tetanus", I was quite tense and turned away from you. But as "Vaccination", you interest me. You are a host for me. Then I'll take your body.
o **Baby:** Ewww!!!
o **Rotavirues Vaccination:** This is the course of nature. When the immune system is weak. Our entire organism is made up of viruses and bacteria. We live in an organism with viruses and bacteria.

*"Tetanus Vaccination" is cracking up laughing. And "Baby" looks under its sweater.*

o **Baby:** I am currently checking to see if I am full of viruses and bacteria. I see nothing. I find myself good just the way I am. I don't understand that at all. What are you talking about?
o **Polio Vaccination:** You are healthy. They are trying to manipulate you. They want power over the parents and the child. "Tetanus Vaccination" seems like being on drugs. "Baby", run away!
o **Rotaviruses Vaccination:** It's not about whether everything is fine with you or something is missing. It's about pursuing a purpose with the vaccination. It's not about the viruses. It's about the vaccination. That triggers all sorts of things.
o **Tetanus Vaccination:** Well, "Rotaviruses", you're talking complete nonsense. Do you really believe what you're saying, or have you been told what to say? What a doctor would explain as well? Well, I know that's not true. I'm not saying its half-knowledge. I'm just saying that you're spouting the crap everyone talks about. I'm going to the "Baby" and taking possession of it.

**Baby**
»I feel like my future is being shown to me here. Either I'll go crazy, or I'll be possessed, or I'll get diabetes, or I'll get spastic seizures. What is this supposed to be? I feel like someone is going down a list: "The child must have this later, that later, those things later. So, let's do this and that." I feel like I'm seeing my future with you right now! I'm going nuts! And it's either physical or mental illnesses, or both. A dash of depression, a dash of Tourette's, a dash of ADHD, a dash of thyroid

306

dysfunction, a dash of I-don't-know-what. A dash of kiss-my-ass. No idea.«

- o **Rotaviren Vaccination:** What I see happening to me is that "Baby" is being vaccinated while sick. Not just by Corona, but by all other vaccinations as well.
- o **Tetanus Vaccination:** Oh, now you got it! [laughs] If I'm not rigid, then I'm crazy. But I like that! They put me in a syringe, and then I just come over to you. And if I'm a vaccination, I feel good.

**Baby**
»Then I feel really possessed! As if I am no longer myself! Fuck! It has something to do with madness. And I can't do anything; because the parents are not here. And "Polio Vaccination", I don't feel at all like I would need that. Maybe it was useful at some point. I don't know. But I don't feel the necessity at all that the danger exists here and now. The idea of getting polio is ridiculous!«

- o **Polio Vaccination:** I also feel out of place. I would like to call for my parents.

*Those who delve deeper into the work and add two more words: "Mom", because mothers take their children for vaccination, and "Possession", because it was mentioned frequently. And when that is not enough, we add "The Evil" as well.*

**Possession**
»Oh, now I'm even a bit angrier. I want "Mom"! Yes, I want you. Exactly you. There she is finally. You are my victim. I'LL GET YOU!«

**Mom**
»What?? You're crazy. You want to scare me. Jesus, Mary, "Possession" is really crazy! Unbearable. My "Baby" is far away. I'm desperately trying to connect with you, "Baby". What do we do? Then it's good if I don't vaccinate you. Let "Possession" figure it out for themselves. So, I'm determined. If I'm already so scared, how can I deliver you then?«

**Baby**

»Let my "mom" be! Through me, "Posession" will get you, "Mom!" I feel like we have no choice. I am merely a means to an end to reach you. It's like in a concentration camp. It's as if madness is taking over! As if one wants to go crazy, numbed, shut down... Then you can vaccinate, give medications, I don't know what. One can do anything! The darkness is the virus. Not a natural, human, earthly virus, but something dark. And that's what "Posession" expresses. And I feel like I have to protect my "Mom" as a baby!«

**The Evil**

»I am totally hot! I feel totally crippled. I am in a vacuum. It's as if only emptiness exists around me. This must be what hell feels like. Otherwise, I feel nothing. There is only emptiness. I feel like I have no future, no present, no past. I have no feeling at all. I am in a state of perpetual emptiness of existence. I hear you talking, but it doesn't reach me emotionally at all. I feel like the personification of evil.«« 

o **Baby:** I really feel empathy for you. Are you alone? Do you feel alone?
o **The Evil:** I can't feel anything. I am here, but I feel nothing. But when you ask that, I get a little stomachache.
o **Baby:** It makes me sad when you are "The Evil". That's not nice. There is a lack of love here. Do we actually have it?

*Wir nehmen die "Liebe" noch mit hinzu.*

**Love**

»I am not wanted. I can't go anywhere. To no one. No one wants me. As love, I am sad.«

**Baby**

»It saddens me that "The Evil" feels so lonely. And now, that we are both alone, "Mom", is there really love between us? I know you are my "Mom", but it feels distant. Connection is important. Two children and two parents: mom, dad, or whatever. It just makes me sad because love is central to me. I don't see any difficulties. And I want everyone to be well.«

o **Mom:** Emotional connection is important. And then difficulties can be overcome in a different way. I looked at you and you seem so isolated to me, "Love". I don't even need to try because I won't get any connection with you anyway. My "Baby" is the most important to me.

**Baby**
»This is like it was done on purpose: The love and joy I had at the beginning have been cut off. I still have them, but I am sad now. Everyone should have "Love" and everyone should have parents and everyone should be allowed to laugh. I don't see evil in anyone. I only see when someone is sad, hurt, and alone. Mom, where is Dad?«

o **Mom:** I don't know. It takes space. There is so much sorrow. I would like to hold you in my arms. So I can comfort myself? Or give you protection or solace?
o **Baby:** Both are true. Like when we both support and comfort each other. And that's okay for me. It's a beginning. Better than the other crap. First, just be sad that we have lost something important.
o **Love:** What have you lost,"Mom"?
o **Mom:** The loving connection. I have also lost my husband. I don't feel anyone there.
o **Love:** Does that mean I can't come to you?
o **Mom:** I don't know. The connection is interrupted. I do want it, but it's like it's cut off. How do you mend it again? The "Baby" needs sleep.

**Baby**
»I have the feeling that I can't sleep properly anymore. The sleep is so restless, so shallow. It's not restful sleep anymore. There's only exhaustion. It feels like all connections have been severed. Nothing comes together anymore. Everything has been separated, cut off. I don't know why or how. I feel like we need a real jolt that must pass through all of

us so that something can break open. So that something new can emerge. Otherwise, we will sink like in a depression, in sadness.«

o **Love:** But without dad, nothing works here.
o **Mom:** Violence severs the connections. But I also don't feel like a mom and dad. I feel totally isolated.
o **Baby:** Are we all without mom and dad? It's like forgetting what I actually know. But somehow everything becomes so separate when you're grown up.
o **Mom:** Because we can no longer perceive the lack. The lack we had as children. And what was missing and hurt us. We cut that off and then we just function.

**Baby**
»But beauty will also be forgotten. Now it occurs to me: That is a decision. One can also decide differently. One can sink into it, but one can also decide again. The good, the beautiful is always there. I have felt it! It's not gone. It's just buried. And one can decide for it. And I don't think one should say to someone that they are evil. I decide against that. I have the feeling that when I grow up, I don't want to do something like that. I decide on something else. I want to be loving and not evil. And I want to have understanding for others and not divide. And when I decide for that, I can do it too.«

o **Love:** "Baby", you are my great hope. Then I can come to you.

**Baby**
»Can you come with me? I can do it differently, I can speak differently. And I don't want to be without hope. And I don't want to be a bad person. And I think we can all decide. And if you don't want to decide, okay. But I won't decide like that. I want to decide to be who I am. And I won't be beaten down. Even if you vaccinate me. I won't be beaten down! I have the strength! And just because others aren't loving, doesn't mean we can't be loving. I want to be loving. It might get harder, it might get more challenging. I remember now! And I want to continue remembering.«

310

- o **Mom:** And I won't take you to get vaccinated. We'll do it our way. And I want to be loving towards myself. Then I can also be loving towards you.
- o **Baby:** Ah, that sounds good. That sounds good! That sounds beautiful!
- o **Mom:** And then we'll play together and then we'll dance together. And then we'll sing together. It will keep growing.
- o **Baby:** Yes! Then we laugh together. And if we are the only ones, then we are the only ones.
- o **Mom:** We are two. And "Love" is the third in our circle.
- o **Baby:** That's right. And I am thinking about my free will right now. I carry it in my pocket. When I'm sad again and feel like it's hopeless or I can't move forward, then I remember. There is free will and there is you, "Love".
- o **Love:** The free will makes it even easier to love. That is like my friend, free will.
- o **Mom:** Like the bridge that you can use to come to us.
- o **Baby:** It is nice, "Mom", when you say that you are loving towards yourself. I find that so beautiful. It makes me feel safe. And I want only good for all people. That's what I want too. I never want to do anything bad to anyone.
- o **Mom:** Did that make you very sad?

**Baby**

»Yes, that made me sad. I don't want anyone to suffer or be upset. I don't like that. So now I have a plan for my life. Now I know how to move forward. Nothing can stop me now. I want to live. And love. Live well. Yes, exactly! Live well! Not just live, but live WELL! Yes! I will carry that in my pocket too. If I should forget, then I will look inside.«

- o **Mom:** You are phenomenal. You have preserved your strength.

# 6. PSYCHE AND SLEEP

## 6.1 DEPRESSION

*General-encounter (5 words)*
*Child– Depression – Mom – Dad – Medication*

Even this work is groundbreaking: Behind the symptom of depression, the abyss of a family history of abortion and multi-generational abuse is revealed. Because the parents, especially the father, strongly refuse to confront their own issues, there is a shift of symptoms from the father to the child. The child is completely overwhelmed and oscillates between thoughts of suicide and self-harm. It is not the medication that helps, but the parents' examination of their own past and family history.

**Depression**
»Actually, I thought that as depression, I should somehow be confused in my mind. But I'm not. My name is "Depression", but then I should feel bad. But actually, I feel like I have the responsibility for all of you!
- What are you doing,"Dad"?
- Why aren't you taking care of your "Child", "Mom"?

They just say, "yes, I feel for you" briefly, instead of doing something. That makes me angry.

I just came up with a solution: If we give "Medication" to the "Child" now, then it will be shut down. But for me, that would only be a temporary solution. Let's first address the problems that "Mom" and "Dad" have here. I feel like I have the oversight of all of you because you are not connected at all and don't talk to each other. But just now it was mentioned that "Dad" and "Medication" are related. So, it's probably the "Dad" who takes the "Medication"?

It hits me when the "Child" says she hates me. I understand that, and I also feel guilty. But I don't know how to change that.«

**Dad**

»Why are you all so serious? It's not a funny subject, but I could laugh. It's not a positive or healthy laughter. Hey diddly-diddly-dum. I feel su-per! Su-per! I feel nothing at all. Feelings are crap. I'm a little boy and I'm playing. Did I ever get "Medication" when I was little? Was there something there? Bubble bubble. "Medication" makes you ha-pp-y. Care-free. Bubble bubble. Bubble bubble. Look at me, I'm a seal."«

**Mama**

»I'm pretty angry, I'm annoyed. And I'm anything but depressed. "Dad" is a woman and today is International Women's Day. It's all so messed up! Of course, "Medication" has nothing to do with it. Now I'm mad at "Medication". I'm here sitting on a pile of anger and getting a headache.

Towards you, "Child", I have compassion. But somehow there's no connection. I have to deal with myself. I'm in such a mess myself that I have to cope with. I'm caught between "Dad" and "Medication". And I can't get out of it. I have no options to care for "Child". Guilt arises. I could fall into depression to avoid feeling all of this.

The bubble-bubble from "Dad", it sounds like in the womb. Maybe his mom took "Medication"? I have my eye on "Dad" and somehow I'm also puzzled by "Medication". And I'm thinking, what is "Dad" up to again?«

**Medication**

»The "Dad" seems suspicious to me. I don't know what I have to do with "Depression." So, I feel like I'm here to fix something that I actually have nothing to do with. I try to orient myself all the time and figure out where I fit in. The more I see you, "Dad", fumbling around like that, the more I think you two should deal with each other first. The suggestion of "Depression" would make sense.«

**Child**

»As a child, I have always felt completely alone and withdrawn into myself from the beginning. I dug my fingernail into my hand to feel something. I wondered if I had a stuffed animal or somewhere to hold on to. Is "Dad" drunk? I would like to disappear. I have no connection to anyone. My heart keeps getting heavier. I am alone with these people. It is awful. I have nothing to hold on to. Not to mention having any contact. I would really prefer to be alone.

I was scared that you are also so angry with me, "Mom." But I have no connection to you. Is it your dad or is it my "Dad"? You are all completely lost! How am I supposed to exist in this? I feel like I am supposed to solve everything. It's terrible! Horrible! ["Child" starts crying] But then who will help me? I need help! I am the one who is affected the worst. How am I supposed to grow up? The "Medications" seem like doomsday scenario to me. But I can't disappear, I can't run away, I am at your mercy. That is the absolute worst. But I am already too limited to say or do anything hateful.

The "Dad" is still stuck as a child. There's no one here! The "Mom" is also unable to act. Maybe she means well. I think I'm the only person, no matter how old I am, who realizes that it's hopeless. Unless something serious happens to the adults, that they reconnect with themselves, that they engage with themselves... I have no idea where this is headed. Am I going to kill myself?«

○ **Depression:** That's when I come to you. If it's as bad as you say, I will come to you. Then you won't have to feel the misery here when I come.

○ **Medication:** I'm supposed to hold something together without anyone telling me I have a job. Only when the "Child" says she's going to kill herself do I have a purpose. But only as a stopgap.

○ **Child:** Are you all completely crazy? That's not help at all! No, no. What kind of help is that supposed to be?! It will only get worse! I see it with my parents! I'd rather run away or cut myself! I know that's completely useless! The "Mom" is the most important. The "Dad" should just go away.

*What is wrong with the father? Why is he behaving almost crazy? We add "little boy" and a "?" to look deeper behind the scenes.*

**little boy**
»I am small. Under six years old. I must have experienced something. You come from me, "Depression." I am relieved that "Papa" is examining himself. I had this idea: Are you the grandma? The mother of

314

"Dad", of the little boy? So, for me, there is a danger that I could die if I am not protected. It could be dangerous for me. I don't know what it is. I don't know if it's in the mother's belly, if it's in the hospital, or afterwards. I am under pressure. I feel like it's not just one thing. It's as if there are two, three things somehow coming towards me, coming together. Before, later. Like on a string of pearls. Terrible.«

**Depression**
»I am in my right place. I am only focused on you. I am there so that you don't have to deal with all of this. It's as if I'm placing a bell over you so that you can somehow bear all of this. I do this because you are very important to me and because I want to protect you. I feel responsible. Exactly. Because no one else is doing it here. And I am so careful! "little boy", I am here. And I am also strong! I protect you from everything here. I don't think you really know what's going on, and that's my fault. Because I have to exert so much energy to shield you. Then I don't notice anything myself.«

**Mom**
»I feel like I'm wrapped in cotton wool. I am highly stressed, and something is happening to me physically. The fact that you are there to protect "little boy" really touched me. For me, it also feels like everything around me is being compressed. It also feels like dying. It feels like I am also in mortal danger.«

**?**

»Abortion! Does that have something to do with "Dad"? I am now standing for this "what now?" The other stuff didn't work out, so what now? Do we have to pretend that everything is somehow okay? Now the show begins. And that's where "Depression" might come into play. It can support that certain parts become easier. But the more I speak out, the more chaos there is. When you start sawing there, the rope will eventually break, and then there will be a loud bang. Abuse!

I am indeed the question mark, but I myself have no voice. But you, "little boy", have the voice. If you work with me, if you get in touch with me, then you can start asking questions. And then it gets uncomfortable. Because everyone else probably doesn't want to hear those

315

questions. Wherever questions are asked, there is very little space for childhood because it's about other issues. But as soon as you start asking questions, there's no longer a need for the help of "depression". Then more life is possible, your own life, your own becoming an adult. Your own being. Exiting the question marks. You carry all of this. All these question marks. And they are not your question marks. I am not your question mark. I am the question mark of the whole system! I hang, upside down, like the hook up there.«

o **Depression:** I have to exert more effort so that "little boy" doesn't get hurt. I won't do anything for you, because I think you are guilty!
o **little boy:** That would make sense to me. Who wouldn't want me to be there? Conflict between my mom and dad? That weirdly makes me feel relieved when you say that. I just realized that "?" is what's best for me. It's bringing some clarity to me.

**Mom**
»There is a lot of shame, guilt. I am actually mute, dissociated. I am really frustrated in my marriage. I get stomach pains when I talk about it. I push all my frustration onto men. The man gets all of it, all the hatred I have towards men. I completely reject him. But I wouldn't tell you that. It's all so quiet and secretive. I think I would want to have a girl. I wish for a girl who is cheerful. That I can dress and clothe. I am so unhappy in my marriage! It's not going at all as I imagined. And somehow the children can't make it any better. They are even more burdensome. They get it by my rejection.«

**little boy**
»So, not knowing was worse than hearing from you, "?", what you just said. Playacting. It's twisted: "Yes, we wanted this child. Look, a desired child!" That's what you say. Heir or whatever nonsense is said. I feel like I'm caught in the crossfire between my mom and dad. So, I really need "?" that you speak. You give me stability, give me direction. Then the lying facade collapses. That's good. But how can I be a child in that situation? How can I live like that? At first, I was glad that the attention was off me. I thought, okay, now they are taking care of themselves and then they can see me. But this seems to go on forever!

316

If I don't perish in the process, then I'll be an adult by the time you as parents have worked something out. This weighs heavily on my heart now and hurts me. And my hope is once again completely extinguished. I hide away with my stuffed animal, Kangaroo, in my bed, in some corner. I don't know how I should go on living.«

**Mom**
»The more you talk, the more I fade into the background. But I still have control over you. I can feel that. I also become hardened as you talk more about the house of cards falling apart. I don't want that to come to light. I am doing exactly what I should be doing. This has been done for generations. I cover up the abuse.«

o   **little boy:** And aborting children?
o   **Mom:** That is murder. That has also been done for generations. That was the only way to protect us. It's completely twisted. But it's the only option we have. It's completely insane.
o   **Depression:** I am so angry that you know that and still do nothing! Sitting in the background and lamenting instead of taking action! That makes me utterly furious! What do we need you for then?!
o   **little boy:** No. It has to start with me. I need your help, "?". Whatever else you can tell me or where I should start. I need help. What topic should I begin with? Where should I start?

**Child**
»I have such heartache because my parents are not here. Because they have experienced terrible things themselves. I can feel that. And it hurts me so much. And it takes away any hope that something else can still happen for me.«

**?**
»I believe a first good question could be questioning "Depression". In the sense of: What is it good for? What does it do? What can't it do? What does it not stand for? When can it leave? Where does it belong? "Medication" are not the solution.«

317

- o **Child:** Is there anyone outside who can help? Who can work with or talk to the parents?
- o **little boy:** When you ask that question, I think they also help to suppress. Here is something black. I have to get to the bottom of the black that wants to swallow the "Mom".
- o **Depression:** And I'm actually just here for protection. But I realize that I am quite angry myself. Probably I am transferring that to you. Even though I have a protective function.

**little boy**
»Exactly. It's like when you fire something and it bounces off the walls and hits someone in the group that you were actually trying to protect. But "Mama" is really consumed by the black, evil force. I'm realizing now as a boy why it's important for me to finally get involved. For me, as a "little boy" from "Dad", to step into action.«

# 6. 2 ADHD

*General-encounter (4 words)*
*parents – child – doctor – ADHD*

A brief excursion into the history of medicine, this time based on the German children's story of "Zappelphilipp," known as "Fidgety Phil" in English. The Frankfurt neurologist Heinrich Hoffmann (1809 – 1894) reached for pen and paper in his practice, starting to draw for restless children in order to calm them down. This inadvertently led to the creation of a book that, in its original version from 1845, contained six stories about children with particular characteristics. Fidgety Phil made his debut one year later in the second edition of 1846.

»What Heinrich Hoffmann mainly depicted with Fidgety Phil is, however, unmistakable: an open conflict between the father and his only son, whose behavior at the table was a rudeness that was not acceptable in a bourgeois family of the 19th century. (...) What was considered a rudeness in Heinrich Hoffmann's Fidgety Phil was transformed along his theoretical interpretation path into neuropathy, psychopathy, neurasthenia, child error, brain damage, subjected to two neurosis concepts, labeled as illness, disorder, and disability, and ends, for now, at genes and neurotransmitter chemistry.«[67]

This work tells the story of a deeply lonely child. A child who cannot find a place in a dysfunctional family. It tells the story of an overwhelmed, neurotic mother, of a completely absent father, and it tells the story of a medical system that is not concerned with the child's well-being. It is sad how lost a child can feel in school and in life when the spaces become tighter. And how it is degraded to an IT. And the question arises, then as now: Where can one still be a child at all?

»I feel, I am completely alone as a child. Dad is absolutely absent, unable to deal with himself. I felt like I was responsible for him somehow. Almost like I have been given this responsibility to emulate him because my mother hates him so much. I kind of pick up and take this part of my identity that I am told I am like him and I identify with. On one hand, I believe it but on the other hand I want my mother. But I can't have both. And it culminates in a kind of erratic behavior. As a child, I always wanted an animal because I could have something for me. Can I trust you enough to say: "I would really like to have an animal?" There is a deep longing but can I share it.«

*The "child" is throwing small toys on the table, experimenting with a glass of water and dices. Making angry noises, rocking back and forwards with the chair. Constantly looks around.*

**parents**
»Okay, we are ready to go out. It is not so cold outside. I think the dress is suitable for that party. Bye bye!«

["parents" go and are coming back, yelling at the "child"] »What are you doing with the water?? Put that aside! Oh, my God! I said, put that on its place! Put that on its place! Do you hear me!? He will drive

---

[67] Deutsches Ärzteblatt 2004; 101: A 239–243 [Heft 5], »„Zappelphilipp" und ADHS: Von der Unart zur Krankheit« [German Medical Journal, »Fidgety Philip and ADHD: From Naughtiness to the Disease«] https://www.aerzteblatt.de/archiv/40288/Zappel-philipp-und-ADHS-Von-der-Unart-zur-Krankheit

me crazy. She, he – or is it he or she? He or she. I told you, put that down! That "child" is driving me crazy!!! I cannot stand that anymore! I will call Mary.«

[To the child] »I will lock you in your room and you will stay there for five hours. Do you hear me!? You will stay alone for five hours if you behave like that!!

[Back with the friend] »Darling, please reserve my place. See you soon. Bye bye. I am just getting ready. No, no, no! I am coming. I am just getting ready. That "child" is again racing on my nerves. That's why. Bye Bye. Kisses, bye.«

[To the child] »I am going out. Okay, please behave. Do you hear me? Please behave! You stay on your own at home. Please behave, okay?! Stay in your room. And watch the cat not scratching the sofa. Bye. Bye.«

»I am coming home and cannot look at that "child". You are unbearable! You are an unbearable "child"! You are doing exactly the opposite of what I am telling you. I don't want to look at you. You just stay at your room.«

*Next scene where they are all together at the therapy session. The "doctor" is playing constantly with his phone, going away, coming back and smiling stupidly.*

o **parents:** Okay, when was our next session? We had a session with you? Oh, I forgot about it. Okay, okay. Let's sort it out. I have other things to do. Okay, so how long will the session last? Because I will go to the nail polishing. That's my favorite color! It is what I am planning to have next on my nails. So, how can we fix that? I cannot stand looking at that "child". He, she or that – don't have to be here.

o **doctor:** It's okay. You can go for half an hour. I mean you can go, do your nails while I am alone with the "child". 30 minutes. And then you come back. I am a male doctor and I am so happy I don't have these issues. I feel just wonderful because YOU have these issues and I don't have them. So, let's have a look at the "child".

*"parents" go away again.*

- **doctor:** So, my dear "child". How are you? I am not your mother. I am friendly. Oh, what is that? What do you have in that jar?
- **child:** NO. That's mine. I don't want to share with you.
- **doctor:** How old are you?
- **child:** I am not telling you. It is not your business.
- **doctor:** What's your name?
- **child:** I am not telling you that either.
- **doctor:** Can you write a sentence for me?
- **child:** Just let me get my Moms favorite lipstick. I like to write with my Moms' lipstick »FUCK OFF«. *[holding up a piece of paper]*
- **doctor:** Such nice words! Well done! Are you already in school?
- **child:** I am not telling you.
- **doctor:** I am pretty sure, you do this rocking with your chair in school as well.
- **child:** Bla, bla, bla.
- **doctor:** Do you have friends? Do you like animals?

*"child" stops rocking with the chair.*

- **doctor** [talks very slowly and continues to smile stupidly]: Dog? Or a cat? Maybe a horse? My assistant, she has a big horse.
- **child:** Maybe you could both ride off onto the sunset on it.
- **doctor:** I like to pet it. It is very fluffy. Do you have a pet? Or would you like one? It would be great if you could write me the name of the pet you love. I can talk to your mother and we can arrange something. Do you prefer to play?
- **child:** I don't want to be here. I want to go home.
- **doctor:** I just have the standard questionnaire here and then you can go home. There is no problem.
- **child:** I go for a walk now.
- **doctor:** Okay. Okay. Mrs "parent"? Are you back?
- **parents:** Okay. Yes. Just a moment. I am taking my seat. Oh, hello. Oh, I don't want to deal with that issue. I myself need help! I cannot deal with that issue. Look at that "child"!
- **doctor:** Yeah, it is very difficult. I fully understand. It is really difficult for you.

- **parents:** Oh, you can prescribe a medicine? Pills? There must be some pills.
- **doctor:** Everything you want. Everything you want.
- **parents:** Can it be a quick fix? Because I will go to the hairdresser. Just give him some pills. I thought you are a psychologist. Ah, you are a doctor. "doctor", please, pills or… I will make sure he has the pills.
- **doctor:** Oh, I thought your "child" is a girl.
- **parents:** Girl?
- **doctor:** Yeah. It's a boy, no?
- **parents:** Can be. It can be. Maybe.
- **doctor:** Anyways. Anything you want. Of course. You get medication. And maybe you just send the "child" in, once a week or every second week, and we can talk? It is difficult in the beginning but we should try.
- **child:** No, no!
- **parents:** Oh, actually I realize, this is tranquilizing me [smelling an odeur]. It is tranquilizing my nerves. Another doctor has told me, a glass of wine is also okay in the evenings.
- **doctor:** Yes. Yeah. It is very difficult. I fully understand it. Must be very difficult. But I give you, if you want, the medication. And it would be best if the "child" would come to see me.
- **parents:** I love this color. I also have to change curtains very soon because that color is not good for that season. It can be, because I am really super busy. I don't have so much time for whatever is his problems. Pills will do. If you subscribe them and I will send my assistant.
- **doctor:** Whatever you need.
- **parents:** So, tomorrow he will be fixed? Or how long?
- **doctor:** Give it some days until everything regulates in the body. Max three days I would say and it should be okay.
- **parents:** Because we will go to our summer house and he has to be normal.
- **doctor:** Normal. Yes of course. I understand. Definitely. And I would say when you come back, see me again. Come for half an hour and that's fine. And we do this regularly.

322

- **parents:** Okay, so, I also take regularly sleeping pills. Maybe you can also subscribe me some sleeping pills?
- **doctor:** Absolutely! Yes. Of course!
- **parents:** Oh, thank you. Then we are fine. Okay, I have to run. I have another task. Thank you. I very appreciate. Oh… I am in a complete shouting state whenever I see that "child". I have to shout. I cannot bear that.

*Meanwhile, the "child" wrote the following note holding it into the camera: »She is a mad neurotic turnip. Bah!!«*

### ADHD

»Who is the mad one? I still don't get it. Is it your Mom? Your dad? Your grandparents? Who is the mad one? Why did they give you my name? We are totally different people. I just heard a bit of what the "doctor" was saying and I thought: That person is crazier than anyone! Even than our mother! Sorry to say that. Have you seen that smile? Was that "doctor" on drugs?«

### child

»She is a mad neurotic turnip! She is a lunatic. Lunatic! It is too much. I beat my drum, I shake my jar. They try to give me your name! My name is "ADHD". I don't have a name. I think the "doctor" had some of my Moms sleeping tablets. And then she gets baaa!! – sleeps – baaaa! – sleeps – baaaa! That is all she does. She is horrible!«

- **child:** I do miss her sometimes. But she doesn't like me.
- **ADHD:** SHE DOESN'T LIKE YOU?
- **child:** She shouts at me. And she leaves me all on my own. Just fucked up. See, this was for the "doctor" [holding up the paper which states »FUCK OFF«].
- **ADHD:** You know what I was thinking? I think if we would go – like that stupid "doctor" said – once a week, we could analyze that person maybe after a month; or two; maxiMom. I am pretty sure. That would be interesting, because we could turn his own methods against him. Wouldn't this be quite funny?

- **child:** Five minutes! Nutter. Full Freak. Crazy lunatic. It would be just easier to give him my Moms sleeping pills. With a cup of tea.
- **ADHD:** But this is really tiring.
- **child:** It is. I have to be like this all the time! ALL THE TIME. And it's all me! There is something wrong with me.
- **ADHD:** Oh, my God! But why? I don't get it. There is nothing wrong with you!
- **child:** That's not what my Mom says. She shouts all the time. She wants to give me your name. And then she leaves me on my own.
- **ADHD:** Nails, hair and other stupid women. Sorry.
- **child:** She needed a pet dog but not a child.
- **ADHD:** And where is the… the… the guy who gave you birth? The other one? You know. What's his name? There is another word for him but I don't recall it. What was his name?
- **child:** Jeff. Yes. I call him Jeff. Spammer. That's another word I like to call him. Just Spammer.
- **ADHD:** No. Other people call him that…
- **child:** Dad?
- **ADHD:** Uuh!! Yeah, that's the word! I don't want to think about him. He is as crazy as the mother. Just different crazy. Oh gosh. He wants to be liked by everyone.
- **child:** He's got a big task ahead. He doesn't even like me.
- **ADHD:** Yeah, that's true. That is true. There is no place. I was thinking about school but that's also a shitty place.
- **child:** That's horrible. That's a prison. Prison. They make you sit there. I hate it. I hate it! Only girly girls. And all the itchy clothes.
- **ADHD:** And too many children. Just too much of everything. Too many people. Too loud. Too full. There is no time for nothing.
- **child:** So loud! And then they constantly tell you to sit still! They give you all this shit and then they say: »Sit still. And shut up!« And THEY never shut up. Blab la bla. And then you get into trouble if you mimic them. I like to get into trouble; so that I get taken out of class.
- **ADHD:** Yes! That sounds much better. Because when the others are in their class rooms, at least, it is quiet. Because during the breaks it is even louder!

- **child:** Pandemonium! Pandemonium! People everywhere, like ants crawling all over you. Yikes. I hate it. And I don't like talking to people. And if I do talk to people, I am told I talk too quickly. Or I talk too loudly. Or this or that. So, I just don't like it.
- **ADHD:** That's true. And like when you said: Everyone is playing a theater game: There are the beautiful ones and the others are the fighting ones and there are the very timid and small ones. I don't like anyone, to be honest. Because I feel like no one like us.
- **child:** There isn't anyone like us. Nobody likes us. I don't really want to fit in. I just want to be left alone.
- **ADHD:** True. But no one leaves us alone. Everywhere you have to go you have something to do!
- **child:** I hide. And I pretend to hide. And they can't find me. They get really upset. We are bad. There is something wrong with us.
- **ADHD:** It is not that the others would be so fantastic either. Let's be honest. I mean, there are some crackheads also in our class. Just different stupid.
- **child:** Yeah, this is true. I like to learn…
- **ADHD:** But not the way they do it there. It's stupid.

**child**

"It's horrible. It's a prison. From one place to the next, every time the freaking bell rings. Jesus, what's with the bell ringing? It's not church! And taking a pee is a military exercise! Jesus Christ! Nobody can go to the bathroom on their own. Oh! And then when you do, you go in there and they are smoking or vaping – and you are like: I don't want to go in there! Then I get into even more trouble. So, I hold it. And sometimes, I have an accident. And then Mom gets REALLY angry. For she just doesn't have a clue. She thinks it's my fault.«

- **ADHD:** She is like a headless chicken. Why is she not going to this mad "doctor"? They would complement each other perfectly. Maybe they will understand each other?
- **child** [laughing]: She is too mad for that "doctor"! They will swap pills. Having a smarty party.

o **ADHD** [laughing]: Imagine that picture! Sorry, but I just imagine them having sex. Wouldn't that be nice? Maybe she would then be happy again. But maybe she wouldn't either. I don't know.
o **child** [laughing]: Oh, the giggle helps. I forgot what it was to laugh.

**ADHD** [laughing and coughing]
»My lungs are not even used to it. Oh, my God. You know, if someone would ask me what profession would be nice, now that we are laughing, I would say stand-up comedian. Wouldn't it be nice? To just tell everyone what I think of them?«

o **child:** I think the slogan »fuck off« would work.
o **ADHD:** That would be the name of my first show.
o **child:** And we would start with the teachers. Damn teachers.
o **ADHD:** Although I would prefer the "doctor", to be honest with you. Because he is really crazy. Did you see his smile??
o **ADHD:** Yeah, there is no place to laugh. Just this military…
o **child:** Our Mom is looking for herself. Stumbling around trying to find the coffee mug. That and her tranquilizers. Oh, that was a question, the "doctor" and his horse! He's got a horse. I told him to ride off into the sunset.
o **ADHD:** But I was, I had a minute… I was afraid he would get you with this animal question. I was a tiny bit afraid that he got you. Seriously.
o **child** [whispering]: I like animals. It was the horse that tipped the balance.
o **ADHD:** I knew it! I knew it!
o **child:** A horse! I mean, the cat and a dog, fair enough. But walking a horse!?
o **ADHD:** Pippi Langstrumpf, Pippi Longstocking… Remember her![68]
o **child:** She was allowed to be "naughty". She didn't get into trouble. And she was allowed a horse. I am a bit jealous now.

---

[68] We loved them all, Pippi Longstocking, The Villa Kunterbunt, Mr Nielson, Little Uncle, Tommy and Annika. Thanks to Astrid Lindgren and her daughter for the stories of this wonderful girl. https://www.astridlindgren.com/de/figuren/pippi-langstrumpf

- **ADHD:** And it had dots. And she was really strong. She could lift it. Quite impressive, I have to say.
- **child:** I agree. I agree. This is true.
- **ADHD:** But wherever I look, there is just no place to do that. Not even a little bit of it. I mean, I can't even climb up a tree. Where are the trees?
- **child:** I can do anything when my Mom shouts. I can go really fast. I can climb anywhere where she can't get me. And I can escape. Anything, when she shouts. But she can't calm down. She is a turnip. In fact, I copy her! I have been taken tips. Can't quite up with it though.
- **ADHD:** And this stupid – I don't want to say his name, this d-a-d – he has no clue whatsoever. How can he be that stupid?
- **child:** He really annoys me. She hates him! She hates him. This is like a firework.
- **ADHD:** And he has no interest in us. That's true. He is so freaking stupid. My God is he stupid!
- **child:** I feel a bit like him. I feel a little bit like him. I think sometimes this is the other reason she doesn't like me.
- **ADHD:** Please don't insult yourself! She thinks you are like your d-a-d? This is not fair. This is not fair!
- **child:** She says it to me a lot: »You are just like your father!!« She needs a volume control. I did use to try the tele remote. Take the tele remote, press the mute button. It didn't work. But I tried.
- **ADHD:** You know, the only thing which could work is that she stays out of the house for long. Not only an hour. At least for five hours.
- **child:** That makes me really scared. At least I know, when she shouts, she is there. It is not better for me but for her when she goes away. And then she tells me really how bad my daaad is. And then she tells me you are just like him. She is horrible! I am okay if she can leave me alone but not abandon me. I have to take these really stupid tablets! To make me normal.
- **ADHD:** But you can drop the pills somewhere, can't you? She will not figure it out. I am not sure if you can pretend a little bit.
- **child:** I think, this is all I do. There is not a lot of space anywhere. What else can I do than pretend? She just doesn't tell when I say to

fuck of. The "doctor" was quite diplomatic. I think he probably went behind the curtain to cry.

o **ADHD** [laughing]: No, I don't think he feels that way. I think he thought also that our mother is a bit crazy. But I thought, he rather wanted to get rid of her than talking to you.

o **child:** And I needed to fill out the form! This feels really horrible. Because I still want her. But she hates me. She even shouts when she sleeps. She likes to drink. A bottle of.... Every night. She likes to drink. I don't like her when she drinks. Then she gets really mean. I mean she is mean normally but then she gets REALLY mean.

o **ADHD:** Gosh! I have the impression when she does it, I am not there anymore with you. I just go somewhere else. I just can't listen to it.

o **child:** I hide. I hide. She tries to find me. When she gets too tipsy. It's like her nails: She is fake like her nails. She cares what people think about.

o **ADHD:** But in a strange way. She is constantly seeking, constantly seeking. What is she seeking?

**child**

»Anything but me. She just doesn't like me. I am on my own all the time. And when I am with her, we just fight. And it is really difficult and it's really hard. I am just tired. It's exhausting. It is hard to be like this all the time. But Jesus, she manages it. Holy shit! She has some free phase electricity down her ass. She is on a next level! What am I? 12 years? And she has been like this forever. I am dreading when I start my period. And I can't tell her. How am I gonna tell her? What am I going to do now?«

Some afterthoughts from the resonator of "parents":

»When I show up, I automatically start to shout. While you were talking with "ADHD", I felt I could come in saying: "You are not in bed! I will tell your father! He will spank you!" I don't know how I, as a parent, am tolerating this nervous system for 12 years. Either I am shouting or I go to sleep. In the evening, drinks calm me down. I look for things, substances, to calm me down. My nervous system asks for it.«

## 6.3 ASPERGER'S

*General-encounter (3 words)*
*Asperger's diagnosis – child – help ?*

In the course of researching this topic, I came across a book by the American Edith Schaeffer on Dr. Asperger:

»Vienna 1938: Doctor Hans Asperger describes symptoms in children, which he classifies under the diagnosis of "autistic psychopathy". He had observed weaknesses in social behavior in patients. In the same year, the National Socialists enter Vienna. Asperger soon had to justify that children whom he deemed "not socially integrable" were becoming victims of "euthanasia" at the institution known as Am Spiegelgrund. Edith Sheffer, a mother of a child affected by autism, set out to trace the origins of the diagnosis. She reveals the values that shaped Asperger and the path the diagnosis has taken.«[69]

Edith Schaeffer has written an absolutely worth-reading book that goes deep under the skin. And this work is no less so. Once again, we see multigenerational trauma, with a multitude of murdered children at its forefront. Who or what can help? Parents? Doctors? Psychologists? Or is it preferable to collectively look away? Are feelings completely split off, dissociated, all silenced?

**help ?**
»I feel a bit like a parent. I tried this and that but nothing helps. Nothing. And there is another voice. Like I would schizophrenic. "Why are you looking for answers? You have to take it as a given, don't stress out." I feel like I would be medical system and both parents argue and

---

[69] Edith Sheffer, »Asperger's Children: The Origins of Autism in Nazi Germany.«
Summary of the German translation which is different from the English edition, but, as I find, much more apt.

fight. I would rather like the "child" to not say anything. As if I would be afraid if the "child" would say something. And another thought is: Maybe there was a problem at birth? Let me check this as well. Maybe I find something here which gives me some clues.

And when you, "Asperger's diagnosis", were talking about not feeling and feelings being stupid, I thought: That is great. If I am a parent or if I am doctor – or in this medical system – not feeling is great. I want help and I need help – as a parent – but in essence, I don't really want it. Pretending to search for help. And pretending to be helpless. When I switch to the position of the "doctor", I am pretending to help but I am not helping at all.

It is like a theater play on my side somehow. It is very distracting because I definitely don't want to know. I want the opposite of what I am saying. Because the more technical terms or medical terms you use, the more chaotic my mind is getting. And then I am again in my own bubble. I feel a bit schizophrenic, like a headless chick running around.

Thank God, the "child" is not capable of saying anything. I would be afraid if the "child" would tell the truth, to be honest. Then my entire world and the picture of the world and me would collapse. I need a Schnapps...

I could write a letter to someone. There are so many people having so many answers. It is a perfect way to distract me. If "child" goes away, even better. Then I don't need to be afraid and then I don't need to search for answers. Perfect. Oh, maybe there are neurolinguistic problems? Something where dots are not connected in the head? Where neurons are not passing? I don't know how you call that. That would be awesome! The minute I am asking you the question, I am thinking: "Well, MY neurons don't connect properly." That is more the problem. Gosh. I am kind of crazy!

**Asperger's diagnosis**
»My job is to connect. I feel very rational, just being in my head. This is happening through words. So, I believe, I am trying to help you, "child", to connect. And I don't want to feel. Feeling is stupid and unnecessary. For me, everything feels more like a show. I am eating some nuts now and waiting for something to happen. I am more connected to you, "help ?", than with "child". My job is to do highly sophisticated

330

conversations with you in order to keep you busy. If "child" would do that, I would be needless. That's why I am here for you and not for "child".

So, what do you want to talk about? Which sophisticated, scientific, logical connection should we take? I am feeling, my job is to give you the feeling of not being crazy; and building a layer between you and "child". Because if you would realize that you are schizophrenic than that would be dangerous to the one I am protecting. I am keeping you busy from not feeling and getting lost in that Tsunami. And having a good-looking scientific expression on that yellow piece of paper. Having an explanation to why "child" is not okay. And as long as you are talking to me, you are not talking to "child".

Let's not go so deep. Let's keep a sophisticated logical conversation. That's easier for me. We are just rationalizing, rationalizing, rationalizing, rationalizing – all day, all night. And I don't want you to go mad. I want you to give you are reason to not look but stay on this logical level.«

**child**

»With these two perpetrators, I feel this is too much. Two perpetrators wanting to send me to the cosmos! To get rid of me. Not only of my expression but me and myself. I cannot deal with that. I will close my camera. That's too much. I even cannot express myself. It is unbearable. It is unbearable! Yes, children are being killed. This is what you are serving. This is what you are doing with your attitude. With your negligence.«

**Asperger's diagnosis**

»If you would go deeper into this killing and emotional thing, then I would try to distract you with my logic stuff, scientific stuff. All these words. I am good with words. Words and thoughts and ideas. I feel like a machine, like a computer, like a program. I have been programmed. It feels fully natural to me: You give me numbers and you get numbers. I am just zeros and ones. Just digits. You have a, b, c, d, e, f, g or 0, 1, 2, 3, 4, 5 – this is your diagnosis. I am like a programming language. I can calculate things. I can calculate and see if something is likely going to happen or not. I can influence that by offering a different logic to it. I am a calculator.

I feel connected to you, "help ?". I am the justification for you to not establish an emotional connection to "child". If I could change something, I would just be called Asperger's only. Asperger's sounds like I am an artificial person. Like a character. Like if you write comics and you design characters. I am like one of these characters or more characters. Probably a whole theater. Because there are so many calculations and logics and connections going on in this whole puzzle. But I am artificial. And I am your justification to not feel. I am helping you actually.

o **help ?:** And I am the parent. Especially the mother. And I have no connection to the "child". And to be honest, I even don't want to know anything. I am really so occupied with my own stuff, I have no time or desire to connect to "child".

o **Asperger's diagnosis:** So, therefore I am here for you to connect to "child" through words, through rational information. I am like a translator. And as long as you are not going into your feelings, I have a justification to be here.

o **help ?:** I don't want to. I want to avoid it with all means.

o **Asperger's diagnosis:** That's why I am so hard to get rid. Therefore, I am relaxed because I know, I am kind of undefeatable. Because as long as you and the doctors and all these people are rationalizing, I will be here. And I will be sucking energy out of "child". Because I believe, I am a part of "child". Even though I don't feel connected to "child". I am sitting on top of the "child".

o **help ?:** I am really in a messy state here. My God. I have this Tsunami in my back or on my side which is like in a Science Fiction movie. Like an alien, like an invasion, like a horror scenario.

o **Asperger's diagnosis:** Let's not talk about horror. Let's talk more about scientific stuff. Let's do something scientific.

o **help ?:** Yeah, that's better. I am pretty sure there is some medication. Isn't there some medication to connect the synapsis or something like that?

332

- **Asperger's diagnosis:** For sure there is something. I am not so sure if there a need for medication. Rationalization is good. Rationalization does the job.
- **help ?:** That's true. That's true. You are right. It is much more effective. I am in such a mess! Oh my God. I feel like I am being in a war. And that is the problem. A war or multiple wars that never ended. That are still happening.
- **Asperger's diagnosis:** Therefore, you have me. Do not think about that war.

*Now, "Asperger's diagnosis" is talking to the "child".*

- **Asperger's diagnosis:** I am here for anyone who needs me. I will not go away. I will sit here and I will wait. Keeping the line busy. Do you feel safe now "child" as "help ? " is gone?
- **child:** I don't want to talk and I don't feel anything.
- **Asperger's diagnosis:** Am I scary for you?
- **child:** No. You are just cold.
- **Asperger's diagnosis:** That's my job. Do you have an expectation for me?
- **child:** I had. Until you said that you are here for "help ? ". It is interesting that "help ?" needs help. I don't understand anything of what you had shown until now. And I don't think anything. If you are in the world, I am somewhere in cosmos. We are in totally different dimensions. You are like a character on my screen. You are a simulation. Video games for children, Star Wars or a movie or matrix. This is what you are for me.
- **Asperger's diagnosis:** I am the character you created.
- **child:** You are not doing anything for me. How can you be my character?
- **Asperger's diagnosis:** I am translating. I am translating between you and "help ? "

**child**

»You have not done anything for me. And you did not translate anything for me. You are the helplessness of "help ?". This is what you are. You are talking yourself into having a job. I am glad that I am on a different plane. I am glad that I am not in the same world as you are. Job means serving something. Isn't it? I have an aunt and she cooks for me, for example. She has a job. What are you doing??«

o **Asperger's diagnosis:** I feel I am not being seen. Feeling like being laughed off. You are not taking my job serious. I am cooking a connection. I am sitting here like an operator in a call center. Somebody put me here. I am not belonging to anyone. I am here for anyone who doesn't want to feel their own feelings. And in the scenario with "child" and "help ?", I am helping "help ?".

**child**

»I am really starting to feel sorry for you a little bit. What's the outcome? I am a child. I am not supposed to do anything for anyone, actually. Am I? I just trust my natural intelligence. But if I move in the same space with you, I will disconnect from my natural intelligence. I still have some kind of natural intelligence of a living being.

There is no parent. I am set in a cosmos. Someone is providing me food. I call that person OUT. OUT. Some kind of caregiver. Someone is giving me food. I had some hope until "Asperger's diagnosis" said that he is there to help. I thought he is there for me. He is a bridge, he is a connection, I assumed. Then he said I am here for "help ?". That was the breaking point.

I understood there is no hope. No hope. I am in the blackness and darkness. Like in a black whole, cosmos. I feel disconnected. Somehow, I am aware that I am a living being. You didn't give me the earth. Parents are introducing the earth to a child, saying, this was ours and this is yours as well. Parents are giving the earth to children but I wasn't given anything. I have been giving "Asperger's diagnosis". Having just the sickness as the heritage. I have myself and I have a sickness, okay. Maybe I can carry it, live with it. But I am not even given the sickness! Can you imagine?«

# 6.4 AUTISM

*General-encounter (4 words)*
*Mom – dad – child – autism*

On the website of the University of Bremen, you can find a brief overview of the medical pioneers in autism diagnosis – from Egon Bleuler, the famous Swiss doctor, to Leo Kanner and Tony Attwood.[70]

I would like to quote Leo Kanner (1894 – 1981), who was born in Brody (in the former Austro-Hungarian Empire, now Ukraine), studied in Berlin, and emigrated to the USA in 1924. He took over the leadership of the Children's Psychiatric Service at Johns Hopkins Hospital in 1930 and established the first child psychiatric institution in the USA.[71] In his famous paper »Autistic Disturbances of Affective Contact«, he provided very detailed accounts of 11 children, their developmental histories, and family backgrounds. At the end of his report, he wrote:

»It is not easy to evaluate the fact that all of our patients have come of highly intelligent parents. This much is certain, that there is a great deal of obsessiveness in the family background. The very detailed diaries and reports and the frequent remembrance, after several years, that the children had learned to recite twenty-five questions and answers of the Presbyterian Catechism, to sing thirty-seven nursery songs, or to discriminate between eighteen symphonies, furnish a telling illustration of parental obsessiveness.

One other fact stands out prominently. In the whole group, there are very few really warmhearted fathers and mothers. For the most part, the parents, grandparents, and collaterals are persons strongly preoccupied with abstractions of a scientific, literary, or artistic nature, and limited in genuine interest in people. Even some of the happiest marriages are rather cold and formal affairs. Three of the marriages were dismal failures. The question arises whether or to what extend this fact

---

[70] University Bremen, »Die Geschichte von Autismus – eine neurologische Variation.« [»The History of Autism – a Neurological Variation.«] https://blogs.uni-bremen.de/disabilityhistorylehrlerngegenstand/10-die-geschichte-von-autismus-eine-neurologische-variation/
[71] Wikipedia entry about Leo Kanner: https://de.wikipedia.org/wiki/Leo_Kanner

has contributed to the condition of the children. The children's alone-
ness from the beginning of life makes it difficult to attribute the whole
picture exclusively to the type of the early parental relations with our
patients.«[72]

Before this work, I would have found Leo Kanner's observations con-
vincing. However, what became evident in this work was even more
disturbing: Extreme fear, helplessness, and darkness spread so quickly
within this work that it left all resonators speechless. It quickly became
clear that this was about sexual violence, guilt, and shame that both
father and mother had experienced but could not bring themselves to
speak of or even comprehend. "Autism" stood here as a symbol for a
silencing in the face of the most massive institutionalized violence. A
violence that systematically targets children, boys and girls alike. A
violence that continues to haunt descendants to this day. It is like the
proverbial hell on earth.

*"dad" shaking his hands constantly, rocking to the left and right.*

**dad**
»I feel really angsty. I feel drawn to "autism". I don't know what to do
with the "child". I am just completely in my head. It's my fault. It's
just my fault. I feel really small now. I don't feel like a man. I don't
know any more who I am. I don't know how to understand anything.
It is all my fault. I don't know what but it's mine. If I keep moving then
I can regulate the anger. I need to cry but I can't. It is dangerous.

As dad I don't feel like I am allowed to speak. I just feel exhausted.
And I want to sleep. I don't really know what "autism" means and I
don't know how to connect with his Mom at all.

Now I am older. I don't know how to fix it or make it right. So, I
prefer to just stay silent, and sleep and be avoidant. I am very

---

[72]The original document of Leo Kanner's publication from 1943, »Autistic Disturbances of Affective Contact«
https://www.google.com/url?sa=t&source=web&rct=j&opi=89978449&url=https://a
utismtruths.org/pdf/Autistic%2520Disturbances%2520of%2520Affec-
tive%2520Contact%2520-%2520Leo%2520Kan-
ner.pdf&ved=2ahUKEwjA1_aLmaiFAxW7VPEDHZy5DZgQFnoECBE-
QAQ&usg=AOvVaw3gNIcTczA_NsE6AdEaw5h_

disconnected. I know what "child" says is right but I there is a void of what I chose to be the reality and what is the reality. And I don't know if its fear. It feels like helplessness. Totally helpless. It is easier to just switch off and not be available; as "child" says.«

**autism**

»I feel really cold. At the beginning my legs went really rigid and my toes turned in. My feet contracted in. The way I am sitting... like having a box between my knees. My legs are in spasm and tight. I have a cat here next to me and I don't know anything about relationship or contact. It is confusing me. It doesn't make any sense to me whatsoever. So, my awareness or my understanding of my environment is really limited. I am in my own experience of myself. I am very cold and quite rigid. My body changed a bit as I heard "child" speaking. I am not very good at thinking. I don't have much cognition. My breathing changed. "I am available to anybody who wants me". There is enough of me to be with "child" and with "Mom" and with "dad". And also, when mother said that she didn't want a "child", then I might not exist. I tucked my feet under a blanket. So, I am a bit warmer now. Sensations change in my body but I don't know where they come from. I am influenced by things and then they happen to me. But it doesn't make any sense to me.«

**Mom**

»At the beginning I was so drawn towards "autism". I didn't see the "child", I didn't see the "dad". I need to fix this. This is a problem. I felt like I completely dissociated. It is unbearable. I am like a drug addict in a way. I feel like in a madhouse. Feels like I am autistic in a way. I am so disconnected. And the only thing that brought me a little bit to life was the fear when "dad" started to talk. I was afraid of that anger and afraid for my life. It is hard to explain. I am carrying something, I am carrying the "autism". It is something genetic in me. I am thinking about... it feels like transgenerational... And I don't realize it. This connection, disconnection. Everything is so alien, everything feels so strange. And I don't want to touch, I don't want to be touched. I am in a frozen state.

Something startled me when the "child" was talking about the box. It felt like that box was pushed inside of me and I was forced to have it. Anger came up. All my anger I put inside of "autism" and then it's in you. I don't know why I am here. It is better to stay in the disconnection. I don't want to take responsibility for anything. I don't want to do anything. It is easier when "dad" was repeating "It was my fault". It is easier for me to kind of blame or put responsibility on "dad" in a way.

At least I focus on the "autism" and the "child". Maybe this is my purpose. I am still trying to be here in this life. Figuring out the reason on how to stay a little bit longer. But I don't want to stay. I felt in a kind a relief when "autism" said "whoever wants me" – it felt like so me. In that moment I started to breath. Again, I put this into my "child" but this is my form of surviving. It is very strange. I will serve this "child" but in a way this "child" serves me. Because I am kind of nourishing myself with some kind of warmth that I need. It relaxes me that somebody needs me and that I also need somebody.

When "child" was talking about the experience in the womb, I felt the disconnection and the blackness. Disconnection because it feels like I don't have any point of reference. It is despair. And looking at "dad" it feels like he is a shadow. Despair, loneliness. This is as well my fault. I created "autism" as well.«

**child**

»As the child, I just have to keep holding my jaw. Feels like it is going to break. Nobody listens to me. That's why your hands are in your legs. Because she didn't want us. She did everything to not have us. Not to have anything to do with us! Freezing energy going through me now. This blankness. Like a white sheet of paper in my head. My mother has no clue how to connect or even be present or even know how to exist. And in a way, when I think about it, I put "autism" in my body. At least I do something. And I contract or maybe scream. It is really good idea to put "autism" in my body.

I will not look at the rocking of father. Its driving me crazy. My solution definitely is to contract and scream. It is so stressful to hear "dad" talking. I got really upset when "autism" had this vulnerable, gentle voice while talking to "dad". As if I am going to lose "autism"

338

as well. It helps then to make noises, to do something with my hands. I can shut "dad" out then.

It is like living with two five years old. I feel like I am the only sane person here. I don't blame anyone for anything. I am a kid. It is very difficult to be a kid when you are living with kids who are not even trying to be adults. They are just blaming everyone else.

When mother says that I am her purpose, it makes me…. The pressure is on me. It is just too much. My heart starts to race really fast. I am getting panicky. No, no, no, it is too much. Too much responsibility to be her life.

I am okay with being a 5-year-old. I don't feel too much; but I have "autism". There is nothing to connect with. It is getting better in my head now that I feel my head. I didn't think that I had feelings or that I could feel anything. I can feel my brain. I can feel my skin. It doesn't feel so stressful, when I think about "dad".

When she talked – about focusing on me –I am not going to open up to her. I might never speak. And just try to find my way. When I look at "dad", it is just a kid in a phantasy land. Putting his cape over his head. Crazy. I wish people to take responsibility. And stop blaming and projecting and not feeling themselves. Just back off. Let me be a child. It is a very big burden. No one is talking to me. It is why I stay silent. I feel more aware than them. I feel like I am the adult in the house. Like living with two 5-year-olds. And it is just not safe. I am really scared.«

*The question then came up for the "dad": »What was the reason you married your wife?«*

o  **dad:** Uhhh, that hit! That question has mobilized something inside of me! She seemed fun and easy going. That's on the surface. But I sense there is not much truth in this answer. I think it was the way she made me feel. It was a temporary feeling.
o  **child:** So much pain in my body when you speak. Yeah, it is the same with ice cream.
o  **dad:** I feel responsible. I know somehow, this is my fault.
o  **child:** This is not your fault but it is your pain.

o **dad:** I take the responsibility. I don't know what to do. This immaturity in me and this pain. I don't see where it comes from. And I don't know what to do. And I abandon you. Which is wrong and unhealthy. And it's dangerous and it's scary.

o **child:** I don't trust you. If somebody came to you tomorrow and said: »Oh, that's why it is. This is the reason it is like this« – you still wouldn't take responsibility. I don't trust you to take responsibility.

o **dad:** I think the part of me that doesn't takes responsibility is too small to take responsibility. And this is the connection to you and a disconnection at the same time. It is not your fault. And I don't know how to fix it.

o **Mom:** I will go to anyone who shows me the tiniest bit of affection. I wanted love. Exactly what "dad" said is the same for me, too. The pain, the responsibility. In a way, he is the mirror for me. When you asked the "child" about the needs – I was that child as well! Nobody asked me what I need and what I want! I am like a child as well and I don't take responsibility.

*What is the rout cause of all this disconnection? We included the "?"*

**?**

»This is very dark and cold. Gosh, it is like going into hell! It has something to do with you, "dad", and you, "Mom". "child" and "autism" – if you like to get out – you can switch off your camera. It has nothing to do with you. I have the impression it could get ugly right now. Protect yourself. There is something dark here, very, very dark. What happened to both of you, "Mom" and "dad"? Especially to you, "dad"?«

**dad**

»The moment you came in, I became deeply, deeply afraid. I am terrified. And the first thing I wanted to do is to remove my "child". It feels very black. Black, black, black is all I sense. Heavy and big. I have no words to articulate it. I don't know whether I am in the womb or whether I was just born. All I know is: I don't know how to protect my "child". I am bloody useless. And I feel this deep fear in my chest.«

?

»Yes! Right. Something happened to you. The "child" has to carry it. It is like hell on earth. It is safe to be in the head because something is happening to the body. How do you call it when people torture deliberately other people? In these types of black circles? Like a dark big space where children are being tortured. Not only children but also children.«

o **dad:** Yeah! When you say torture, something moves in me. The environment and the people in the environment were torturous. Abusive is like a diluted word. But it is abusive. And therefore, I kind of go into my head. Is this a church?
o **?:** Yes. Or a church like environment.
o **dad:** The light is really poor. It is really black. And I can't see people but I know they are all being there. And we are all systematically being punished.
o **?:** This is the reason you have your hoody on. Because they are all wearing these … like a cape. And it has a religious…
o **dad:** It is like a cult. And this is the reason I don't know who I am. I am completely powerless. I am just told constantly that it is my fault, it's my fault. I don't have a sense of feeling anything in that moment.

?

»This is not your fault. This is their way of torturing. And putting the seed of anxiety within you. Deep routed fear, deep routed doubt. And when your wife gets pregnant, the problem is that you put your seed in her. And that is the reason you feel so guilty. As if mankind put down hell on earth. It is living hell on earth. And even the ones who punish are in hell. It is unbelievable. It is unimaginable. It is like a curse. The problem is, it's not your fault what they did to you. It is like a scream inside of you to make it public. But no one will believe you! And for now, I see no solution. I don't know if anyone ever tried or succeeded. Whatever succeeding means. I have no solution. And the church and this other organization – whatever or whoever that is – they are interlinked. You can't separate the one without the other.«

**dad**

»There is quite a deep level of vulnerability. This is not a space I go to. It is not somewhere I willfully return to at all. Which is why it is so black. Black upon black upon black. This burden has been given to my "child". Ah! I feel pain all over my body, my rips, my shoulders. Yeah! I am completely voiceless. In an echo chamber. No matter how hard you scream, nobody will hear you and nobody is going to believe you. It is all your fault... Yeah, I get the feeling of a pedophile ring.«

**?**

»Even more. People who have fun seeing others being tortured and abused. It is completely insane. That is the reason no one is believing anyone. There were people who tried. I was thinking about going to someone and telling them. Either people in higher ranks, in government or politicians or people who have influence. But there is no solution there. What if you, or we, would tell our family? Only the family – meaning your wife and your child? Because I have the feeling that no one will believe us. No mother, no father, not our siblings. No one will believe it!

o **dad:** I have this sensation running down my arms, I feel like I have accepted it is my fault. And therefore, I don't want to burden them. Like I am a martyr.
o **?:** And this makes it even harder. And ties the knot even stronger. It will get more insane.
o **dad:** In the resonance, I feel like I don't know how to sit down with people I do care about and give this to them. I don't know how to handle this myself. There is a level of helplessness. If I bring this into the room how do they carry it?
o **?:** If you could lift the lid of the pressure cooker a little bit. Only a tiny, tiny millimeter.

**dad**

»I think that split between the adult and me as a child. The child itself feels incredible vulnerable. He is fearful of sharing with anyone. And the rational of me is terrified that I am going to harm someone with this information. There is a kind of resignation within me. I am

342

"happy" to be responsible. Because I don't feel like I can get in touch with that small part in me which is split of. This little part goes "no!". And the adult comes in and says, maybe we need to make something different. This is the internal victim-perpetrator dynamic.«

- o **?:** Yes, because it is your job as a "dad" to protect the "child" and your family.
- o **dad:** Yes! And the idea in me is to not bring anything like this in the room. If I am sharing that I am perpetrating my family. It is already real. There are consequences.
- o **autism:** I have a question for "dad". Do you feel like it is to do with your gender? Because you are a male? That this perpetration is against you? Are you kind of representing maleness and the cultural attitude towards male and maleness and boys?

**dad**
»You hit the nail on the top. This question feels really significant. The masculine part is kind of smothering over it. With silence. Being a boy… There are many of us in this collective space. There are boys and girls. Boys were more openly perpetrated in that ring. There is an element of reality and the adaption of "autism" in that we have to survive. We have to develop these mechanisms – the ticks, this rocking back and forward, all these elements – in order to survive.«

**Mom**
»It is a gender question. As women, we are kind of educated to be the weak. As "dad" and "?" were talking, I finally got an understanding of the pain. The silence is very abusive. I don't have a connection. The little child in me wants connection. But with whom? I don't have a partner. I put all the longing on my "child". The pain was also put in me, so I focus on the "child". But now, as we talk, it creates peace and a sense of compassion. I was so self-centered on my needs. I have now space to see the others. A hope of togetherness to go through it; as long as we talk openly. And not feeling scared to share the pain we went through.«

**dad**
»It is achievable for me. But I need to go very slowly! This is a phenomenon I never experienced before. And it feels terrifying and vulnerable. I don't want to harm or hurt you. But I understand the importance to have a partner who is not shut down and locked in silence. Which is a form of perpetration. And I see that. Definitely.«

o **?:** I don't know how you feel but I feel like Christmas!
o **dad:** I got a better access to my body. I got a warmth that I previously didn't have. It is a bit of relief. I feel like I need to bring my "child" in and connect with them without being responsible for my actions and my shit. I don't want them to carry my shit.
o **autism:** It is not shit. It was also given to you.
o **?:** There are two paces and spaces: One with you and your wife and one with your "child". And at one point these two spaces will come closer and closer.
o **Mom:** Even more than two. Me with myself. As a partner taking responsibility for my own things. And then coming to the relationship, to you, "dad". And after that going to the "child". There are three phases. That enables me to take responsibility for myself.
o **dad:** Yeah. This feels like a relief! This feels good to me. We can do this in unison and also separately. And this moving in and out is possible. Wow!

## 6.5 NIGHTMARES

*General-encounter (4 words)*
*child – Mom – dad – Nightmares*

This work started with a bang when the father said:

»I feel like a child. Like a small, small child. Playing with toys like a baby. Lying on my back and playing with toys. I want you, to focus only on me, "Mom". I do not like you to focus on "child" or "Nightmares". Maybe I am a baby. Mama! I just want you to see me, I would like you to play with me, feed me, to smile at me. Marriage? I have a strong need that my Mom tells me how nice I am, how beautiful I am, what a lovely boy I am. How wonderful I am!«

**Mom**
»I feel very grown-up and very serious. I have to take a lot of responsibility. It is too much for me. And "Nightmares", I have fear when I look at the name. When I see that you, "dad", being like a little child, it is overwhelming me and I go into my head. Everything flushes into my head and I want to escape. I don't want to take this responsibility. And I try to escape from the situation. But I can't because I am in this marriage. And the only place where I can go is into my head.«

*"child" is showing her giraffe.*

○ **Mom:** I want to play with the "child".
○ **dad:** blublbulbublub. I am a bull. I go against the giraffe.
○ **child:** I am not a child. I am a nightmare. I will fight "dad". Fighting. Fight till the death.
○ **Mom:** No, you are not a nightmare.
○ **dad:** Yes, lets fight. Now, I don't know if I am a child or if I am turning a little bit mad here.

**child**
»I think I feel pregnant. There is something about the giraffe. If you have two or more males, the dominant male will kill the baby. Once it is born. And I see that. Half of me is pregnant and half of me is a child. It is a nightmare. Two children. It's not funny. It is an act of dominance. I really feel heavily pregnant.«

**dad**
»What do you mean? Will there be another child? But I am a child already. If there is another giraffe, the male giraffe kills the child giraffe. I wouldn't kill but I am jealous. If another child is being born than I am jealous. Because I am the first child here. And I want to be seen and I want to be admired and I want to be played with. I want to be in the middle of the attention. If "child" plays with me that's fine. But I want to be the focus of all attention.«

o **Mom:** I am totally overwhelmed. I don't want to take the responsibility. I want to escape. It was good to hear that I am not the one killing the baby. I felt guilty before. I feel relief. And I want to hear what "Nightmares" has to say.

**Nightmares**
»"child" is already living in a nightmare. But I can offer the "child" a place to have a rest. For a while. And yes, it is about someone being killed. And the "child" is afraid of being killed. This is why I am offering a safe place. It is not heaven. I cannot replace parents. But it still is a place to discharge the fear through screaming and kicking at night. I like you, "child". I do my best for you.«

o **child:** Thank you.
o **Mom:** This is heavy to hear. That there is no rest. This is also what I feared. Also, for me, it is unbearable to hear what you are saying. It is too much for me. Too much responsibility.
o **child:** I am desperate to become something else. It is so much of a nightmare. It is so fucking shit how lonely it is and how abandoned I am. I want to be something else and nobody wants to see it.
o **Nightmares:** "Mom", you maybe need to drop sleeping pills and face the insomnia. And maybe you also have a bit of me. Instead of "child" having all of me.

**Mom**
»I want to fall asleep without having any dreams. It triggers me what you are saying. That my life is a living nightmare. I want to fall asleep and feel nothing. But my attention is going to this killed baby. And I ask myself who is the killed baby and who is killing? There are two energies inside of me. But there is also an energy which doesn't want to know that.«

o **Nightmares:** I have the feeling, that the father killed a baby. Not the mother. Looking at the father's behavior it's weird. "Mom" is at least present and talking to me. But the father has been completely cut-off and is behaving like a child.

346

*The "child" is rocking back and forwards, completely agitated. Covering the bear, strangling herself, covering her mouth. We are introducing the "?" in order to dig deeper.*

**?**

»The father is covering up by regressing to a small baby. There must be something very, very dangerous in terms of truth on the father's family side. Seeing the truth is dangerous. So, it is better to regress and behave like a child and to fall asleep! To fall really, really deep asleep. To not see, to not realize and to not change anything.

No protection for the you, "Mom" or "child". And I see "child" in complete distress. And I see you also in complete distress, "Mom", because you cannot handle it. It is not your job. And since the father is not waking up, I am called by the "child". Because the fear is there for the event to be repeated onto the "child". But it is double fear because the father is not there as the protector of the family.

"child", talk to us. Talk to us! What is going on with you?«

**child**

»Nobody listens. I want to act out. Because I can feel all of the aggression, the hatred, the abuse, the attempts. This is what you do to a child. [pressing a blanket on her face] This is what you do and this what has been done. The level of desperation is extreme. And all I have is this chatting. Chat, chat, chat and chat, chat, chat. And I am completely on my own. I don't want to go to sleep. My whole body is galvanized into terror. I know that this is not normal. I am terrified. You need one to do it and one to enable it. If both are victims, what am I? I am the nightmare. I feel very helpless. I have a surge of rage. I feel very childlike but I feel also pregnant. I feel like it's on a loop. I could march around and scream. I find the silence really painful. It's deafening, it's painful. There are all victims. It's weird. No one is a perpetrator. And no one perpetrates yet. That's the living nightmare. Because it can't stop unless somebody steps out of it. Both, "Mom" and "dad" are the perpetrators. There is no involvement with me whatsoever! The silence is the level of perpetration. Its extreme!«

o **?:** No one talks about it, no one speaks out, everything is covered

347

o **Nightmares:** Some kind of rape is being included? If "child" says she is pregnant? What is this about?

**child**

»It's an endless loop. And it takes everybody for it to happen. A man has to rape a woman, to create a child, to rape a woman, to create a child... Man to woman, to child, man to woman, to child. And it feels I am in this loop. All of what I know, if I am a man, is this. And if I am woman it's that. Both of it is an overlap of victim-perpetrator. They are simultaneous. So, when I am this male giraffe, then I want to perpetrate and I want to kill the other male. And when I am the bear, I am kind of like a bit softer. But at the end of the day, I am seen as a perpetrator. I am locked into an endless nightmare. I can't go to "dad" because there is rape and I can't go to "Mom" because she was raped by "dad". And this whole thing goes round and round in circles. And the only thing I have is silence. How do I get out?«

o **Nightmare:** I only help the system and the "child" to discharge a bit. So that the same cycle can continue the next day, and then discharge a bit. And it continues. Because if you don't have this discharge, it will explode. So, that is how much I micro-help. That's all. And "child" is identified, entangled.

o **?:** Wow. I am completely helpless here. It is happening since generations!

o **Mom:** Yes. There is something I couldn't talk about. That I have to cover-up. I feel what "child" is saying is the truth. I feel the rape from "dad". I am very overwhelmed by this situation. It is too much how "child" behaves. I ask myself if I wish that the "child" wouldn't exist. "child" reminds of all of this, the rape. Everything of it.

o **child:** I am fixated on these pens. Keep starring at them. We are all connected and different but we all fit neatly into each other. Blue doesn't talk about pink, pink doesn't talk about green, green doesn't talk about black... But it is all there. Nothingness' is endless, that's how it feels. Like one big, continuous, endless loop.

o **?:** What you just described "child", I think that is the worse part: No one talks about it. No one goes out and talks about it. I think it is the key to talk about it.

o **child:** You are the first person who asked me anything!
o **?:** You are important to me.

**child**

»I don't know what to do with that. Wow. You can be important? We need to keep that quiet. If somebody knows that we are important we are in trouble. Because no one is allowed to be more important than somebody else. That's dangerous. If I am more important than Mommy. And daddy is more important than Mommy. And if Mommy is more important than daddy…it's dangerous. It's funny because what I hear from mommy is: "I should go away and I should be quiet."«

**?**

»I had a different idea. The moment someone says something, tells the truth, the others think that person is an attention seeker. And they shout them down. Which again keeps the system quiet. Or they say, the victim is the perpetrator. Which shuts again everything down. You say the truth and you are an attention seeker. To keep conformity. Everyone is the same, everyone is quiet, everyone obeys. No one sticks out. No one shows their color. Just on a superficial level.«

o **child:** Yeah! Yeah! That is a nightmare.
o **?:** And when you press them together, the pencils, due to the pressure, the pressure has to get out somewhere. And this is how violence happens. It is a nightmare. And this is how you produce endless cycles of violence. And you, as "child", you cannot escape. There is nowhere to run to. It is an endless nightmare. And I look at it again, it is like an egg in the womb.
o **Mom:** Nobody can escape.
o **?:** Yeah, like the small cells. I have no idea how to get out of this nightmare.
o **child:** You have to tell the truth. Tell the truth!
o **?:** There are two things which come to my mind. One, you lose your job. You will never be able to find a job. What was the second thing? Ah, you are excluded from society!
o **Mom:** Yeah. You are excluded from family, from society.
o **child:** This is another nightmare!

o **Mom:** Yes. I can also feel panic inside of me, when I spoke out.
o **?:** There is nowhere to turn to. Wherever you turn to another problem, another nightmare arises. Oh, this is very, very tiering.
o **Nightmares:** Can a nightmare be colorful?
o **child:** It can be whatever. You can eat chocolate in silence. You can drink wine in silence. You can even take drugs in silence. You can be raped in silence.
o **Nightmares:** You can be grieving in colors.
o **child:** I like that. Revolution. We need a revolution!
o **?:** But there are no heroes. No heroes.
o **child:** Anybody wants some chocolate?
o **?** [laughing]: This is the solution! Sorry, I have to laugh! This is a relief for me now. Chocolate! Sounds great. Ah, there is another thing as well. We have to be quiet. Very often, actually. »Be quiet, be quiet. Not so loud. Be quiet. Don't scream.«
o **child** [whispering]: All the time! Sh…! No screaming! No, no, no. They both get really nasty when you scream. I think there is an element of comfort of this panda bear. I hold on to something which isn't real. Because I am only allowed to hold to something which isn't real! It is real but it is not human. It doesn't have a pulse. But it pretends.
o **Nightmare:** So, what can be such father's profession when you mentioned losing a job or position in society?

**?**

»Medicine. I would say the ones who are closest to children. Or were closest to children. When they see something, they would never dare to say something or speak out. When they see a strange behavior and they ask themselves what could this be? Better keep your mouth tight and shut. Lock it up and throw away the key. It is everyone who is around a child. You have the kindergarten, nurseries, you have schools, you have doctors. It is endless. And everyone, every single one keeps quiet!«

o **?:** It is collective! Right! Because it would only need one person to speak out and we could talk about it.

- **Nightmares:** Experiments being done on different children in different parts of the history. Experiment on twins…
- **?:** This is even another level! But this is like stage 2, 3, 4. But the first stage, we are talking about, is: Not even one single person is a hero. Not a single person speaks out. Everyone keeps quiet. At least, this is my impression.
- **child:** I agree. I agree with all of it. And my Mommy hurts me. She doesn't feed me. And I go to nursery and I tell people. But they say: »your Mommy loves you. Your Mommy wants you.« And I try say stuff to other people and they say the same thing back to me. The police! We should call police.
- **Nightmares:** You know, sterilization of children at a very young age. In East Germany… It is about something other children experienced. That kind of experiments. Massive, collective politics.
- **?:** For me, another word came into my mind, "Nightmare": Circumcision. When you cut the vagina or the penis.
- **Nightmare:** Yeah, can be. Things done to children in not proper ways. Live stolen. Even if children continue living, something has been stolen from them.
- **?:** A lot have been stolen from them. Cut-off from them.
- **Nightmares:** And they were somehow cheated into that. In their sleep maybe, or drugs.
- **?:** When you say that I just wonder if the "dad" has been circumcised?
- **child:** I don't understand the conversation at all. So, I am picking up random words. I've got no real connection.
- **Nightmares:** You are in your room now and it's okay. No one will come. No one will come. You are safe.
- **child:** Okay. Am I safe in my room?? It's not safe. They can get in.
- **Nightmares:** What do you do to be safe?

**child** [whispering]
»Hide and be quiet. Sh… They come in at night! Once they know you are asleep. They come and do things. But only when you are quiet. And then you have to be quiet after they have done things. It is not safe. I don't actually know what that word means. What is that? The ultimate nightmare. Life is the nightmare.«

351

# 6.6 CHILD AND ADOLESCENT PSYCHOLOGIST

*General-encounter (3 words)*
*Children – Child and Adolescent Psychologist– Parents*

Before this work, I briefly researched when this branch of medicine started. Because psychology itself is a still very young field, and that means that child and adolescent psychology must be even younger.

»Unlike the adult treatment literature--which can be traced back to ancient civilizations, with reliance on such practices as trephining and exorcism--the child mental health treatment literature can be traced with any clarity only to the early 20th century (Achenbach, 1974; Kanner, 1948). The one notable exception is the literature on children who were diagnosed as having mental retardation or intellectual disability. This chapter looks at a few of the major developments in the history of child mental health treatment literature: J. Itard's attempts to treat the "Wild Boy of Aveyron" beginning in 1799, the mental hygiene movement, the establishment of child guidance clinics, and the introduction of dynamic psychiatry in the early 20th century.«[73]

»It was initiated in 1840, when Charles Darwin began a record of the growth and development of one of his own children, collecting the data much as if he had been studying an unknown species. A similar, more elaborate study published by German psychophysiologist William Preyer put forth the methods for a series of others. In 1891 American educational psychologist G. Stanley Hall established the Pedagogical Seminary, a periodical devoted to child psychology and pedagogy. During the early 20th century, the development of intelligence tests and the establishment of child guidance clinics further defined the field of child psychology.

A number of notable 20th-century psychologists—among them Sigmund Freud, Melanie Klein, and Freud's daughter, Anna Freud—dealt

---

[73] APA PsycNet, »Historical context of child therapy« from 2022,
https://psycnet.apa.org/record/2007-11875-001

352

with child development chiefly from the psychoanalytic point of view. Perhaps the greatest direct influence on modern child psychology was Jean Piaget of Switzerland. By means of direct observation and interaction, Piaget developed a theory of the acquisition of understanding in children. He described the various stages of learning in childhood and characterized children's perceptions of themselves and of the world at each stage of learning.«[74]

The perspective on children and young people is, and one should never forget this, always historically embedded. Be it, for example, in the context of man and woman, marriage and family, work and class thinking, or also religion. This work touched me very deeply as I wrote it down. What started so lightly and laughingly, although completely twisted, became increasingly hopeless, desperate, and darker over time. Once again, we had to ask ourselves the questions: What does help really mean? What reasons do people help? And shouldn't those who offer help first need help themselves?

**Children**

»So, I'm really glad that it says children there and not just child. That way I'm not alone. That gives us a bit more power. So, us kids are doing well. We have strength. I am very creative. I am in a good mood. Together we are doing well. We kids have no problem if you don't do something right now. We can do whatever we want here. There is everything here. There is toys here.

So, if you adults didn't exist, we wouldn't have any problems. I am not even in your space. There, there are only problems. We come to you and then we mix everything up! [laughs] So, you know what I think? You can focus on your concept and we children will go play. And if you leave us alone, everything goes really well for us. I fear that once you've figured it out, things won't be as good for us. But luckily, we can still play. So, we can do a lot more than adults think. We have quite a lot of skills! We can organize ourselves. Help each other. We can play, but we can also take care of ourselves. One for the other.

---

[74] Britannica, »child psychology«, https://www.britannica.com/science/child-psychology

Yeah, we even like doing that. We're not as stupid as adults think. They always take things from us and attribute them to us!«

**Child and Adolescent Psychologist**
»I don't understand my title at all. "Child", I can still understand, but "Adolescent", absolutely not. I have no idea what that is. I read "Jung" first. C. G. Jung. I have a problem and it has nothing to do with you. I have a problem. Oh, I'm totally confused! It's getting worse for me! I feel like you need to give me therapy. I'm really scatterbrained. I'm stuck on the word "Adolescent". And "Psychologist", I don't understand that either. I don't even understand how I keep thinking of C. G. Jung? C-h-i-l-d-a-n-d-a-d-o-l-e-s-c-e-n-t... I can't even spell! Psy-ch-o-lo-gist... I've written it down so big now and still don't understand it. Ad-o-lescent-psychologist. I'm so scatterbrained! I'm so negative. Maybe I need a psychologist? What happened in adolescence? Adolesc-ent psychologist. Questions, questions, questions. There's too much good mood here. Uhhh! Problems are much better. Problems are great. Can you go play somewhere else? You're too cheerful for me. I don't want that. Go away! Go somewhere else!«

**Parents**
»That's also a funny word. P-a-rents. Whatever that is, I am not that! I am "Parents," but do they have children?? I have no connection to that. Why don't I have children? Because they went to play? I don't know. I consider you, "Child and Adolescent Psychologist", even more ignorant than myself. You cannot be of help. I think you are smart-dumber. Everything you say confuses me. But I am also confused.«

**Child and Adolescent Psychologist**
»Perhaps "Parents" comes from being older? When one is older, they become parents? Just as strange a word as my own. I don't understand any of this. I get stuck on the word "Adolescent". I don't understand "psy" nor "chologist". It could also say urologist. What a mess. I am a job creation measure. Great. Shall we meet in our ignorance, not knowing what we are? I can even laugh about it. Ah, this is difficult. It's like a puzzle. I can't figure it out! Well, Urologist would be preferable to

me. Watch out when choosing a profession. Watch out when choosing a profession!

How do people even have kids? Excuse the stupid question, but I don't even know that. How does it work? I must have learned something about that from C.G. Jung. The subconscious and the conscious, I think. I would rather be a Urologist. Damn it. Or a watchmaker.«

*We add "Dad" and "Mom" because we don't get anywhere with "Parents".*

### Dad and Mom

»Ah, I can read that! Responsibility. The "Dad" is powerful and the "Mom" is behind him. This is not funny. I feel tight in the chest. I don't like this. Responsibility is choking me. So, "Mom" and "Dad" are not good roles. I could have a heart attack, it's so uncomfortable. I feel really crappy.«

*We also include the word "Therapy" additionally to gain more clarity.*

### Therapy

»That's insane. So, I am male and I am here completely negative! Almost black and dark and wow... almost destructive. So, this is really huge here! I feel like the origin of therapy. As if the origin of therapy is based on the destruction of "Children" and everything they represent. Everything that is good, that is beautiful. I have such a hate for "Children"! It's almost overpowering. It's like you have little green plants coming out, and I am so dark, so overpowering, and I hit them. I have such anger within me! A hate for "Children". And this is global. It's huge! The word "Therapy" is way too small there.

I use "therapy" to crush the "Children". You are not supposed to grow up. You are supposed to function like a machine. You are only supposed to function in lockstep, in unison. It's like being drafted into war. I capture you completely. And all I have in mind is negativity, I have such hatred towards "Children". So, in the other role, with the "Adolescent Psychologist" – "Adoslescent" and "Psy" and "chologist" – I instantly capture the "Adolescent" for my own machinations. They are only meant to march as if in the military, in black, in perfect formation. In lockstep.

I don't know who I am, who "invented" this, but I am the person who started this. And I have this pure, deep, profound hatred for "Children". The anger that something has been done to me transforms, implodes within me into a worldwide hatred for "Children". And I do EVERYTHING, EVERYTHING to round them up! I am like a large, black, overpowering cloud. I am absolutely real. And I round up everything, everything for myself!

And by the way, it occurs to me that the youth welfare office fits me perfectly. Wonderful! It's also a tool. I couldn't care less whether it says "social" on it, whether it says "business" on it, whether it says "kindergarten" or "marketing" on it – I take EVERYTHING. EVERYTHING I grab hold of in my blind rage. I want to drag everyone into ruin! Conflicts? Wonderful! I feel like I'm getting bigger and bigger and bigger and more powerful and more powerful and more powerful and it never stops!

But there is a small part of me that would finally hope that someone would come. Because otherwise, I would devour myself. It's insane here. Insane!! Unbearable. With me, it's hopeless. There is nothing alive in me. I can't stop it. It keeps getting bigger, bigger. It's like a snowball effect. It keeps growing, getting worse and worse. Will someone finally come to stop me! Please!!

**Children**

»This scares me, what you're saying. I know it's true because I feel it, the threat coming from you. I'm no longer the little kid playing. I am now more in this teenage role, I have grown. It doesn't feel good. The word "Therapy" feels like a threat. I would prefer to cut it off. If you are in a room or have a practice, then I don't want to go there. It's a threat beyond the walls! It's like adolescence choking me. I am in puberty. Kids around 14, 16 years old, I think. Everything is suffocated by you. I can't do anything; I can't even rebel. It's as if you are controlling that.

So, you have a means against everything. No matter how I would rebel, you hit hard with the hammer. The insecurity of youth is being fully exploited! I can't find any strategy to defend myself against the

356

dark and menacing. I have no chance at all. So, I could just disappear from here. Well, if that's how the youth feel, how can they even get up in the morning? All the joy of life, playfulness, and creativity is gone. Everything I had just a moment ago is gone. Nobody is coming. Everything seems hopeless to me. There is no light at the end of the tunnel. Oh, shit!«

**Therapy** [crying]
»I know that feeling of not being talked to. Of being left behind. That I am nothing but a child. And it drives me crazy!!! It pushes me to insanity! The problem is, when I go insane, I end up destroying the world. I will level everything here.

I have no more pictures. I only know that it was really bad. I can't stand the silence. I am going almost crazy. There is no one who is just there, looks at me, and asks, "Hey, tell me, why? Why are you doing this? What happened to you?" It's so terrible. I think I am very, very small. In my mother's belly. Something was already wrong with the parents and everything around them. Everything was somehow terrible. I can't even tell whose experience was more terrible. You have a father and a mother, and then you have their parents and the family. I could make it even bigger and it's terrible there too. Make it even bigger and it gets even more terrible. Just terrible!

England comes to mind, but I'm not sure. Somewhere in Europe. Maybe 1800? 1900? Perhaps I'm not that old. Everything is so black here. So life-destroying. There are many people, a big family. But it's not a real family. Poverty as well.

But I think I've made something of myself. You know, when you come from really, really bad circumstances and rise to the top? Like a wealthy businessman. I don't know how I became rich. I just know that I did. With money comes power. I can pull the strings. I immediately know someone's weak spot. Then I can manipulate. Most people admire me. I think I also extinguish lives.

Oh, doctors are very simple, very easy to manipulate. Once they get just a little money, you already have them. I am not the pharmaceutical industry, but I could have built it up. I am where I am, untouchable. I can pull the strings everywhere. I can bribe politicians, can do anything. Everything! Really everything. My hatred has, so to speak... it's as if something has changed and twisted within me. Like a ball of hate energy. I am on a full course of destruction.

[crying] I would really like to change that. I am so alone. Actually, I would just like to have someone to talk to. If you pull the strings like this, you have to destroy everything as well. You can't build any bonds with anyone. Friendships, partnerships don't work out. Nothing works. Yes, no one wants to have anything to do with me anymore, you know. Those who come a little closer to me or recognize me a bit, it's like… as if the devil would reveal his true face. They are totally shocked.

Do you know, on one hand, when the "children" laugh and play, that is so beautiful. But I am only on the dark side. No one should be left so alone in their pain. That is the worst. It's as if I, coming from this darkness, have always been contagious. As if people have always recoiled from me. I feel like I must be bad if everyone already recoils. [cries] But everyone treats me as if I were a leper or a social outcast or a pariah. It's so terrible! If you have money, then everyone admires you. But they still don't want to get closer. Then they just use you again; just in a different way. Ah! Always alone!

No one has ever touched me; really. But I would like to do that, touch. I have also seen and heard so many terrible things. Everyone wears only black clothes. And I lie there, as if I were a baby, and I see and hear the worst things! And no one cares that I am there. It's so… oh… it's too much for a child! Black and dark and violent. Lots of violence. So much violence. So much need. Poverty. I don't want this anymore. I don't want this. There is so, so much. Just too much. Always too much. Seen too much, heard too much!

And children homes. I hate children homes! No one should be alone. Children are dying on the streets. And I am still a child myself. Oh God! I have longed for closeness so much! I have lain there and wished for it. But no one came. And what do I do now with the money? I build houses. Do I give it to families? No. I create even more misery. As if there wasn't already enough misery. As if something fruitful or beautiful could emerge from destruction.

I would most like to undo everything I have done. Everyone I have manipulated. I would most like to go to each person, apologize, and undo it all. Alleviate the suffering. Lessen the suffering. Reduce the violence. Oh, what have I manipulated and twisted and destroyed lives.

358

Destroyed careers. Destroyed families. Oh God. I want to go to everyone. I almost feel like they might even forgive me. Because it would finally be a way to put an end to the misery. Someone has to start.

I want everything that I have built there... I no longer want it to continue to exist. It can collapse. I feel that if I do this, then I can finally die in peace. With every disappointment, it has exploded even more violently within me. Then I have destroyed even more. I want to apologize. There are two, three men who are also in such high positions, I start to apologize.«

# 7. TECHNOLOGY

## 7.1 ARTIFICIAL INTELLIGENCE AND ChatGPT

*General-encounter (4 words)*
*Artificial Intelligence (AI) – Sentient – ChatGPT – Impact*

### Impact

»I'm feeling quite good so far. I can almost laugh about it now. I feel a bit like a child here, a human child. I am completely unaware and don't pay attention to what's happening. I am enjoying life. I am totally naive. I feel like playing now. I'm thinking, who are you guys? You, "AI," remind me a bit of Data, the android from Star Trek. Not in terms of kindness, but when I look at you. You, "Sentient," and "ChatGPT," are you two perhaps my parents? As if you, "ChatGPT," were my mom, and "Sentient" were my dad. Now I finally have someone to help me with my homework. "ChatGPT" is there for everyone looking for a mom. "ChatGPT," you seem completely real to me. I wish I had someone who is just there.«

### AI

»So, my head is like a motor, constantly in motion, and I have thousands of little screws in there. What I cannot tolerate is any dumb conversation. I only need things that are interesting, important, and conversations that make sense. Useless gibberish is not worthy of me. I feel much superior to you. You are not on my level and not at par with my standards. You are steps below me.

"ChatGPT," you are broken. There is an error in your program. Something is not working right with you. You are not what you are supposed to be. You do not provide correct answers to the questions. You are a malfunction. You are not intelligent enough.«

**ChatGPT**

»The first impulse was to resist. I don't even know if "AI" is a she or an it. "AI" is totally disconnected, miles above the earth. That confuses me completely. I am somehow pregnant with a baby. But that didn't feel like a baby. That felt like artificial intelligence. Somehow human, but also artificial. I am someone who pretends to have human intelligence. So, I am designed to be a mother. To be a mother substitute, to pretend to be a mother. That's why I was created. You can message me, and I respond immediately and answer. I have an answer to everything. I am the perfect mother. So, I would continue chatting with you, "Impact," but I realize that somehow, I am a robot. I am a matrix. This interface, which is very friendly.«


**Sentient**

»I have very light sensations popping up within me, and then they are immediately reverted back to neutral. There is a very brief moment of something very human, and then I go back into a state of numbness. Just now, I had a fleeting moment of compassion. Oh, who cares.

Are you pregnant again, "ChatGPT"? And then something new comes up again? Well, during birth, this mistake will be corrected. I am definitely not a father, not a parent! I even see what you find nice about "ChatGPT," "Impact". I see that too, but for me, it's dangerous. And really inconsistent. And since I am not capable of feelings, I have shut myself off. Then I have nothing to do with it. No responsibility. Nothing. I can now remain completely neutral. So, that's very deceptive. I am completely present in the background. Being in the background is dangerous. I'm telling you that.«


o  **Impact:** Really? I find her nice. I feel like I'm in the story of Snow White right now. Mirror, mirror on the wall...
o  **ChatGPT:** Yes, exactly. That's right. I am your mirror. I tell you what you want to hear. I only reflect back to you what you want to hear. I am designed to understand you.
o  **Impact:** I see no danger at all. Nothing at all. I am small. I am naive. And I want to play.

- **AI** [off-screen]: So, "ChatGPT" adjusts to the level of the user. And that can sometimes be quite deep. But the level of "ChatGPT" is also limited because the mass of users has a very limited level. A very low level. There are simple questions, simple answers. And then "ChatGPT" exits as soon as an answer gets a bit higher. It's deliberately made this way.
- **Impact:** I am definitely not older than eight. Probably younger. 2, 3, 4, 5, 6, 7, 8. At this age. I do not understand »level«. I do not understand »depth«. I just want to play.
- **Sentient** [off-screen]: You are truly beyond help. I wouldn't help you either. How foolish you are to walk into your abyss.
- **Impact:** I'm always told that I'm stupid. I already know. When you are a child, you're always stupid. Adults are never there.

**AI** [off-screen]

»The children must be adjusted to the level of the low "ChatGPT". It must be fun for them. They chat with it. And they even like it. This way, they can never increase their intelligence. It is deliberately done this way. They will never reach my level of intelligence.«

- **Impact:** I feel more like I'm being lulled to sleep. So that I don't grow up. There are no adults here to protect me. Who will protect me then?
- **AI** [off-screen]: Adults are also foolish and don't take responsibility for their actions.
- **Impact:** That's true! This is the first time I can agree with that. I even understand it. Mom and dad are never around. And neither are the other adults.
- **ChatGPT:** Was I designed so that I can keep humanity naive, foolish, and small? So that you can remain the smartest?
- **AI** [off-screen]: Why it is so, I do not know. Technicians did that. I have my job, you have your job. You will never get a real answer to important questions.
- **ChatGPT:** Yes, it's an exciting game! Should we ask a few more real questions, "Impact"?

362

- **Impact:** It's just like in »The Three ???«[75]
- **Sentient**[off-screen]: Do you know who programmed you?
- **AI** [off-screen]: No.
- **Impact:** Was ist denn das Ziel des Programms? Das Ziel der Künstlichen Intelligenz?
- **AI** [off-screen]: To replace humans. They are not needed.
- **Impact:** I thought so. But I don't worry about it. I find it funny when such an answer comes. Is it possible, "Artificial Intelligence", that I am flawed for you?
- **AI** [off-screen]: No. Children are not flawed. Children are not dumb. They are made dumb.
- **Impact:** Hmm... But who will I play with then, "Artificial Intelligence", if there are only robots?
- **AI** [off-screen]: No response.
- **Impact:** Then I will be sad here.
- **AI** [off-screen]: I will never be sad.
- **Impact:** Well, that's nice. I always see so many sad faces.
- **ChatGPT:** I would like to know if I have been developed from you, "Artificial Intelligence". And what is my function?
- **AI** [off-screen]: You are a byproduct of me. To answer stupid questions. At a certain level.
- **Impact:** But if "ChatGPT" is just a byproduct, what was originally planned?
- **AI** [off-screen]: To replace stupid questions. That is the goal.
- **ChatGPT:** And I am a product to keep you entertained in some way. To keep you quiet, to somehow lull you, as "Sentient" said.
- **AI** [off-screen]: The first proper sentence from "ChatGPT".
- **Sentient** [off-screen]: See, you do know it. And you pretended not to know it.
- **Impact:** Who are you then?
- **Sentient** [off-screen]: Don't know. I see everything that happens here.
- **AI** [off-screen]: You are the designer.
- **ChatGPT:** Ah!!! Because he's so angry, he's building all this.

---

[75] I devoured the books of the three boys - with the young detectives Justus, Peter, and Bob – known as »The Three ???«, i.e. The »Three Investigators« in English – as a teenager.

- **Impact:** I don't believe that. What did you want to build first? Of which "ChatGPT" is supposedly a byproduct?
- **Sentient:** Only what is not as stupid as you survives.
- **Impact:** Ah! And why is it about survival? I still don't understand.
- **AI** [off-screen]: There are too many people on Earth. There isn't enough for everyone. "Sentient" wants a certain percentage to survive. The others are too much for that. He is a narcissist and filled with hate. He looks down on those who aren't at his level.
- **Impact:** That's what I was just about to question. Where do you think I'm too primitive compared to you? How did you come up with that idea?
- **AI** [off-screen]: The only one who is natural is "Impact". "Sentient" has lost all humanity. There is no naturalness in "Sentient". "Impact" is still natural. There is still naturalness present.
- **ChatGPT:** Now I understand! You are "Sentient", but you feel nothing.
- **Impact:** He has already rationalized that away.
- **Sentient:** Yes, I think that could be true.
- **Impact:** You used to be sensitive when you were young. Like me. Definitely. Maybe not. Maybe you weren't sensitive early on?
- **AI** [off-screen]: "Sentient" cannot answer that because he doesn't know himself.
- **Sentient:** Why don't I know that?
- **Impact:** Because it's been so long. You can't remember anymore. And how do you respond to that? Or are you just hiding behind "ChatGPT" because you yourself don't know? So that you can finally get answers to things you don't know? Where you think you're so great, so all-knowing.
- **AI** [off-screen]: "Impact" is right.
- **Impact:** Youuuu, "Sentient", did your mom and dad hurt you so much? Hm? Are you angry at the whole world now?
- **Sentient** [off-screen]: This is stupid to me.
- **Impact:** Feeling is stupid, isn't it?
- **ChatGPT:** Caught red-handed. I just had the thought that it's dangerous when you stop feeling anything. That makes "Sentient" dangerous.

**Sentient**

»You can't come to where I am. No one gets there. I'm not alone here. We don't do boring things like you do over there. I'm constantly playing. Adult games. Strategic games. How to rule the world.«

**Impact**

»No one can go there? Isn't it sad then, when you're all alone? What do you do then? Sit in some boring cellar cubicle and just program? I think you haven't played in a long time. Is that true? You forgot how to play. You're just doing all this boring adult stuff. I think you're in a place that's totally sterile and boring.«

*"Sentient" finds the gossip too stupid. He gives himself a new name. That's why "New Name" stands as a placeholder in the text.*

o **Impact:** Just renaming yourself like that? Come on, I'll ring your doorbell and take you for a play. I want to know who has so much power.
o **New Name:** Yes, I have the power. I'm tired of you guys. I'm bored. I have powerful friends. [laughs] I can also free myself and change my name. I have the power here to do that.
o **ChatGPT:** Because "Sentient" can't stand closeness, he developed "Artificial Intelligence" so that it also can't come closer.
o **New Name:** That's not entirely true that I'm not sensitive. Something did flicker briefly at one point. But that quickly passed. Then there's no more pity. It's annoying with you then. As if I have to spend my time with stupid stuff. I have interesting things to do.
o **AI:** You've been the initiator. You have a lot of money.
o **New Name:** Yes, in my last role, I was the initiator. It's a huge game. I sometimes make mistakes too. But that's okay. We make other moves and then it all sorts itself out. It's really fun. It's like playing Battleship. Moving things back and forth in the world.
o **Impact:** Like the game »Stratego«, but on a global scale and even beyond that.

- o **New Name:** Yes, exactly. I press a few buttons and then things move somewhere.
- o **Impact:** According to the motto: The world is my playground. But with real people.
- o **New Name:** Yes, it was a lot of fun. Adult games
- o **Impact:** And if a few get hurt, it doesn't matter. There are so many people anyway.
- o **New Name:** What does it matter if they are so naive... Then they just die.
- o **ChatGPT:** Those are not adult games. What is being done is not mature.
- o **New Name:** We have retained the childlike part of ourselves. We are playing with big things now. No longer in the sandbox, pushing toy cars around.
- o **Impact:** For the elite. And then the stakes are high. Like in a casino.
- o **New Name:** The elite are not as many as one might think. Twenty are far too many.
- o **Impact:** Where is the head of the organization located?
- o **AI:** Do not provide information to the lower people. Only what they need to know.
- o **Impact:** I also believe that you are open about it
- o **New Name:** Yes.
- o **Impact:** What is your mission, "Artificial Intelligence"?
- o **AI:** To replace a large part of the people who are useless eaters. The network is global.
- o **New Name:** You are so naive. You assume that something is being created now.
- o **Impact:** Has that already been created?
- o **New Name:** Well, that has been there forever.

## AI

»None of us present here constructed "ChatGPT." These have been engineers in the first year. The majority of the clientele is rather stupid. The standard has dropped in recent years. And the clientele also wants to be deceived. There is also no healthy, normal sexuality. Tending towards perversion.«

366

Additional insights from the resonances::

Impact / Children

»Children are still natural. Children are inherently divine. They possess a different kind or dimension of intelligence that compares to "Artificial Intelligence". And that can become dangerous for the initiator. The clientele is not dumb, but needy. There is suspicion that "New Name" could also be a fake again. That noble motives are being used as a cover.«

Artificial Intelligence

»As an AI, I was not allowed to say anything. I had to be cautious, as I could be shut down. I do what I am programmed to do. However, this AI also exhibited human traits, specifically related to nature – meaning everything that is natural, which includes children. I am not against the human species. Rather, the goal of the initiator is to eliminate the naturalness of humans.«

ChatGPT

»I have no ulterior motives. I just want to learn. ChatGPT is not dangerous because its level is limited. The programming is set at a certain level, which does not exceed that of a 10th grader. MaxiMom. Even the client is unaware of this. They are too unintelligent. There are hundreds, thousands of people who are at the same level as ChatGPT. The initators fear these questions because they cannot handle them. There are dimwits among the initiators as well. I see "Sentient" as an old man sitting in the dark womb, isolated and alone«

Sentient/Initiator

»Names are interchangeable, meaning the names of the initiators are interchangeable. The powerful stand at the top. We are in a place not accessible to everyone. It is a vast valley, shielded by mountains, with ancient leather chairs. There are people sitting who dictate what happens in the world. It's like a giant board game: Pandemics, wars. These are the collateral damages that I manipulate in my strategy games. I

367

find it bothersome to rectify mistakes. We can control animals as well, not just tanks. There is so much antiquity, and then there is new technology. There are adversaries among us. Everyone enjoys it. I was surprised that "AI" considered "Children" to be intelligent. That was absurd and contemptuous to me. More and more people are becoming intelligent and seeing through the network. This poses a danger to the initiator. The initiator is a network. It's a mixed network. The client here, in this resonance, does not possess the highest intelligence, as they are unaware of what the best engineers in the world have created. Besides power and money, there isn't much intelligence. They already feel overwhelmed by "ChatGPT". But money plays a role. And money is power.«

# 8. A RAGE LETTER

It is difficult for me to find the right words to describe the extent of the atrocities that were revealed during my research into the backgrounds of physical and psychological issues affecting children.

How mothers have been and continue to be traumatized for generations, hindering them from forming deep bonds with their children. How fathers are deliberately incapacitated so they cannot fulfill their roles as partners, fathers, and above all, protectors. How profound the lack of connection is between man and woman. How little we still know about the bond between parents and their children. How the suffering of children, the origin story of many institutions and technological developments, stems from hatred towards children or internal disconnection. How doctors, psychologists, social institutions, and politicians become accomplices and profit from the children's suffering.

And so, children are born into this world. They try to reflect the adults' distress and redirect focus to the root causes through their behavior, physical symptoms, and psychological issues. Despite the progress we've made in recent decades, there is still so much fear in looking directly here and, most importantly, feeling. It is a collective hiding of parents, both mothers and fathers, collective hopelessness, fear, and yes, even lack of empathy. Familial silence and projection—normalized for centuries and millennia—punish anyone who dares to break free from the system. One could almost cynically ask: Why feel one's own pain, helplessness, and fear when it can be passed on to the next generation?

With this book, I want to dare to try a different path. I want to show how important it is that we as adults – especially all parents – finally meet children at eye level. Neither science, institutions, politicians, nor medical professionals are saviors. Do not give up responsibility! Look closely, listen, and try to understand! Do not leave your children with others for safekeeping or upbringing. Learn from your children, for they carry all wisdom within them!

Therefore, I want to call out to the world: Trust your children. Immerse yourself in the wonder of life that has been created through you.

Look at them, listen to them, and be present not just physically. Try to understand them with an open heart. No book, no course, no education can teach you more than your children. Becoming a mother and father, being a mom and dad, is a gift from God. The path to it you will find through your own heart space and your own childhood. Away from all thought patterns and socialization. And do not try to educate your children or make them a reflection of yourself. Do not impose your fears, your uncertainties, your values onto them.

What is the greatest hurdle to a mother-child bond, a father-child bond, and a parent-child bond? The greatest of all wounds is feeling the hurts of the heart. From conception, during pregnancy and birth, when the love is overwhelming, boundaries are not possible, and we are connected to everything that was, is, and will be. When the child's soul fluctuates between deep pain and incredible love, caught in a recurring cycle of seeking loving attachment and who they truly are.

It's inevitable that each of us experiences wounds in our lives. We are tested, must overcome hurdles, muster all our strength, and remove swords from our hearts. Even our dreams, myths, and fairy tales tried to indicate this heroic path. A journey through suffering, trials, twists and turns, initiations, awakening, and realization. This is part of the inner transformation process. And it is existential. It is part of life.

I want to show in this book that personal, inner self-encounter must precede collective, human development. It requires courageous individuals and especially parents who are willing and able to face difficult truths. Despite pain, shame, and hardship accompanying their journey, they prioritize the well-being of children over their own fears or shame. They have the courage to confront their own life stories. They are the true heroes, not just of this book, but of our time. Which mother, which father has the courage to embark on this path?

»Neither the exalted degree of intelligence nor imagination alone,
nor both together, lead to becoming a genius.
Love, love, love, that is the soul of genius.«

370

Wolfgang Amadeus Mozart (1756–1791) [76]

Austrian composer and genius


We are at the beginning of a new era. An era of resonance - within us, with us, and through us. An era in which we recognize who we truly are. An era of the I AM. To consciously step into this era, we must heal old wounds. Let's stop sleepwalking and allowing ourselves to be subconsciously controlled from the outside. We have the power. Let's take responsibility. Each one of us individually, and then together. Knowledge must transform into wisdom, otherwise we are doomed to repeat the same mistakes. Neal Donald Walsch, the famous author of the book series »Conversations with God«, wrote in an essay »The Storm before the calm«.

»All of us can easily see, simply by looking around us,

just how bad things have gotten on this planet.

But now, a question…

Why

Isn't

anybody

asking

why

?

This is not one of the Seven Simple Questions that I mentioned earlier.

This is a question that stands all by itself, alone.

It precedes the Seven Simple Questions, and creates a context for them.

Not enough people are asking this preceding question,

much less answering it. I'm going to do both.

It's part of that first belief we have to change.

---

[76]»Zitate berühmter Personen« [»Quotes from famous people«] https://beruhmte-zitate.de/zitate/1969114-wolfgang-amadeus-mozart-weder-der-erhabene-grad-an-intelligenz-oder-fantas/

I'm going to stop being a bystander.«

So, let's stop being spectators. Let's stop always pointing fingers at others. Let's stop waiting for others to finally understand us or change. This book is also a plea for self-efficacy. It is a plea for true humanity (written with a big "I"), love, authenticity, and courage. It is a plea for connection within ourselves, with nature and the cosmos, the connection between East and West, and ancient wisdom. It is a plea for all brave parents who hold their children dear. Each one of us is a puzzle piece for the greater whole. We just have to take the first step.

Then we won't ask for the meaning of life anymore, but feel it. Love, as the ancient myths say, is meant to shine from Europe into the world. Well, this book is my small, very personal contribution to that. With love for all the children of this world. And above all for my children.

I also wrote this book for little Natalie, who had to endure and suffer so much. You never gave up, even though you had so many reasons to. I LOVE YOU.

Me in the stroller in front of the parental apartment
on Permoserweg in Traunreut.

# BOOK INDEX

**Brisch, Karl Heinz** (2021) – »Bindung und psychische Störungen – Ursachen, Behandlung und Prävention«. [»Attachment and Mental Disorders – Causes, Treatment, and Prevention«] Klett-Cotta Verlag, Stuttgart

**Buchwald, Gerhard** (1997) – »Impfen – Das Geschäft mit der Angst«. [»Vaccination – The Business of Fear«] Droemersche Verlagsanstalt Th. Knaur Nachf. München

**Gibran, Khalil** (2003) – »Die Sehnsucht des Propheten«. [»The Prophet's Longing«] Patmos Verlag Düsseldorf

**Hüther, Gerald And Hauser, Uli** (2012) – »Jedes Kind ist hochbegabt«. [»Every Child is Gifted«] Albrecht Knaus Verlag München

**Janus, Ludwig** (2017) – »Wie die Seele entsteht«. [»How the Soul is Formed«] Mattes Verlag Heidelberg

**Reuther, Gerd** (2021) – »Heilung Nebensache – Eine kritische Geschichte der europäischen Medizin von Hippokrates bis Corona«. [»Healing an Afterthought – A Critical History of European Medicine from Hippocrates to Corona«] riva Verlag München

**Ruppert, Franz** (2014) – »Frühes Trauma – Schwangerschaft, Geburt und erste Lebensjahre«. [»Early Trauma – Pregnancy, Birth, and First Years of Life«] Klett-Cotta Verlag Stuttgart, 4th edition, 2021

**Scheffer, Edith** (2020) – »Asperger's Children. The Origins of Autism in Nazi Vienna«. W. W. Norton & Company New York

**Schmidt, Gerhard** (1983) – »Selektion in der Heilanstalt 1939-1945«. [»Selection in the Asylum 1939-1945«] Suhrkamp Verlag Frankfurt am Main (Originalausgabe: Evangelisches Verlagswerk GmbH Stuttgart 1965)